POVERTY AND FUNDAMENTAL RIGHTS:
THE JUSTIFICATION AND ENFORCEMENT OF
SOCIO-ECONOMIC RIGHTS

Poverty and Fundamental Rights: The Justification and Enforcement of Socio-Economic Rights

DAVID BILCHITZ

OXFORD
UNIVERSITY PRESS

OXFORD
UNIVERSITY PRESS

Great Clarendon Street, Oxford OX2 6DP

Oxford University Press is a department of the University of Oxford.
It furthers the University's objective of excellence in research, scholarship,
and education by publishing worldwide in

Oxford New York

Auckland Cape Town Dar es Salaam Hong Kong Karachi
Kuala Lumpur Madrid Melbourne Mexico City Nairobi
New Delhi Shanghai Taipei Toronto

With offices in

Argentina Austria Brazil Chile Czech Republic France Greece
Guatemala Hungary Italy Japan Poland Portugal Singapore
South Korea Switzerland Thailand Turkey Ukraine Vietnam

Oxford is a registered trade mark of Oxford University Press
in the UK and in certain other countries

Published in the United States
by Oxford University Press Inc., New York

British Library Cataloguing in Publication Data

Data available

Library of Congress Cataloging-in-Publication Data

Bilchitz, David.
 Poverty and fundamental rights : the justification and enforcement of socio-economic
rights / David Bilchitz.
 p. cm.
 ISBN 978–0–19–920491–5 (alk. paper)
 1. Civil rights. 2. Civil rights—Political aspects. 3. Equality. 4. Poverty. I. Title.
 K3240.B54 2007
 362.5'5614—dc22

2007002220

Typeset by Newgen Imaging Systems (P) Ltd., Chennai, India
Printed in Great Britain
on acid-free paper by
Biddles Ltd, King's Lynn, Norfolk

ISBN 978–0–19–920491–5 (Hbk.)
ISBN 978–0–19–955216–0 (Pbk.)

1 3 5 7 9 10 8 6 4 2

For my parents, Cynthia and Reuven Bilchitz

Foreword

In the very first socio-economic rights case to come before the Constitutional Court, former Chief Justice Chaskalson made the following pertinent observation:

We live in a society in which there are great disparities in wealth. Millions of people are living in deplorable conditions and in great poverty. There is a high level of unemployment, inadequate social security, and many do not have access to clean water or to adequate health services. These conditions already existed when the Constitution was adopted and a commitment to address them, and to transform our society into one in which there will be human dignity, freedom and equality, lies at the heart of our new constitutional order. For as long as these conditions continue to exist that aspiration will have a hollow ring.[1]

With this book David Bilchitz has made a vital contribution to filling out that hollow ring so that our constitutional bell can ring loud, proud, and honestly, for all to hear.

Building from first principles, he has constructed an impressive account of how we should think about socio-economic rights and what that means for our implementation of those rights. The argument that the fundamental justification for civil and political rights is in reality the same as the justification for socio-economic rights challenges traditional thinking on the subject and can only serve to enhance the influence or status that socio-economic rights have in both legal and political thought both in South Africa and across the globe. This is followed up with a nuanced and compelling account of the limitations or conditionality of rights and a powerful argument for judicial review in the realm of socio-economic rights.

These ideas, whether we agree with them or whether they spark further engagement with the theory of socio-economic rights, will undoubtedly take us all closer to what is the driving force behind David's efforts—a deep desire for a society where no person is left hungry or thirsty, homeless or uneducated, lacking medical treatment or social assistance. This passion is immediately clear to anyone who has spoken to David and the book itself is infused with his unrelenting conviction that we must all strive to make this country and this world a better place for all who live in it.

A large section of the book is devoted to a criticism of the South African Constitutional Court's 'reasonableness' approach to socio-economic rights and an argument for a 'minimum-core' approach. As a Court, we can only count ourselves privileged to have warranted such a careful, honest, and critical evaluation of our work. It is vital to the health of our constitutional democracy that there is a robust debate in legal circles and civil society at large about the work of the courts

---

[1] *Soobramoney v Minister of Health, KwaZulu-Natal* 1998 (1) SA 765 (CC) at para 8.

and the content of the rights enshrined in the Bill of Rights. David's contribution will undoubtedly force all this country's judges, lawyers, and academics to think long and hard and to talk frankly about whether the path that we are currently on is indeed the best route to the destination we all wish to reach. I can offer no greater praise for this book than that.

Pius Langa
Chief Justice of South Africa

Johannesburg, South Africa
October 2006

Preface

On a daily basis in South Africa, I have met individuals suffering from severe economic hardship, who lack sufficient food, clothing, shelter, or life-saving health care. Millions more people around the world live in similar or even worse conditions. Some of these people perish; others live a life of hardship. South Africa made a commitment in its 1996 Constitution to addressing their plight. Most countries in the international community have signed and ratified the International Covenant on Economic, Social and Cultural Rights. Whilst working on the *Grootboom* case at the South African Constitutional Court, I realized that socio-economic rights, suitably interpreted and enforced, have the potential to help alleviate much of the suffering of those in desperate need. I was troubled by the nagging question: why is it that individuals are allowed to starve in a country with ample food, to die on the streets of hypothermia in a country with vast tracts of land? And why is it that violations of these socio-economic rights are treated with less urgency than violations of civil and political rights, such as the right to freedom of speech or to vote?

These questions stimulated me to write my doctoral thesis on the subject of the justification and enforcement of socio-economic rights, upon which this book is based. In the process, I found that the normative priority accorded to civil and political rights could not be justified, that the philosophical base for both rights was similar, and could be used to provide a theory of content that could assist in the interpretation and enforcement of socio-economic rights. That theory of content most importantly provides an argument for the fundamental interests of the worst off in society to be accorded priority by politicians, civil servants, and judges. That priority can best be expressed in legal terms through a modified version of the 'minimum core' approach to socio-economic rights, which has important policy implications both nationally and internationally. This book was written in the hope that decision-makers around the world will not be satisfied with politically expedient rhetoric but will, as a matter of urgency, adopt policies designed to ensure that the basic needs of all individuals are met. That may require revisiting some of the assumptions that have come to dominate economics, law, and politics in the recent past. The possibilities of a different and more just world were strongly underlined for me through my experience of having grown up in South Africa during its remarkable period of transition from a society founded upon injustice and inequality to a constitutional State based upon the values of democracy, fundamental rights, and social justice. I hope that this book may contribute towards greater priority being given to the needs of those who are worst off, thus paving the way for the eradication of dire poverty in the near future, a goal that is wholly achievable.

I would like to express my deep gratitude to the supervisors of my doctoral thesis, Matthew Kramer and Christopher Forsyth, for their assistance, continual encouragement, and support. Their incisive and challenging comments have played an important part in the development of this book and I am highly indebted to them. Onora O'Neill gave me outstanding guidance during my MPhil and helped provide me with direction for my academic pursuits. St John's College, Cambridge provided me with the wonderful, congenial atmosphere in which to develop my thinking.

The Bradlow Foundation provided the main financial support for my doctoral studies at St John's College and I am deeply indebted to them. The Skye Foundation, Wingate Foundation, and University of the Witwatersrand Appeal Fund also provided significant financial contributions towards my studies in the United Kingdom, for which I am most grateful.

Pius Langa, the Chief Justice of South Africa, for whom I worked in 2000, encouraged me to pursue my post-graduate studies and is the exemplar for me of a humane, wise, and thoughtful judge. I am deeply indebted to him for writing the foreword to this book. I am fortunate to have been provided with an outstanding secondary education at King David High School, Linksfield and both superb under- and postgraduate tertiary education at the University of the Witwatersrand. In particular, I would like to thank Mark Leon, David Zeffertt, and Sharon Seftel, who have been important intellectual influences in my life. Ross Kriel has recently provided me with superb guidance upon my entry into legal practice at his firm Ross Kriel Attorneys, and I am indebted to him and Hazel Gumede-Shelton for allowing me leave to make the revisions necessary for publication of this book.

I am most grateful to Rebecca Smith of Oxford University Press, who has from the start provided me with so much support for the publication of this book and who has offered me such helpful guidance through the publishing process. I would also like to thank John Louth for his involvement and advice. Hugh Logue has deftly and efficiently guided me through the production process, for which I am most appreciative. I would also like to thank Deborah Hey for her detailed copy-editing, and Robert Spicer for his excellent work on the index.

Finally, and most importantly, I would like to thank my wonderful parents, Reuven and Cynthia Bilchitz, and brother, Leonard Bilchitz, for their continual love and caring that has formed the bedrock of my life. It is impossible to articulate how much this work emanates in so many ways from the stimulating atmosphere they created at home, and their devotion towards ensuring that I was provided with all the opportunities I could have wished for. I would like to make special mention of both my loving and unique grandmothers, Minnie Bilchitz and Muriel Kaplan, who passed away during the period I was writing my thesis in Cambridge, and my grandfather, Shraga Bilchitz, who passed away shortly after my return. My surviving grandfather, Morris Kaplan, remains an inspiration for my academic pursuits through his sharp, enquiring mind. I am grateful to our devoted domestic worker, Jemaima Mabanga, who has always sought to create extremely conducive conditions in which I could work. Our beloved pet, Simcha, also has had a special place in my life. I have derived wonderful nourishment too from my extended family, academic and work colleagues, partners, and friends. Thank you for providing the web of support that has enabled me to endeavour to work towards a better world.

D.I.B.

Acknowledgements

The author would like to thank the following for permission to include material from the following publications in this book:

Juta Law Publishers

Bilchitz, D. 2001. 'Giving Socio-Economic Rights Teeth: The Minimum Core and Its Importance'. *SALJ* 119: 484–501.

—— 2003. 'Towards a Reasonable Approach to the Minimum Core: Laying the Foundations for Future Socio-Economic Rights Jurisprudence'. *SAJHR* 19:1–26.

—— 2005. 'Health'. In Woolman *et al. Constitutional Law of South Africa* (2nd ed.). Cape Town: Juta and Co.

Oxford University Press

Bilchitz, D. 2003. 'South Africa: Right to Health and Access to HIV/AIDS Drug Treatment'. *International Journal of Constitutional Law* 1: 524–34.

Contents

Table of Cases

Introduction

'While formalized in many legal instruments, economic, social and cultural rights remain the normatively underdeveloped stepchild of the human rights family.'[1] Socio-economic rights are widely regarded as aspirational goals, rhetorically useful, but having few practical implications for government policy and hence the distribution of resources within a polity. It is, therefore, not surprising that socio-economic rights have been systematically neglected, regarded as having little to offer a world filled with severe poverty and inequality.[2]

Eight hundred and fifty-two million people in the world are chronically undernourished.[3] Ten million people die each year from hunger-related causes.[4] Malnutrition and hunger-related diseases cause the deaths of six million children in the developing world each year.[5] 1.1 billion people in developing countries lack access to safe drinking water.[6] It is estimated that over one billion people worldwide lack adequate housing whilst 100 million people are homeless.[7]

Against these facts, it is sobering to note that the world's richest 500 individuals have a combined income greater than the poorest 416 million.[8] Of the world's population, 11.6 per cent—those who live in the United States and the European Union—are responsible for 60 per cent of the private consumption expenditure in the world.[9] It is estimated that to provide clean drinking water for all would cost around USD 10 billion, whilst eliminating hunger and malnutrition would cost USD 19 billion. Against these statistics, it is interesting to note that USD 14 billion is spent on luxury cruises a year and USD 18 billion on make-up.[10] Statistics such as these demonstrate vividly how many individuals are unable to attain the very basic essentials of life, whilst others are able to afford numerous luxuries. They also tend to show that the task of meeting the basic needs of individuals is not impossible and can be achieved.

---

[1] Woods, 2003: 767.

[2] I shall focus upon a sub-set of these rights, what I shall term 'subsistence rights': rights to food, housing, and health care.

[3] See <http://www.fao.org/newsroom/en/news/2005/1000151/index.html>.

[4] See <http://www.wfp.org/aboutwfp/introduction/hunger_who.asp?section=1&sub_section=1>.

[5] See <http://www.wfp.org/aboutwfp/facts/hunger_facts.asp>.

[6] See <http://www.unicef.org/wes/mdgreport/waterCoverage0.php>.

[7] See Report of the Special Rapporteur on Adequate housing, Miloon Kothari at <http://daccessdds.un.org/doc/UNDOC/GEN/G05/117/55/PDF/G0511755.pdf?OpenElement>.

[8] <http://hdr.undp.org/reports/global/2005/pdf/hdr05_summary.pdf>.

[9] See <http://www.worldwatch.org/press/news/2004/01/07/>.

[10] Ibid.

Socio-economic rights have been recognized at the international level since the 1948 Universal Declaration of Human Rights[11] and enshrined in an international treaty—the International Covenant on Economic, Social and Cultural Rights—in 1966.[12] However, even the few statistics that have been quoted are sufficient to indicate that these rights are more honoured in the breach than the observance. Why have these rights been accorded such low priority when they deal with such critical matters as the most basic needs of individuals? Moreover, why have people tended to give priority to civil and political rights whilst regarding socio-economic rights as of lesser importance?

There are many reasons that can be given for this sorry state of affairs, ranging from the self-interest of those who stand to gain from disparaging these rights, to the real difficulties in ensuring that they are properly implemented. However, perhaps one of the most important causes of their neglect has been the failure by the philosophical and legal communities until recently to provide a clear under-standing as to why their recognition is of importance and what their implications are for legal doctrine and government policy. Much of the academic writing today still evidences confusion as to their normative import and proposes very weak doctrines and mechanisms for enforcement, evidencing perhaps a sense that such rights are somehow not really deserving of the name.

This book attempts to counter this tendency by providing a clear understand-ing of the normative justification of socio-economic rights. Such a justification, it will be shown, lies in a general philosophical theory of fundamental rights that provides the foundation for both civil and political, and social and economic rights. Neither is to be regarded as having greater priority and, in this way, attend-ing to the justification of fundamental rights can help ensure that socio-economic rights achieve the status they deserve alongside civil and political rights.

It has often been charged that socio-economic rights lack determinate content and thus cannot be enforced.[13] This work will focus on providing an analytical framework for understanding the content of socio-economic rights. Where judicial review exists, having an understanding of their content will allow the development of legal doctrine as to how these rights should be enforced by the courts. Even where judicial review does not exist, an understanding of content will assist states to comply with their international (and possibly domestic) obligations in this regard.

Moreover, only when a clearer understanding of the content of these rights is obtained will it be possible to work out how these rights should be enforced and the policy implications that such rights have. It should be evident that this project involves both theoretical and practical considerations. Attending to the normative basis of such rights will render it possible to provide real-life consequences to

---

[11] See Article 25 in particular. The Declaration can be found at <http://www.un.org/Overview/rights.html>.

[12] The Convention was adopted on 16 December 1966 and entered into force on 3 January 1976.

[13] For instance, see De Wet, 1996: 42.

them.[14] However, the constraints and considerations that emerge from the realm of practice can also help modify and develop the theory. Thus, this book seeks to achieve a 'reflective equilibrium' between theory and practice[15] and thus to develop the best analytical approach possible for the enforcement of socio-economic rights.

The first half of this book consequently considers the philosophical justification of socio-economic rights. The justification that is developed provides a common normative basis for both civil and political rights, and socio-economic rights. Moreover, the theory aims to provide a justification that could be assented to by a diverse range of individuals and allows for a plurality of conceptions of the good. As such, it is constructed upon a minimal set of assumptions and based upon broad factual and normative truths that can command wide-ranging agreement. The theory that is developed here is thus a wholly general philosophical theory that seeks to provide an account of the substantive content of rights. It also has a range of applications beyond the particular sphere of socio-economic rights that cannot be developed in this work but, for instance, include implications for civil and political rights and our treatment of non-human animals.

The chapters in this section are generally structured by first considering one or two of the leading theories in the area and, then, through considering some important objections to these theories, building upon them to provide more adequate theoretical foundations for fundamental rights. Given that the ultimate aim is to provide an argument for an overall theory of fundamental rights, and to trace its implications for legal doctrine and policy, it is not possible to canvass all the philosophical complexities that arise from each chapter exhaustively.[16]

The first chapter of this book is concerned with understanding the principled basis upon which we can make judgments about what is of importance in the lives of sentient beings. All sentient beings are included in this discussion, as there appears to be no adequate justification for why the interests of human beings alone should be considered in this regard. I shall also be concerned to address the question of how we can make judgments of priority within the class of what is of importance to such beings. I shall argue that there are two main sources of value in the lives of beings: experiences and purposes. There are some general capabilities and resources which are necessary prerequisites for individuals to be able to realize their own experiences and purposes. Individuals can be said to have fundamental interests in these capabilities and resources. Even in relation to these interests there are two thresholds that can be identified, the first having a greater normative priority than the second. Individuals have a priority interest in the first threshold which involves being free from the general conditions that threaten a being's survival.

---

[14] As will be seen, this is a matter of some complexity given the range of issues that are engaged by these rights.   [15] This approach draws its inspiration from Rawls, 1999a: 18.

[16] Indeed, books have and could be written relating to each chapter of this work; yet these books often do not trace how all the elements of a theory of fundamental rights fit together, nor the implications of such a theory for legal doctrine and policy.

Individuals also have an important interest in the general conditions necessary to realize a diversity of purposes.

The second chapter will consider how we move from an account of interests or value to an account of rights and obligations. I contend that rights arise from the demand that a society based upon law must treat the lives of each individual being with equal importance. An argument is provided as to why equal importance must at least require that individuals be guaranteed the necessary preconditions for living lives of value to them.

The third chapter establishes that the rights that were argued for in the previous chapter are not absolute and can be overridden by other weighty normative factors. An important distinction is drawn between 'conditional rights' and 'unconditional rights'. It is argued that Chapter 2 provided a justification for the conditional rights of every individual, but such rights only become unconditional after a range of other important normative and pragmatic considerations are taken into account. Five of the factors involved in translating conditional into unconditional rights are discussed in this chapter: they are scarcity, urgency, sacrifice, effectiveness, and allocation. Ultimately it is argued that, in determining the unconditional obligations upon the State, an all-things-considered consequentialist judgment must be made as to which state of affairs best succeeds in treating individuals with equal importance.

Given the complexity of reaching such a judgment, it becomes of importance to understand who within a society is tasked with making such decisions. Chapter 4 involves an argument for judicial review: allowing judges to make final decisions in relation to matters concerning fundamental rights. The focus of this book is not upon justifying judicial review; however, the argument in the previous chapters concerning the content of rights provides a powerful argument for supporting judicial involvement and decision-making concerning the enforcement of fundamental rights. That argument requires a theory concerning which institutions within a democracy are most likely to make the best decisions regarding fundamental rights. Reasons are provided for thinking that in relation to principled questions concerning fundamental rights, the judiciary may be best placed to make final decisions in this regard. Similar arguments are often accepted in relation to civil and political rights; many commentators, however, balk when it comes to allowing the judiciary to review legislation and policies for their conformity with socio-economic rights. The chapter concludes by applying the general justification provided to the case of socio-economic rights.

This sets the scene for the second half of the book, which focuses upon the approach that should be adopted towards determining the content of socio-economic rights in law. A detailed analysis is conducted in the fifth chapter on the approach of the South African Constitutional Court towards enforcing socio-economic rights. South Africa is the focus of this applied discussion as directly justiciable, express socio-economic rights are included in its Bill of Rights. It thus represents an important case study for considering the content of socio-economic rights and their implications for the policy of a government faced by significant poverty. I shall discuss some of the important case law that has developed concerning these rights and, in particular, the 'reasonableness approach' of the Constitutional Court. This approach is found wanting in several respects: perhaps the most important defect is its failure to provide much determinate content to such rights.[17]

The sixth chapter will be concerned with providing an alternative approach to interpreting and enforcing socio-economic rights. The approach I advocate is a modified version of the 'minimum core approach' adopted by the United Nations Committee on Economic, Social and Cultural Rights in its third General Comment. However, the normative basis of the minimum core approach has not been adequately developed, nor have its full implications been properly considered. These problems can be addressed by basing that approach upon the philosophical theory that was developed in the first part of this book. The approach then involves distinguishing between the two thresholds of interests that individuals have and giving priority to the realization of the first threshold. Any failure to meet the first threshold places a heavy burden of justification upon the government to explain why the most basic interests of individuals have not been met. The government also has obligations to take measures progressively to realize the second threshold and is required to justify its actions in this regard. A range of objections to this approach are considered and the approach is developed in the course of responding to these objections. Thus, I shall seek to show how an understanding of the normative basis of socio-economic rights can assist judges and other actors in society to determine the content of these rights and thereby contribute to their effective enforcement.

A decent theory or doctrine should not just mirror the world we live in where such a world contains so much man-made misery and injustice. It must also provide a path to reform these injustices and to address the suffering. One of the chief virtues of the minimum core approach is that it has a number of important implications for the policy of governments. In order to render the doctrinal discussion more concrete, the concluding chapter considers briefly some of the policy implications of the minimum core approach for the United States, the United Kingdom, India, and South Africa. This discussion engages a number of the important issues involved in translating the approach from theory into practice. It is hoped that this discussion will demonstrate the importance of adopting a robust approach to the enforcement of socio-economic rights and highlight the possibilities such rights, when properly interpreted and understood, hold out for governments and the international community as a whole to address the most fundamental interests of individuals.

[17] Where content is given to the rights and good results obtained, they are generally derived from the normative foundations of the minimum core approach.

1

Towards a Thin Theory of the Good

1 Introduction

In the course of our lives, we differentiate between the value of different goods and capabilities for us. Being able to acquire food is generally thought to be more important than being able to acquire perfume. Having warm clothes is generally thought to be more important than possessing an ornament.[1] These examples highlight two important features of our lives. First, we regard certain resources and capabilities as having value for us. Secondly, we regard some resources and capabilities as having greater value than others. This chapter focuses upon trying to understand the deeper basis for these two types of judgment.

That basis is of central importance to a theory of fundamental rights. To explain why individuals require the protection of rights, it is necessary to have an understanding of what is of value to individuals. Since rights apply across a range of diverse individuals, this requires an understanding of the common grounds of value for such individuals. Certain constraints must, however, be placed on the theory of value that is developed. First, the theory of rights must take account of the fact that in every society, individuals differ in a large number of ways. The theory should aim to be true, and provide an accurate account of what in fact are the common grounds of value in the lives of a diverse range of individuals. It should not aim to impose commonality where none exists. It is likely that the area of overlap between the goods for different individuals will require that the theory be fairly general and limited. Secondly, a theory of rights such as the one which is developed in this book is directed at influencing the way in which rights are used and interpreted in a diverse political society, and as such should be designed so as to command as much agreement as possible amongst a range of diverse individuals. Agreement is not necessarily an indication of truth, but it is necessary if members of a society are to regard themselves as bound by the schema of rights

[1] We often attempt to capture this difference in the distinction between necessities and luxuries. However, the distinction appears to be too crude. A computer, for instance, does not seem to be a necessity, but it also does not appear to be a complete luxury in the modern world. Computers serve a number of functions: they aid communication, information acquisition, writing papers, research, and much else. They do not appear to be essential to living; yet they have the power to affect our lives significantly.

that govern a society. In turn, such agreement would lead to greater stability and social cohesion. For these reasons, this chapter attempts to arrive at a 'thin' theory of the good.[2] Such a theory is not exhaustive, in that it specifies the common sources of value in the lives of individuals, despite their differences. Moreover, such a theory attempts to avoid, as far as possible, bringing in assumptions that cannot be justified from the perspectives of different individuals.

I shall thus proceed by analysing what is involved for something to be of value to a being.[3] I shall offer an argument for recognizing that the primary notion of value refers to what is of importance to beings capable of having subjective conscious experiences of the world. This argument limits the scope of creatures to which such judgments apply. It also provides reasons for thinking that the quality of the subjective experiences that beings have will be important when providing an account of value.

I then turn to the accounts of value offered by Nussbaum and Rawls that also seek to provide a true account of the common sources of value shared by diverse beings that can command widespread assent. It will be argued that neither of these accounts alone provides us with a wholly satisfactory account of value in the lives of beings. In developing a more adequate account, I shall argue that it is important to attend to the empirical characteristics of beings which have an evaluative dimension. I shall focus on two such characteristics—the ability to experience and to have purposes—and attempt to demonstrate how an account of value can be rooted in certain very general natural features of beings.

Given this general account of value, it is necessary to determine whether it is possible to arrive at a 'thin' account concerning which goods or capabilities can be said to be of particular importance to beings. A theory of rights cannot possibly ensure that each individual is guaranteed everything that he values, and must attempt to determine which goods have a particular urgency for individuals. I shall conclude the chapter by arguing that there are two significant thresholds that can be identified, the first having a greater urgency than the second. The first threshold involves a priority interest in having the resources and capabilities necessary to be free from threats to survival. The second threshold involves an important interest in having the general resources and capabilities necessary to have and realize a wide range of purposes.

2 Value and Point of View

Let us first then consider the idea that there are resources and capabilities that have value for beings. This idea presupposes the notion that there is some way in which

---

[2] The notion of a 'thin' theory of the good can be originally traced to Rawls, 1999a: 348ff.

[3] In the course of this discussion, I shall try to understand the primary sources of value judgments in the world. It is a mistake to confine oneself at the outset to the human case without justification.

a being's life can be better or worse. Resources or capabilities that have value for beings are those which contribute to rendering a being's life better or worse.

It is important to recognize that there are two senses in which things can go better or worse for a being: the one sense is 'primary' and the other sense 'derivative'. In order to grasp the difference between these two senses, let us consider the case of plants. It is conceivable that someone might claim that life can go better or ill for a plant: if one deprives a pot-plant of water, for instance, it generally wilts, and if placed in sunlit, moist conditions it usually thrives. How then is one to make sense of the idea that life can go better or worse for a plant?

The real difficulty in making such judgments relates to the fact that a plant lacks a point of view. The lack of a point of view means that the plant itself lacks a perspective from which harm can be judged. This fact entails that we cannot know what constitutes harm from the point of view of a plant. In order to judge whether a plant is harmed or not, we therefore have two possibilities. The first possibility is that harm to the plant can be judged relative to our interests. Consider an example where Mary enjoys eating fresh tomatoes and thus daily picks tomatoes from the plant growing in her garden. If the tomato plant wilts and dies, then Mary will be unable to pick and eat her fresh tomatoes. We can thus claim that the tomato plant is harmed if it perishes, as it is unable to produce tomatoes for Mary's consumption, something that she values. Yet, it is clear that the harm to the plant in this case is derivative: it is wholly dependent on Mary's capacity to be harmed, which is primary.

The second possibility is that there is some objective method of establishing when a plant is harmed. The most plausible attempt to explicate this idea involves making sense of the notion that a plant is harmed when it is unable to fulfil its biological function. 'Life going well for x' can be conceived of in terms of a biological (or mechanical) function that is specified independently of the point of view of a creature or living thing. We attempt to capture the standards that are appropriate to a particular kind of species or being and define good or bad functioning in relation to those standards.[4] In the case of plants we specify that there is an end to be achieved (continuing to live), and evaluate various states of affairs in relation to that end.

The problem, however, is to specify why the fulfilment of a certain type of biological functioning is valuable in itself. The problem with assigning primary value to entities such as plants or rivers is that it is we who identify the ends and standards in terms of which their flourishing is to be judged. Ultimately, there is no point of view from which something is bad for a plant other than some externally imposed framework. If a plant wilts and dies, it is unclear why its biological function should be regarded as valuable anyway. Our ability to make value

---

I shall use the term 'beings' to refer to those creatures that have subjective conscious experiences of the world.

[4] See the discussion of Attfield and Taylor in Sumner, 1996.

judgments about plants is thus dependant upon standards that we adopt in relation to such entities. This need not imply that plants are only valuable in an instrumental way when they fulfill our needs. They may also be intrinsically valuable in the sense that we value them for certain qualities that are components of the good life for us—they provide beauty, for instance, or a sense of gratification.[5] Either way, however, the capacity to make value judgments about plants is dependant on the existence of beings with subjective conscious experiences of the world for whom such entities can have value or who can specify the standards according to which their value is to be judged.

Once subjective consciousness emerges, however, a being has the capacity to be benefited or harmed in its own right. I adopt Nagel's[6] explication of what is involved in being a subject: there must be 'something it is like to be an x'. The emergence of a distinct point of view entails that there is not merely an external perspective from which harm can be judged. A being with subjective conscious experiences of the world can experience life as going badly for her independently of what anyone else says about what harms her or not.

The reason subjectivity is so important is that it forces us to consider that there are things that are of value and disvalue from the point of view of the being concerned. Once a point of view emerges, there is a clear perspective from which value can be judged: the subject's own point of view. Such value is not dependent upon the existence or judgments of any other being. Thus, the notion that something is valuable for a being has primary application in relation to beings that have subjective experiences of the world. The fact that other living and material entities lack a point of view means that there is no criterion by which we can judge or know what constitutes harm to such entities in their own right. As a result, any judgments of value that we make concerning such entities will be derivative of what makes the life of a being with subjectivity go better or worse.[7]

---

[5] Raz (1986: 177; see also 1999: 296) distinguishes between ultimate value—value which does not derive from its contribution to something else—and intrinsic value—value that is not instrumental: it does not derive its value from the value of its consequences. In Raz's terms, I wish to draw attention to the fact that plants could have intrinsic value without being of ultimate value. I have not employed Raz's distinctions as I have doubts about whether there is a sharp distinction between intrinsic and instrumental value. Both types of value are valuable in the sense that they contribute to the lives of beings with ultimate value: the difference is in the way they contribute to the lives of such beings. An instrumentally valuable thing is one that is a means to a valuable end; whilst an intrinsically valuable thing is one that forms part of or constitutes the valuable end pursued.

[6] Nagel, 1979a: 166.

[7] Having reached this conclusion, it is important to question whether it is possible to understand what it is about the point of view of beings with subjective consciousness which allows them to be benefited or harmed in their own right. The existence of a point of view is integrally connected with certain characteristics of beings, which I shall argue later are the common sources of value for such beings. First, the existence of subjective consciousness is generally accompanied by the capacity to have experiences. These experiences have a particular quality which can be either pleasant or unpleasant for the beings that experience them. Beings generally find experiences that have a pleasant phenomenological feel desirable and those that are unpleasant are regarded as undesirable. Thus, the capacity to have experiences of a particular quality could be closely linked to an account of what is

I shall be concerned in this chapter with the question of value in the sense in which it has primary application to beings. I turn now to consider two accounts concerning the common sources of value in the lives of beings. These accounts concentrate on the particular case of human beings and this explains why the focus in what follows is on the good for human beings.[8]

3 Nussbaum and the Notion of a Human Life

3.1 The capabilities approach: Sen and Nussbaum

Martha Nussbaum has offered a theory of the human good which she sees as a development of Amartya Sen's capabilities approach. The capabilities approach attempts to carve out a space in between a 'welfarist' view of the good and a 'resourcist' view. It does not ask only whether a person is satisfied with what she has or does; nor, is it merely concerned with the resources at a person's disposal. Rather, value in an individual life is to be understood in terms of functionings and capabilities: 'we ask not only about the person's satisfaction with what she does, but about what she does and what she is in a position to do (what her opportunities and liberties are)'.[9]

Sen characterizes functionings as representing 'parts of the state of a person—in particular the various things that he or she manages to do or be in leading a life'.[10] This is a very broad notion and includes passive states of the person such as being well-nourished and being healthy, as well as activities that a person engages in, such as debating or playing the piano. Capabilities, on the other hand, represent sets of alternative combinations of functionings that a person can attain.[11] The concept recognizes that there are alternative courses a person's life may take, and that the choice between these courses is an important value for those capable of such a choice. The notion of a capability also recognizes that the achievement of functionings is limited by a number of factors, including individual abilities, the resources at an individual's disposal, and the existence of social, environmental, and physical constraints.

For Sen, the life of an individual is to be seen 'as a combination of various "doings and beings", with the quality of life to be assessed in terms of the capability to achieve valuable functionings'.[12] The central question of the capabilities

---

valuable in the lives of beings. Secondly, many beings with subjective conscious experiences are able to form purposes which they act upon. They hold the achievement of these purposes to be desirable and the frustration thereof undesirable. Thus, a second general characteristic that can be a source of value for a being is its capacity to have and fulfill its purposes. I shall elaborate on how I take these two general features to ground an account of what is of importance in the lives of beings later in this chapter.

[8] I regard this as a mistake and, as will be shown, this starting point accounts for some of the defects in these views.   [9] Nussbaum, 2000a: 70.

[10] Sen and Nussbaum, 1993: 31.   [11] Sen, 1992: 40.

[12] Sen and Nussbaum, 1993: 31.

approach is thus whether a person is capable of being or doing X. However, put in this way, the central incompleteness of Sen's approach can clearly be seen. Sen offers us little guidance in determining which functionings and capabilities can be said to be valuable. Yet, it is simply incorrect to assert that all states of being and doing enhance our lives. Some functionings have a minor impact on our lives: for instance, being able to choose a particular brand of washing powder that is much like any other washing powder is unlikely in and of itself to enhance an individual's life.[13] Other functionings have negative value and detract from our ability to live well: being nauseous, being obsessive, and being highly strung. Thus, we need some basis upon which to judge which capabilities are important to us, and whether there are different degrees of importance amongst capabilities.[14]

Nussbaum attempts to resolve this problem by providing an account of the principled basis upon which to evaluate the importance of various functionings and capabilities to human beings. She claims that there are two distinct thresholds which delineate the value of functionings and capabilities to human beings.[15] The first threshold concerns those functionings that are particularly central in human life: their presence or absence is typically understood to be a mark of the presence or absence of human life. Nussbaum contends that those who display a severe deficiency in their ability to reason, think, speak, move around, or recognize a loved one would fall below this threshold.[16] The second threshold delineates those functionings that characterize a flourishing human life, one that is 'worthy of a human being'.[17] This threshold is based on the idea that it is of importance for us to exercise the various capabilities in a manner that is truly human: that is, in Nussbaum's view, through the use of the powers of sociability and practical reason which distinguish human beings from other animals.

On the basis of the notion of what it is to live a human life and further, a good human life, Nussbaum develops a list of central human functionings and capabilities that determine what is of importance to human beings and how well off they are. In arriving at this list, she does not believe that she has arrived at some external pre-ordained ahistorical truth about the human good.[18] Rather, the list is drawn up on the basis of a discussion amongst human beings and an analysis of narratives and myths in different cultures that give content to the notion of what it is to live a 'truly human life'. Through this method of discussion and analysis that is tentative and open-ended, Nussbaum believes that human beings will arrive at an overlapping consensus concerning what it is to live a human life, and a flourishing human life.[19] She proceeds to outline a list that she has compiled through her cross-cultural discussions. The list is fairly extensive and ranges from 'being adequately nourished' to 'being able to use imagination and thought in connection with experiencing and producing self-expressive works and events of one's own choice, religious, literary, musical, and so forth'.[20]

---

[13] Williams, 1987: 98.   [14] Ibid: 100.   [15] Nussbaum, 1995: 81.   [16] Ibid: 82.
[17] Nussbaum, 2000a: 73.   [18] Ibid: 74–7.   [19] Ibid: 76.   [20] Ibid: 78–80.

There are many virtues to Nussbaum's account. Unlike Sen, she attempts to grapple with the difficult issue as to how different capabilities can be valued. Through the notion of the two thresholds, Nussbaum also recognizes differing levels of priority amongst capabilities.[21] Nevertheless, I shall argue that both her methodology and her principles that determine the value of differing capabilities are defective.

3.2 The factual notion of human life

Nussbaum specifies her first threshold in terms of the claim that there are certain functions that are particularly central in human life, 'in the sense that their presence or absence is typically understood to be a mark of the presence or absence of human life'.[22] The core notion here is the idea of what constitutes a human life.[23] Now, there are two possible ways to understand the idea of a human life to which Nussbaum is referring. The first possible understanding thereof involves reference to those functions that factually mark the presence of a life that meets the biological characterization of the species *homo sapiens*. For instance, a human life typically involves the ability to move around using two legs. A human being unable to move around on two legs would lack a central capability.

There are several problems with trying to use this factual notion of the human being to provide us with an account of what is of value in human life. First, human beings are typically able to do many things. A human being can typically spit at someone. He can procreate. She can abstain from food. The ability typically to do something does not alone tell us whether something is of value for human beings or how much value it has for them. A person who cannot see we regard as lacking a capacity of value; a person who cannot whistle is not generally regarded as being deprived in a similar way. Moreover, the importance of not having a capacity typically possessed by human beings very much depends on an individual's purposes. For instance, though the ability to procreate is typical of the human species, many people engage in relationships where procreation is not a possibility or choose not to have children. The lack of a capacity to procreate, although typical of human beings, may well not be important for some people. Thus, the fact that our species can typically perform certain tasks naturally fails to delineate which tasks are of importance to members of our species.

Secondly, if Nussbaum's view is construed in this particular way, it leads to triviality: any function that can be performed typically by a member of the human species can be regarded as one that marks the presence or absence of human life. Therefore, all functions that human beings can typically perform can be said to meet Nussbaum's first threshold, and it thus fails to mark out those functions that

---

[21] Here I disagree with Alkire and Black, 1997, who regard the two thresholds as an 'unnecessary complication' (at 266).   [22] Nussbaum, 2000a: 72.
[23] My critique here shares commonalities with that of Antony, 2000.

human beings can typically perform which are of *particular* importance to human beings. Thus, Nussbaum's first threshold fails in its task to provide us with a principled basis upon which to select the functionings that matter.

These arguments suggest that there is a more general problem here: if we appeal to general facts about the human species which lack an evaluative dimension, then it seems unclear how such facts can serve to generate evaluative judgments about what is valuable for members of that species.[24]

Finally, Nussbaum's first threshold on any understanding of it is objectionable in that it characterizes beings as not human if they lack typically human characteristics. Human beings who lack two legs, or cannot stand upright, or lack the mental abilities to reason are not regarded as being fully human. Yet, this is mistaken. On a purely factual level, the lack of certain capacities does not determine which species one belongs to. Physically or mentally disabled people still belong to the species *homo sapiens*.

Furthermore, although the treatment of a being need not automatically differ as a result of being characterized as less than 'fully human', the category of being human is critical in Nussbaum's thought. It is only to human beings that one owes the duty to act according to the principle that one should treat each person as an end in themselves.[25] Thus, in Nussbaum's system, the characterization of a being as either human or not indicates what sort of treatment is owed to such a being. Apart from failing to provide us with any idea as to how we are to treat non-human animals, such a system would create a stratification within the realm of the human species: between those that are 'truly' human and those that are not. Such a distinction is not well-motivated, and has, in the past, been at the heart of some of the most morally reprehensible systems such as Nazism and Apartheid.[26]

3.3 The evaluative notion of human life

It seems therefore that Nussbaum needs to go beyond the factual characterization of a particular species and develop some kind of evaluative notion of human life that can serve to determine what is of value to us. Indeed, in a later article, Nussbaum claims that her project involves reference to a 'concept of the human being (person) that is . . . evaluative and, in the broad sense, ethical: for among the many things we do and are, it will have to single out some as particularly central,

---

[24] See Antony, 2000 at 15, who puts the point in relation to ethical value.

[25] Nussbaum, 2000a: 73–4. In her Tanner Lectures delivered at Cambridge University in 2003, Nussbaum did recognize duties to beings that are not human or not 'fully human'. However, her revised view is still vulnerable to the charge that it focuses on the category of being 'human' or 'truly human', in a way that stigmatizes and de-emphasizes the unique value that resides in the lives of those that are less than 'fully human'.

[26] This illustrates the fine line that can exist between theory that supports progressive outcomes and that which has repugnant consequences: by understanding how the latter are generated through, for instance, unjustified hierarchical assumptions present in Nussbaum's work, we can attempt to provide more solid ethical foundations.

as so important that without those we don't think that a human life exists any longer'.[27] We have to ask ourselves about the importance of certain capacities such as reasoning and sociability to human life, and she claims that there is a broad consensus that a life without these qualities is not a truly human life.

First, it is important to note again that Nussbaum's terminology is very confusing. She retains as her central ethical category the notion of human life, asking us to evaluate what in our view is central to being human. Yet, there is a real question as to why the species we belong to should determine what is important to us. Though we may be creatures of a certain sort, it may be that what is important in our lives is connected with what is important in the lives of other species. It is unclear why what differentiates our species from others should come to define what is most important to us. For instance, we share the ability to have pleasurable and painful experiences with many other animals and that appears to be an important part of the good for us.

Moreover, it may well be that there are differences between members of the same species. It is again unclear why what is most valuable to an individual must track what is common between members of a species. Thus, Nussbaum presupposes a link between 'the category constructed by asking me what I value most deeply about my life and the biological category that will classify me together with many others whether I want to be so classified or not. But, it is the link itself that needs explaining.'[28] Nussbaum fails to explain why the central ethical question is 'What makes your life a human life?', rather than the question 'What makes your life important to you, what makes it a life worth living for someone like you?'.[29]

This objection raises the question as to the role that species should play in defining the good for creatures such as us. As shall be argued later in this chapter, it is important to recognize that it is not the species we belong to that defines the good for us; rather, it is the possession of certain abilities and characteristics—most notably the ability to experience the world and engage in purposive behaviour—that leads to our valuing certain capabilities and resources. The actual experiences and purposes that are valued will vary often as a result of belonging to different species, and in some instances will lead to different capabilities being valued. A dolphin lives in the water and performs all activities central to its life in the water: its ability to swim is thus central to its ability to experience and act in the world. The same would apply to a whale or shark. On the other hand, a human being cannot live in water: being able to swim is thus less of a central capability for a human being. The same is true of a vervet monkey or elephant. Thus, in all these cases, what is centrally important is the having of positive experiences and the fulfilment of our purposes. These features transcend any one species and thus ensure that the species to which we belong does not determine the source of value in our lives. Since the type of experiences and purposes that a being values will often vary

---

[27] Nussbaum, 2000b: 119.   [28] Antony, 2000: 34.   [29] Ibid: 34.

in accordance with the species they belong to, the species barrier may nevertheless be a convenient indicator of the importance of certain resources or capabilities to particular beings.

A further problem with Nussbaum's evaluative notion of human life is that it is supposed to provide the principle by which we identify what is important and valuable in our lives. Yet what is the evaluative notion of human life if not itself already a view of what is of central importance in human life? Defining what is of value in human life by reference to an evaluative conception of human life is thus question-begging. What we need is an account of why a life lived in a sociable manner and employing practical reason is better for a particular human being than a life in which a person deliberately tries to live according to his emotions or withdraws from society with others.

Thus, the real question involves deciding how to arrive at an evaluative conception of human life. Nussbaum's method of answering this question rests on our judgements that certain types of life are 'worth living' and others are not. In order to identify what can truly be called our shared 'evaluative' notion of human life, Nussbaum claims that we must attempt to arrive at an overlapping consensus of human beings. The idea of an overlapping consensus that Nussbaum employs has been borrowed from Rawls, who developed it in the context of outlining a theory of political liberalism that is supposed to be free of controversial metaphysical assumptions. The idea according to Rawls is that all citizens living in a democratic society and with different visions of what it is to live a good life can, for the purposes of setting up a basic structure of society, agree on certain basic assumptions from which to begin constructing a system.[30] Being aware of problems with the Aristotelian method of ascertaining the human good, Nussbaum attempts to use the method of achieving an overlapping consensus involving *all human beings* to attain an account of the human good.

Yet, there are several problems with trying to arrive at an overlapping consensus as the basis of an account of the human good. First, it is not clear how Nussbaum wishes to judge whether or not the overlapping consensus exists concerning the human good. She claims tentatively that her fairly determinate list could form the basis of such a universal consensus. Yet, it is not clear how extensively she has consulted and how one could reach a position where universal consensus is obtained. Rawls limits his claims about consensus to a specific context—a bounded democracy.[31] His claim about arriving at an overlapping consensus is more plausible as it is more limited in scope.

Secondly, a presupposition of Nussbaum's methodology is that an overlapping consensus is possible. Yet, there seems no basis for believing that such a consensus will arise unless there is some deeper metaphysical truth regarding the 'essence' of human nature that we can all converge upon. Thus, an overlapping consensus is

---

[30] Rawls, 1993: 15.   [31] Ibid: 12.

likely to happen only if there is some deeper metaphysical truth about human nature.[32]

Thirdly, if there is such a deeper truth, then it is unclear why an overlapping consensus would provide the best epistemological access to such a truth. An overlapping consensus will surely also include persons with mistaken or unreflective conceptions of the good, including those with racist or exclusivist conceptions. To achieve consensus, an account of the good would have to aim for the lowest common denominator between the diverse conceptions of the good in a society. As a result, it is unlikely to be the best way to discover the truth in this regard.[33]

The overlapping consensus in Rawls functions not as a means to discover the truth but as a means of arriving at agreement on the principles of justice in a diverse society. If agreement is all Nussbaum is aiming at, then it is possible for the consensus to overlap in the wrong way such that it merely expresses the prevalence of a shared ideology that is mistaken about what is in fact valuable for individuals. For instance, many patriarchal assumptions that differentiated between the good life for men and women failed to capture what was of importance to many women despite having been almost universally shared in the past. Thus, the project of defining the good for human beings is not merely concerned with what we agree to be good—which may be mistaken—but with what actually is good.

The final problem with Nussbaum's view is that it seems unlikely that an overlapping consensus will be forthcoming on a fairly detailed evaluative conception of human life such as she provides. In a diverse world, there are likely to be substantially different conceptions of what is valuable in human life, and these will vary according to people's philosophical and religious commitments. One of the central assumptions underlying Rawls' work is his acceptance of the reasonable pluralism in a democratic society regarding determinate conceptions of the good.[34] There is strong reason to think that comprehensive conceptions of the good differ quite considerably even about the requirements for lives that can be said to be 'human' or 'truly human'.

Consider, for example, the fact that in Nussbaum's view, persons with certain severe forms of mental disability are not living 'truly human lives'.[35] There are a number of religious and secular views that would be in sharp disagreement with Nussbaum's position. Many forms of Judaism and Christianity, for instance, regard any member of the human species as having a divine spark which is the only status that is relevant in those particular systems of thought. Some ideologies in our society also deny the status of human to those who do not share the same

---

[32] The problems with reaching consensus without any grounding in the actual nature of human beings would be akin to those I identify in relation to Rawls' heuristic conception of the person below.

[33] I attempt to establish here merely that consensus is not the best way to *discover* the truth; nevertheless, it is a desirable outcome for a political theory that will hopefully be arrived at by recognizing the truth.   [34] Rawls, 1993: 36.

[35] Nussbaum, 2000a: 73.

beliefs ('Jews', for instance) or a certain status ('female', for instance); others may see some practices or characteristics as not 'truly human' (certain dogmas regard homosexuality in this way). O'Neill[36] points out that such differences occur within Aristotelian ranks. Whilst recent Anglophone Aristotelians like Nussbaum tend to view human flourishing as highly variable and sensitive to context, more traditional Aristotelians often have a view of human flourishing that is quite determinate and exemplified by the Thomist vision of the good. Quite different value judgements would be endorsed by these differing conceptions of the good and thus a method is required to break the deadlock between them. Appeals to an unavailable consensus about what it is to be truly human cannot do so. It is thus doubtful that we share an evaluative concept of the human being that has sufficient content to distinguish between what is valuable and what is not.

In my discussion of Nussbaum, I have thus attempted to show that the notion of a 'human life' cannot perform the work she wants it to. A 'thin' factual conception fails to provide criteria as to what is of value in human life. Yet, a 'thick' evaluative notion of human life fails for other reasons, chief amongst which is its inability to command the consensus that Nussbaum seeks. The diversity of human beings renders it unlikely that consensus will be achieved on a determinate, detailed conception of value. Thus, it seems that only a 'thin' evaluative theory can perform both the functions of outlining the important sources of value in life and achieving significant agreement. I turn now to an evaluation of Rawls' concept of the person to see whether it can offer us a more satisfactory account of what renders a life valuable for human beings.

4 Rawls and the Concept of the Person

In order to arrive at his principles of justice, Rawls requires some understanding of what people value in life. Yet, at the same time, he wants to regard the principles of justice (or right) as constraining people's ability to pursue their conceptions of the good.[37] He also recognizes that there are numerous divergent conceptions of the good, and wishes to establish principles that do not rely on what he terms a controversial comprehensive notion of the good. Thus, he attempts to develop what he terms a 'thin' theory of the good which is restricted to the bare essentials necessary to arrive at principles of justice.[38]

Fundamental to Rawls' theory is a conception of the person and a well-ordered society.[39] A person, he claims, is to be viewed as being moved by two highest-order

---

[36] O'Neill, 1995: 145.   [37] Rawls, 1999a: 347.   [38] Ibid: 348.

[39] In providing an account of Rawls' views, some complexity is introduced by the fact that the way he characterizes his view has changed over time. I focus on Rawls' account as laid out in his article 'Social Unity and Primary Goods' (1982). In his Revised Edition of the Theory of Justice (1999), he points to this article as being his fuller statement on the subject (at xiii).

interests to realize and exercise the two powers of moral personality: the capacity for a sense of justice (the capacity to honour fair terms of cooperation) and the capacity to decide upon, to revise, and rationally to pursue a conception of the good. Moral persons also have a higher-order interest in advancing their determinate conceptions of the good.[40] The latter interest is subordinate to the highest-order interests in the sense that the pursuit of one's good as well as the demands one can make on others must conform to public principles of justice that all can reasonably be expected to accept. '[T]his conception of the person gives regulative primacy to the two highest-order interests, so that moral persons are said to have both the capacity and the desire to cooperate on fair terms with others for reciprocal advantage'.[41] A well-ordered society in turn for Rawls is one where all individuals cooperate for mutual advantage on the basis of fair terms which all can be reasonably expected to accept. How then are we to conceive of each person's advantage?

Rawls develops his account of 'primary goods' in order to answer this question. Primary goods, Rawls argues, are defined relative to the highest-order interests that people have, and are the means for realizing these interests. Thus, primary goods are the necessary conditions for realizing the powers of moral personality and are all-purpose means for a sufficiently wide range of final ends.[42] They include basic liberties—for instance, freedom of thought, speech, and association—freedom of movement and job opportunities, the ability to assume public office, income and wealth, and finally, the social bases of self-respect. The interests Rawls identifies as part of his conception of moral personhood do not only single out the primary goods, but also specify their relative importance. Thus, the priority of liberty over the difference principle in Rawls' theory reflects the 'pre-eminence of and the relation between the highest-order interests in the conception of the person'.[43]

4.1 The concept of the person as a heuristic device

In specifying these interests and the priorities between them, Rawls provides a general 'thin' account of what in his theory is to be regarded as valuable in human life. What is important to recognize, however, is that Rawls' conception of the person is in fact heuristic and defined for the purposes of setting up his theory of justice. Rawls refers to his use of primary goods as a 'reasonable social practice which we try to design so as to achieve the workable agreement required for effective and willing social cooperation among citizens whose understanding of social unity rests on a conception of justice'.[44] Thus, he does not claim that the concept of the person he is working with actually describes what we regard as valuable. Rather, his notion of the person is in fact a model designed for the purpose of fitting into a theory designed to achieve social unity.

---

[40] Rawls, 1999b: 365.   [41] Ibid.   [42] Ibid: 367.   [43] Ibid.
[44] Ibid: 386–7.

There is a tension here between defining a theoretical conception of the person and relating it to the more empirical notion of how we are and what we regard as valuable.[45] I shall argue that Rawls faces a difficult dilemma here: either his account is purely a theoretical construct of limited use in the world of politics, or, when understood as an account of what is really valuable in human lives, it becomes controversial, is incomplete, and is, in some respects, mistaken.

Let us first consider the problems with regarding the model of the person as purely a theoretical construct. First, if the model of the person does not relate to what we do in fact value, then the model will be of little relevance to the world in which we actually do live. Why should we choose principles of justice which are based on a theory of the good that is dissociated from what we actually do value?

Secondly, if the model is not defended on the grounds that it mirrors best what we do value, then there is the real question as to why we should adopt any particular construct over any other. If Rawls merely provides one model of the person which need not be accepted, then it is open to political societies to adopt a different model which would lead to different principles of justice. Acceptance of the Rawlsian principles of justice becomes contingent upon accepting this particular model of the person. A religious society such as Iran, for instance, could argue that the model of the person it adopts is of a being that conforms its will to the will of G–d (as expressed in the Koran). Similarly, an illiberal society such as China could argue that it regards the person as an entity whose chief function is to contribute to the collective good. Thus, there are several different and incompatible heuristic conceptions of the person. In order to decide between these conceptions, and come up with a theory that applies universally, we need to make claims about whether such conceptions accurately reflect what is in fact important in our lives. Otherwise, it is unclear why only a society founded upon Rawls' conception of the person should be considered just.

A final problem with a purely heuristic conception of the person is that it does not explain why persons are conceived of as valuing the particular things they do value. The starting point seems relative to the particular theory that is desired: in Rawls' case it involves specifying a theory of social cooperation. 'When the notion of cooperation . . . is applied to the basic structure of society, it is natural to take the two moral powers as the essential features of human beings.'[46] However, it is unclear why a theory of social cooperation necessitates adopting the particular conception of the person that Rawls does. Hobbes, for instance, outlines a theory

---

[45] Given the influence of Kant upon Rawls, it is not surprising that Kant faced a similar difficulty. In the context of a discussion of 'equality', Williams, 1972: 116 captures this tension when he argues that the Kantian transcendental conception of all persons as equally rational agents seems empty, 'when the question, for instance, of men's responsibility for their actions is one to which empirical considerations are clearly relevant, and one which moreover receives answers in terms of different degrees of responsibility and different degrees of rational control over action'.

[46] Rawls, 1999b: 385–6.

of social cooperation employing a very different conception of the person: individuals are conceived as being restless, egocentric, and concerned primarily to protect their interest in self-preservation.

Thus, in order for Rawls' model of the person to be a plausible basis upon which to construct a theory of justice, it must connect up with an account of what are in fact the sources of value in our lives. However, Rawls' account fails in large measure to capture accurately what our highest-order interests are.

4.2 Social cooperation

I shall concentrate firstly upon Rawls' claims regarding the centrality of social cooperation within the structure of human preferences. Rawls contrasts his conception of the person with an alternative view: '[i]n justice as fairness the members of society are conceived in the first instance as moral persons who can cooperate together for mutual advantage, and not simply as rational individuals who have aims and desire they seek to satisfy.'[47] However, moral persons do not simply have the capacity to cooperate but it is one of their highest-order interests: 'citizens in the well-ordered society of justice as fairness have both the capacity and the regulative desire to cooperate on fair terms with others for reciprocal advantage over a complete life'.[48]

The idea that one of the highest-order interests of persons is in social cooperation places a controversial and highly contestable notion of the person at the foundation of Rawls' theory. I am not denying the importance of social cooperation: after all, a human being is born into society with other human beings and thus rules regulating the relationships between persons are going to be important for individuals, whatever their conceptions of the good. Yet, there is a major difference between theories that regard human beings as having a primary interest in social cooperation and theories that regard an interest in social cooperation as deriving its importance from other interests that are of primary importance to people.

Hobbes, for instance, views individuals as primarily self-interested. They aim to ensure their self-preservation, and to achieve what they regard as best for themselves even at the expense of others.[49] Their interest in social cooperation arises as a result of the fact that social coordination will better enable individuals to achieve their important ends than a situation in which such coordination is absent. The Hobbesian view has been influential and, it could be argued, much of modern economics is based on a similar view of the person. Rawls, as I have indicated, in his initial assumption directly contradicts the Hobbesian view, by placing social cooperation as one of the primary interests that human beings have. The first problem with this approach is that it builds a highly controversial assumption into the foundation of Rawls' theory of justice that is supposed to convince people

---

[47] Rawls, 1999b: 385.   [48] Ibid: 386.   [49] Hobbes, 1991: 87.

with diverse philosophical convictions. This runs counter to Rawls' liberal project of attempting to found a theory of justice upon slender and relatively uncontroversial basic premises.[50] Anyone who did not share Rawls' view about the place of social cooperation within the structure of human interests would thus not be persuaded by his account. If possible, it would thus be preferable to have a theory of value that avoids placing such a contestable claim at its centre.

Nevertheless, the fact that Rawls' view is controversial does not mean it is mistaken. Yet there are strong reasons for thinking that social cooperation is not best classed as one of the primary values in the life of individuals. Though the Hobbesian notion of human nature is too bleak, the Rawlsian view is too optimistic. Social cooperation involves being prepared to work together towards common goals. Having a primary interest in social cooperation would imply that if one's own purposes conflict with the cooperative enterprise, one would be prepared to subdue those purposes in order to further cooperation. If very slight personal interests could cause people to act in ways which violate the terms of social cooperation, then it would appear that the latter interest is pretty weak.

It is evident that there are numerous instances within our range of experience where people are not prepared to subdue the pursuit of their personal purposes for the sake of cooperation. Many people are prepared to gain benefits for themselves at the expense of others. For instance, if people can find methods to evade paying taxes unlawfully, many will attempt to do so, despite such a course of action being inimical to a society based on social cooperation. The enforcement agencies in our societies are kept busy precisely because people place the pursuit of personal advantage above the furtherance of social cooperation. Thus, there are numerous instances in the world which indicate that the demands of social cooperation appear to have little weight for many people when they decide what to do. This suggests that social cooperation is not in fact a primary interest shared by all people; rather, it is the pursuit of their own experiences and purposes that is fundamental for all. Rawls' view is thus not only controversial: it seems in significant respects to be mistaken.

In *Political Liberalism*,[51] Rawls has recast how the concept of the person is to be viewed. In that work, he argues that the concept of the person is to be understood as a moral notion latent in the public culture of a constitutional democracy. The concept of the person is not just a theoretical construct but rather an evaluative notion that lies at the heart of modern democratic societies and which could form the basis of an overlapping consensus within such societies.

However, this revised understanding of Rawls' concept of the person also suffers from several shortcomings. First, the justificatory power of the concept of the

---

[50] Rawls' view could also be said to be contrary to the liberal project of being neutral between competing comprehensive conceptions of the good by enshrining a particular conception of the good based upon social cooperation within his theory. It would seem to be prejudiced against those who do not view social cooperation as a fundamental project of theirs and wish, for instance, to lead solitary lives.   [51] Rawls, 1993: 13–14.

person has been significantly limited by this revised understanding. Rawls' project was to outline what a just society would be like.[52] Yet, his recent methodology assumes a certain model of society is just and then attempts to interpret which model of the person is latent therein. The concept of the person that is arrived at will merely reflect the nature of the system it is derived from. Thus, it is not surprising that Rawls' concept of the person emphasizes personal and political freedom because it is drawn from an analysis of the latent assumptions of societies that emphasize such freedom. The fact that the concept of the person is derived in this way thus means that it cannot really function to justify a particular system—constitutional democracy—as it is derived from an analysis of that very system.

Furthermore, a theory of justice arrived at on the basis of a conception of the person derived in this way cannot provide the basis for criticizing societies which do not share the same conception of the person. The theory of justice one adopts thus becomes relative to the type of society one lives in. Moreover, Rawls' method of arriving at a theory of justice is also likely to lead to conservative conclusions even within the domain of constitutional democracies. By basing the theory on the current assumptions of particular societies, it is likely that the theory which results will not deviate too significantly from the current status quo.

It is also debatable whether Rawls has correctly identified the presuppositions of constitutional democracy. Many constitutional democracies exhibit sharp divergences of wealth between the rich and poor. The United States, for instance, has significant problems of homelessness and food insecurity.[53] People who are homeless are generally unable to compete on fair terms with others. Yet, socioeconomic guarantees have often not been provided ensuring that people will be housed and thus able to enjoy the opportunities that others have. In some countries, the welfare state is being cut back. It is doubtful whether the desire of each to cooperate on fair terms is presupposed where the constitutional structure allows for a situation in which the most basic socio-economic needs of citizens are not met. Certain constitutional democracies may be better understood to be premised on a conception of persons as highly competitive creatures who are willing to benefit at each other's expense. On such a view, the rules of the basic structure are merely there to preserve a framework in which people's competitive natures can be expressed in ways which do not defeat their primary interests in having positive experiences and realizing their purposes. Thus, it is not clear that Rawls is correct to interpret all modern constitutional democracies as presupposing a model of the person that places the desire to cooperate on fair terms as one of the highest-order human interests.

I have thus attempted to show, through a critique of Rawls' 'thin' account of value, the limitations of a heuristic conception of the person with little application to what people do in fact value. When Rawls' theory is considered as an account of

---

[52] More accurately, he wishes to understand which principles of justice would regulate the basic structure of a just society.   [53] See the concluding chapter of this book (Chap 7).

what we actually do value, I have argued that his claim that social cooperation on fair terms is a primary interest of all human beings is controversial and, possibly, mistaken. I have not thus far criticized Rawls' identification of the second highest-order interest of persons: an interest in being able to decide upon, revise, and rationally pursue a conception of the good. Though Rawls has identified a value of importance, there are two reasons why a more adequate account needs to be developed.

First, Rawls offers us an overly intellectualized vision of people's highest-order interests. Many individuals, even rational ones upon whom Rawls focuses, do not have a fully coherent 'conception' of the good. They have a number of projects and purposes they wish to fulfil, lacking a comprehensive overall understanding that would comprise a 'conception'. For some, these aims and desires are quite haphazard. As a result, it is likely that many rational individuals lack an overall 'conception' of the good but rather have a variety of aims, goals, and preferences that are valued by them and contribute to their well-being.[54]

Moreover, Rawls' account of this highest-order interest automatically excludes both human and non-human beings that are not fully rational. A 'conception of the good' seems to require the ability to have an explicit understanding of what is valuable in one's life. Though non-rational creatures may lack such an explicit understanding, it is unclear that this precludes their lives from having value for them. Non-rational creatures can also form purposes, and experience the fulfilment or frustration thereof in ways which affect their well-being. Their situation in this regard seems analogous to the fulfilment or frustration of a rational being's conception of the good. It is thus unclear when developing a theory of value why it is necessary to restrict ourselves to a consideration of rational beings. Consequently, it would be preferable to find a way of describing this interest without assuming that it need involve a coherent, explicit, and reflective 'conception' of the good. I shall argue below that the notion of purposiveness can better describe this fundamental interest.

Secondly, Rawls emphasizes the importance of moral autonomy, being able to make decisions and to fulfill one's goals.[55] However, he fails to recognize that it is not only what we succeed in achieving that is of value to us, but also the manner in which we experience the world. It shall become evident, when I defend my own account of value, that Rawls' claims concerning a person's highest-order interests are seriously incomplete as a result of omitting the experiential dimension.

5 Drawing Fact and Value Together: Experience and Purpose

Thus far, I have argued that we cannot read off directly from factual accounts of what constitutes a human being to what is of importance to us. The two evaluative

---

[54] I am indebted to Onora O'Neill for this point.
[55] In this, Rawls falls within a tradition of liberal theorists, from Kant to Raz.

conceptions of the person I considered also have not provided a satisfactory basis upon which to determine what is of value to us. Louise Antony attempts to specify a general problem faced by all attempts to provide an account of value rooted in human nature: 'appeals to external accounts of human nature can be expected to garner interpersonal agreement that's independent of normative judgments but, for that very reason, will not be able to generate reasons for accepting ethical propositions about what human beings should or should not do. Appeals to internal accounts can generate ethical conclusions, but the crucial premise about human nature will only be acceptable to someone who antecedently endorses the value judgments embodied therein, rendering the appeal itself otiose.'[56]

In posing this dilemma, Antony constructs a strict opposition between factual and evaluative notions. Indeed, the history of philosophy has seen many philosophers distinguish sharply between fact and value and criticize others for making illicit inferences from fact to value.[57] I do not wish to dispute that there are occasions when the distinction is important: what I do wish to suggest, however, is that fact and value are not as separate as is often made out, and it is this recognition that will allow us to make progress in identifying what is of central importance to beings.

In any field of enquiry, there must be an end to derivation or inference.[58] Although our starting points for ethical enquiry will have a special epistemic status, we need to provide some justification for commencing with them. Just as our knowledge about the world around us begins with sense experience, it seems to me that the starting points for ethical inquiry can be found in observing features of the world around us. What is interesting is that when we do so, we are able to find general factual characteristics of beings that are intimately tied to the evaluative dimension of their lives.

5.1 Experience

Consider the case of pain. Pain involves a particular type of phenomenological experience, one that can be regarded as having a particular descriptive content. If it did not have that 'feel', it would not be pain.[59] Yet, pain is also a state which all beings with subjective conscious experience find unpleasant: it is an experience such beings regard as undesirable. My claim is that the undesirability of such an experience is integrally linked to the particular phenomenological content of the experience. To experience pain is to have an experience of something that is of dis-value to a being.

---

[56] Antony, 2000: 15–16.   [57] See, for instance, G.E. Moore, 1965: 19 and 67.

[58] This assumes that our model of justification for ethical or political theory must connect up with the world in some way.

[59] Putnam, 1975: xi states that 'anything that a normal person who is paying attention cannot distinguish from a pain . . . is necessarily a pain . . . the term "pain", like many other sensation terms, has the appearance-logic'. Kripke, 1980: 152 expresses a similar point as follows: '[p]ain, on the other

To support this claim, two methods of corroboration seem possible. First, each individual can be asked to evaluate whether this claim is true for her from the first-person point of view. Secondly, the linguistic and non-linguistic behaviour of beings that accompanies painful experiences can provide evidence as to how they regard those experiences from the first-person point of view. These methods provide, in my view, overwhelming evidence upon which to conclude that phenomenological experiences of a certain type (which we refer to as 'pain') are regarded by beings that have subjective conscious experiences as having disvalue for them.[60]

However, pain is only one particular type of experience. There are many types of experience: frustrating experiences, boring experiences, exhilarating experiences. Each type of experience is associated with a particular phenomenological feel: yet, it is also associated with either a state that is valuable to us—one which enhances our lives—or which has disvalue for us—one which harms us. Once one is conscious, things can either go better or worse for one. What applies to pain thus applies also to many other types of experience: there is a tight connection between the content of such experiences and their value for us.

In section 2 of this chapter, I defined a being that has conscious experiences as one for which there is 'something it is like to be x'. My contention is now that 'what it is like to be x' at various points in time involves not only having a particular phenomenological experience, but that such an experience also involves a particular qualitative state that has either positive or negative value for that being. Thus, the ability to experience the world consciously provides a bridge between fact and value: our phenomenological experiences of the world are themselves one important source of value in our lives.[61]

The fact that the existence of conscious experience is closely linked with an evaluative dimension provides some explanation for the earlier claim that the notion of value has primary application to beings that can experience the world. It also provides a non-arbitrary reason for including within the scope of an enquiry into value all beings that can have subjective conscious experiences of the world. It

---

hand, is not picked out by one of its accidental properties; rather it is picked out by the property of being pain itself, by its immediate phenomenological quality.'

[60] There are cases such as that of the ascetic and sado-masochist that exhibit some complexity, which I discuss below.

[61] J.M. Coetzee, 1999: 44–5, the famous South African author, alludes to this important point when he writes: '[W]hat is it like to be a bat? Before we can answer such a question, Nagel suggests, we need to be able to experience bat-life through the sense-modalities of a bat. But, he is wrong: or at least is sending us down a false trail. To be a living bat is to be full of being; being fully a bat is like being fully human, which is also to be full of being. Bat-being in the first case, human-being in the second, maybe; but those are secondary considerations. To be full of being is to live as a body-soul. One name for the experience of full being is *joy*.' I understand this passage to mean that we need not understand exactly what the particular experience of another entity is like in order to be aware that there is a quality which the experiences of other beings have that makes them like our own. I endorse Coetzee's further claim that for conscious beings, there are no neutral experiences: being able to exist and be free from negative experiences would mean being in some form of positive state: what he terms 'joy'.

is an empirical matter as to which beings have this capacity that will depend on a judgement based upon suitable behavioural and physiological evidence.[62]

5.2 Purposiveness

A second characteristic of beings which involves an intimate link between fact and value is the ability to have purposes and to act on those purposes. There are many creatures that act for certain ends or purposes. The frustration of such purposes is of disvalue to such beings and the fulfilment thereof valuable to them. Alan Gewirth[63] develops this idea as the starting point for his theory of human rights. By considering his theory, I shall attempt to explore the complexity involved in the notion of having 'purposes' or a 'conception of the good'.

Action as conceived by Gewirth has two primary features: voluntariness and purposiveness. Voluntariness involves an action being under the control of an agent's unforced and informed choice. Purposiveness involves acting for some end or purpose which is a person's reason for acting. People who engage in voluntary behaviour control their movements for reasons of their own. These reasons or wants are the purposes of action.[64] All forms of wanting involve a pro-attitude towards something, which involves selective attention to a purpose, attempts to attain the purpose, and a favourable attitude to attaining the purpose. Thus, aiming to perform an action involves a purposive being in having some pro-attitude towards doing it.

Beginning with this conception of action, Gewirth constructs an argument for fundamental rights. I shall be concerned in this chapter with the first two steps in his argument. His first claim is that every agent makes an implicit judgement that the purposes for which he acts are good.[65] In acting, an agent envisages some outcome he wishes to achieve. In acting voluntarily, he regards this goal as worth pursuing, and thus values the goal sufficiently to act upon it.[66]

Since an agent values the attainment of his purposes, he must also value the generic features of all action—voluntariness and purposiveness—which are central to his ability to pursue any purposes at all (Gewirth refers to these features under the heading of 'freedom'). In addition to these features of action, he must value three other kinds of goods. First, 'basic goods' are those necessary preconditions for his performance of any and all of his actions. They include food, physical security, clothing, for instance, without which he would not be able to act for any purpose or good at all. Secondly, he must value 'non-subtractive goods': abilities and conditions that ensure one's level of purpose-fulfilment is not diminished.[67]

---

62 Some philosophers of mind investigate how it is possible to know which creatures have similar qualitative experiences to our own. I have defended an account thereof in Bilchitz, 1998. We can justifiably attribute conscious experiences to mammals, some birds, and some reptiles for instance, whilst it is doubtful that insects have such experiences (see, for instance, Wise, 2001: 133).

63 Gewirth, 1978.　　　　64 Purposes may be dispositional and not clearly in view: Ibid: 38.
65 Ibid: 52.　　　66 Ibid: 49.　　　67 Gewirth, 1982c: 56.

These involve, for instance, not being lied to, and not being subjected to debilitating conditions of physical labour or housing. Finally, he must value 'additive goods': the abilities and conditions required for increasing one's level of purpose-fulfilment. These include having his self-esteem protected, access to education, and not being discriminated against.[68] The valuation of one's general ability to fulfil one's purposes is thus the ground for valuing these three other types of goods which Gewirth refers to as comprising a person's 'well-being'.[69] Thus, 'freedom' and 'well-being' represent together the most general and proximate necessary conditions for an agent's purposive action. Since an agent values her purposes, she must also be committed to achieving that which is necessary to achieve her purposes. Consequently, we arrive at the second proposition: every agent must be committed to having the freedom and well-being that are necessary for achieving her purposes.[70]

5.3 Does purposiveness imply reflective awareness?

I shall not reconstruct the rest of Gewirth's argument in this chapter.[71] Since purposive action is the key notion in Gewirth's theory, it is important to consider further what is involved in this notion. For Gewirth, it is only beings capable of using language and following logical entailments that are capable of purposive action. His reason for making this claim lies in his conception of action which does not simply consist in bodily movements but also involves thought processes such as choosing and intending. Such thought processes, he claims, are connected with language. Thus, if one can attribute intentional action to a being, then that being must be capable of making judgements expressible in language.[72]

Yet, this claim suggests that Gewirth is working with a narrow and simplistic conception of agency. The crucial point to recognize is that it is possible to act for a reason without recognizing and being able to formulate a linguistic judgement which captures that reason. Consider two examples. First, let us consider the development of a child. In the initial stages of a child's life, it moves around a lot, and much of the movement appears involuntary. As the child matures, but prior to its acquisition of language, the child will often point to something that it wants (a bottle or a toy, for instance) and make an effort to grab hold of it. In explaining such actions, we typically attribute a desire or purpose to a child—that she wants her bottle, or toy—without claiming that she is able to recognize the reason for her action in linguistic terms. As the child develops, she will (hopefully) grow to

---

[68] Ibid.

[69] In Gewirth's view, there is a hierarchy in relation to the three kinds of goods which make up a person's well-being which could be linked to the varying degrees of urgency for individuals. The basic goods have the highest degree of necessity as without them no purposes can be fulfilled. The additive goods, on the other hand, have less necessity as their absence precludes increasing purpose-fulfilment, but allows for some degree of purposiveness. [70] Gewirth, 1978: 63.

[71] The rest of the argument will be discussed in Chap 2. [72] Gewirth, 1978: 42.

be able to become a competent user of language and recognize linguistic judgements. However, even when we reach adulthood, not all our actions stem from the self-conscious recognition of our purposes. Strong emotions such as anger or passionate desires for food or sexual pleasure may well drive us to act without a self-conscious examination of our reasons for doing so.

The second example concerns documented cases where chimpanzees use certain tools (such as the bark of a tree) to crack a nut. In explaining such actions, we typically attribute a certain intention to the chimpanzee: that she desires the nut and believes that using the bark of the tree will allow her to eat it. It seems plausible to refer to the chimpanzee as an agent, who acts in the world to achieve her purposes.[73] Yet, the chimpanzee cannot generally formulate or recognize these judgements in the linguistic forms we use.[74] Of course, in all likelihood, it also has a type of language, or system of representation that allows it to process cognitive information. This system of representation does not, however, appear to be such that we can say the chimpanzee is aware of a linguistic proposition and can follow logical entailments of the sort Gewirth requires for thought.[75]

There are thus beings who have intentions and appear to control their actions in accordance with purposes, yet are not self-conscious about their purposes, and do not deliberate in linguistic form regarding the course of action they will pursue. Into this category fall children at least up to the age of language acquisition, many mentally ill people, and many non-human animals. There is also, as we know, a category of beings who have intentions and control their actions in accordance with their purposes, but who are capable of self-consciousness about their purposes and who do deliberate in linguistic form about which course of action to pursue. As far as we know, only adult human beings who are not mentally ill fall into this category. Let us call the first category 'non-reflective beings', and the second category 'reflective beings'.

Gewirth claims that reflective beings need not be self-consciously aware of the judgements and inferences he attributes to them in order to derive his supreme moral principle. We can attribute commitments to such beings, even though they are not aware of them. This is in fact a centrally important feature of his 'dialectically necessary method' that involves analysing what an agent is necessarily committed to by engaging in action.[76] It importantly relies on being able to attribute

---

[73] See, for instance, Regan, 1988: 74–5.

[74] There is indeed a dispute in the philosophy of mind as to whether language is required in order to be able to think. Gewirth simply glosses over this debate and seems to assume that only those able to express judgments in language can properly think: 'it has long been recognized that language is connected with thought, as expressing and communicating it' (1978: 42). The truth seems to me to be much more complex and requires separating out mental states which allow us to operate in the world, from the self-conscious recognition of these mental states. Language may be required for the latter recognition, but is not required for the former beliefs. My position is opposed to that adopted by Davidson, 1984 in 'Thought and Talk', which I have criticized in Bilchitz, 1998. Some animals may even be capable of higher-order thoughts: see the examples given by Dennett, 1983.

[75] See, for instance, Malcolm, 1991: 458; and Wise, 2001:158–9.

[76] Gewirth, 1978: 42–4.

a judgement to an agent even if the agent herself does not recognize the judgement: 'the method operates to trace the judgements and claims every agent logically must make from within his standpoint.'[77] Thus, an agent may not be self-consciously aware of the inferences Gewirth draws; yet we can still claim that such a person is committed to such judgements.

However, if this is so, why could we not also attribute such commitments to beings who are non-reflective? The difference between the two cases is that the one group can become reflectively aware of these judgements whilst the other cannot. Yet, if there are members of the former group who never do become reflectively aware of these judgements, and we still attribute these judgements to them, it is not clear that *in respect of these judgements* they differ in any relevant way from beings that can never become reflectively aware thereof. It is clearly the case that there are people who have never become reflectively aware of Gewirth's judgements about what they are committed to: after all, since his theory involves an element of originality, no one presumably ever drew these exact inferences. Thus, if we can still attribute these commitments to those who never consciously recognized them, then we can do so in relation to beings that can never become reflectively aware of them.

This argument may initially seem strange in that it involves attributing judgements to those who cannot become reflectively aware of them. The important point to consider is the role of reflective awareness in Gewirth's theory. The crucial characteristic of a being that allows Gewirth to attribute judgements to it is that it is a purposive agent. Gewirth ties purposiveness to the possession of language. I have attempted to prise these two characteristics apart, and show that one can be a purposive agent without possessing a human language.[78] If this is so, then it is possible that Gewirth's argument could apply to reflective as well as non-reflective beings.

Let us consider the two claims of his argument in light of what has been said. A purposive agent, Gewirth claims, is committed to the positive valuation of her purposes. A non-reflective being could not be self-consciously aware of this valuation, but by the mere fact that she pursues a particular purpose we can infer that she judges it in a favourable light. Thus, any form of creature to whom purposes can meaningfully be attributed embraces only what is favourable to it and avoids what is harmful.[79] Since such creatures value their purposes, each non-reflective creature must also wish to have the necessary goods involved in realizing her purposes.

---

[77] Ibid: 44.

[78] See, for instance, also the fascinating examples of human beings that only developed language later in life, and reported that they had had thoughts and purposes of their own prior to acquiring language: see Wise, 2001: 158ff.

[79] It is important to distinguish between beings that merely respond to stimuli, and those which are able to engage in properly purposive behaviour. It seems to me that such a distinction must rest on the difference between having an end that can be identified but is aimed at without any act of

If this line of reasoning makes sense, then the question becomes why has Gewirth limited himself to the class of reflective beings? There is indeed a powerful reason why a theory of morality must address itself to reflective beings. A being that is not reflectively aware does not consider her purposes in light of morality, and does not deliberate as to the correct course of action to follow. It is only a being that is reflectively aware that can consider the demands of morality upon her action, and thus regulate her conduct in accordance with Gewirth's theory. A theory of morality will thus address itself to reflective beings.

Accepting this truth, however, is quite different from accepting that the subject matter of morality concerns itself only with reflective beings or that life can go better or worse only for beings that are reflective. Gewirth in fact provides us with powerful reasons for thinking that the realization of purposes for any being that has them is morally significant. I have thus attempted to highlight some complexities in relation to the notion of what constitutes a purposive agent which Gewirth does not consider. These complexities allow us to recognize that it is possible for both reflective and non-reflective beings to have purposes whose fulfilment is of value to the individuals in question.[80]

6 In Defence of the Proposed Theory of Value

I have attempted to identify two general characteristics of beings which provide the grounds for judgements about value and disvalue in their lives: the ability to have conscious experiences with a particular quality and the ability to will the fulfilment of one's purposes.[81] By situating the sources of value in certain natural features of beings, the theory provides a criterion as to which creatures fall within the scope of our moral concern. It offers principled reasons for its focus on beings that can have subjective experiences or purposes, and does not arbitrarily exclude non-human species from the sphere of moral concern.

It should be evident that the theory I propose has both objective and subjective elements. Features of the world—such as consciousness and purposiveness—are objective in the sense that they exist in beings independently of anyone's perspective. In turn, these features provide us with an objective basis upon which to recognize the sources of value within the lives of beings. Whether something

---

'endorsement' by the organism, and the conscious and willing pursuit of a particular end. For instance, only creatures that exhibit some flexibility in their behaviour and the capacity to learn can be said to engage in properly purposive behaviour (see, for instance, the sphex wasp's behaviour, which appears to exhibit merely a stimulus-response mechanism (Dennett, 1984: 11)). A fuller account of purposiveness would have to address such issues in the philosophy of mind, but for reasons of length I cannot hope to address all these matters here.

[80] As a result, this notion also solves certain of the difficulties raised in connection with Rawls' account of locating value in a 'conception of the good'.

[81] It may be that it is possible to identify further features; however, the ones I have identified seem to me to be the most important and plausible candidates for performing this role.

in particular is of positive value or not, however, can usually only be judged by considering what the experience is like for the being in question or whether such a being regards certain purposes as important to her.[82] This feature of my account thus allows us to recognize common sources of value in the lives of beings, whilst at the same time being able to take cognizance of the diversity of the experiences and purposes in the world. The content of what constitutes 'positive experiences', for instance, will vary according to the 'form of life' of creatures, their societies, their individual natures, and circumstances.

These features enable the account I have developed to meet the requirements for an account of value that were outlined at the outset of this chapter. In this regard, it is instructive to compare my account to that of Rawls. First, in a previous section of this chapter, I have attempted to show the difficulties with the heuristic and constructivist nature of Rawls' account. The account I have offered is not merely a theoretical construct but aims to be a true account of the sources of value in our lives. It has a naturalistic element which ties value to the possession of certain characteristics exhibited by creatures in the world. It thus can be evaluated in light of empirical features of the world, and is not defined in relation to a particular theory or the wishes of a corrupt regime. This naturalistic feature of the theory allows us to root our theoretical constructs in the world.

If it is true that certain naturalistic features of the world are the sources of value in our lives, then it is also more likely that individuals will be able to reach a consensus about the sources of value in life. Arriving at consensus does not in and of itself determine what is of value in the lives of beings. That fact is determined by actual features of the world: however, the existence of such objective naturalistic features renders it likely that individuals will eventually be able to reach agreement about these issues. As in the case of scientific theory, it is still possible for a mistaken consensus to arise; yet, the existence of certain hard features of the world means that such a consensus is likely to be disrupted when it fails to take account of such features and, thus, errors are likely to be discovered.

The theory I have proposed also seeks to outline a general, minimal account of the common sources of value in the world. It does not, however, require agreement about the value of specific experiences or purposes and thus allows for individual opinions to differ regarding these issues. It thus seeks to define a small space of commonality whilst recognizing the wide-ranging diversity of individuals. This feature will hopefully enable it to command a large degree of consensus.

---

[82] We need not be confined to examining what actually is the case for the being in question, but what could be the case for such a being as well. Thus, my view allows for the possibility that we can make predictions that a certain state will be of greater experiential value for a being even though that is not her current state. The difference between the value of the actual states she experiences and the ones it is possible for her to experience opens up the possibility of criticizing an individual's own understanding of what is best for her. The difficulty of making judgments about when others would be better off would correctly lead to circumspection in this regard, and may partially explain our reluctance to make such judgments in relation to others. For purposes of this chapter, it is not necessary to develop these points further. I make a similar point later in connection with purposes.

These considerations count in favour of the theory I have proposed. Moreover, there is a further argument in favour of this account based upon another interesting feature of the world: despite the diversity of different creatures, it is striking that we are to a large extent mutually intelligible. Were individuals completely different, valuing nothing in common, it would be impossible to understand one another. Davidson claims that '[t]he process of making the beliefs and other propositional attitudes of others intelligible to ourselves necessarily involves our fitting others into our scheme to some degree'.[83] Thus, in order to understand one another, it is necessary that we have at least some shared framework of values.

John Finnis[84] provides an account of the human good that can be understood as an attempt to identify this shared framework that is necessary to understand one another. He identifies seven basic values in human life: life, knowledge, play, aesthetic experience, sociability, practical reasonableness, and religion. These values can be identified, he claims, through the use of practical reason: employing reason in 'identifying the desirable'.[85] That entails analysing human action and understanding the general commitments and purposes which generally render such action intelligible.

However, in order to understand each other, we do not need a detailed or specific account of the good such as is provided by Finnis. Consider a dictator such as Robert Mugabe. Let us attempt to explain why he went to such lengths to rig the March 2002 election in Zimbabwe. Let us say that our explanation is: 'Mugabe wished to retain political power.' That is a familiar form of motivation that we often attribute to political leaders and serves to provide a plausible account of their behaviour. Thus, our very ability to understand others does, it seems, depend upon their conforming to certain patterns of behavioural and motivational assumptions that are recognizable to us.

However, the example highlights two problems with Finnis's account. First, the desire for power is not included amongst his seven basic values of human life. Though he could merely have made a mistake about this, the omission suggests a serious problem with identifying an exhaustive and specific list of the basic values in human life given the diversity of individuals. Secondly, and more seriously, it is unclear that in attempting to explain Mugabe's behaviour, we must share the *specific* value lying behind his action: of wishing to retain political power. Similarly, it is unclear that we must share the specific value of knowledge or aesthetic experience in order to understand the actions of others who pursue these values. What is necessary to explain the actions of others does not appear to be certain shared *specific* values.

What we require is rather a minimal account of certain *general* sources of value we share with others who have certain similarities to us. In my view, the identification of experiences and purposes as the general sources of value is sufficient to enable us to understand the actions of others. Mugabe is intelligible to us because

---

[83] Davidson, 1986: 205.   [84] Finnis, 1980.   [85] Finnis, 1983: 35.

we understand that he is attempting to fulfil his own purposes, even though we regard his *specific* purposes as warped. A drug addict's actions are intelligible to us as we can understand the desire for positive experiences, though we may regard his actions unfavourably. Thus, the thin theory of the good I have defended identifies the shared framework of value necessary to render the actions of others intelligible. It does not go beyond what is strictly necessary for this purpose and thus avoids some of the controversial territory that more specific accounts of the good—such as that of Finnis or Nussbaum—traverse.

6.1 Objection 1: Nozick's experience machine

I have thus far provided reasons for favouring the account of value I have proposed. One of the features that distinguishes my account from that of Rawls is the fact that it does not regard all value in life as deriving from the achievement of goals and purposes. I have also sought to draw attention to another clear source of value in our lives: the ability to have experiences that are of a particular quality.[86]

Finnis,[87] however, claims that it is a modern mistake to think that experience plays an ineliminable role in accounting for what is valuable in human life. He employs Nozick's famous thought-experiment—the 'experience machine'—to support his case.[88] Imagine that one is given the choice to plug into an 'experience machine' which stimulates one's brain whilst floating in a tank and thus provides one with all the positive experiences one could wish to have. One must, however, plug in to the machine for a lifetime or not at all. Finnis claims that no one would choose to plug into such a machine as each person 'wants to *do* certain things (not just have the experience of doing them), one wants to *be* a certain person through one's own authentic, free self-determination and self-realization'.[89]

It is important to be clear about what exactly the 'experience machine' establishes. This thought experiment relies on our intuitions about the quality of a life that is plugged into such a machine. Even if people generally would not wish to plug into the experience machine,[90] that does not mean that there would be no value in the lives of those who choose to become connected to it. It is precisely because there is some attraction to an existence of pure pleasure that the thought experiment is so powerful. Those connected to the experience machine would have positive experiences and so have some form of value in their lives. Yet many think that other features of the situation overshadow the experiential value that is derived.

In specifying what those features of the situation are, we are not led to conclude that experiences lack intrinsic value in the lives of beings. All the thought

---

[86] It is not the case, however, that both characteristics must be present in order for there to be value in the lives of beings. One of the characteristics is sufficient. [87] Finnis, 1980.
[88] Nozick, 1974: 42. [89] Finnis, 1980: 95.
[90] The thought experiment relies on people sharing this intuition. In my experience, the reaction of people to it is not as uniform as Finnis or Nozick would like.

experiment succeeds in establishing is that we regard it as being important that the quality and content of our experiences are connected with the way the world is. Yet this does not in any way imply that experience is somehow unimportant; rather, it shows that a good life is one in which one has positive experiences that connect up reliably with the way the world is. The fact that one does not wish to live in a dream world does not mean that one does not place value upon having positive experiences of the real world.[91]

This point directs our attention to the fact that value in the lives of beings that have a subjective consciousness but live in an external world involves considering the interrelationship between beings and the world. We cannot ignore the component we bring to the world (our experience), but we want to be experiencing things about the world, and doing things in the world itself. The account of value I have developed can recognize this point by providing that experience must connect up reliably with the world.

The second component of value I have identified already implicitly requires there to be a connection between purposive agents and the world. The fact that beings have purposes and wish them to be fulfilled means that they are not satisfied where there is the mere 'illusion' of having their purposes fulfilled. Only the actual realization of their purposes can be a source of value to them. Thus, the fact that purpose fulfilment is one of the sources of value in my account means that individuals would not generally be satisfied by a life lived in the hallucinatory world of the experience machine.

6.2 Objection 2: Is pain always bad?

In defining one of the sources of value as lying in experience, I have suggested that there are some types of experience that virtually always are of negative value to the individuals who experience them. It may be objected, however, that even in the case of painful experiences, there are those who regard them as positive. For instance, sado-masochists regard painful experiences as 'positive'; ascetics regard the experience of starving as 'good'. Thus, it could be argued that an experience is only negative if one regards it as such. Whether one regards an experience as negative can be affected by all sorts of factors, such as one's purposes and the society in which one lives. As a result, there are no experiential states that can be identified uncontroversially as being 'negative'.

Contrary to this argument, I wish to defend the claim that there are in fact certain experiences—such as pain and starvation—that are negative for all beings that experience them. The critics usually accept that this may be the case in most instances but point to exceptional cases to disprove the general claim. I shall offer an alternative explanation for two exceptional cases—the ascetic and the

---

[91] It is an interesting question why it is that we wish our experiences to be connected to the world. I cannot deal with this question here.

sado-masochist—that does not require us to believe that pain in certain instances is 'good'.

What then about the ascetic? In response to this example an element of complexity is added to my account. Beings such as human beings are able to have experiences and choose the purposes they wish to fulfil. Sometimes, there is a conflict between these two sources of value. At times, we choose to undergo experiences that are negative in order to fulfil our purposes. We may be prepared to suffer the momentary pain of a vaccination to allow us to have a vacation on a tropical island. Similarly, we may be prepared to suffer the pain and injuries that often happen when preparing to run a marathon, in order to attain the health benefits thereof or succeed in a personal goal. What is important to recognize is that the negative experiences we subject ourselves to do not become 'positive' merely because of this act of choice. They remain negative, but there is another domain—in relation to the fulfilment of purposes—wherein they can be regarded as positive. The case of the ascetic is thus best explained, in my view, by saying that she has many negative experiences but regards them as valuable in that they accompany the fulfilment of certain purposes that she has freely chosen. In turn, the realization of the ascetic's purposes generates certain positive experiences (that generally accompany the fulfilment of her purposes) in her. In this case, the two dimensions of value I have identified clash, with one superseding the other.[92]

The case of the sado-masochist may, however, appear to be more difficult for my account. Here, an experience most would usually regard as negative is valued as positive by the sado-masochist. There are three possibilities consistent with my account that can explain such a case. First, it could be that the usually painful experience is in fact pleasurable for the sado-masochist. In this instance, there is no clash with my account as in fact there is only a 'positive experience'. It seems unlikely but sado-masochists may just be hard-wired differently from the rest of us.

Alternatively, it could be that sado-masochists experience pain as we do. Yet, such an experience triggers in them a pleasurable experience as well. The phenomenon is a genuinely mixed one: pleasure and pain combine in one experience. Since the pleasure exceeds the pain, sado-masochists subject themselves to such experiences.[93]

The other possibility is that we have a case such as that of the ascetic: sado-masochists have certain purposes—subjecting themselves or others to pain which they see as good—and this dimension of value conflicts with the experiential

[92] The value to the creature of fulfilling his various purposes will have to be judged against the disvalue of the negative experiences. The relative importance of the purpose or the experience for the being will often determine which course of action the being pursues. One's attitude towards commensurability will affect whether one thinks clear-cut judgments can be made in each instance as to which source of value will take precedence.

[93] Thus, when deciding what to do, a particular course of action may lead to both negative and positive experiences. So long as the experiences are commensurable, individuals will prefer that course of action that will tend overall to produce the experience which is maximally positive.

dimension of value. Whichever of these interpretations is accepted of the sado-masochist's experience, it remains possible to identify certain experiences such as pain that are of disvalue to all who have them. This is, in my view, a basic feature of all creatures that are conscious.

Some object that pain in fact is 'good' for a being as it has survival value. However, it is precisely the 'negativity' of pain that leads beings to avoid phenomena that are harmful. The 'benefits' of pain arise precisely from its 'negativity': having a painful experience leads us, in general, to avoid further similar painful experiences, and, in this way, we are enabled to lead lives that are filled with positive experiential value and the fulfilment of our purposes. For most individuals, living in a continual state of pain would be a miserable existence, having little value.

6.3 Objection 3: Mistaken purposes and adaptive preferences

As with the experiential component of value, there are several objections that can be lodged against purposiveness as a source of value. I shall briefly consider two objections that must be mentioned, though cannot fully be answered in this book. I shall suggest responses only insofar as is necessary for developing my theory of fundamental rights.

The first problem relates to the fact that an individual's purposes may vary in accordance with her information and rationality. An individual may initially want to smoke. However, upon finding out that smoking causes lung cancer, the individual would decide that she no longer wishes to smoke. Thus, when deciding upon what is of value to individuals, the question becomes whether we consider an individual's current purposes as determinative of what she values. The alternative is to consider what she would value under certain favourable conditions of evaluation such as full information or rationality.[94] Both accounts that exclusively focus on actual purposes and those that make counterfactual judgments about a being's real purposes face difficulties that need not be resolved here. All I have sought to establish in this chapter is that the fulfilment of purposes is a source of value in the lives of purposive agents: this brief discussion has suggested that we need not be confined to our actual purposes in evaluating this value in the lives of beings.

The second problem concerns the fact that beings often accommodate their subjective purposes to their particular conditions. A being may thus come to be satisfied in conditions that are tremendously meagre. Yet, most people would judge that individuals in such situations do not live well. Consider an example

---

[94] Certain desire accounts of well-being do not focus on actual desires but a person's 'true' desires which are defined as those 'he would have if he had all the relevant factual information, always reasoned with the greatest possible care, and were in a state of mind most conducive to rational choice' (Harsanyi, 1982: 55). See also, Griffin, 1986: 11. For a critique of these accounts, see Scanlon, 1993; and Rosati, 1995.

mentioned by Nussbaum: women in India living in the desert area outside Mahabubnagar were severely malnourished and lived in conditions which violated basic United Nations norms for health, sanitation, and the provision of clean water.[95] Despite such conditions, these women had no desire to change their circumstances and merely accepted that this was their lot in life. They adapted their purposes to fit their position in society.

Accounts of value that include a subjective component are forced to accept the individual's own account as to which purposes or desires are valuable for her. That very determination by an individual is liable to be influenced by the environmental conditions in which an individual finds herself. Thus, accounts of value with a subjective component are bound to legitimize tyranny and validate judgements which merely reflect an accommodation of human expectation to circumstance. 'Consider a very deprived person who is poor, exploited, overworked and ill, but who has been made satisfied with his lot by social conditioning (through, say, religion, or political propaganda, or cultural pressure). Can we possibly believe that he is doing well just because he is happy and satisfied? Can the living standard of a person be high if the life that he or she leads is full of deprivation?'[96]

This problem is often termed 'the adaptive preference problem'. It has been one of the prime motivating reasons to develop an objective account of the good. If a person's own subjective purposes cannot be relied on to determine what is good for them, then it is necessary to go behind such purposes. However, when we consider the components of value in our lives, it is clear that value is in fact in large measure tied to the subjective experiences and purposes of a being. Allowing room for subjectivity in an account of value also allows us to take cognizance of the diverse nature of the good for different individuals. It is thus implausible to remove subjectivity completely from the picture. Yet, any account that retains a room for subjectivity faces the adaptive preference problem in some form or another.

I cannot hope to offer a complete response to this problem here and thus merely wish to point to resources within my own theory that mitigate the force of the problem and may offer the possibility of a solution. First, several philosophers have attempted to examine the conditions under which our preferences, valuations, or purposes are formed. It is often argued that what we need is the ability to identify conditions under which purposes can be formed autonomously such that they are regarded as those of the person themselves.[97] The theory I have proposed situates the source of value in the fulfilment of a being's *own* purposes. A plausible development of the theory could thus provide that it is only in circumstances where purposes are formed autonomously that the fulfilment thereof is valuable for a being.

---

[95] Nussbaum, 2000a: 113.   [96] Sen, 1987: 8.

[97] In this regard, see Arneson, 1990; Sumner, 1996; and Christman, 1989. This strategy will depend upon developing an adequate account of 'autonomy'.

Secondly, the theory I have proposed is not a pure subjectivist theory and includes objective claims about the two sources of value in individual life. I shall argue shortly that there is a further objective element in my account of value that allows us to identify features of the world that are of particular importance to beings. These features of the world are certain objective necessary conditions that must exist in order for beings generally to be able to have positive experiences and fulfil their purposes. These conditions arise as a result of certain facts about the physical, psychological, and social nature of beings that affect their capacity to lead valuable lives. As such, they are not susceptible to much variation between individuals and so provide a ground for judging that, in their absence, individuals will generally be badly off.

This allows for a partial response to the adaptive preference problem. In the exposition of the problem, it was clear that it is most acute where we are led to judge via a subjective theory of the good that an individual is well-off despite being severely deprived. If we can identify objective conditions that are necessary for the very possibility of fulfilling purposes, then it will be possible to judge that individuals are badly off where these conditions are absent, even if their actual purposes have adapted to their circumstances. Yet these objective conditions cover most of the circumstances of severe deprivation. Thus, once we eliminate the possibility that individuals can live well even where these objective conditions are not present, we have succeeded in strongly reducing the force of the adaptive preference problem.

It is important to point out that these objective conditions are identified by considering what is generally necessary for a particular species (or several species) to have the sources of value in their lives. It is the physical or psychological similarities between beings that allow for the identification of such conditions. The generality of such conditions provides a safeguard against rendering such judgements relative to the particular circumstances of an individual. Where these conditions are not met, we judge that individuals will generally be badly off. Where individuals maintain that they are well off despite these objective conditions not being present, we will need to analyse whether this is as a result of a freely chosen lifestyle choice or an adaptation of their purposes to a pre-existing situation of deprivation. The similarity of individual physical and psychological natures would lead us to be sceptical, for instance, about accepting individual claims that they are well-off even when malnourished. It is to the task of identifying these objective conditions that I now turn.

7 Judgements of Priority

I have thus far argued that there are two sources of value in individual lives: the first source of value is in having experiences with a positive phenomenological content; the second source of value is in the fulfilment of a being's purposes.

However, individuals also characteristically make judgements about different levels of importance that various goods have for them. Those judgements can have a number of sources: they may, for instance, vary with individual purposes and experiences, and so prevent us from drawing any conclusions about what is of particular importance to beings in general. The question in this section concerns whether it is possible to identify certain general features of the world that beings must generally regard as having particular importance for them. If we can answer this question in the affirmative, it will be possible to judge that individual lives go particularly badly where such features of the world are lacking in their lives.

The general argument in this section shall be that in relation to all physical beings with consciousness, it is possible to identify certain general and essential preconditions that are required for such beings to realize the sources of value I have identified. If we can identify such preconditions, we can identify what must necessarily be realized in order for beings to lead lives of value to them. I shall argue that we can identify certain objective preconditions which can be divided into two thresholds. Both are of significance in the lives of beings but the first threshold has a greater urgency than the second threshold for individuals. The importance of recognizing different thresholds within the class of objective preconditions and the greater urgency of the first threshold will be argued for in Chapter 6.

7.1 The necessary preconditions for being free from threats to survival

One clear precondition for having experiences or purposes at all is survival. Since existence is a necessary condition for the realization of what is valuable in our lives—experiences and purposes—it too must be of central significance in the lives of beings. The ability to maintain one's existence can thus be identified as a particularly important interest of beings.

There are many goods and resources that are necessary for maintaining a being's survival. Some of these will depend upon the type of beings that we are concerned with. A certain level of food is necessary for the survival of all beings. For human beings, some shelter too is necessary for survival. These goods and resources can thus be termed 'survival needs' and are clearly of particular value to any being.

It is important to recognize that survival needs will generally be fairly minimal. A very small amount of food can keep an individual alive. An individual may have sufficient food to maintain her survival but lack sufficient food to be free from malnutrition. Similarly, an individual's environmental conditions can be adequate to keep her alive but not be adequate to keep her healthy. These states of malnutrition or ill-health would themselves be of general disvalue to beings as they would prevent individuals from having positive experiences and impair the realization of their purposes. As a result, it is clear that the interest in having the necessary resources to be able to survive does not exhaust the objective preconditions that can be identified as necessary for living lives of value.

However, it is important to point out that in many of these instances—of severe malnutrition or ill-health—there would in fact be a strong threat to the survival of beings, and thus their ability to have any value in their lives whatsoever. Chronic malnutrition may not kill immediately but progressively over many years. Thus, the first threshold I have identified is best specified as requiring that beings be in such a position as to be free from the general conditions that threaten their survival.[98] That would involve having access to a higher level of resources than that merely required to maintain bare survival.

7.2 The general necessary preconditions for the fulfilment of purposes

However, being free from the general conditions that threaten survival does not exhaust the objective preconditions that can be identified which are necessary for realizing the sources of value in the lives of beings. In trying to define a sphere of objective interests that are of primary importance, Rawls' account of 'primary goods' is often regarded as a natural starting point. He argues that the primary goods are the 'necessary conditions for realizing the powers of moral personality and are all-purpose means for a sufficiently wide range of final ends'.[99] I have already criticized Rawls' conception of the ends that the primary goods aim to fulfil; however, now I wish to consider whether a range of particularly important interests can be identified by the idea of identifying objective necessary conditions for realizing a being's purposes.

7.2.1 Defining the threshold

A famous objection has been made to Rawls' account of primary goods. It has been argued that if one is to be fair between differing ends, then the primary goods, understood as all-purpose means, must help to promote each end to the same extent. However, it has been contended that the primary goods fail to promote each person's purposes to the same extent. As such, they are not 'all-purpose means' but rather means of realizing particular conceptions of the good. The primary goods, it is argued, will be differentially useful to people depending on their final aims, and in particular will be biased towards those with individualistic goals.[100]

---

[98] It is necessary to add the caveat that these conditions must be capable of being eliminated without restricting the person's ability to achieve the sources of value. Thus, legislation to prevent people driving motor vehicles owing to the threat they pose to survival would be impermissible as a result of the fact that such vehicles also provide the mobility necessary to fulfil one's purposes.

[99] Rawls, 1999b: 367.

[100] Nagel, 1973; Schwartz, 1973; Arneson, 1990b: 429. Rawls has replied to this claim, and there have been responses to his reply: see Arneson, 1990b.

In responding to this objection, it is important to point out that in considering these particular preconditions, I am not attempting to examine the content of the purposes that beings have or how far each is able to realize their particular purposes. Rather, it is important to understand whether there are certain general shared conditions that must be realized for beings to be able to fulfil their purposes. If there are such conditions, then these will be of particular importance to each being, whatever their particular purposes. There do in actual fact seem to be such general conditions. Being in a state of health, for instance, will be of importance to anyone wishing to fulfil any purposes whatsoever and, similarly, having an adequate amount of food will be of great importance to any purposive being. Thus, it is possible to identify certain general conditions necessary for beings to fulfil any purposes whatsoever.

It could be objected, however, that satisfying these conditions that are necessary for the fulfilment of any purposes whatsoever does not take us much beyond the level required for survival. Once a being is alive and capable of minimal functioning, he or she is capable of realizing at least some purposes. Also, some individuals may actually decide to adopt purposes that are self-denying and thus may only require what is necessary for a very minimal level of survival. Thus, it is unclear whether in identifying these general conditions we have merely succeeded in reformulating the first threshold—the necessary conditions to be free from the general conditions that threaten survival—in a different way, without substantially increasing the level of provision and goods required to meet this threshold.

Setting this standard so low is, however, problematic. It only identifies what is of particular importance to those with purposes that require minimal resources to realize them. It thus fails to identify general conditions necessary for the realization of a diversity of purposes. Yet it is that set of objective conditions we must identify if we are to find a common interest between a set of diverse beings. The reason for this is that beings differ and, as a result, their purposes differ. To identify a shared interest that is of particular importance to the full range of beings, it must be an interest in having access to general conditions that are necessary for the realization of a *diversity* of purposes, rather than merely a minimal range of purposes.

Individuals might also change their purposes throughout their lives. If this is so, then it is of particular importance that individuals be guaranteed the objective conditions that would not only involve the fulfilment of their current purposes, but also place them in a general position to be able to change their purposes.[101] If this threshold is too minimal, then it is unlikely to enable individuals to realize different purposes in their own lives should they so wish.

However, it is then arguable that the converse problem arises. Some people have purposes that require a lot of goods and others require only a minimal amount of goods. Thus, some people will regard having a television as a necessary

---

[101] Buchanan, 1975 has put forward an argument to this effect in his defence of Rawlsian primary goods.

precondition for realizing their purposes, whilst others will only require a small amount of food and minimal shelter. To enable each to realize the full range of purposes would involve essentially providing everyone with everything they could conceivably want. The threshold would collapse into the statement that each person must have all the necessary resources to fulfil her purposes. In such an instance, no general shared objective conditions would be identifiable that would be of particular importance to a wide range of individuals.

In response, however, an important distinction should be drawn. Each creature no doubt has an interest in the fulfilment of his or her particular purposes. In order to do so, however, certain general conditions must be met. These conditions are of priority as, in their absence, the creature cannot attempt to fulfil or realize the particular purposes he has or adopts. They are also of particular importance as these conditions are not only implicated in the fulfilment of one particular purpose, but they are instrumental in satisfying various other purposes as well.[102] Thus, there is a difference between the fulfilment of particular purposes and achieving certain states of the body and control over resources which enable beings to realize a diversity of purposes. These general conditions are the ones that provide the opportunities to fulfil a range of purposes, and are thus of particular importance to all purposive beings, even if they do not share many particular purposes.

Are there any such general necessary conditions that can be identified? Two points are important here. First, our ability to identify such conditions may depend upon restricting our focus to beings of a certain type. If the nature of beings of a particular type diverge too much, then it will not be possible to identify shared general conditions necessary for the realization of a wide range of their purposes. There is thus important empirical work to be done in attempting to identify the similar natural and social conditions that must obtain in order for creatures of a particular type to be enabled to realize their purposes. What we need to do is to analyse the similarity in structure between the nature of certain beings and their purposes in order to arrive at the general conditions necessary to realize a diversity of purposes.[103] Secondly, it is important to recognize that no being is prejudiced by having certain conditions met that are greater than necessary to realize his particular purposes. Since one is not compelled to use these resources, there is no prejudice should one be provided with more than one needs.

7.2.2 Capabilities or resources?

It is important now to consider an example as to whether these considerations actually allow for the identification of a level of provision that is of priority and falls between the first threshold relating to survival needs and the complete

---

102 Goodin, 1988b: 39 explicates the priority of needs over wants in this way.

103 Thus, Rawls states (1993: 180) that we need to identify a 'partial similarity in the structure of citizen's permissible conceptions of the good'. In order to have a shared idea of rational advantage, it is important that people require roughly the same primary goods to advance their ends. 'We suppose

fulfilment of beings' particular purposes. Before doing so, however, it is necessary to consider the manner in terms of which this level of provision is to be specified. The issue arises in the context of Sen's objection that Rawls makes a fetish of primary goods. Rawls, he claims, is guilty of regarding the achievement of equal levels of primary goods as desirable in itself.

However, Sen contends that equal levels of primary goods would have a differential impact on different people. A disabled person, for instance, would require more resources in order to be able to move around than a person without such a disability: 'while goods and services are valuable, they are not valuable in themselves. Their value rests on what they can do for people or rather, what people can do with these goods and services.'[104] We should not as a result be interested purely in the level of primary goods that each being has but rather, Sen suggests, whether such goods enable people to function in a valuable way. Thus, the threshold that determines what is of particular importance to beings should not be specified in terms of access to certain goods but in terms of the functionings and capabilities of beings.

It is clear that the threshold I have identified is concerned to articulate the general conditions necessary for beings to be able to realize a diversity of purposes. Thus, ultimately, what we are concerned about are the abilities and capacities of beings. We are not simply interested in whether a being is provided with a certain amount of food for its own sake, but about whether such food provides a being with the general capabilities necessary to enable them to fulfil a diverse range of purposes. Thus, my account can be said to require specification in terms of certain objective functionings and capabilities.

However, even though this is true, the matter is a little more complex. There are certain resources that are generally necessary to enable beings to achieve these capabilities. Whilst we wish to achieve the general capabilities that enable us to realize our purposes, we can also identify particular goods that are necessary conditions for realizing these capabilities. The capabilities alone are fairly abstract and fail to provide sufficient detail as to what is of particular importance to beings. That is why, in specifying the threshold of priority in question, it is necessary to make reference both to certain goods and to the capabilities that we are concerned with. I shall proceed in what follows by examining an example of a capability with which we are concerned, and then specifying the goods necessary to realize that capability.

In order for a being to have purposes and realize them, two types of conditions are necessary. The first is that certain conditions must be fulfilled in relation to the internal workings of a being. In order for beings to be able to realize their purposes, they must be in a state of physical and psychological health. To maintain

---

that all citizens have a rational plan of life that requires for its fulfilment roughly the same kind of primary goods'(at 181). In saying this, he claims, 'we rely on various common sense psychological facts about human needs, their phases of development and so on' (at 181).

[104] Sen, 1984: 510.

health and bodily functioning, certain goods are necessary. For instance, it is crucial for human beings that they are provided with food adequate to meet the nutritional requirements of a human being. Here, it is interesting to note that one cannot just be provided with that level of food necessary to be free from threats to one's survival. As has already been mentioned, such a level of provision may well keep one alive but still undernourished. A person who is undernourished, however, will be hindered in the pursuit of a wide range of purposes. As such, if we wish to protect the conditions necessary to pursue diverse purposes, we must make sure that people are not undernourished and constantly hungry. In such an instance, the food must be sufficient that human beings have the energy and vitality necessary to pursue a range of purposes. The level of food required does not entail that individuals share a priority interest in such luxuries as ice cream and caviar. However, it does mean that individuals have a priority interest in well-balanced nutritional food that enables them to be healthy and physically vigorous, thus being capable of realizing a wide range of purposes. In turn, it is important to realize that recognizing this threshold of priority does not determine exactly which foods will be provided. Having nutritional food is consistent with providing different types of food, and which types of food are chosen will no doubt depend on the tastes and preferences of the individuals concerned.

Similar remarks could be made in relation to human beings about having access to housing, clothing and medical care. Such goods all concern the bodily and mental states of an individual that must be obtained if they are to be in a condition such that they are able to realize a wide range of purposes. However, in describing these necessary conditions, it is not sufficient to focus purely upon the bodily states of individuals but we need to consider the social conditions in which they exist as well. If one is in excellent bodily shape, but will be imprisoned if one attempts to realize one's purposes, then one is frustrated in the pursuit of one's purposes despite being in peak bodily condition.

Thus, it seems that certain protections for individual liberty are necessary conditions for realizing a wide range of purposes. Individuals will be unable to pursue a range of purposes if hindered from doing so through fear of harm to their sense of bodily security. Moreover, human beings typically require the liberty to express themselves and to act according to their purposes if they are to have a hope of realizing them. Thus, protection of freedom of speech and action is a necessary precondition for realizing a diversity of purposes. Similar points could be made about freedom of association, and freedom of belief. In addition, there is a general need for individuals to have control over some of the resources in the world in order to realize a range of purposes. Beings with a highest-order interest in purpose-fulfilment will thus have an interest in a system that allows them control over some resources.

It is thus possible to attain a fair degree of specificity as to the functionings, capabilities, and resources that are necessary preconditions for being able to realize a wide range of purpose. Even the fairly general analysis above has indicated that the level of provision necessary to meet this threshold will exceed that which is required to meet the first threshold of survival. To achieve more specific determinations as to the practical meaning of this threshold requires additional empirical facts (regarding what constitutes sufficient nutrition, for instance). Such facts will mean that, to some extent, the actual necessary conditions for realizing a variety of purposes will vary in accordance with the particular circumstances of beings. In a rural town where distances are very small, people will be able to achieve a range of purposes without having access to a system of transport. On the other hand, in large cities where one cannot achieve much without being able to move around over larger distances, the existence of a system of transport will constitute a necessary precondition for realizing a wide range of purposes for the affected people.

It is thus possible to specify a threshold of priority at a level greater than that required for survival, but which does not involve the complete fulfilment of each being's particular purposes. The ability to specify this threshold is of immense importance to the task of specifying the level of provision required in a society that recognizes socio-economic rights. It is also of great importance in our judgements about individual well-being, as without the fulfilment of these conditions, it becomes clear that individuals are impaired in their ability to realize one of the sources of value in their lives.

A similar threshold could also be developed in relation to the other source of value: experiential value. There are certain shared conditions that generally give rise to negative experiences and would prevent a being from having positive experiences. There is a strong degree of overlap between the general conditions identified by a threshold focused on experiences and one focused on purposes. For ease of use and simplicity, I shall thus focus on the threshold that I have specified as involving the general necessary conditions for realizing a variety of purposes.

7.3 Shared purposes

I have argued that the source of value in the lives of beings does not lie in the species we belong to but rather certain characteristics we have. These characteristics—being able to experience or have purposes—are shared by many species. It is to be expected, however, that in specifying the content of the experiences and purposes that are valued, similar types of creatures will find certain similarities between what they regard as valuable. Thus, most human beings are likely to share certain characteristics that lead them to regard certain activities and practices as valuable.

It is interesting to note that in almost all known human societies, some form of music has developed. Similarly, we note that across diverse nations, there is a shared interest in sport. The shared and widespread nature of these goods suggests that they have some specific importance for human beings on either or both of the experiential or purposive dimensions of value. The mere fact that they are shared cannot, however, determine that they are of positive value; rather, the shared and universal nature of these purposes provides evidence of what human beings typically regard as being of value to them. In deciding which purposes to adopt oneself, or which purposes to promote in a society, such evidence may be of great significance. Thus, beyond the thresholds I have identified, there may well be other features of our lives—such as music and sport—that are of particular importance to beings of a certain type. The identification of these things may depend upon empirical and contextual factors that are not amenable to theorizing of the type exhibited in this chapter.

8　Conclusion

Thus, I have attempted to offer solutions to two important questions in this chapter. The first problem concerned how to arrive at an account of what is of value to beings. I have suggested that this can be done through identifying two general characteristics of beings—the ability to have experiences with a particular quality, and the ability to fulfil purposes—which both have an essential evaluative element. The second aim of this chapter has been to try to understand whether there are features of beings' lives that can be said to have particular importance for them: these features may be termed the 'urgent interests' of beings. I have attempted to use the account of value developed in this chapter to argue for the existence of two thresholds concerning shared interests that are of particular importance for beings. These conclusions are useful not only in providing us with a deeper understanding of what beings value but also in guiding decisions about what we ought to do. The next chapter attempts to understand the relationship between the thin theory of the good that I have developed in this chapter and the entitlements that a society must recognize that beings have.

2

The Justification of Fundamental Rights

1 Introduction

In the previous chapter, I attempted to offer a theory of value for beings with a subjective experience of the world, and to develop an account of what can be said to be the 'urgent interests' of such beings. The question that I am concerned with in this chapter concerns the relationship between the claim that 'x is an urgent interest for a particular being y' and the claim that 'y has a fundamental right to have x satisfied'.

In this chapter, I shall first consider Gewirth's attempt to derive fundamental rights from the basic presuppositions of human agency. After pointing out a fundamental flaw in his argument, I shall consider the possibility of using an argument by Nagel to plug the gap. Ultimately, Nagel's argument does not succeed in solving Gewirth's difficulty. Nevertheless, it suggests an important insight: if we are to avoid solipsism, there must be an impersonal perspective from which we can understand and make statements about the lives of other beings with a subjective consciousness.

The second part of this chapter attempts to provide a more successful argument for fundamental rights. It is contended that from the impersonal perspective Nagel identifies, the value present in the life of each sentient being must be regarded as equal to the value present in the life of any other sentient being. That impersonal perspective in turn is the one that should be adopted by a society in deciding upon the basic framework of rules to govern it. Thus, a society is bound to recognize the equal value of each sentient being's life. When this idea is combined with a theory of urgent interests, I shall contend that it is possible to generate a powerful argument for fundamental rights. The last section of this chapter will respond to objections that can be made against this theory.

2 The Presuppositions of Agency and Fundamental Rights

2.1 Gewirth's argument

Fundamental rights are recognized in the constitutions and institutions of a wide range of societies today: the South African Constitution, for instance, recognizes amongst others the right to freedom of expression, the right to life, the right to freedom of association, the right to have access to adequate housing, and the right to have access to sufficient food and water. Most of these rights are also enshrined in a number of International Covenants. Why are individuals said to have these rights? A common claim is that individuals have certain compelling interests in being able to speak freely, to live without a violent threat to their survival, to have their basic needs taken care of. These interests are of such importance that they justify being given protection by rights, which ensure that individual freedoms are respected, and that basic needs are provided for. Nussbaum, for instance, states that '[t]he basic intuition from which the capability approach begins, in the political arena, is that certain human abilities exert a moral claim that they should be developed'.[1]

However, more needs to be said about the step from the fact that beings have certain fundamental interests to the claim that they have a right to have those interests satisfied. There seems to be a clear difference between recognizing that some ability or interest is good for a being and that the being has an entitlement against others to have it developed or realized. On the theory of value I have presented in the first chapter, it is clear that pleasant mental experiences are good for beings, though it is a completely different matter whether one is entitled to claim that others must provide one with pleasant mental experiences. It is thus unclear how interests and abilities in and of themselves justify strong entitlements without any further premises.

Alan Gewirth has presented an argument that attempts to bridge the gap between interests and entitlements. In the first chapter, I considered the early stages in Gewirth's argument for human rights. The critique did not pierce to the heart of the theory and merely sought to raise certain complexities about the notion of purposiveness that Gewirth's theory could accommodate and still remain intact. I now wish to consider the remainder of the argument Gewirth provides for human rights, and shall subject it to a critique that is more damaging.

The first two steps in the argument have been discussed in Chapter 1. First, Gewirth claims that every agent makes an implicit judgement that the purposes for which she acts are good.[2] Secondly, every agent must value 'freedom' and 'well-being', which are collectively the most general and proximate necessary conditions for an agent's purposive action.[3]

The next step in Gewirth's argument is to claim that an agent who regards freedom and well-being as necessary goods is logically committed to holding that others ought to respect and provide her with these goods. His basic argument for this proposition is as follows: an agent is committed to regarding her purposes as good. Endorsing the goodness of her purposes entails endorsing having freedom and well-being, the necessary goods for purposive action. Each agent who judges

---

[1] Nussbaum, 2000: 83. Similarly, Raz states that '[t]he specific role of rights in practical thinking is . . . the grounding of duties in the interests of other beings' (1986: 180).
[2] Gewirth, 1978: 52.   [3] Ibid: 63.

that she ought to do X must also be committed to judging that she ought to have the necessary conditions that can enable her to do X. Each agent is thus committed to judging that others must not interfere with her freedom and well-being, and if necessary, provide her with these goods. She can thus be said, on Gewirth's view, to have a prudential right to freedom and well-being.[4] At this point in the argument, the judgement that she has these prudential rights is relative to what each agent must necessarily believe about what she requires in order to realize her purposes.

In order to generate a supreme moral principle that is binding on all agents, Gewirth invokes the logical principle of universalizability: 'if some predicate P belongs to some subject S because S has the property Q (where the "because" is that of sufficient reason or condition), then P must also belong to all other subjects S1, S2 . . . .Sn, that have Q.'[5] Thus, if one person has a right because she has a certain quality Q, and Q is the sufficient reason for having the right, then all others with such a quality Q must also be held to have the right (otherwise Q is not the sufficient reason for having the right). In Gewirth's theory, the property Q that justifies any particular person claiming rights in her own case is the fact that she is a prospective agent with purposes to fulfil (and thus requires freedom and well-being as necessary conditions for purposive action).[6] But, if this is so, we can invoke the principle of universalizability to infer that each person is committed to holding that all other prospective agents with purposes to fulfil also have rights to freedom and well-being. Thus, we reach the conclusion that all prospective agents with purposes to fulfil have rights to freedom and well-being.

Those subjects who are affected by one's actions are termed 'recipients' by Gewirth. Where these recipients are prospective agents, they must, according to the above argument, be recognized to have rights to freedom and well-being, and this attribution of rights to recipients requires the agent to comply with these rights.[7] Such rights involve a negative component of not coercing or harming recipients, and a positive component of assisting them to attain freedom and well-being where they cannot otherwise have them. Gewirth terms the supreme moral principle which expresses these claims, 'The Principle of Generic Consistency: act in accord with the generic rights of your recipients as well as yourself'.[8]

Gewirth's case for fundamental rights can thus be summarized in the following schematic argument.

(1) Purposive action has two central features: voluntariness and purposiveness.

(2) An agent who acts voluntarily and purposively makes an implicit judgement that the purposes for which she acts are good.

(3) Since an agent values her purposes, she must also be committed to achieving that which is necessary to achieve her purposes. Freedom and well-being are necessary goods for achieving an agent's purposes; thus, every agent must be

---

[4] Ibid: 79–80.   [5] Ibid: 105.   [6] Ibid: 109.   [7] Ibid: 146.
[8] Ibid: 135.

committed to having freedom and well-being as necessary goods for achieving her purposes.

(4) An agent who regards freedom and well-being as necessary goods is logically committed to holding that all other people must refrain from interfering with her (and must provide her with) freedom and well-being. This is tantamount to asserting she has a 'right' to freedom and well-being.

(5) The logical principle of universalizability holds that 'if some predicate P belongs to some subject S because S has the property Q (where the "because" is that of sufficient reason or condition), then P must also belong to all other subjects S1, S2....Sn, that have Q'.

(6) Since the sufficient reason for an agent holding that she has rights to freedom and well-being is that she is a prospective agent with purposes to fulfil, she must recognize that all other prospective agents with purposes to fulfil also have rights to freedom and well-being.

(7) Thus, each prospective agent with purposes to fulfil is obligated to act in a way that respects and fulfils the rights of other agents to freedom and well-being.

2.2 The gap in Gewirth

I now turn to consider whether the argument Gewirth provides for the recognition of fundamental rights is valid. In particular, I wish to focus on the step, where he moves from the claim that each agent must judge, relative to her standpoint, that others ought not to interfere (must provide her) with her freedom and well-being, to the claim that each agent ought to respect the freedom and well-being of every other agent.

A crucial feature of Gewirth's theory is the fact that his method is dialectic and not assertoric: more simply put, he attempts to reach conclusions from statements that arise relative to a particular point of view, namely, that of the agent. His reason for doing so relates to two problems he imputes to naturalistic theories of rights. Naturalistic theories, he claims, attempt to make assertions about the value of certain purposes based upon certain natural facts about people's desires, interests, or strivings. This leads to the illicit attempt to move directly from facts to values and thus the so-called 'naturalistic fallacy'. The second problem is that of relativism. Where agents have different and conflicting purposes, not all of these can be regarded as good. The problem is that people differ according to what they regard as good, and so it is unclear what is actually good on naturalistic theories.[9]

Gewirth's dialectical method, on the other hand, attempts to portray action and its purposes as these are viewed by the purposive agent herself from within her conative standpoint. Thus, the difference is between naturalistic claims of the form 'A does X for purpose E; therefore E is good' and dialectical claims of the form 'A does X for purpose E; therefore, A thinks (or holds) that E is good'.[10]

---

[9] Gewirth, 1978: 159–60.   [10] Ibid: 160.

The latter statement is less controversial than the former statement, and thus Gewirth proposes to erect an ethical theory on the foundation of such dialectical statements.

However, working from the standpoint of the agent[11] raises problems all its own. The difficulty lies in moving from a statement about what an agent judges to be in his interest—a prudential statement—to a moral statement whereby an agent is bound by a moral obligation whether or not it is in his interest to perform. A number of philosophers have claimed that Gewirth fails to show how one can move from the prudential to the moral, and that this represents a critical gap in his theory.[12] I shall concentrate on the problem as laid out in its most recent form by Kramer.[13]

The problem arises at step four in the schematic argument I presented above. At this point in the argument, Gewirth wishes to establish that an agent must claim rights to freedom and well-being as a result of her recognition that they are necessary goods to achieve her purposes. Yet, it is crucial to recognize that at this point the rights-claim merely reflects what the agent must judge, *relative to her standpoint*, as being required of others if she is to attain her purposes. '[I]n making his rights-claim, the agent is thus not claiming that other persons have their own prudential or other reasons for according him the rights in question; he is saying or implying only that he has his own prudential reasons for holding that he has these rights against other persons.'[14]

Clearly, the particular agent is committed to judging that she should have freedom and well-being in order to act. But, if a moral principle is to be generated, we have to understand why each agent must accept that she should respect the rights of **others** to freedom and well-being. Why then, on Gewirth's theory must each agent recognize the rights of others to freedom and well-being? Kramer claims that an analysis of the necessary conditions of agency for each agent cannot in itself generate a moral principle to respect those conditions in the case of others. The fact that as an agent I must will that I have freedom and well-being provides you with no reason to comply with what I want. The problem is that the judgements to which purposive agents are committed do not provide reasons for action to other agents when those judgements are addressed to those other agents. There is no reason of self-interest that is provided at this point for recognizing the generic rights of others, nor has a moral principle yet been generated. This leads Kramer to reject Gewirth's usage of the notion of a prudential right:[15] '[a]n agent cannot correctly hold that other persons ought to abstain from interference, while admitting that the others have no reason to abstain.'[16]

---

[11] These problems also attach to the possibility of recasting Gewirth's argument as working from the idea of what experiencing beings must necessarily value.

[12] See, for instance, Lomasky, 1981 and Hare, 1984.   [13] Kramer, 1999a: 174–99.

[14] Gewirth, 1980: 65–6.

[15] See Scheuermann, 1987 for a discussion on the concept of a 'prudential right'.

[16] Kramer, 1999b: 177.

Kramer, in my view, overstates his case when he claims that the agency needs of an agent provide no reason for other agents to respect such needs, unless their interests converge. He tends to divide having reasons into two categories: the prudential and the moral. If a person has neither moral nor prudential reasons, he is then said to have no reason at all.[17] Kramer qualifies this claim in a footnote and it is important to stress that human beings can be motivated by altruistic reasons: the fact that a particular action is in the interests of others may be sufficient reason for persons to act thereon. John may decide to buy a sweet for the child in the queue behind him at the supermarket merely because it will cause her happiness. The interests of others can motivate us even if we are not bound by a moral obligation or act in our own self-interest.

Recognition of this point is not sufficient, however, to save Gewirth's theory. For Gewirth wishes to generate a moral judgement about what rights all agents ought to respect from the fact that each is committed to a strong claim that she should have freedom and well-being. Yet, the fact that X may recognize that Y's claim to have her agency needs met may provide some (altruistic) reason to act in accordance with those needs does not imply that X is obligated to satisfy Y's agency needs. Gewirth wants to generate a rights claim, and altruistic motivation merely gives X some reason to realize Y's agency needs, without giving him a conclusive and binding reason to do so. Gewirth's argument also becomes much more tenuous if it is dependent upon altruistic motivation to generate rights. People who do not recognize altruistic reasons or are not motivated by them would then have no reason to recognize such rights. Yet Gewirth wishes to claim that all agents are logically committed to respecting the generic rights of others merely by virtue of their being purposive agents.

Kramer goes on to argue that, when the initial rights-claim in Gewirth's argument is relativized to the standpoint of each agent, the process of universalization cannot generate the supreme moral principle. The reason for this is as follows: universalization moves us simply from the judgement that each agent must will that others should not interfere with his freedom and well-being to the universal claim that every agent must will that others should not interfere with his freedom and well-being. However, this does not say anything about whether each agent ought to comply with what his fellow agents must will. Consequently, the universalized judgement is not an other-addressing prescription, but merely a statement about the necessary conditions of agency.[18] Kramer admits that, when the interests of a number of agents converge, then they will each have reasons to respect the rights of others; but equally, where they conflict, they will lack binding reasons to do so. Thus, Gewirth's attempt to derive a supreme and universal moral principle collapses. This problem is a direct result of rendering the initial judgement that one has a 'right' relative to the standpoint of each agent. The problem lies in seeing

17 Kramer, 1999b: 189.   18 Ibid: 184.

why others who do not occupy the same standpoint as the agent should accept his judgement regarding his entitlements.

It seems that one response is to reject the claim that agents do not occupy the same standpoint. The problem is that the dialectically necessary method does not operate from such a shared viewpoint. The judgements we make are not universal judgements for all agents, but judgements from our own perspectives and in our own interest. Is there a way to bridge this gap? Thomas Nagel has put forward such a theory. He claims that reasons have both a personal aspect and an impersonal aspect to them, and that the reasons each accepts from his own standpoint can also be applicable beyond this standpoint. Nagel's theory would have the result that if I, as an agent, have a reason for claiming that others ought to respect my rights to freedom and well-being, then there is a reason for all agents why they ought to respect my freedom and well-being. It is clear that Gewirth requires a position like this in order to generate his moral principle.[19] It is therefore important to investigate Nagel's position in more detail.

3 Nagel's Strategy: Impersonal and Personal Reasons

3.1 Nagel's argument

Gewirth argues for the position that each individual agent must will that others not interfere with (or provide her with) the necessary conditions of her agency, namely, freedom and well-being. That is a reason that Nagel would refer to as a personal or subjective reason: it relates to seeing the world through a particular perspective, making a judgement from a certain point of view. Nagel claims, however, that 'we are also able to think about the world in abstraction from our particular position in it'.[20] He refers to this as the impersonal standpoint on the world. The reasons that we generate from the impersonal standpoint on the world can be agent-relative or agent-neutral. An agent-neutral reason is a reason that can be given a general form but which does not involve essential reference to the person who has it. If the general form of a reason does include an essential reference to the person who has it, it is an agent-relative reason. Thus, if we say that anyone has a reason to do something because it is in her interest, then this is a judgement made from the impersonal point of view, but it is agent-relative.[21]

Nagel considers the particular examples of pleasure and pain, and accepts that almost everyone takes the avoidance of pain and the promotion of pleasure as personal reasons for action. He then questions what we can say about the value of pleasure and pain when viewed in abstraction from our personal perspectives.[22] First, he claims that we must at least recognize from the objective point of view

---

[19] Lomasky, 1981: 252, for instance, suggests that Gewirth pursue Nagel's strategy.
[20] Nagel, 1991: 10.   [21] Nagel, 1986: 153.   [22] Ibid: 157.

that pleasure and pain are good or bad for us. This is because we cannot 'from an objective standpoint withhold a certain kind of endorsement of the most direct and immediate subjective value judgements we make concerning the contents of our own consciousness'.[23] To hold otherwise would imply, for instance, that one is required from an objective point of view to recognize that one has no reason to relieve a headache, even though one is subjectively motivated to do so. Since this seems absurd, Nagel claims that there are at least agent-relative reasons to 'seek pleasure and avoid pain'.

The question then arises whether the promotion of pleasure and avoidance of pain can provide agent-neutral reasons from an objective point of view. Nagel makes the following two arguments to establish that pleasure is good and pain bad no matter whose they are. First, as an objective spectator, we acknowledge that X has a reason to want pain to stop, but if the reason is only agent-relative, one can see no reason from anyone else's point of view for wanting the pain to stop. However, the pain 'can be detached in thought from the fact that it is mine without losing any of its dreadfulness. It has, so to speak, a life of its own. That is why it is natural to ascribe to it a value of its own ... [I]n its most primitive form, the fact that it is mine—the concept of myself—doesn't come into my perception of the badness of pain.'[24] This supports the view that the badness of pain can provide an agent-neutral reason to avoid it.

Secondly, Nagel argues that if we assign impersonal value to pleasure and pain, then people are committed to judging that pain is bad and should be avoided, and not only that each person from his own perspective has reason to want it gone. On the other hand, if 'we limit ourselves to relative reasons, he will have to say that though he has a reason to want an analgesic (for instance), there is no reason for him to have one, or for anyone else to be around to give him one'.[25] Nagel claims that there is a fundamental dissociation that occurs to an individual in such a circumstance which arises from accepting two claims: the attitude that X has reason for wanting the pain to stop, but that there is no reason why it should be stopped which others should accept. This dissociation that occurs as a result of the failure to accept the agent-neutrality of pain is, according to Nagel, akin to committing ourselves to a type of solipsism about the world. I shall now elaborate on his argument for this claim.

To recognize others fully as persons requires a conception of oneself as identical with a particular inhabitant of the world, among others of a similar nature. According to a solipsist, all descriptions of situations are personal and essentially related to one's own point of view. There is no way to translate statements from one's own point of view into statements about others who have different points of view on the world. A central assumption of our lives is that we are not solipsists. A rejection of solipsism involves a commitment to a world in which there are others like us, and to concepts which apply beyond the realm of our own experiences and circumstances.

---

[23] Nagel, 1986: 158.   [24] Ibid: 160–1.   [25] Ibid: 160.

In the practical realm, this implies that we are committed to principles that can be understood in a way not fundamentally tied to a particular perspective. We thus require practical motivational principles that can be impersonally formulated.[26] Agent-relative reasons only justify a desire for things bearing a certain relation to oneself. And although agent-relative reasons provide a justification from an impersonal point of view, they can only provide the motivation to act from the personal perspective. 'The motivational content which forms an essential part of a first-person practical judgement is therefore missing entirely from an impersonal judgement about the same individual, if that judgement derives from a subjective principle.'[27]

Thus, agent-relative reasons provide us with reasons that motivate from the personal point of view alone. From the impersonal point of view, we could not explain why agents were motivated by such personal reasons. If this is so, however, one would be forced to recognize that these motivational reasons are fundamentally tied to a particular perspective. That in turn would entail an analogue of solipsism in the practical realm: since one could only explain one's motivation from the personal point of view, one would be committed to viewing the personal realm as fundamentally inaccessible to others and dissociated from them. If we are to regard ourselves from the perspective of being one individual amongst others, however, then it is necessary that we do not see our motivational reasons as linked solely to the personal realm. In order for this to be true, however, it must be that for each agent-relative reason there is in fact a corresponding agent-neutral reason.

I shall now attempt a schematic summary of Nagel's argument.

(1) Solipsism is the view that there are no others besides oneself. It often involves the supposition that the concepts which one applies to one's own experience do not include the possibility of application in the same sense to anything which is not one's experience.

(2) We are not solipsists.

(3) The rejection of solipsism involves a commitment to a world in which there are others like us, and to concepts which can apply beyond the realm of one's own experience. Therefore, we are committed to the existence of impersonal concepts: those that are not tied to one perspective alone.

(4) In the practical realm, to avoid solipsism, we must have concepts that are potentially applicable beyond the realm of our own perspectives.

(5) If there are only agent-relative reasons for action, then the reasons we have motivate only from the personal perspective.

(6) In order to explain why they motivate from the personal point of view alone, we must make reference to concepts that are purely personal. But then we are assuming solipsism: we are committed to viewing ourselves as fundamentally disconnected from others.

---

[26] Nagel, 1970: 99–115.   [27] Ibid: 117.

(7) To avoid viewing ourselves as solipsists, we need to be able to explain the motivation of reasons from an impersonal perspective. Hence, we need, agent-neutral reasons.

(8) We cannot view ourselves both as solipsists and not as solipsists.

(9) To avoid a radical dissociation between different ways in which we view ourselves, we must accept that each agent-relative reason has a corresponding agent-neutral reason.[28]

How is Nagel's position relevant to Gewirth's argument? Well, Gewirth's problem is to move from an agent-relative reason to an agent-neutral reason. He argues that there is reason for each agent from his own perspective to will others to recognize obligations not to interfere with (or provide him with) the necessary conditions of his agency. The problem is to understand why other agents should endorse such a reason that is relative to the perspective of each agent. However, if there is a corresponding agent-neutral reason to each agent-relative reason, then each agent will have a strong impersonal reason to recognize an obligation not to interfere with (or provide) another's agency needs. The reason that was tied to a particular perspective becomes a reason for all agents irrespective of their particular perspective. The principle of universalization would then allow us to conclude that every agent has an impersonal reason to recognize an obligation not to interfere with (or provide) every other agent's freedom and well-being. Such a process of reasoning would take us a long way towards justifying Gewirth's supreme moral principle. It is thus crucially important to examine whether each agent-relative reason is accompanied by an agent-neutral reason as Nagel claims.

3.2 Nagel's problem

First, I shall consider Nagel's first argument. It is not clear that this argument is anything other than a restatement of what Nagel has to prove: that pain provides an agent-neutral reason. After all, his claim that the badness of pain is detached from the concept of myself need not be accepted. It does not seem far removed from reality to imagine a person who hears about someone in pain, and is totally unmoved. Moreover, one can accept that a person cannot detach himself from his own pain and must will that it cease. Yet, is it impossible that such a person might also recognize that others have no reason to help ease his pain? Even in the case of pain, it is not clear why a personal commitment to ending pain must lead to an impersonal judgement that pain *per se* is bad and must be relieved. I do not deny that most of us make the impersonal judgement: but the question we are considering is the justification of such a judgement, and Nagel's first argument does not provide such a justification.

---

[28] Nagel has subsequently recanted on the full generality of this claim, and rather confines these reasons to the particular context of pleasure and pain (1986: 159).

The second argument is a more elaborate attempt to show that we can only reject such impersonal reasons by giving up a fundamental assumption concerning how we view the world: that each of us is one person among many others with similar natures. How does this argument fare? Clearly, this argument does not dispose of solipsism as a philosophical worry, and does not attempt to refute it. Yet, Nagel is correct to claim that a fundamental part of our world view is that we are not solipsists. If his argument can demonstrate that in order to avoid solipsism we are required to accept the existence of agent-neutral reasons in every case where there are agent-relative reasons, then it would indeed have much strength.

The fundamental question is: does the rejection of solipsism require a transition from agent-relative to agent-neutral reasons? I do not think so. What Nagel's argument shows is that a rejection of solipsism requires that our concepts at least be potentially accessible to others, but it does not show that each agent-relative reason be accompanied by an agent-neutral reason. To see this let us consider an example. Todd claims that he has a reason X to become a Muslim. In order to avoid solipsism, our concepts must be applicable beyond ourselves. Thus, Todd's reason to become a Muslim must not only be comprehensible from his own perspective. Moreover, the motivational force of his reason must also be understandable by others. It is thus necessary that we are able to understand from an impersonal point of view that 'there is reason X for Todd (someone particular) to become a Muslim'.

However, it is the next move that is problematic: from this it does not follow that 'there is reason (for anyone) to become a Muslim'. The avoidance of solipsism does not require that all agent-relative reasons become reasons for everyone. It only requires that these agent-relative reasons be understandable from an impersonal perspective. There is a difference between being able to understand a reason and its motivating force from an impersonal perspective, and endorsing that reason and motivation from that perspective. This is the fundamental gap in Nagel's argument. Nagel's argument establishes the need for agent-relative reasons that can be viewed from an impersonal perspective. However, it does not establish the need for agent-neutral reasons that correspond to those agent-relative reasons. In order to avoid solipsism, we must be able to adopt an impersonal standpoint, and be able to understand why others are motivated by particular practical principles. However, this does not imply that those practical principles must themselves motivate from the impersonal point of view.

4 Equal Importance and the Justification of Fundamental Rights

4.1 The equality premise

There thus is a fundamental gap in both the theories of Gewirth and Nagel. The gap occurs in trying to move from principles that apply relative to a particular standpoint, to those that apply generally, and are not relativized to a particular standpoint. That gap has meant that the arguments thus far have failed to generate a fundamental principle of equality: that each individual's life is to be treated as being of equal importance to that of every other individual (what I shall term 'equality premise'). Such a premise is important for constructing a successful argument for fundamental rights. Together with the premise that there are certain necessary conditions to realize lives of value, it would allow us to generate the conclusion that each being ought to be entitled to the equal provision of the necessary conditions required to live lives of value. In this section, I shall attempt to provide some grounds for accepting the 'equality premise'.

The 'equality premise' does not seem to flow from what has been termed by Nagel the personal perspective of the individual.[29] From such a perspective, each individual can always seek to claim priority for his own interests and the interests of those he cares about over the interests of others. The special ties and affections we grow up with and cultivate—in relation to our loved ones, friends, and partners—are generally taken to justify departures from the principle of equal importance. Perhaps the clearest case is that parents are seen to be justified in treating their children as having special importance and, indeed, we would regard someone as a defective parent were they to maintain a strict impartiality between their own children and those of other people. Shue renders such intuitions more visual with his idea that the common-sense duties we have are akin to the image of a pebble being dropped in a pond which generates concentric circles that become fainter the further removed they are from the pebble. The strongest duties are to those closest to us and the further away we move the weaker they become.[30]

It seems that in order to be a plausible principle, 'the equality principle' requires us to adopt a perspective which abstracts from our individual positions. Sidgwick famously made reference to a 'point of view of the universe' from which it could be said that the happiness of individuals mattered equally.[31] Of course, there is no literal 'point of view of the universe' and so it seems that Sidgwick must rather have been referring to the ability of individuals to abstract from their own perspectives and to consider questions from an impartial standpoint. Sidgwick admitted that he could not provide a reason for individuals to adopt this standpoint in guiding their actions.

Nagel too identifies an 'impersonal standpoint' which generates a powerful demand for universal impartiality and equality.[32] This standpoint is one in which we abstract from our particular positions in the world without prioritizing any one set of concerns over any other. He claims that 'ethics and political theory begin when from the impersonal standpoint we focus on the raw data provided by the individual desires, interests, projects, attachments, allegiances, and plans of

---

[29] Nagel, 1991: 11.   [30] Shue, 1988: 691.   [31] Sidgwick, 1981: 421.

[32] Nagel, 1991: 10. It is necessary that we are able to adopt such an impersonal standpoint in order to avoid solipsism. I have accepted that Nagel succeeds in establishing this proposition in the argument discussed above, but not the further proposition that the rejection of solipsism requires the existence of an agent-neutral reason that corresponds to each agent-relative reason.

life that define the personal points of view of the multitude of distinct individuals, ourselves included. What happens at that point is that we recognize some of these things to have impersonal value.'[33] It seems to me that Nagel makes a mistake in this passage. It is not that, when viewed from an impersonal standpoint, suddenly desires and interests come to have some form of impersonal value, distinct from their personal value. It is rather that this standpoint leads us to recognize that desires and interests have value for each creature with a personal perspective, and that there is no basis, from the impersonal standpoint, upon which to distinguish between the importance to each creature of their lives.

Since I am engaged in a process of reasoning, reference may be had to certain presuppositions of rational enquiry. One of these presuppositions is that like cases must be treated alike.[34] Since the impersonal perspective provides us with no basis upon which to judge that the personal value in one creature's life is greater than that in the life of another, we are required from that perspective to regard the personal value in individual lives as being equally important.[35]

More could indeed be said about the impersonal standpoint and its importance in our lives.[36] Nagel situates the personal and impersonal perspectives within each individual and thus faces the difficult problem of reconciling the demands of each.[37] Throughout his argument, however, it remains unclear what the force of the impersonal perspective is, and why individuals should accept that at times it can override the personal perspective.

I wish to argue that the impersonal perspective is the perspective appropriately adopted in the design, formulation, and implementation of the background rules governing the distribution of benefits and burdens within a society. In defending this claim, it is important to understand that there is an implicit assumption being made that human beings are social beings born into associations of different kinds whose rules are designed to govern the interaction of a range of individuals. For virtually all human beings in the world today, the question is not whether we form rule-based societies from a state of nature. Rather, we find ourselves within such societies, and there is virtually no individual today that is unaffected by the rules

---

[33] Ibid: 11.

[34] Harrison, 1993: 182: 'if a reason can be given, justifying a particular course of action, this will be because of some feature of the action itself, or of the situation in which it occurs. Yet, if these features serve as a reason justifying this particular action, they will also serve as reasons justifying the same kind of actions wherever else they apply. If we get the same features again, we get the same reason. Of course, other features may differ between the two cases, providing other, countervailing reasons. But, as far as it goes, if our actions are to have reasons and be justified, then we are committed by the sheer nature of reasons to treating the same kind of case in the same kind of way.'

[35] From the fact that we have no grounds upon which to distinguish the value of creatures' lives from the impersonal perspective, it does not follow, however, that as a matter of metaphysical fact, their lives are of equal value. Our epistemic inability to determine the relative value of individual lives from the impersonal standpoint, however, entails that we are forced to treat individuals *as if* their lives are of equal importance to them. To act in any other way would involve arbitrariness, and violate rudimentary notions of fairness.

[36] Defending some such notion may indeed be fundamental to any theory of morality: see Sen, 1992: 17. Though I cannot attempt to defend this here, such a justification may require referring to the importance in our lives of a capacity for sympathetic identification.   [37] Nagel, 1991.

of a society. Thus, the question of utmost importance today concerns the nature of the rules that should be adopted by a society.[38]

I shall provide three arguments for thinking that the impersonal perspective should be adopted in formulating these rules. First, it may be understandable why an individual would adopt a personal perspective to assess his own actions.[39] Yet, the rules governing a society are by their very nature not concerned with the actions of a particular individual but are designed to regulate the distribution of benefits and burdens to a group of individuals. As such, the formulation of such rules must take place from a perspective that is able to take account of the lives of a number of individuals rather than that of any one individual. To do so, however, requires abstracting from the point of view of any one particular individual to take account of the impact of the rules on a number of differing individuals. Such a perspective that is not tied to the perspective of a particular individual is the impersonal perspective that Nagel identifies.

Thus, when we are concerned with the rules for a society, it does not make sense that we should adopt the perspective of any one individual in formulating these rules. Otherwise, such rules would be suitable only for a particular individual rather than for a group of diverse individuals. That may explain why we regard it as singularly inappropriate where a particular individual manipulates the rules of a society for his own interest. We can object that corrupt leaders such as Saddam Hussein and Mobutu Sesi Seko do not design rules for a society—a group of diverse individuals—but for themselves. They thus commit a form of 'category mistake', attempting to apply rules only justifiable from their own perspectives to a completely different context: a society whose rules are designed to govern a group of individuals. Thus, the very nature of societal rules imply that they should be formulated from the impersonal perspective.

Secondly, it is possible for a group of diverse individuals to agree to formulate rules to govern a society on the basis of overlapping personal reasons. Hobbes and Gauthier, for instance, attempt to provide theories which show why it makes sense for individuals from the personal perspective to accept certain societal rules. However, in the absence of a miraculous convergence on rules that meet the personal demands of each, the individuals in question will be forced to abstract from their own perspectives so as to consider rules for a society that would be acceptable from the perspectives of others. Thus, in attempting to design and formulate rules for a society—even where these are seen to be the outcome of a contract—individuals are forced at some point to adopt an impersonal perspective. Of course, in arriving at these rules, the personal perspective may still at times be

---

[38] A further question is the nature of the rules that should be adopted by groups of societies. I cannot deal with this question here but it should be evident from the arguments provided that the impersonal perspective would apply to the rules at the international level as well.

[39] I state this claim weakly as it may be argued legitimately that when deciding how to act morally, an individual should adopt the impersonal perspective even in regulating his own actions.

followed by individuals in preference to the dictates of reasoning from the impersonal perspective. Nevertheless, the fact that reaching an agreement about rules for a society requires adopting a perspective that takes account of others' perspectives suggests that the impulse to society is strongly connected with the impulse to adopting the impersonal perspective.

Finally, many of our practices support the claim that we require those representing the society to adopt an impersonal perspective in their reasoning. Consider the following examples. The judiciary is often required to decide between competing individual interests. Judges are expected to adopt an impartial perspective and to attempt to achieve the result that is required by a fair application of the law and reasoning. Were judges to decide a case on the basis that they personally would profit from the success of one of the litigants, we would regard this decision as biased and unjust.

Secondly, in relation to our elected representatives, once they are in a position of power, we expect them to take decisions that are not only justifiable from their own personal perspectives. There have recently, for instance, been persistent objections that the President of the United States, George Bush, makes decisions on the basis of personal preferences and his connections with the oil industry. Similar objections were lodged against the actions of the former President Bill Clinton who, prior to leaving office, granted pardons that were connected with large contributions to his political campaigns. Such objections indicate a shared understanding that when making public decisions, we do not expect our elected representatives to adopt reasons that can only be justified from their own personal perspectives. Finally, there are a number of occasions where we recognize that a society may justly make a decision that is in the interests of that society as a whole yet which may be objected to from the personal perspectives of particular individuals. For instance, a society may have a policy of refusing to negotiate with kidnappers who are motivated by political grievances even though the families of the hostages would be strongly in favour of negotiations.

Thus, I have attempted to provide reasons for thinking that in formulating the rules of a society, the impersonal standpoint should be adopted. Yet, we have seen that from the impersonal standpoint, the personal value in the life of each being must be treated as being of equal importance to the personal value in the life of every other being. Thus, those formulating the rules for a society will be required to treat all those who have personal value in their lives as being of equal importance. Hence, we can conclude with Dworkin that '[e]qual concern is the sovereign virtue of a political community'.[40]

Though formulated slightly differently in different theories, the idea of equal importance is foundational to most moral and political systems.[41] Its roots run

---

[40] Dworkin, 2000: 1.

[41] See, for instance, Barry, 1996: 267; Anderson, 1999: 295; Dworkin, 1977: 182; Dworkin, 2000:1 and Appiah, 2001: 2.

deep and, as a principle concerned with the equal status of each human being, it is widely accepted today.[42] I have attempted to provide reasons for thinking that those concerned with the design of rules for a society are bound to treat each sentient being with equal importance. Others have provided different grounds for its acceptance which I mention briefly. Some have sought to ground the equality premise in the fact that moral and political discourse requires us to be capable of justifying our actions to others which can only take place on an assumption of moral equality to them.[43] Others have sought to provide support for this assumption by contending that without it people would not be motivated to cooperate with one another, and its acceptance is thus said to be necessary for social cooperation to take place. Dworkin, for instance, has claimed that it is only upon some such assumption that people can be motivated to participate in a political society.[44] Finally, it has been contended that the equality premise can be traced to the requirements of rationality.[45]

4.2 Equal rights

Whatever our reasons for accepting the 'equality premise', it is important now to turn to the question of its implications for the foundational rules that should be adopted to govern a society. These rules establish the framework within which beings can live lives of value. One of the assumptions made thus far is that we are concerned with a society composed of a group of diverse beings. It is simply a feature of the world in which we live that individuals differ and have different paths to leading a good life. As such, a society which seeks to treat the lives of each being with equal importance cannot favour any particular way of life as that would privilege the lives of some over others. There are several other reasons why it is undesirable for a diverse society actively to promote a particular understanding of the good life. First, adopting a particular 'thick' conception of the good life would involve imposing one such conception on society, despite the fact that many do not share it. Over thousands of years of debate, both in philosophical literature and individual discourse, there has been no consensus on what it is to live well. The intractability of disputes surrounding the good life suggests that it would be better to avoid coercing others into one view that may well be mistaken. In fact it seems quite possible that given the diversity of beings, different forms of life may well be good for different beings. An individual who has grown up as a Jew may find that it is only Jewish practice that she finds life-enhancing, whilst a Hindu may find such practices a curiosity and only find Hinduism meaningful.

---

[42] I do not believe a more searching analysis of this principle can sustain a focus on human beings alone. See Regan, 1988, Singer, 1995, DeGrazia, 1996, and section 5.3 below.

[43] See Sen, 1992: 17–18 and the sources he quotes in n 12, at 18.

[44] See Dworkin, 1983: 33.

[45] Arguably, Kant's second formulation of the categorical imperative could be a form of this principle that mandates treating each rational being as an end in him- or herself and not merely as a means. See Kant, 1996: 79–80.

Secondly, it is not clear why those who do not share a particular idea of the good life should endorse public institutions that entrench that conception of the good. In order for societal institutions to be fair to all citizens, and to maintain stability in society, it would seem that the framework of society should allow for a plurality of reasonable conceptions of the good life.[46]

Thus, a diverse society founded upon the equality premise should not seek to prioritize a particular vision of the good life. As such, it must try to develop a 'thin' theory of the good which can apply to all beings. As I have argued in the first chapter, the 'thin' theory provides us with the broad general features that are the sources of value in the lives of beings. Yet, though the sources of value will be the same—purposes and experiences—the particular goals and experiences that beings value will differ. It may be suggested that instead of favouring a particular way of life, the goal of a society should be to create rules that favour the particular goals and experiences of each being to the same extent. However, an attempt to design basic social rules along these lines would be undesirable as well as impractical.

First, it would be impossible to formulate general rules that could serve to fulfil the particular goals and experiences of each being to the same extent. The goals and experiences of different beings often conflict. If the rules sought to realize the goals and experiences of each being equally, then that conflict would be enshrined in the very rules themselves, rendering them contradictory and incapable of clear application.

Secondly, it would be virtually impossible to measure whether individual goals and experiences were furthered to the same extent. As such, any rules would be open to the charge that they were favouring one individual over another, thus violating the principle of equal importance. A further corollary of this point would be that it would be unclear how to ensure that such rules would in fact exemplify rather than violate the principle of equal importance.

Thirdly, no framework of rules could possibly guarantee that individuals realize their goals and have positive experiences. Achieving these ends is often largely within the power of the individuals concerned and dependent on many subjective factors. Thus, it would not be possible for a society to ensure that individuals feel joy, or succeed in becoming great writers. These are simply not states of affairs that can be guaranteed by the rules of a society. These rules can only seek to enable individuals to have the capabilities such that they may realize their own projects and attain their own happiness.

Finally, there is a real question about whether the rules which govern a society should be designed to ensure the fulfilment of individual projects, even if the aim

---

[46] See Rawls, 1993: 10. It has been objected that this liberal approach favours individualistic conceptions of the good over communitarian ones (Nagel, 1975: 9–10; Rodewald, 1985). A reply to this charge lies beyond the scope of this chapter, though I am inclined to follow the approach of Rawls, 1993: 193–200.

is to achieve equal fulfilment.[47] Such rules, it may be said, must generally have a social purpose: for instance, divide resources so as to treat each being with equal importance, and minimize conflict. To identify these rules with the realization of individual projects would remove them from their primary social function. As such, they should properly provide the framework in which individuals may pursue their individual purposes, rather than aiming to realize the actual purposes of individuals themselves. This understanding of social rules allows for a division of responsibility between individuals and the state. Moreover, it does not envisage a state that is so massive and overreaching that it is capable of ensuring the realization of individual projects. It allows a space for individuals to pursue their own projects and to take responsibility for their success or failure therein. As such, it respects the integrity of individuals.

For all these reasons, a society should not seek to ensure the equal fulfilment of individuals whether it be in relation to their purposes or experiences. Rather, it should focus upon what lies within its power: to create the enabling conditions for beings affected by its rules to live a good life by their own lights. To do so, and thus to recognize the equal importance of each life, it must guarantee to each being the necessary prerequisites for realizing a life of value.

In the first chapter, I identified two different thresholds: the necessary preconditions for being free from the general conditions that threaten a being's survival, and the necessary preconditions for the fulfilment of a wide range of purposes. It is quite clear that all sentient beings require certain resources to be free from threats to their survival. Without the resources to be free from starvation or malnourishment, for instance, no being can live a valuable life. However, a being may not be malnourished yet have so little food that he feels continually hungry. In order to be capable of realizing their purposes, beings must have access to a higher level of provision than that required by the first threshold, which would include, for instance, well-balanced nutritional food that is sufficient for a being to be physically strong. Similar points can be made in the case of human beings in relation to housing, clothing, and the need for liberty.

Thus, I have argued that a society must in its background rules treat the lives of beings as having equal importance. Since it should not seek to realize the particular goods of such beings, it must concentrate on ensuring that its members are provided with the enabling conditions in which to live lives of value to them. To do so requires guaranteeing to each individual the necessary prerequisites for realizing a life of value. Thus, for a society to provide protection for such enabling conditions in its background rules would require that, in the case of human beings,

---

[47] An allied point concerns whether responsibility for realizing the projects of individuals should be partially or wholly removed from them and placed on the state. Dworkin (2000: 5), for instance, assumes a principle of special responsibility: 'though we must all recognize the equal objective importance of the success of a human life, one person has a special and final responsibility for that success—the person whose life it is.'

individuals are guaranteed the basic freedoms—including those of speech, religion, and political participation—as well as sufficient resources—including adequate food, housing, and water—to enable them to realize a wide variety of goals. Thus, a society that recognizes the equal importance of individual lives must recognize each individual's basic rights to claim the necessary prerequisites for living a life of value.

5 Objections

5.1 Objection 1: Does equal importance support basic rights?

It may, however, be objected that the argument has moved too swiftly from the claim that the rules of a society must be formulated from a point of view that recognizes the equal importance of beings' lives to the claim that these rules must involve the recognition of the basic rights of beings.[48] I shall consider two alternative interpretations of the principle of equal importance which will help to clarify the nature and meaning of this principle in my theory. The first rival interpretation would claim that a society may recognize the equal importance of the lives of beings by offering no entitlements whatsoever to any being. Everyone is treated equally in the sense that they are not able to claim anything from the society, and, it may be argued, that this is consistent with recognizing the equal importance of each being's life.

In responding to this objection, it must be recognized that the principle of equal importance combines two elements. The first element is a claim about the fact that the lives of beings have value, and I have provided a 'thin theory' as to what this value consists in. The second element is a claim that the value in each being's life must be treated as being equal to the value in the life of any other being. The objection in question attempts to divorce the element of equality from the value claim. It involves the contention that a society where each is given no entitlements is a society in which the equality of beings is respected. We can concede this point but still insist that the principle of equal importance is not designed to protect bare equality of treatment. It involves protecting the *value* that lies within the lives of individuals: such value rests in the ability of individuals to have positive experiences and to fulfil their goals. A society which failed to recognize basic rights would be one in which individuals could be allowed to starve to death, be severely malnourished, and lack the general capabilities necessary to realize projects of their choosing. Such a society would thus be one that could allow the value components of individual lives to diminish greatly and in some cases disappear altogether. Such a society could not be said to protect the equal *importance* or *value* of individual lives.

---

[48] I am indebted to Dr Alison Hills for raising this objection powerfully in the course of a seminar.

Moreover, if we take cognizance of certain uncontroversial empirical evidence, it is clear that individuals differ in their abilities, talents, and characteristics. A society that failed to protect basic entitlements would in essence allow those with characteristics that were advantageous to dominate over others with less advantageous characteristics. The strong would be able to outmanoeuvre the weak and often be able to realize their own projects whilst depriving the weak of the ability to realize their projects. The value components of the lives of some would thus come to be privileged over the value components of the lives of others. Taking account of these natural differences allows us to recognize that a situation in which there were no basic entitlements would be likely to lead to a situation in which there was great inequality in the extent to which individuals could lead lives of value to them. Though there may be a degree of formal equality in a situation of no basic entitlements, in substance, the ability of individuals to lead lives of value in such a situation would differ greatly. This would clearly violate the concern by a society to ensure that individual lives were treated as being of equal importance.

A second rival interpretation of the principle of equal importance would claim that a society which accepts the principle would adopt maximizing utilitarian principles to regulate the basic structure. Utilitarianism embodies the basic assumption that 'each is to count for one and only one'. In making decisions, political societies must seek to maximize utility in the society and, in doing so, it must count every individual equally.[49] Such a method of political decision-making would be one in which, it could be claimed, each being's life is treated with equal importance as no one's interests are given priority over any other being's interests in the utilitarian calculus. Thus, the principle of equal importance would not lead to the background rules of a society being formulated in accordance with equal rights but rather to their being designed by an application of the principle of utility.

Of course, this argument does not exclude the possibility that such a utilitarian basic structure would recognize basic rights. It may well be that utilitarian principles would require the recognition of basic rights in the basic structure and so those rights would be derived through this extra step of mediation by utilitarian reasoning. As will be seen in Chapter 3, I believe some form of complex consequentialist judgement will ultimately be required in deciding upon the current 'unconditional' obligations of a political society. Yet I do not believe that the argument for basic rights needs to be mediated by aggregative utilitarian reasoning, nor should it be. Basic rights can be derived directly from the principle of equal importance, and the form of consequentialism that I endorse is one designed to achieve a state of affairs in which equal importance is realized rather than attempting to maximize a measurable quantity of utility.[50]

---

[49] There are different versions of utilitarianism, and I shall only focus upon the most common aggregative version. [50] See the end of Chap 3 for a defence of the latter claim.

One of the traditional objections to utilitarianism is that despite its good intentions and the attractive fact that it counts everyone equally in its calculus, it is consistent with widely unequal results. In the process of aggregation, it loses sight of the value of each individual, and 'does not take seriously the distinction between persons'.[51] A community allocates according to what would provide the greatest net utility and 'in itself no distribution of satisfaction is better than another'.[52] Utilitarianism could thus lead to a situation where one individual is deprived of liberty on the grounds that this would make the rest of society feel safer. It could also allow for a situation where some are deprived of very basic resources as their use by others who are better off would lead to a greater level of utility in the society.[53]

If this is so, then such a result is not consistent with the assumption of equal importance as I have described it. Equal importance does not simply involve the fact that each being is counted equally in an equation to decide upon how the rules of a society should be formulated. The equal counting of a being alone is not sufficient; rather, the resultant state of affairs must be such that the being's life is actually treated as having equal value in relation to the lives of other beings. Otherwise, a society can treat the principle of equal importance as a purely formal matter, with little concern for the substantive situation of individuals. However, a society that truly takes the principle seriously must ensure that the framework of its rules is designed so as to ensure that beings *in actuality* are treated with equal importance. Utilitarianism can lead to situations in which the lives of some individuals are substantively treated with little respect for their value.[54] It can also lead in its operation to some individuals being vastly privileged over others. In translating equal consideration of interests into aggregate utility, the equal importance of lives can get lost. As such, we need to find a way in which a society can preserve its focus on the equal *value* of individual lives. To do so, I have argued, a society must recognize certain basic entitlements of each individual which can help ensure that each being's life is treated with at least a certain level of importance.

5.2 Objection 2: Why not an overall equality of resources?

It could, however, be objected that my conclusion is too minimal, and that we can achieve a more expansive conclusion working with the same premises. A society that treats each being with equal importance should, it could be claimed, distribute all its resources equally and not just those required to meet the thresholds I have identified. A society that cannot seek to realize the particular projects of individuals ought to distribute all resources equally.

However, in attempting to make this more expansive argument, matters become more complicated, as it can be claimed that the assumption of equal importance does not automatically lead to a situation where a society ought to distribute its

---

[51] Rawls, 1999a: 24. [52] Ibid: 23. [53] Scheffler, 1988: 2.
[54] This may not be a problem for all forms of utilitarianism, but I cannot here, for instance, deal with indirect utilitarianism and the possibilities it raises.

resources equally. It may be argued, for instance, that once the necessary prerequisites of living a life of value have been guaranteed to each, treating everyone with equal importance requires that additional resources be focused as far as possible on attempting to equalize the welfare of individuals. That, in turn, may require an unequal distribution of resources.[55] Alternatively, it could be argued that a society should be seeking to equalize certain valuable capabilities of individuals. Since different individuals would require different amounts of resources to achieve the same capability, such an aim would again involve distributing resources unequally amongst individuals. A further position that could be adopted is that a society ought not to concern itself with the distribution of resources beyond ensuring that everyone is provided with sufficient resources to meet the thresholds I have identified. Thus, equal importance does not unequivocally support an equal distribution of resources, and it is a matter of much dispute amongst philosophers which form of overall distribution should be aimed at by an egalitarian.[56]

An individual who lacks the prerequisites for leading a life of value cannot even begin to realize the two major sources of value in life: the having of positive experiences and the fulfilment of purposes. A society that fails to guarantee an individual these necessary prerequisites thus can be said without any doubt to fail to treat that being's life as having importance. As a result of the differing degrees of urgency represented by the two thresholds, such a failure is a matter of degree. Failing to guarantee the resources necessary for being free from general threats to survival virtually negates any claim of the society to respect the importance of a being's life; failing to guarantee a being the general conditions necessary to realize her purposes displays little respect for the importance to a being of her own purposes.

Thus, the principle of equal importance at least implies that each being should be equally entitled to the level of provision necessary to meet the thresholds I have identified. Beyond this point, the assumption of equal importance could be compatible with a number of different theories of equality. I have sought to draw out the minimal implications of such a principle which must at least be enshrined in the rules regulating the basic framework of a society. It may well be that the principle of equal importance can be shown fairly decisively to favour one more comprehensive ideal of equality over another. If this is so, then such a view will at least embrace the two thresholds I have identified. These may still be of importance in identifying the course of action that should be followed where it is necessary to make decisions about the priorities of a society under conditions of scarcity.[57] On the other hand, if there is no decisive argument in favour of

---

[55] Some of the arguments I have made above for the focus on the thresholds I have identified would also suggest that an ideal of 'equality of welfare' is unattractive. For a further critique of this view, see Dworkin, 2000: 11–64.

[56] See, for instance, the different positions of Cohen, 1989; Arneson, 1989; Sen 1992, and Dworkin, 2000.

[57] The exigencies of the real world will almost always require that such decisions be made.

a particular interpretation of equality, then it will have been of great importance to identify at least the minimal implications of such a principle. Since the debate over which conception of equality is favoured by this abstract principle has not been decisively concluded, the conclusion I have reached may well be of use in establishing a fixed level of distribution that a society must at least achieve if it is to take the principle of equal importance seriously.

Furthermore, it seems that the more minimal implications of such a view are less utopian than the more extensive conceptions of equality tend to be. Our world currently embodies severe inequalities between rich and poor within most societies, and between such societies. The idea of equalizing the resources available to each individual seems beyond the realms of possibility. It is an ideal that also lacks any serious political backing in the current world. On the other hand, the attempt to specify minimum standards of provision for individuals that can be guaranteed by states and international organizations is a goal that seems both attainable and is currently the focus of world attention. Developed countries have, for instance, made promises in their commitment to the Millennium Goals to halve the number of people suffering from such maladies as malnutrition, lack of access to clean water and sanitation. Within societies, a number of states have succeeded in setting up welfare systems to ensure that each individual is provided with at least a certain amount of resources and has certain capabilities.[58] Thus, there seem to be good practical reasons for focusing upon a project of justifying and specifying the content of minimum guarantees that societies ought to provide to individuals.[59]

5.3 Objection 3: Who is included within the scope of the principle of equal importance?

It may be objected that I have been assuming that the principle of equal importance should be applied to all beings. Yet, the arguments I have made thus far have not justified exactly who is included within the scope of the principle. The fact that the impersonal perspective must be adopted when dealing with a group of individuals does not specify who is included within this particular group. Our practices also seem to limit the range of application that the principle of equal importance has. Many accept the principle, for instance, in relation to human beings but would not extend it to non-human animals. Similarly, individuals in society are often most concerned with those within their society and would not treat the lives of those beyond the boundaries of their society as having equal importance.

---

[58] Most European states have some form of welfare system, some of the most successful of which exist in Scandinavia.

[59] A further practical reason for focusing on more minimal guarantees is that these tend to suffer from less measurement difficulties than those proposals concerning the overall distribution of resources in a society. For instance, the actual implications of an ideal of 'equality of resources'

To answer this challenge, it is necessary to consider the point that the background rules of a society govern the distribution of benefits and burdens to a group of diverse individuals. The question that has been raised concerns who is to be included within this group. If our rules are not to be arbitrary, as is a presupposition of engaging in rational enquiry about them, then there must be reasons for formulating these rules in a particular way. To justify rules in a diverse society requires having reference to reasons that others can accept from different perspectives.[60] Social rules will affect all those who have value in their lives. As such, deciding the question as to who should be included within the sphere of social concern requires a decision to be made about who should be regarded as having value in their lives. Given the diversity of views amongst rational humans, it seems likely that it will be necessary to find a shared principled basis upon which to decide this question. In Chapter 1, I attempted to develop an account as to the sources of value in the world that could command widespread assent from a diverse range of perspectives. That 'thin theory' found two major sources of value in individual life: having positive experiences, and the fulfilment of purposes.

The principle of equal importance requires a decision to be made as to who counts as being equally important. Yet, the 'thin theory' provides a natural answer to this question: all those that are capable of leading lives of value according to that theory. In applying the principle of equal importance to the background rules of a society, we are thus required only to have reference to a theory that can be justified from the perspectives of a diverse range of individuals. The 'thin' theory of the good is designed to meet this criterion. The rules that are developed on this basis will thus apply to all those capable of leading lives of value. That in turn will involve non-human animals, non-rational humans, rational humans, and also those who are affected by those rules and live beyond the boundaries of a particular society. Thus, the 'thin theory' provides us with a principled basis upon which a society with diverse perspectives can justifiably seek to outline the scope of the principle of equal importance.

Thus, the scope of the group whose rights must be protected will coincide with the group that is identified by the 'thin' theory of the good as capable of leading lives of value. Yet it may be objected that such a conclusion seems extreme. It could, for instance, be taken to suggest that in the formulation of its rules, a society must be concerned to treat every being in the world today with equal importance. Since there is a large amount of interaction between individuals and societies in the world today, the background rules of one society may have an impact on beings that do not live within that particular society. Can a society

---

are most difficult to understand in a world that cannot easily go back to an auction of all resources such as that described by Dworkin, 2000: 68. The suggestion of an equal basic income may be the most attractive development of this idea (see Van Parijs, 1995), though there are difficulties involved in setting the level of income. In this book, I cannot hope to develop these points any further.

60 See, for instance, Rawls, 1993: 226–7; 236; and Scanlon, 1998.

really be required to treat all beings with equal importance and guarantee the rights, for instance, of those living even beyond its borders?

It is important to make two points in response. On the one hand, the principled concern with all, even those beyond the boundaries of a society, can be said to be an attraction of the view. It entails that a society cannot promote the interests of its own members at the expense of others who do not live within it. Since these other individuals also have lives of value, it is not permissible to exclude their interests from consideration merely on the grounds that they are not of a particular society. Thus, for instance, the environmental and labour implications of policies must be considered in relation to all those affected by such policies. Similarly, such a view would ensure that the rights of refugees are respected, as a society is not allowed to limit the concern of its rules to its own members alone.

On the other hand, the extreme impartiality required by such a view is mitigated by the fact that in our world today there are a number of different societies which assume special responsibility for the lives of beings that lie within their domain. Each individual thus has a society whose framework of rules should be specially concerned with ensuring that he is treated with equal importance and guaranteed the necessary prerequisites for living a life of value.[61] Within this current arrangement, it is justifiable for a particular society to focus largely upon the position of those beings that fall within its borders. [62]

Moreover, in such a system, the rules of a particular society only have force generally within the domain of that society. As such, those rules primarily have the power to affect the individuals that fall within their domain of operation. Since they have a greater impact on the lives of those within their domain, they can justifiably be concerned particularly with those individuals. It does not violate the equal importance of other individuals, as these rules are primarily designed to have an impact only on those individuals that lie within the society. The less the impact of the rules on the way a being lives their life, the less that these rules need to take the interests of such beings into account. To the extent that there is an impact beyond a society's borders, the interests of all affected must be given equal consideration.

[61] The idea here has similarities to the 'assigned responsibility' model that Goodin, 1988a: 679ff develops: special responsibility for compatriots is justified on his view as the most efficient method of realizing certain general duties we have towards one another. In my discussion, however, I assume that the world is divided into societies each primarily responsible for those within its domain, and make the conditional claim that in such a situation it is justifiable for a society based upon a principle of equal importance to devote its primary attention to those who lie within its domain. Where the boundaries of societies are less rigid, and the rules of a society or group of societies affect individuals beyond the borders of a particular society, limiting the scope of these rules to a particular society may not be justifiable. Although not the focus of this book, global institutions would also be required to develop rules that treat individuals with equal importance.

[62] It is obviously a matter of some complexity to decide what type of system would be most conducive to treating each being with equal importance across the world. At the moment, each state assumes responsibility for those within its domain to achieve this end. Alternative models could be imagined, such as the formation of regional or world government, though, it is unclear that these would succeed better than the current model.

5.4 Objection 4: Individual duties to comply with societal rules?

The argument for rights that I have provided has focused on the fact that the formulation of the rules of a society must take place from an impersonal perspective that requires the lives of each being to be treated with equal importance. However, it may be admitted that this is true, yet individuals from their personal perspectives have little reason to comply with these rules, particularly when they conflict with their personal interests. As such, whilst society has a duty to treat each individual with equal importance, I have not shown why each individual would be motivated to comply with this societal duty.

In response, there is a good argument for the rules of a society to include a number of sanctions and incentives that encourage individuals to comply with them. As such, these rules would be designed as far as possible to ensure that individuals would find it against their own personal interests to violate these background rules.

However, insofar as this is not possible, there may indeed be a clash between the personal perspectives of individuals and the claims of society. Nevertheless, the theory still allows there to be reasons that can motivate an individual. To the extent that the individual is rational, the argument provided has attempted to show why he or she should respect rules of a society that enshrine a principle of equal importance. As such, to the extent that a rational and moral argument can motivate, individuals have good grounds for complying with the societal duty.

Moreover, as has been argued earlier, engaging in a society involves taking account at least to some extent of the perspectives of others. Having a society has many benefits from the personal perspectives of individuals: it provides an ordered framework for cooperation, for instance. To fail to comply with certain of the fundamental background rules of a society could undermine some of the benefits societies have for individuals. Thus, the individual has some personal reasons to comply with such rules and support the social structure.

Finally, it is a mistake to assume that individuals are wholly self-interested and lack the ability to empathize with others, and act altruistically. The motivation for obeying societal rules may thus not be purely rational but involve empathy and altruistic elements as well.

5.5 Objection 5: Obligations rather than rights?

I have thus attempted to establish that a society that recognizes the equal importance of each being ought to recognize the rights of such beings to have their basic liberties and needs met. Onora O'Neill[63] has been a powerful critic of the discourse of rights and has argued for a moral perspective that focuses on obligations rather than rights. She claims that '[t]he perspective of rights provides a perilous

---

[63] O'Neill, 1996: 134.

way of formulating ethical requirements since it leaves many possible obligations dangling in the air'.[64] Whilst rights provide rhetoric for political change, their weakness, she claims, is that, in not attending to obligations, it is easy to forget about the actual demands they place on agents. They also fail to specify which agents are responsible for the fulfilment of rights. The perspective of obligations, on the other hand, has less political resonance, and is often harder to articulate; it has the advantage, though, of being more realistic about the burdens it places on agents, their justification, and allocations. If the content of obligations can be identified, they will have implications for action and the design of institutions. Those who claim rights, on the other hand, but do not know who bears the counterpart obligations, grasp 'thin air'.[65]

O'Neill points to many unanswered questions raised by a theory of rights that focuses on interests. O'Neill claims at one point that such rights only have rhetorical value, and that they are a 'bitter mockery to the poor'.[66] She fails, however, to mention the work that a theory of rights performs. Such a theory renders it clear that the source of our obligations to others lies in their urgent interests and a concern for treating their lives as being of importance. It recognizes that an infringement of these interests renders such individuals particularly vulnerable. A theory of rights thus focuses attention on the most urgent interests of beings, and recognizes the importance of their being provided with strong protections that help to end their vulnerability. It is simply not true that such a theory lacks any action-guiding consequences. The importance of fundamental rights is that they impose a responsibility upon societies to ensure that the urgent interests of beings are effectively protected. The urgent interests of beings provide the reasons for many of our duties to others.[67] Talk of duties alone fails to indicate that it is our connection to others who have interests that is of critical importance and which imposes obligations upon us.

Consider an example that a person should generally refrain from torturing another.[68] Focusing on the fact that an individual has a right not to be tortured emphasizes the fact that the reason lying behind this requirement is the tremendous suffering caused by torture to the victim thereof. However, it may also be pointed out that the 'deliberate infliction of suffering debases and degrades the torturer, derogating from his humanity and undermining his rational integrity'.[69] Providing such a reason against torture places the focus on the perpetrator and his duties. Yet, to focus on the perpetrator alone and the impact on his humanity

---

[64] Ibid.   [65] Ibid: 135.   [66] Ibid: 133.

[67] Raz, 1986: 180 in fact states that '[t]o assert that an individual has a right is to indicate a ground for a requirement for action of a certain kind, i.e. that an aspect of his well-being is a ground for a duty on another person'. This formulation renders rights prior to duties, and thus suggests that they are not strictly correlative. It would be better to regard urgent interests (together with a principle of equal importance) as the grounding of both rights and their correlative duties. The argument has been that talk of rights serves particularly well to highlight their grounding in the fundamental interests of beings, something that talk of 'duties' fails to disclose so readily.

[68] I take this example from Waldron, 1984: 13.   [69] Ibid.

or rationality is to de-emphasize the victim and her interests. Such duty-based reasons alone tend to be fairly self-serving—they are about avoiding a harm to the perpetrator after all—and sterile.

Thus, these thoughts suggest that neither the perspective of agency—which favours a focus on duties—nor that of recipience—which favours a focus on rights—ought to be prioritized. The perspective of obligations focuses on the agent, and what she is required to do. It must provide reasons for the agent to act in the way that she does and explain what she is required to do. In providing reasons that are moral or political, however, it is necessary to refer to the interests of others. The perspective of rights focuses our minds not only on ourselves and the duties we must fulfil, but also on others with whom we live, interact, and cooperate in this world.

6 Conclusion

In this chapter, I have considered the justification for recognizing fundamental rights. I have argued that such a justification can be grounded in the principle that a society should treat the lives of individuals as having equal importance. The argument thus far has focused on the perspective of rights and the urgent interests that are protected by them. The next chapter will be concerned with the perspective of agency and the duties which arise from a recognition of these fundamental entitlements.

3

Determining Our Unconditional Obligations

1 Introduction

In the last chapter, I provided an argument for recognizing fundamental rights to the necessary prerequisites for living a life of value. When attempting to derive practical duties from such rights, however, a number of additional considerations need to be taken into account. In this chapter, I shall seek to outline an analytical framework for arriving at the actual duties which arise from a recognition of fundamental rights. First, I shall provide certain reasons for thinking that we cannot move directly from the argument for recognizing fundamental rights to practical duties to implement such rights. Secondly, I shall argue that, as a result of these difficulties, it is desirable in our analysis to distinguish between 'conditional' and 'unconditional' rights. Thirdly, I shall outline five important factors that must be taken into account in moving from conditional to unconditional rights: they are scarcity, urgency, sacrifice, effectiveness, and allocation. Finally, I conclude with an argument that the overall framework in which a decision should be taken about the content of our practical duties to implement fundamental rights is a complex consequentialist framework.

2 Unanswered Questions About the Content of Rights

The argument in Chapter 2 was designed to show that the background rules of a society must recognize certain basic entitlements of beings to the necessary prerequisites for living a life of value. Yet, if the content of rights is specified in this way, then it seems that a society would always be in breach of its obligations unless everyone's basic needs were met. However, holding such a position is implausible and leads to a number of practical and principled problems.

First, such a theory of rights fails to answer crucial questions as to who has the obligations to realize these rights. Whilst it has been contended that a society has the general obligation to realize these rights, there is no further specification as to who is responsible within the society for their implementation. In particular, it is unclear to what extent individuals are to take responsibility for meeting their own basic needs. There thus needs to be greater attendance to the question of the agents who are required to realize these rights.[1]

Secondly, the theory of rights says nothing about the possibility of realizing the rights in question: significant scarcity may prevent anything from being done to uphold these rights. Since at times the failure to realize fundamental rights may be as a result of factors beyond the control of a society, it seems mistaken to claim that the society would be in breach of an obligation it cannot fulfil. The common-sense ethical principle that one ought to do only what lies within the realm of possibility seems to rule out an obligation to do what lies beyond the power of humans to achieve.

Thirdly, the theory of rights does not seem to place any limits upon the demands that can be made upon individuals and institutions. Even a society that has made massive sacrifices to realize the basic needs of all may still be in breach of its obligations if anyone remains below the threshold required to realize their rights. The theory thus says nothing about the extent of the demands that may be placed upon individuals and institutions. However, it is entirely possible that the achievement of basic capabilities for all under conditions of moderate scarcity may well require that all of a society's resources be spent upon realizing such basic capabilities. Arts, culture, sports, and much else may need to be sacrificed in a society that recognizes such rights.

Consider the provision of expensive medical procedures such as heart transplants or kidney dialysis. Though these procedures are required to ensure that people have the most basic capability—the very ability to live—their cost is often exorbitant.[2] If all people are to be brought to the point where their basic capabilities are equally realized, most, if not all, of society's resources could then be devoted to achieving this aim.[3]

This would seem to have two effects. First, since some will need a much greater level of resources in order to ensure that they have the basic capabilities necessary to meet the thresholds I have identified, a society will end up spending vastly disproportionate amounts of resources on some rather than others. That, it could be argued, would lead to some lives being treated as more important than other lives. Nevertheless, it may be responded that such a situation would be acceptable in order to ensure that everyone has the basic capabilities that the rules of a society must protect. Equal importance would entail that each person is to have the same minimum capabilities, and, as such, the differential spending of resources would be mandated rather than forbidden by this principle of equality.

---

[1] O'Neill's critique of rights (1996) that was discussed briefly in the previous chapter fails to show that we should replace talk of rights with that of obligations; but it highlights the need to include a discussion of issues concerning the allocation of obligations, for instance, within a theory of rights.

[2] This difficult problem arose in the South African case of *Soobramoney v Minister of Health (Kwazulu-Natal)* 1998 (1) SA 765 (CC) that is discussed in Chapter 6.

[3] See Dworkin, 2000: 308 for an explanation of how high-cost medical technologies even in developed countries will need to be rationed to avoid this result.

The problem with this reply, however, is that it does not do justice to the very case that has been made for valuing basic capabilities. The point is that we want basic capabilities to enable us to live lives that go well beyond the realization of such capabilities. We want capabilities and resources to enable us to live valuable lives: have positive experiences and realize our purposes. Basic capabilities are the necessary conditions for realizing valuable ends. To devote all of society's resources to achieving equality of basic capabilities would be to elevate the means to a valuable life to the status of ends in themselves.

Frank Michelman[4] has eloquently made a similar point by distinguishing between what he terms basic goods (broadly analogous to the ones I have outlined) and residual goods (broadly those which go beyond the basic). He puts the point as follows:

[I]t is true that for anyone below L on the basic-good side residual goods have no value— or, as we can say, an unfulfilled basic need exists. But, it seems equally true that for anyone lacking residual goods, satisfaction of basic needs has no point—yielding only a foundation with no possibility of a superstructure, or a self with no possibility of realizing its aims. Extreme shortage of residual goods thus seems to signify disadvantage no less severe than does existence of basic need. There is no clear aim in satisfying the basic needs of some when the cost is eliminating the residual goods of others.

This problem arises for anyone committed to a conception of value that recognizes a sphere of urgent interests which are necessary conditions for the realization of those aspects of living that give value to our lives. In fact, Fishkin[5] presents a general argument designed to show that two of our basic moral assumptions conflict whenever we are dealing with positive obligations on a large scale. First, he claims that there is a general recognition that we have at least some positive general obligations to assist one another. Fundamental rights that have a positive dimension would perform this function in the theory I have developed. Secondly, he claims we recognize that there 'are limits on what any other person can demand of us as a matter of duty or obligation'.[6] However, when we are concerned with, for instance, the poverty in a society or globally, then even recognizing very minimal positive obligations will entail extremely onerous sacrifices of individuals and this would violate the second assumption. Thus, Fishkin identifies what he takes to be a general problem that our basic moral assumptions conflict in such cases.

Fishkin does not, however, seek to explain the source of these seemingly different moral assumptions and merely suggests that they are fixed points in our moral thinking. In the latter contention, he seems to be correct. Yet, in my view, the source of this conflict become clearer when we recognize that it arises not in virtue of conflicting and divergent principles of morality, but rather in virtue of a common core conception of value. The point is that a society that respects the principle of equal importance must protect the ability of individuals to lead valuable lives. To do so entails protecting their urgent interests in meeting the thresholds

---

[4] Michelman, 1975: 338.   [5] Fishkin, 1982.   [6] Ibid: 7.

I have identified. The problem is that in ensuring everyone reaches these thresholds, a society may prevent individuals from actually achieving valuable lives, being forced to content themselves with only that which is necessary to meet their basic needs.[7] The importance of meeting needs is, however, defined in relation to values that go beyond the basic: thus, an obligation to meet basic needs comes to prevent the fulfilment of values which provide the very reasons for regarding the meeting of needs as important.[8]

The argument thus far attempts to establish that in determining the obligations that result from a recognition of fundamental rights, it makes no sense to require that individuals be reduced to the level at which they only have the basic necessities. There must be a space in which people can hope to have positive experiences and realize projects and purposes that they value. This space may be regarded as intimately connected with the value for individuals of living lives of their own in which they can realize values that are of importance to them. The crucial question that is raised by this discussion and is most difficult to answer is the extent to which individuals should have a space to pursue their projects beyond the basic, whilst other individuals lack even the basic necessities. The argument thus far has attempted to establish the need for such a space, but has not answered the question as to its range or extent.[9]

3 Conditional and Unconditional Rights

The difficulties with the theory of fundamental rights I have outlined suggest that we cannot simply move from an argument concerning the need for a society to recognize such rights to actual obligations to realize such rights. A number of additional practical and normative considerations need to be factored in that may modify the actual obligations that a society may be expected to fulfil. It is thus important to develop an analytical framework that allows us to arrive at conclusions concerning the practical obligations that a society which recognizes fundamental rights must fulfil. In this section, I shall be concerned with the way in which we should structure our enquiry into the content of these obligations.

One way of avoiding this problem is to hold that it is mistaken to separate out the content of practical obligations from the question concerning the content of fundamental rights. It could be argued that instead of specifying the content of such rights in the way I have suggested—by referring to the fundamental interests

---

[7] Dworkin, 2000: 309 makes a similar point when he states that 'it is preposterous that a community should treat longer life as a good that it must provide at any cost—even one that would make the longer lives of its people lives barely worth living'. He fails, however, to explain the deeper reasons for this claim.

[8] The problem arises even if one accepts that there is some intrinsic value in meeting basic needs. It is implausible to suppose that the *only* intrinsic value in the life of beings is the realization of basic needs. As long as the meeting of needs remains at least partially instrumental to the realization of other sources of intrinsic value, it will be objectionable to focus on meeting such needs alone.

[9] That question will be dealt with later in this chapter.

of individuals—the content of such rights should be specified in a way that immediately takes account of all relevant practical and normative factors that relate to a particular context and thus avoids the difficulties I have outlined. Such an inquiry would mean that a whole host of factors must be brought into the picture immediately when assessing the content of a fundamental right: in addition to the interests of the individuals that are at stake, we must take into account the limits of the obligations that can be imposed on individuals, the scarcity of resources, the possibility of sharing the burdens, and much else. Ultimately then, there is no separation between the rights that a society recognizes and the practical obligations it has to realize such rights. There is only one enquiry and the content of both rights and obligations is determined by a balanced all-things-considered judgement that takes account of a variety of different factors in a particular context.

The difficulty with adopting this analytical strategy is that by determining the content of rights in one step, one can easily lose a sense of what rights are for, rendering their content subject to a conglomeration of factors each of which are brought together as a result of a wide variety of justificatory considerations. The urgency of fundamental interests, and the equal importance of beings must be balanced together with a concern for the freedom and integrity of an individual, the possibility of realizing moral demands, and the influence of a social setting upon such demands. The complexity of reaching such an all-things-considered judgement can obscure what I have argued is the central feature of a fundamental right: that it offers protection for an urgent interest flowing from the concern of a society with the equal importance of each life.

The problem is similar to one that it has been contended arises in general with ethical principles. Since universal principles are abstract and at times come into conflict with competing considerations, they cannot in and of themselves determine what action ought to be performed in a particular circumstance. Consequently, it is argued that such principles are empty and cannot in fact guide action.[10] Instead, our focus, it is claimed, should be on making all-things-considered judgements in particular contexts where we consider various descriptions of particular courses of action and evaluate how they accord with our moral sense. Ethics and political philosophy, it is contended, would be better doing without general principles and should simply require a form of ethical judgement to be exercised in particular cases.[11]

However, as O'Neill points out, 'the fact that principles underdetermine action means only that they do not provide those who adopt them with an auto-pilot for life, and not that they do not structure and constrain it. Judgement is always needed in using or following—and in flouting—rules or principles; but principles

[10] See O'Neill, 1996: 78.

[11] This seems to be one of the main arguments that lies behind some of the criticisms of the minimum core approach to socio-economic rights and in favour of the 'reasonableness' approach, which stresses context above all else and seeks to dispense with the need for determining the content of more specific principles. See Chapters 5 and 6.

are none the less important.'[12] The problem with the view which attempts to discard principles concerns how to identify and guide action. Where context and particularity is stressed above all else, the question becomes what lies behind the ethical decisions that we are to make in such contexts? Principles may not determine action but they provide the normative framework in terms of which we judge what to do in particular contexts and what is relevant in such contexts. They also provide the framework in which discussions concerning particular cases can take place and in which we can articulate intelligent disagreement about particular cases. O'Neill summarizes the importance of general principles in our moral life as follows: 'without them, we would drift through the flotsam of available descriptions, and perceptions, unable to orient ourselves on a course of action or life, to navigate among existing possibilities or institutions, to chart our way to new ones, or to reason with those with whom we are not already in agreement.'[13]

Thus, it is important to retain our focus on the general normative features of the political world that are of importance in particular contexts. To do so has an impact on how we structure our enquiries into rights. Consequently, in order to ensure that the considerations that motivate recognizing fundamental rights are given their due weight in our moral discourse, it is important to separate out the stages of our enquiry into the content of the rights that we have. These two stages correspond with a distinction I shall draw between the content of 'conditional rights' and the content of 'unconditional rights'. A 'conditional right' focuses on the perspective of recipience: each individual has certain fundamental interests that are the necessary prerequisites for leading lives of value. A concern by a society with the equal importance of lives will entail that each being ought to have their fundamental interests protected.[14] Whenever the fundamental interests of a being are infringed, that being suffers severe harm and has a *prima facie* case that society ensure that these fundamental interests are protected.

An 'unconditional right' focuses on the perspective of agency: it concerns the fact that respecting and upholding conditional rights may take place in circumstances of scarcity, and involves action by agents who have their own interests. There are thus morally relevant features of the world in which rights are to be realized that would, in several circumstances, justify a failure to realize fully the conditional right. Such a notion requires that attention be given to questions of

---

    12 O'Neill, 1996: 78.   13 Ibid.: 89.

    14 It is usual to think of a right as a relation between two parties, one having a claim on the other to do certain things. Sen argues, however, that there is some advantage 'in characterising [goal] rights as a relation not primarily between two parties but between one person and some capability to which he has a right, for example the capability of person "i" to move about without harm'(1988: 200). This suggestion ties in nicely with the rationale for conditional rights: that important interests are involved in justifying the recognition of such rights. It also emphasizes the point that in relation to conditional rights there is an emphasis on the recipience-based perspective rather than the agency perspective. However, ultimately, it seems that such a notion lacks coherence. Sen has made the mistake of identifying an 'interest' with an 'entitlement' (Kramer, Simmonds, and Steiner 1998: 44). It seems unclear that we can make sense of the notion of entitlement without some idea that the entitlement is directed to some other. The specification of a capability or interest does not require consideration of any other person; a claim about the right to have a capability protected does.

efficiency and the allocation of burdens. The determination of a society's current obligations can only take place after all these practical and normative factors have been taken into account. Thus, I refer to this notion as an 'unconditional right' or 'unconditional obligation', which signals that it is this notion that ultimately conveys what must be done in a particular circumstance.[15]

The difference between these two notions can be clarified by considering a number of useful distinctions made by other authors in relation to rights. Kramer[16] considers an objection to his view on the correlativity of rights and duties by Raz and MacCormick. They argue that we can attribute a right to someone before we have explicated it fully or even specified against whom the right is held. In order to explain how this feature of rights can be accommodated by his view, Kramer[17] introduces three important concepts. First, he makes reference to the concept of a person's interests. Secondly, he refers to what he terms 'inchoate entitlements'. These consist in the judgement that 'certain interests deserve moral and legal protection as yet unspecified'.[18] Thirdly, he makes reference to 'defined entitlements', which consist in the forms of moral or legal protection that are actually bestowed. To say someone holds a right even though nobody knows what it involves is to say, according to Kramer, merely that a certain interest is worthy of moral or legal protection. In moving from inchoate entitlements to defined entitlements, Kramer argues that two conditions have to be met. First, the kind of legal protections that are to be offered must be properly defined. Secondly, it must be specified against whom the right is held. In recognizing the necessity for further definition, he recognizes the problems which authors such as O'Neill lodge against fundamental rights discourse in general. However, as he points out, many of these problems beset only the stage of inchoate entitlements.

What justifies the introduction of a conditional right is, I have argued, a concern for the equal importance of lives together with the recognition that beings have certain fundamental interests. Such a right can have practical consequences: after all, a necessary corollary of such a right is that effective means be adopted to realize the interest that it protects. To this end, it may require specified things to be done: for instance, food ought to be provided to those who lack it. Nevertheless, it is conditional in the sense that the right will only impose a binding, unconditional obligation to act in cases where certain further relevant considerations do not modify the practical requirements imposed by the conditional right. Where operative, these further considerations may, depending on the circumstances, have two main effects on the obligations imposed by conditional rights. They may dictate that the right not be realized at all. Given the importance of the interests protected by the right, this is an unlikely scenario. Alternatively, they may require that a right be realized partially and thus modify the practical obligations that a conditional right may impose.

---

[15] Since this notion is action-orientated, I shall generally prefer the locution 'unconditional obligation'.   [16] Kramer, Simmonds, and Steiner, 1998.
[17] Ibid: 46.   [18] Ibid.

Even though a 'conditional right' can thus have its own practical implications, these may be modified or negated by considerations that must be brought in when determining the practical obligations of a society. Thus, in some sense, the practical consequences of 'conditional rights' are 'undefined', to use Kramer's locution. However, the lack of definition is not the central feature of these conditional rights: it has been contended that such rights do in fact have their own clear practical consequences. It is rather the fact that they are subject to modification by a variety of considerations that leads to such a lack of definition. Thus, it is preferable to specify the distinction I am attempting to capture in terms of 'conditional' and 'unconditional' rights rather than between 'inchoate' and 'defined' entitlements.

This distinction captures another important feature about conditional rights: that they are generally not absolute. As a result, theorists have spoken about 'prima facie rights' which may be overridden by another right, obligation, or other considerations.[19] Aiken[20] argues that there are two different ways to deal with *prima facie* rights. The first is to say that such rights only look like rights and do not constitute a right until a complete judgement is made. If my *prima facie* right to have control over my goods overrides your right to my assistance, 'then I have a right and you no longer have anything—you cease to have a legitimate claim against me. Rights are in effect determined by right actions.'[21] The problem with this approach is that it fails to explain why we regard the initial *prima facie* right as having some moral force and why such force vanishes completely once other considerations are factored in. It is also likely, as mentioned before, to confuse several different considerations rooted in different justificatory perspectives.

The alternative is to see *prima facie* rights as legitimate but defeasible moral claims. 'When these claims come into conflict and we must choose to act on one, the other (overridden) one remains a legitimate claim even though it would be wrong, in the circumstances to act upon it.'[22] Consider an example where A holds a gun to the head of B threatening to kill him if he does not assault C. C's *prima facie* right not to be assaulted remains a legitimate claim yet, in such a circumstance, it seems that B may be excused from honouring it. The point of recognizing conditional rights is partially concerned with the fact that such rights retain a moral force even where one is not required to act upon them. Thus, conditional rights can be seen to be *prima facie* rights in this second sense which Aiken describes.

Conditional rights protect those interests that we have particularly strong reasons to value and which require strong countervailing considerations to outweigh

---

[19] The term 'prima facie' can have two meanings: first, that phrase can mean 'upon initial consideration' or 'after taking into account only some relevant factors'; secondly, it may mean 'susceptible to being outweighed by more pressing considerations'. These meanings are not mutually exclusive, nor are they equivalent. The term as used in this section is meant to refer to the second meaning. See also Ross, 1930.   [20] Aiken, 1977b.

[21] Ibid: 94.   [22] Ibid.

them. Scanlon, for instance, recognizes the problems of rendering rights as absolute moral bars and prefers a 'balancing view, according to which such a right merely represents one important value among others, and decisions must be reached by striking a proper balance between them'.[23] These ultimate decisions are akin to the notion of 'unconditional rights', which arise as a result of the judgement one makes about the content of a society's duties towards beings after taking into account all relevant features of a situation.[24]

Such a structure of moral reasoning is not particular to the rights context. Jonathan Dancy, for instance, argues that moral reasoning in general requires reference to the notion of a contributory reason. 'A contributory reason is a feature whose presence makes something of a case for acting, but in such a way that the overall case for doing that action can be improved or strengthened by the addition of a second feature playing a similar role.'[25] There could also be contributory reasons favouring an alternative or opposing course of action that ultimately defeat the contributory reasons in favour of a particular course of action.

Dancy explicates the notion of a contributory reason in terms of favouring: that I promised to do an action, for instance, is a reason in favour of doing it. Not all reasons, in his view, represent favouring reasons; some are enabling conditions for a particular favouring relation. Thus, if a promise was given under duress, then the initial contributory reason no longer favours the keeping of one's promise (in his terms, it disables what would otherwise be a reason). However, the fact that a promise was not given under duress does not itself provide a reason for doing something; it merely enables the reason (that I promised to do X) truly to favour a particular course of action. The presence or absence of some reasons are thus necessary for others to do their favouring job. Moreover, some reasons are not reasons in and of themselves for a particular course of action but intensify or attenuate the primary reasons for performing a particular task. These are all useful ways of capturing the idea that there are different ways in which reasons may provide support for or count against a particular course of action. These distinctions consequently assist us to understand the impact that certain reasons should have on the fulfilment of conditional rights and are thus important to bear in mind when considering the various factors that are of relevance to translating conditional rights into unconditional obligations.

4 Translating Conditional Rights into Unconditional Rights

Having drawn this distinction between conditional and unconditional rights is of course not sufficient to show anything about our actual duties towards others.

[23] Scanlon, 1984: 146.

[24] Ross, 1930: 19ff and Melden, 1977: 4ff also refer to the concept of *prima facie* obligations and all-things-considered obligations. Dancy's (1993: 106) notion of contributory reasons also has relevance in this context.   [25] Dancy, 2004: 15.

I have tried to establish that this two-stage structure of an enquiry into the content of rights allows us to retain our focus on the interests of beings whilst not forgetting other crucial moral and pragmatic considerations. It also retains a role for universal moral principles without collapsing a rights enquiry into a groundless, particularistic judgement. I have already provided one possible justification for conditional rights in the last chapter. What remains in this chapter is to discuss some of the most important factors that must be brought into consideration in translating conditional rights into unconditional rights. The discussion in this section assumes that it is not sufficient merely to recognize that conditional rights alone will not determine action; we must understand the key normative and practical considerations that arise in real-life contexts and have an impact on our ability to translate conditional rights into unconditional obligations upon a society.

4.1 Scarcity

One of the main factors that render the realization of conditional rights complicated is the fact that there is a moderate scarcity of resources.[26] Were there to be a complete abundance of resources, the basic capabilities of all could be realized to a minimum level and all could still be able to realize a wide range of purposes. There would be no need to impose sacrifices on some for the sake of others, and conditional rights could generally be realized without any countervailing problems. The world, however, does not contain an abundance of all the resources that we need to fulfil all our conditional rights. Although the problem of resource scarcity is more acute for some societies, even affluent societies in the world such as the United States and the United Kingdom operate under some constraints imposed by resource scarcity. If expensive, life-saving health care were to be provided for each, and vast research undertaken to realize the basic capabilities of every being, it is likely that virtually all of a government's budget could be used up on such activities. Thus, in almost all countries, some form of health care rationing is necessary.[27] In determining the resolution of such problems, it is thus necessary to have some understanding of the resources that are available to a society to realize basic rights.[28]

These levels of scarcity will vary in relation to different resources. In relation to the resources necessary to provide the health care every individual requires to be

[26] Rawls regards the moderate scarcity of resources as one of the objective circumstances that leads to problems of justice in the first place: 'the circumstances of justice obtain whenever persons put forward conflicting claims to the division of social advantages under conditions of moderate scarcity' (1999a: 110). Moderate scarcity in turn entails that '[w]hile mutually advantageous arrangements are feasible, the benefits they yield fall short of the demands men put forward' (ibid).

[27] See, for instance, Dworkin, 2000: 308.

[28] In making such a determination, it may be necessary to specify how world resources are to be distributed between different societies. It is by no means evident that a society is entitled to claim all the resources which lie within its domain and it may be that transfers between societies will be important in determining the extent of the scarcity in a particular society. See, for instance, Pogge, 2002, who deals with this question.

able to realize a wide variety of purposes, the scarcity that exists is such that a choice has to be made between meeting this threshold for all and retaining some ability for individuals to realize projects beyond the basic. On the other hand, in relation to the resources necessary to provide for certain other basic needs, it is possible to guarantee everyone access to these resources without jeopardizing the ability to realize projects beyond the basic. Thus, ensuring each being has adequate nutrition does not require that we reduce the amount of food resources to a point where each only has the minimal amount of food required to live. It may, however, require certain changes in the way we produce food that do impose certain sacrifices on people: in order to reduce scarcity, it may be that certain types of food cannot be provided due to their inefficient use of resources.[29] People may thus be required to give up certain foods in order to ensure that everyone at least has adequate nutrition.

This previous point suggests that we must distinguish between different types of scarcity. Some forms of scarcity cannot be changed as a result of any actions on our part: the total amount of natural oil or land in the world is fixed and cannot be increased generally by any of our actions.[30] We may refer to such scarcity at the outer limit as 'absolute natural scarcity'. However, even in these examples, it is possible for humans to regulate their usage of these resources. For instance, people can regulate the amount of activities that go into extracting oil from the natural world. We can expend greater or lesser effort in searching for oil and, when we find it, we may choose to exploit the resource in different ways. We can also regulate to an extent our reliance on oil-based technologies and thus the degree to which we use oil. Our decisions will thus impact on the extent to which absolute levels of a resource are exploited and the extent to which trade-offs must be made between individuals.

Similarly, much talk of scarcity arises in relation to the fact that certain goods are particularly expensive, and thus a society is limited in terms of its ability to acquire these goods. The reasons that such goods are expensive may vary. At times, the production of an expensive good may involve much time and expertise, which few people have. Since time, effort, and expertise can be scarce resources, our ability to produce such goods is in fact limited. That could explain their expense.

On the other hand, a number of goods are expensive due to the structure of the modern market place, and the fact that certain companies are given monopolies

---

[29] Meat is an incredibly inefficient form of food. We use farmland to grow a vast quantity of grain, but then feed this to animals and then eat the animals. We 'have to feed the animals eight pounds of protein in the form of grain to get back one pound in the form of meat, for a wastage of 87. 5 percent' (Rachels, 1977: 184). In the US, 78 per cent of all grain is fed to animals (ibid: 185). This argument would suggest the need to reduce meat consumption to ensure adequate nutrition for all. Such an argument exists independently of any argument against eating meat that arises from the principle requiring us to respect the basic rights of non-human animals.

[30] This is assuming humans do not develop new techniques to develop oil from other sources. Land, too, may at times be extended by natural occurrences (volcanoes) and, on occasion, by human effort to extend the land into parts of the sea (such as is occurring currently in Dubai).

over the production of certain goods. Life-saving medical drugs often fall into this category where these goods become particularly expensive due to the patents that are held by pharmaceutical companies in relation to them. Whilst patents may reflect large research and development expenditure, the price of the drugs often far exceeds the cost of their production. As such, the shortfall of life-saving drugs that is attributed to 'scarce resources' may not result at all from 'absolute natural scarcity' but monopolistic structures in a market.

Distinguishing the types of scarcity is important as it has an impact upon the obligations that a society is required to perform in order to ensure that conditional rights are fulfilled. On the one hand, the principle that one generally ought to do only what one can do implies that where absolute natural scarcity exists, we will have to tailor our obligations to the level of available resources. On the other hand, where scarcity results from certain human decisions, a discussion can then be held about our obligations to change our behaviour in a way that helps to reduce the scarcity of the resource in question and to realize conditional rights.[31]

4.2 Urgency

In light of the fact that we are faced in the real world with situations of scarcity, it becomes important to outline certain considerations that play a vital role in making judgements about the extent to which conditional rights should be achieved and at what expense. There are several important factors I shall identify that are of central importance in making these judgements.

The first concerns a matter I have already discussed in the first chapter, and that is the urgency of the interest that is involved. I have argued that there are two differing thresholds of urgency that can be identified. Since it is true that the higher the urgency the greater the level of importance an interest has for a being, a society founded on treating each being with equal importance will attempt to prioritize the meeting of interests that are of the greatest urgency to beings.[32] Thus, a society will require a stronger justification for failing to provide shelter for those people who have no protection from the elements, than in respect of its failure to provide for those who are protected from the elements but lack comfortable housing. This is because the implications for the individuals are far more severe in the former case than the latter, and such individuals thus require special attention in order to ensure that they are treated with equal importance to others. In turn, the level of sacrifice required of people in a society will vary in accordance with the urgency of the individual interests that still must be realized therein.

---

[31] This may be very important, for instance, in relation to the availability of expensive drugs to combat diseases such as HIV, where a treatment exists that can be produced relatively cheaply and absolute scarcity is not present. For a fuller discussion of this issue in relation to the availability of anti-retroviral drugs in South Africa, see Sprague and Woolman, 2006.

[32] I shall expand on what is meant by the notions of 'urgency' and 'priority' here in Chap 6.

4.3 Sacrifice

The next important factor involved in deciding upon the unconditional obligations of a society under conditions of moderate scarcity concerns the extent of the sacrifice required of individuals in a society in order to realize conditional rights. The guiding principle would be that as the level of sacrifice required of individuals increases, so does the permissibility of failing to realize the conditional rights of individuals. The reason for this lies in the point made earlier that the very justification of conditional rights requires that there be a space beyond the meeting of basic needs in which individuals can realize their own forms of the good life. Where the very existence of such a space is jeopardized, there may be justification for failing to realize conditional rights. However, that reason also implies that the lesser the extent to which the ability of individuals to lead valuable lives is affected, the less is the strength of the justification for failing to realize conditional rights.

Difficulty arises, however, in that a number of factors will play a part in determining the extent of any particular sacrifice for any particular person. Consider an example where a society requires each individual to devote one morning a week to helping those less fortunate than themselves. An individual who must effect a vigorous daily practice routine in order to realize his life dream of becoming a successful ballet dancer may find it a large sacrifice to devote one morning a week to a charity organization. On the other hand, a commercial lawyer may have to sacrifice very little in terms of her life projects by having to devote one morning a week to legal aid work. The example suggests that the nature of one's life projects may well affect what constitutes a large sacrifice and what does not.

The extent to which certain practices form part of one's identity may well also have an impact upon what constitutes a large sacrifice: a religious individual may find that having to forgo church or synagogue to contribute towards a charity organization constitutes a substantial sacrifice for him, whereas other individuals may feel little loss in such a case. Thus, the extent to which religion, art, and sport, for instance, are valued in a society will determine the extent to which a reduction in such activities constitutes a serious sacrifice for that society.

These considerations raise a difficult question as to whether the extent of the sacrifice individuals make should be evaluated subjectively or objectively. It is possible, for instance, that a person who ties his projects very closely to buying clothes and being fashionable may well regard it as a substantial sacrifice to have to forgo buying expensive clothes. Someone else may regard such a project as having little worth, and not requiring much of a sacrifice. Singer, in his discussion on global poverty, wants to take a more objective line on this question: he states that '[w]hen we buy new clothes not to keep ourselves warm but to look "well-dressed" we are not providing for any important need. We would not be sacrificing anything significant if we were to continue to wear our old clothes and give the money to famine relief.'[33] His interpretation of significance depends upon one adopting an

---

[33] Singer, 1972: 235.

objective interpretation thereof whereby buying new clothes could not form a significant part of the projects of an individual. However, it is difficult to see how one could come up with a general objective account of what constitutes significant sacrifice beyond the realm of basic needs that could be accepted by everyone in a society with differing individual forms of the good.[34]

A society, however, adopting a policy as to the sacrifices it will require of its members will need to adopt a uniform way of measuring the sacrifices required of individuals upon some simplifying assumptions. A society that treats each individual with equal importance must aim to impose an equivalent level of sacrifice upon each individual. To do otherwise would mean that greater burdens are placed on some rather than others, suggesting that the lives of some individuals are less worthy of respect than the lives of others.

The discussion thus far has recognized that where the unconditional obligations of a society place burdens upon individuals, the extent of these sacrifices may vary in accordance with the differing goods of individuals. If we wish to respect the goal that equal burdens be placed upon each individual, then it seems that the contributions required by each individual to meeting these unconditional obligations must vary. There are, however, numerous problems with adopting such a policy. First, any such procedure would be extremely invasive, requiring a society to find out very detailed information about each individual in order to work out the level of sacrifice that ought to be imposed upon her. Secondly, such an inquiry would be virtually impossible to perform across a large society. The time and effort involved would be prohibitive. Thirdly, any such procedure would be unworkable in that it would violate the generality of laws and policies. Fourthly, measuring the levels of sacrifice and making comparative judgements has no clear criteria and is no exact science. Across a society, it is likely that serious mistakes would be made in trying to equalize the level of sacrifice made by each person. Finally, it could have certain counterintuitive results in that those people for whom the marginal utility of wealth is high would be required to give up less wealth, for instance, than those people for whom the marginal utility of wealth is low. That could have the result that some of those in the most privileged positions who are used to a grand lifestyle might be expected to give up the least amount of their wealth given the high level of sacrifice a reduction in their living standard would entail for them.

Thus, in order to avoid such impossible calculations and undesirable consequences, a society will be forced to adopt certain simplifying assumptions that allow it to estimate what constitutes an equal level of sacrifice. In relation to the control over resources, a reasonable assumption to adopt, given the shape of the typical person's utility curve, would be one of 'diminishing marginal utility': as an individual's income and control over resources increases beyond the realm of basic

---

[34] *Contra* Singer, a fashion designer or model, for instance, could regard buying fashionable clothes as an important part of the good for them.

goods, their marginal utility diminishes from each extra unit of income or resources. If we wish to ensure that each individual bears an equivalent level of sacrifice, such an assumption would support a policy of progressive taxation whereby those with greater amounts of resources would be required to contribute more. Thus, although an objective notion of sacrifice is difficult to arrive at beyond the realm of the basic, a society will have to use certain objective proxies for determining the subjective sacrifices required of each of its members.

4.4 Effectiveness

Thus far I have considered various factors involved in determining the nature and content of the unconditional obligations to be imposed upon a society. Conditional rights, it has been argued, inform us that we have a conditional obligation to each to ensure that certain fundamental interests are realized, such as being provided with adequate food. Conditional rights do not, however, generally inform us *how* we should realize these obligations. In arriving at unconditional obligations, it is thus necessary to engage with questions concerning the manner in which such rights are to be realized. These questions, in turn, can at times modify the actual obligations and the form that they take.

Conditional rights are silent on whether, for instance, each individual in a society has an obligation to provide every needy individual with adequate food. It merely states that each is to be provided with adequate food. However, we can deduce from such a right the obligation to adopt effective methods of realizing the right to food of every person. Conditional rights thus contain within them an implicit appeal to effectiveness as a norm that must be taken into account when determining unconditional obligations.

Effectiveness places a number of additional conditions upon realizing rights. First, given the fact that each individual is limited in terms of her own capacities to realize rights, it is evident that in order to be maximally effective, individuals must combine their energies. In order to uphold rights, a society will thus be required to ensure that individual efforts are coordinated and that an institutional structure is provided in which adequate food is provided to each. A society can be said to be conditionally obliged to realize the right to food of individuals; the best and only feasible method of realizing such a right for all is to coordinate the actions of different individuals with one another. 'Cooperation and coordination can be achieved by organising, and they can be achieved over the long term through the establishment of institutions.'[35]

Secondly, effectiveness may also provide another reason for limiting what can be expected of individuals. A situation in which individuals have overwhelming obligations that prevent them from fulfilling their own goods can in fact be counterproductive, leading to apathy, despondency, and resentment. Thus,

[35] Shue, 1988: 695.

effectiveness norms may themselves suggest the need to allow individuals a space beyond the realm of necessities in which to realize their own goods.

Thirdly, effectiveness norms will also require that in moving to unconditional obligations, there is a greater level of specification as to the particular obligations that flow from a recognition of conditional rights. O'Neill[36] incorrectly suggests that it is only positive rights that require such specification. In relation to the right to free speech, which is regarded traditionally as a 'negative right', it is often claimed that each agent is merely required not to interfere with the speech of any other rational agent. However, there are circumstances when interference will be justified and these must be at least partially defined.[37] Secondly, as O'Neill admits, even in the case of 'negative rights', it is unlikely that particular obligations upon a society will stop at non-interference, and, indeed, it is likely that such a right will at least involve an obligation to set up enforcement agencies to ensure that the right is protected. Obligations may also arise, for instance, to provide positive assistance to those who, for whatever reason, are relatively powerless to ensure that their views are aired in the society. On the other hand, in relation to a traditionally 'positive right' such as the right to adequate food, non-interference may also be sufficient in many cases, simply allowing each being to provide their own food for themselves. Positive obligations would arise where individuals need others to ensure that they have adequate food and it is then necessary to coordinate the activities of individuals and to form institutions that can provide the required goods and services.

Thus, the traditional distinction between 'negative' and 'positive' rights offers a highly incomplete specification of the duties that follow from recognizing conditional rights. A more satisfactory analysis has been provided by Henry Shue,[38] who argues that '[t]he complete fulfilment of each kind of right involves the performance of multiple kinds of duties'. He claims that every right, both negative and positive, contains three correlative duties: duties to avoid depriving, duties to protect from deprivation, and duties to aid the deprived. Thus, the right to adequate food, for instance, contains three duties: a duty not to eliminate an individual's only available means of acquiring food (the duty to avoid depriving); a duty to protect individuals against deprivation of their only available means of subsistence (the duty to protect from deprivation); and a duty to provide the food for those unable to do so themselves (the duty to aid the deprived). Thus, according to Shue, each conditional right entails duties to refrain from interfering as well as duties to perform specific positive actions.[39]

---

[36] O'Neill, 1996: 134.

[37] I do not argue that we must be able to specify each and every circumstance where such interference would be justified in advance. To determine the content of an unconditional right to free speech, however, requires at least some understanding of its range and the permissible limitations that may be placed thereon. The exact content of such a right will need to be specified when a specific issue arises, such as the permissibility of hate speech or pornography.   [38] Shue, 1980: 52.

[39] As will be discussed in Chap 6, Shue's analysis has had a great influence on the approach adopted by the United Nations Committee on Economic, Social and Cultural Rights. The relationship

Shue's analysis of the duties that arise from conditional rights seems to contradict the idea that rights and duties are correlative. There are, however, two alternative ways to view the situation which preserves the symmetry between rights and obligations in each case. The first route, suggested by Fabre,[40] is to argue that all rights and duties are on the same level and that each duty has a correlative right. Thus, each of Shue's duties would be correlative to different rights. For instance, there would be no one right to bodily security but rather several rights: a demand that we not be assaulted would be encapsulated by a negative right not to be assaulted, and a demand that we be protected against assaults would be encapsulated by a positive right that the state take steps to protect us from potential attackers. However, there are two problems with adopting this strategy. The first is that it would lead to a proliferation of a confusing number of distinct rights. The second problem is that it fails to recognize that there is a unifying feature to the rights relating to bodily security: each of these rights is designed to protect the same interest.

Thus, a second and preferable route to follow if one wishes to preserve the correlativity of rights and obligations is to distinguish between *abstract* rights where the obligation is specified in abstract terms, and *concrete* rights, which are essentially further specifications of these abstract rights. Each of these concrete rights would also give rise in each situation to a correlative obligation. This suggestion thus takes on board the insight of Fabre's suggestion, but there is an attempt to solve the difficulties with her view. The resulting deontic structure would be one in which there are differing levels of rights and corresponding obligations. Identifying an abstract right would allow for recognizing the particular interest that provides the justificatory basis for the right; concrete rights would provide the further specifications necessary to ensure the effective protection of this interest. Kramer puts the point as follows: '[a]n abstract right that is strictly correlated with an abstract duty can comprise or undergird any number of concrete rights, each of which will of course be strictly correlated with a concrete duty.'[41] In this way, we can take on board the virtues of Shue's analysis without losing the correlativity between rights and duties.

5 The Assignment of Duties

In specifying unconditional obligations, however, it is crucial not only to determine what must be done but who has the responsibility for doing it. One of the problems with conditional rights was said to be their failure to specify who is obliged to realize them. O'Neill, for example, argues that claimants of conditional

between the minimum core approach to socio-economic rights and Shue's approach will be discussed there.

[40] Fabre, 2000: 52.   [41] Kramer, Simmonds, and Steiner, 1998: 43.

rights do not know who bears the counterpart obligations and thus grasp 'thin air'.[42] Though it is true that one cannot arrive at an allocation of obligations directly from the conditional rights, it is clear from the argument presented thus far that the primary obligation rests upon a society.[43] As has been argued, a requirement of effectiveness is implicit within an injunction to realize conditional rights. Effectiveness would require that duties be allocated within a society to those particular individuals and institutions most suitably placed to fulfil these duties. A programme of action designed to realize each right will need to be adopted so as to ensure that individuals and agencies are delegated clear responsibilities. Such a flexible structure of allocation based upon effectiveness may well have an advantage over an overly rigid specification of responsible agents that does not evolve with developments in the world and our knowledge of how best to achieve conditional rights. As a result, it will be a matter for empirical determination as to what the most effective allocation of responsibility is.

5.1 The role of individual responsibility

Some general conclusions can, however, be derived from a theoretical consideration of this issue. The first question concerns the role of an individual in meeting his own needs. It is clear that an individual will have an important part to play in realizing his interest in acquiring adequate food, for instance. Individuals often know best what they need and are best able to provide for themselves. Delegating responsibility to individuals for meeting their own needs also gives them a major incentive to succeed in this endeavour, thus helping to reduce the overall burden on society. It is also conducive to self-respect that an individual be responsible, where possible, for realizing his own needs. These considerations provide strong reasons for a society to allocate primary responsibility to individuals for meeting their own needs.

Adopting such a policy will, nevertheless, entail certain responsibilities that the society must assume: it must, for instance, prevent some individuals from interfering with the ability of others to meet their own needs. It must also provide a legal and institutional framework in which each has the opportunity to do so. Such a framework would require, for instance, that individuals are able to meet

---

[42] 1996: 135.

[43] The notion of a society has been used as a shorthand expression for the primary collective political grouping that designs, forms, and enforces rules which govern the distribution of benefits and burdens to individuals and thus largely determines the ability of individuals to lead lives of value. Most societies in this sense today take the form of nation states and the focus of this book is upon the responsibilities of such states and the institutions within them. It is recognized that there are collective groupings beyond the nation state with the power to formulate and enforce rules that impact significantly upon individuals. It is thus also an important project to consider responsibilities beyond the nation state. Exactly which bodies are responsible for realizing rights in a globalized world is a matter of some controversy among philosophers: for an interesting collection of articles on this question, see Kuper, 2005.

their needs without being coerced into taking jobs that are contrary to their life projects. Protecting the ability of individuals to meet their own needs in a market-based system would also entail that a society must take steps to enable individuals to be employable: education and training may be necessary to achieve this end. Thus, in order to ensure that the allocation of responsibility to individuals for meeting their own needs will be effective, there will always be an area of residual responsibility that must be assumed by societal institutions.

There are, however, certain circumstances in which individuals should not bear responsibility for meeting their own needs and be able to claim direct positive assistance from their society. The most obvious instance where this is so is where an individual is unable to meet her basic needs through her own effort. It would be an entirely ineffective method of allocating responsibility to require someone to do something they were unable to do. Inability may be due to some condition of an individual—such as illness or disability—but it can also importantly be due to a number of social factors. A homeless person may be technically capable of acquiring a job; yet her lack of access to facilities in which she can take care of her personal hygiene may mean that no employer is prepared to employ her.

Inability may also be psychological: an individual may have some mental illness, or alternatively, lack a sense of self-worth which renders him unable to look for work. Similarly, inability to find a job may not be an individual problem, but rather due to societal conditions: for instance, there may simply not be sufficient jobs available to ensure full employment. Under such conditions, which embrace many of the circumstances in which people cannot meet their basic needs, it seems clear that responsibility for meeting their needs should not fall upon the individuals themselves. The society is required to coordinate an effective plan so as to help those in need.

A complication, however, arises in that individuals are unable to meet their needs for a variety of reasons. Some of these are due to factors beyond their control; however, past irresponsible and reckless choices may also be the reason for their current deprivations. Given that a person must be allowed to choose to live an ascetic lifestyle, we cannot force a person to meet their basic needs if they do not wish to do so. I am concerned, however, with a different set of circumstances: where someone has made choices in the past (such as to spend their days surfing) that result in their currently being in a position of need that they do not wish to be in. Is a society obligated to provide for the basic needs of such individuals?

Certain leading theories of distributive justice would deny that a society is required to provide for the basic needs of persons in such situations. Dworkin,[44] for instance, claims that inequalities in the holding of resources are justified when they arise because of choices that people make for which they can be held responsible. People should be compensated, however, for inequalities that result from

---

[44] Dworkin, 2000: 6.

aspects of the self for which they cannot be held responsible. For Dworkin, responsibility is a deep principle embedded in the foundation of his theory.[45]

I have, however, thus far argued that the responsibility to meet one's own basic needs arises as a result of being the most effective allocation by a society of its duties to ensure that everyone's basic needs are met. Where such an allocation is no longer effective in that a person cannot meet their basic needs through their own efforts, then the theory would justify imposing responsibility upon society to organize positive assistance for such persons. The fundamental entitlements are thus justified directly through the principle that a society is required to treat the lives of beings with equal importance. As a result, responsibility does not form part of the deep structure of the justification of conditional rights. This implies that individuals would not necessarily lose their entitlements through their own recklessness. However, this matter is one of some complexity and importance and consequently requires further elaboration below.

5.2 The limits of responsibility

My position, outlined above, could help explain an intuitive distinction made by Scanlon. He points out that it is important to distinguish between two different senses in which we use the notion of 'holding a person responsible for their choices'.[46] On the one hand, this phrase may mean that someone is the proper subject of praise or blame for performing an action. On the other hand, it may mean that it would be a justifiable policy to make him bear the consequences of his conduct. These two senses of the term can come apart. Tort law, for instance, may find that a person has been negligent and is thus to blame for a motor vehicle accident; yet, it may limit the person's (or insurer's) liability to direct harm caused to the other motor vehicle. A court is unlikely to place liability upon a person for the full consequences of his actions where, for instance, a direct result of his negligence was a pile-up of 100 cars on a motorway. Even though a person may be worthy of praise or blame, we do not always insist that a person bears the full consequences of his actions.

This distinction points to a difficulty in Dworkin's theory. He appears to conflate the two usages, and suggests that people should bear the consequences of any action for which they can be praised or blamed. However, that position is too strong. Take the case of being infected with HIV through engaging in unsafe sex. The majority of people who contract HIV in the United Kingdom are educated about how HIV is transmitted and yet some still engage in risky sexual activity. Strictly speaking, people choose freely to have unprotected sex and thus accept the

---

[45] There are several reasons to avoid giving responsibility such a central role in political theory. I mention one main argument here, and have defended others in my MPhil dissertation (2001).

[46] Scanlon, 1995: 2–3.

risk of contracting HIV. Were they to contract HIV, they could be praised or blamed for contracting the disease where this was preventable.[47]

Yet, many of us would judge that individuals should not bear the full consequences of their choices in such instances. HIV drugs are notoriously expensive. If individuals had to be impoverished in order to acquire these drugs, Dworkin's theory would require them to bear the loss, placing no obligation upon the society to help such individuals. Similarly, if individuals lost their jobs due to the incapacitating effects of AIDS, Dworkin's theory would not require that a society devote any extra resources to helping them. This approach is hard-hearted and harsh. It does not accord with the basic intuition to help individuals in such situations and would allow sick individuals to perish under awful conditions. As such, there seems to be a difference between what we are prepared to blame people for, and which costs we require them to bear as a result of their conduct.[48]

A similar problem arises in relation to poor caretakers.[49] Most of these people— mostly women—do not command a market wage for the work they do in raising children or caring for the ill. This leads to economic dependence on others (usually a partner). These caretakers are usually no less talented than those who work in the marketplace, yet they often choose their path of life. As such, Dworkin's theory (and libertarian theory) will hold them responsible for their choices and deny them any compensation for the loss of resources sustained through choosing their path of life. Yet the services caretakers perform are socially valuable. Their economic dependence on others is a recipe for domination and exploitation. Furthermore, the burden of caretaking, in general, falls disproportionately on women and contributes to their inequality in society.[50] Scanlon's distinction allows us to recognize that these people are in fact autonomous choosers and so can be praised or blamed for their decisions; but it also allows us to deny that they should bear all the social costs (measured in material resources) for their choices.

Scanlon's distinction can be seen to accord well with the line of reasoning I have advocated. It may well be that if we allocate responsibility to someone for meeting their needs, and they fail to do so as a result of their own choices, we can blame them for the situation in which they land up. Nevertheless, since their entitlements arise from the principle of equal importance rather than from any philosophical notions of desert or responsibility, people do not automatically lose their rights as a result of inadequate choices. Their entitlements remain despite their being partially or wholly responsible for their position. A society founded upon the principle of equal importance is thus not only concerned with whether the position of each person reflects their responsibility or otherwise; rather, it is

---

[47] Though one can be said to be responsible for one's choices here, I think that one hesitates to attribute blame to people in these circumstances. This may suggest that Scanlon's distinctions do not exhaust the different senses in which a person can be said to be responsible.

[48] Scanlon, 1995 also criticizes Roemer, 1995 for conflating these ideas.

[49] I owe this example to Anderson, 1999: 297–8.   [50] Ibid: 298.

concerned with the effect that different holdings of resources have on people's lives and on society.

The emphasis upon responsibility in Dworkin's theory also overemphasizes the separation between chosen and unchosen aspects of the self. When we recognize that choice is only one important aspect of a person, then it becomes clear that there will be cases where a person's choices will require them to bear the costs thereof and cases where this will be implausible, where some other aspect of the person or their context requires that they be indemnified against the effects of their choices. People's lives cannot be neatly divided into the chosen and unchosen aspects of self. Even the faculty of choice is not itself chosen. Once this is recognized, then it seems that the foundational principle of a society requires us to treat individual lives—considered as a union of the chosen and unchosen aspects of the self—as being of equal importance. However, then it would not sanction allowing individuals to perish or experience severe suffering purely as a result of their own choices.

5.3 Reconciling rights and responsibility

On the other hand, it may be objected that the theory I have proposed thus far places too little emphasis upon individual choice. People who have the capacity for rational choice are capable of making decisions for which they should be held responsible. To indemnify them against all the effects of their choices would be to treat them with disrespect and fail to acknowledge adequately their capacities for choice.

Moreover, two additional objections may be made against a position that allows fundamental entitlements to be completely unaffected by individual choices. First, it seems unfair to guarantee all individuals the same level of provision regardless of whether they landed up in a needy position as a result of their own choices or not. Ensuring that individuals are able to realize their rights is not cost-less and places burdens on other members of society. By making reckless choices that imperil their rights, individuals shift the burden of providing for their needs from themselves to other members of society. A greater amount of societal resources would then have to be spent on providing for the reckless individuals than if they had provided for themselves. That, in turn, entails that greater burdens are placed upon other 'prudent' members of society as a result of the choices of reckless individuals. To allow such a situation to obtain would be to allow individuals to determine the distribution of resources in a society according to their own choices. Yet to do so could in fact violate the principle of equal importance that, amongst other things, requires that the benefits and burdens in a society fall equally upon each individual. It would, for instance, place greater importance on the lives of reckless individuals if they were allowed to realize their own life projects by placing a disproportionate burden on other members of society.

Secondly, if a society continually has to raise a person to the same threshold despite an individual being implicated in willingly allowing himself to fall below that threshold, there would be little incentive for some individuals to maintain themselves above the threshold. They could always fall back on societal provision. Individuals who reasoned in this way and did not mind a relatively low standard of living could thus be led to risk their ability to meet their needs, in the secure knowledge that others would pick up the tab. That, in turn, would encourage reckless behaviour and lead to a greater overall burden being placed upon other individuals in the society.

Thus, there are reasons internal to the principle of equal importance that would justify providing a lower level of entitlements for individuals who are responsible for failing to realize their basic needs. On the other hand, the principle requires that there be a minimum basic level of provision below which no one can be allowed to fall. To do otherwise would be to allow individual lives to degenerate to the point that they either die or become worthless. No plausible interpretation of the principle of equal *importance*—that places value upon individual life—could allow such a situation to arise.[51]

To resolve these conflicting tensions within the principle of equal importance, it is important to consider the fact that the theory I have developed involves identifying two different thresholds that, taken together, specify the necessary preconditions for leading lives of value. That feature of the theory allows for a guarantee to be provided that individuals will not perish whilst ensuring that reckless individuals do not receive exactly the same entitlements as those who, through no fault of their own, are unable to provide for themselves. Thus, a society under such a scheme would be required to guarantee each individual the resources and capabilities necessary to realize the first threshold (being free from threats to their survival), irrespective of their choices. However, a society would not be responsible for ensuring that reckless individuals be raised repeatedly to meet the second threshold (being provided with the necessary conditions to realize a wide range of purposes). The latter threshold is the one most concerned with individual choice, and thus it is fitting that individual responsibility may affect whether or not it is met.

Thus, a society will generally be required to guarantee the second threshold for all, but in most cases will allocate the responsibility for maintaining themselves at this level to individuals. Where individuals can be blamed for falling below it, the principle of equal importance itself will mandate that society need not raise these individuals above the first threshold. In this way, it is possible to ensure that no one falls below a basic minimum in a society, yet no one is insulated against the effects of his reckless choices, and allowed to burden others at whim.[52]

---

[51] See Chap 2, where I make this point.

[52] I have been discussing responsibility in relation to certain minimum thresholds. In relation to the holding of resources beyond the basic, I would generally agree with Dworkin's position that, after an initially equal distribution of resources, and with safeguards for those disadvantaged by nature, an individual's level of resources must be allowed to increase or diminish in accordance with her choices.

6 The Overall Decision Framework

I have thus far discussed a variety of considerations—scarcity, urgency, sacrifice, efficiency, and allocation—that must be dealt with in defining the content of the unconditional obligations of a society. It is necessary, however, in determining the content of these obligations, that there be some framework within which all these factors are to be evaluated. The theory I have proposed does not allow a clear inference to be drawn from the recognition of conditional rights to the claim that certain particular actions need to be performed. However, in the absence of some general framework within which such decisions must be made, the theory fails to provide crucial answers to the most central question: what ought a political society to do as a matter of its obligations to individual members?

I do not propose to answer this question in a way that offers a specific solution to the problem in every situation. At the general level, I have argued that we must recognize the central importance conditional rights must have in our deliberations, and we can isolate several factors that must be taken into account in arriving at a decision about our unconditional obligations. The decisions will have to be taken in particular contexts with particular facts and circumstances playing a part in determining exactly which obligations a society must fulfil. To paraphrase the words of Aristotle, 'determinations of this kind depend upon particular circumstances, and the decision rests with our (moral) sense'.[53] However, in deciding what concrete actions must be taken in particular circumstances, it is necessary at least to have an understanding of the general moral framework within which such decisions must be made. If this is not so, the particular judgements will lack any reference point and it will be difficult to see upon what basis such judgements are made. In arriving at such a general framework, it is important to draw on the basic animating moral vision behind the theory I have proposed, which has two central components. The first component has been a theory of value which recognizes that ultimate value inheres in the experiential and purposive dimensions of individual lives. The second component has been an idea that a society should treat the lives of beings as having equal importance. In evaluating all the factors I have outlined and arriving at determinate judgements in particular contexts, the ultimate question must be one concerning which specification of the content of rights will best realize the values recognized by the moral theory I have proposed. This will translate into the making of a complex judgement about which state of affairs would be one in which the value components of every individual life in the society could best be said to be treated with equal importance.

The theory I propose thus has two tiers, with the idea of equal importance coming in at two levels. The first level concerns the meaning and justification of equal

---

[53] Aristotle, 1962: 51.

importance and involves the contention that, other things being equal, a concern for equal importance will require that a society should aim to realize the conditional rights of beings. At this level, conditional rights are not justified directly by consequentialist reasoning but are rather derived from the principle of equal importance.

The second tier of the theory involves analysing the range of factors that are presupposed in the 'other things being equal' clause. It takes into account the operation of these factors in particular contexts and attempts to determine overall which specification of obligations would be most conducive to realizing the ideal of equal importance in a world of scarcity and trade-offs.

The latter judgement will be consequentialist in nature as it seems that only such a theory is able to allow for the consideration of a host of relevant factors within a common framework. However, the consequences, according to this theory, will be evaluated in terms of whether individuals are treated as being equally important. This accords with a proposal by Scanlon that was made in order to render leading consequentialist theories such as utilitarianism more sensitive to the distribution of goods amongst individuals. Scanlon argues that a complex consequentialism should take into account considerations concerning 'equality of distributions and fairness of processes . . . [which would be] . . . among the properties that make states of affairs worth promoting'.[54] Sen has also argued that it is possible to integrate a consequentialist theory of moral reasoning with rights-based reasoning. Whether or not a being's conditional rights are fulfilled, he claims, can become a central part of the evaluation of outcomes.[55] Taking these suggestions seriously in the context of my theory will mean that in making the overall judgement as to which unconditional obligations we have, strong weight will be given to the fulfilment of conditional rights. This is not a surprising result as considerations of equal importance support the recognition of conditional rights.

It is important, however, to be aware of the nature of the consequentialist theory I am proposing and the complexities involved in arriving at the overall consequentialist judgement to determine unconditional obligations. Such a theory is no classical utilitarianism. The locus of value in such a system lies clearly in individual lives and thus any judgement that is made will oppose any attempt at aggregation that fails to respect the separateness and integrity of individuals. The aim is not to arrive at the maximum utility but the best state of affairs that can succeed in respecting the value and importance of each individual equally. Such a judgement will not allow for vastly disproportionate sacrifices between individuals. Classical utilitarianism has often been criticized for possibly allowing some individuals to fare very badly if that would increase the total utility. The equal importance of individuals would not be upheld if the life projects of some were being sacrificed for the sake of others.

---

[54] Scanlon, 1984: 142.   [55] Sen, 1988: 199.

On the other hand, the theory I have proposed does not rule out some hard choices and provides answers in cases where rights conflict. It may mean that even the most basic interest in life itself can at times justifiably be denied to someone. Such cases will be extreme: circumstances, for instance, in which there is no option but to kill one person in order to save 20. Strong deontological theories would not allow the person to be killed; yet they have been criticized for being unable to cope with such difficult situations. It seems irrational to forbid inflicting 'one uncompensated harm in order to prevent even more such harms'.[56] To hold that one person should be saved at the expense of 20 others would be to elevate that person's life above the life of others, and so fail to respect once again the equal importance of each life. Of course, in such a situation, that individual who is killed will not be respected—this is the reason that such situations represent tragic choices. Yet, the very situation we are faced with places us in a dilemma either to fail to respect the value of 20 lives or the value of one life: if we allow 20 to die for one individual to live, that would be to place his life as far more important than the other lives.

Under less extreme conditions, the equal importance of persons will require, as I have argued, that conditional rights be respected and upheld. In an ideal situation, such a principle supports the full recognition and fulfilment of conditional rights. However, taking into account the variety of factors I have mentioned, it is clear that there are conditions where the full realization of conditional rights may lead to a number of practical and principled problems. In order to ascertain what actions should be undertaken by a society, it will be necessary to evaluate which actions best respect the equal value of individual lives, having particular reference to the urgency of the interests involved and the extent of the sacrifices required. As a general rule, the greater the urgency of the need, the greater the likelihood that a particular action will be required; the lesser the sacrifice, the more likely it is that a particular action will be required. Thus, such an overall enquiry will generally give priority to those in the worst-off situations, and yet allow for a space in which all individuals can freely pursue their own projects.

7 Conclusion

This chapter has sought to defend the following important propositions.

(1) Fundamental rights impose conditional correlative obligations upon a society which can be understood by considering their normative basis alone.

(2) The obligations imposed by fundamental rights are situated, however, within a real-life context in which there are constraints that give rise to competing normative and practical considerations.

---

[56] Scheffler, 1988: 10.

(3) Consequently, the unconditional obligations of a society must be determined both by reference to fundamental rights and these competing considerations. A number of factors and principles were outlined to guide decision-making in this area.

(4) It was argued that ultimately the unconditional obligations of a society will be determined by a complex consequentialist judgement as to the course of action that will best realize the equal importance of beings.

Thus far I have attempted to provide an understanding of the normative foundations of fundamental rights, as well as the principled and pragmatic considerations involved in determining the content of both conditional and unconditional rights. It is clear from the discussion that ultimately decisions as to the actual obligations of a society are complex ones which involve the balancing of competing considerations. We can identify principles and rules that guide our actions, but ultimately, judgement will be required in translating these into particular actions and obligations. Immanuel Kant, for whom rules were of great importance, recognized that 'though understanding is capable of being instructed, and of being equipped with rules, judgement is a peculiar talent which can be practised only and cannot be taught'.[57]

Determining these unconditional obligations is of great importance and will admit of varied responses. It is thus of crucial significance to understand which institutions within a society should ultimately be responsible for making these decisions. This question is the subject of the next chapter.

[57] Kant, 1933: A133–134/B171–172.

4

Justifying the Judicial Review of Fundamental Rights

1 Introduction

In the last chapter, it was argued that determining the unconditional obligations of a society that respects fundamental rights involves making a complex judgement in the face of competing normative and pragmatic considerations about the course of action that would ensure that every individual in the society could best be said to be treated with equal importance. The question, however, arises as to which bodies within a society can best be entrusted with making such decisions. A natural starting point in a democratic state would be to argue that this judgement should be made by a society through a majority of its members. In most democratic societies, decision-making could not be made directly through a majority vote of people in the society and would be made through a majority of the elected representatives of individuals who are chosen by democratic vote. Ultimately, the decisions concerning the unconditional obligations of a society imposed by fundamental rights are to be made by the majority of the community's representatives. It could be claimed that this *procedure* would treat the opinions of each individual in the society as being of equal importance.

However, the problem with such a solution is that there are several reasons for thinking that majority decision-making may be likely in many cases to fail *substantively* to treat the lives of all individuals in a society as being equally important. In response to this problem, the leading alternative model for a democratic society is to place ultimate decision-making concerning fundamental rights in the hands of highly experienced judges in a constitutional court.

In this chapter, I shall be concerned with the justification for judicial review with a particular focus on the judicial review of socio-economic rights. There has been a lengthy debate in academic literature on the legitimacy of judicial review, as well as the particular relationship between judicial review and socio-economic rights. The focus of this book is not on this question but rather on content of socio-economic rights;[1] however, the particular theory of content that has been given provides a powerful argument for supporting judicial involvement in

---

[1] The argument in this book is designed to develop the justification for fundamental rights—with a particular focus on socio-economic rights—as well as to provide an analytical framework for determining

decision-making concerning the enforcement of rights in general and socio-economic rights in particular.

The first section of this chapter considers broadly the different justifications that have been offered for judicial review and I argue for a 'rights-based' justification thereof. The second section considers elements of Jeremy Waldron's critique of such justifications: in particular, his argument that the foundations of fundamental rights support assigning decision-making concerning such rights to majoritarian institutions, particularly in the face of disagreement concerning these rights. Waldron's central argument is shown to be self-defeating; further, it is argued that unrestrained majoritarianism is by no means clearly the best method of dealing with disagreement in society. The section concludes with an argument that some shared values and standards of assessment are necessary in order to construct any theory of legitimate institutions. The third section argues for a 'thin' theory of judicial review that restricts the range of agreement required to what Rawls terms certain 'constitutional essentials'. I argue that such essentials include a theory of fundamental rights and a related theory concerning the assignment of decision-making to particular institutions. I sketch the outlines of such a theory. The fourth section builds on this discussion by outlining certain general epistemological features of good decision-making which suggest that the judiciary is likely to reach better decisions concerning fundamental rights than majoritarian institutions. This in turn would support assigning final decisions concerning fundamental rights to the judiciary. Whilst the justification for judicial review offered in this chapter is applicable to all rights, judicial involvement in decisions concerning socio-economic rights has been regarded as particularly objectionable by some academic writers. The chapter ends by addressing some of these concerns and relating them to the general theory outlined in this chapter.[2]

2 Theories of Judicial Review

The institution of constitutional judicial review involves allowing judges to scrutinize legislative or executive acts[3] for their conformity with a bill of fundamental

---

their content and thus their effective enforcement. The central claims of this book thus apply irrespective of whether one believes that the judiciary should be involved in enforcing these rights. Indeed, the normative importance of socio-economic rights and their implications for a society have often been obscured by the preoccupation in the literature with whether they should be subject to judicial review or not. As will be seen in this chapter, I believe that judges do have an important role to play in determining the content of such rights and enforcing claims based upon such rights. However, other branches of government equally have a critical role to play in ensuring that these rights are realized.

   [2] I shall not, however, rehash the many arguments and counterarguments that relate specifically to the involvement of the judiciary in adjudicating matters concerning socio-economic rights. The burden of this work lies in improving our understanding of the content of socio-economic rights (and other rights). This project in itself offers the possibility of providing principled limits to the involvement of the judiciary in socio-economic policy and as such offers a possible response to some of the objections raised.

   [3] Acts can be said to denote legislation, policies, programmes, or particular actions with which these bodies are involved.

rights, and then to rule that such acts are invalid if they do not so conform. Such powers allow judges to provide authoritative interpretations of a bill of rights and often to render the acts of majoritarian institutions invalid if they violate these rights.[4] It is important to recognize that judicial review does not involve the replacement of majoritarian decision-making by judicial decision-making; rather, it usually involves the judiciary reviewing, on a number of limited and specified grounds, the decisions already taken by majoritarian decision-makers. Judicial review shifts the locus of final decision-making from majoritarian institutions to judicial ones. The counter-majoritarian difficulty arises as a result of the fact that a final decision concerning a particular matter may be imposed by judges against the will of the majority in a society and, thus, the power of judicial review is often regarded as being in conflict with democracy.[5]

In response to the counter-majoritarian difficulty, theorists have offered two main categories of justification that have generally been provided for granting review powers to judges. The first category may be termed 'democracy-supporting' justifications for judicial review. These justifications attempt to show that, far from being in conflict with democracy, judicial review in fact enhances democracy.

There are two sub-categories of 'democracy-supporting justifications'. The first sub-category is 'process-based justifications' of judicial review. Let us say, for instance, that democracy is understood to require that each individual is able to vote for representatives of his choice, with decisions in society being taken by a majority of these representatives. The problem for democracy arises as a result of the fact that once a majority has acquired power, it can tend to marginalize minorities in such a way that minorities are effectively unable to express their views and compete for power on equal terms. For instance, even if minorities retained the ability to vote, a statute which prevented those with minority opinions from campaigning politically would in effect deprive them of the ability to influence others and so change majority opinion. In order to guarantee that the preconditions for majoritarian representative government are fulfilled, unelected officials are required to police the 'borders of democracy'.[6]

The second sub-category of democracy-supporting justifications are 'substance-based justifications'. A substance-based justification is one that involves the contention that counter-majoritarian processes can be countenanced as they are

---

[4] This description refers to the way judicial review has been traditionally conceived in constitutional democracies such as the United States and South Africa. A weaker form of judicial review exists in the United Kingdom. There the judiciary may not overrule acts of parliament but only issue a 'declaration of incompatibility' where these acts are found to be inconsistent with human rights provisions. In this chapter, I offer a justification for granting strong review powers to judges that allows them to make final determinations concerning certain fundamental issues in a society.

[5] There is much literature dealing with this question: probably, the most famous recent attack on judicial review has come from Jeremy Waldron, 1999. In the South African context, Patrick Lenta, 2004a at 1, 13 has recently argued that 'judicial review suffers from a deficit of democratic legitimacy' and that the 'allocation of certain collective decisions to the judiciary constitutes a usurpation of a decision that democracy demands should properly have been made by the people or their representatives'.

[6] The most famous proponent of such a view was Ely, 1980.

required by the best understanding of what democracy in fact is. Ronald Dworkin, for instance, argues that the essence of democracy is not that the majority rules, but that 'collective decisions be made by institutions whose structure, composition, and practices treat all members of the community, as individuals, with equal concern and respect'.[7] In most cases, this core notion of democracy will require majoritarian institutions. On special occasions, however, where the equal status of citizens can be better served by non-majoritarian institutions, then this theory of democracy supports the establishment of such institutions. Dworkin's theory thus represents an attempt to divorce democracy from what he terms the 'majoritarian premise': that decision-making must be made according to the will of the majority.

The second category of justifications for judicial review may be termed 'rights-based' justifications. This view involves the claim that there are fundamental rights that must be guaranteed to all individuals in any just society, whether or not the majority agrees or wishes to recognize these rights. Certain institutional features of the courts render them more likely to provide adequate protection for such rights than representative institutions such as legislatures. As a result, we should assign the power to protect rights to judges, who are justified in overruling decisions of majoritarian institutions where these conflict with fundamental rights.[8]

The difference between democracy-supporting justifications and rights-based justifications for judicial review rests largely upon a different attitude to the conflict of values. The former category of justification denies that there is any conflict between democracy and other values in the institution of judicial review and argues that there is only ideal—the true democratic ideal—which, properly understood, determines all the institutions that should exist. A rights-based justification, on the other hand, recognizes that there may, at a certain level, be a conflict of values associated with the institution of judicial review, but provides reasons for thinking that the moral benefits of the institution—such as the greater protection offered for fundamental rights—outweigh the moral costs thereof—removing certain decisions from the final control of the citizenry and allowing the will of the majority to be overridden.[9] The choice between these two types of justification thus rests on whether one thinks it plausible to recognize a conflict between different values at stake in this debate.

Chapter 3 has already drawn attention to the fact that there are often competing normative considerations in determining the content of rights. It is not surprising, therefore, that competing considerations might arise in deciding upon the institutional structure that is best suited to decision-making concerning fundamental rights. In my view, the rights-based approach should be preferred for several reasons. First, the counter-majoritarian difficulty has been one that has exercised political theorists for much of the past 50 years.[10] It is implausible to

---

[7] Dworkin, 1996: 17.
[8] See, for instance, Moore, 2002: 211; Spector, 2003: 295–304, and Raz, 1998: 45, 52.
[9] See Moore, 2002: 221.   [10] See Friedman, 2002.

suggest that there is no conflict of important considerations at stake that has generated such a robust debate. Secondly, some democracy-supporting justifications risk obscuring the real objections people have to judicial review. By redefining democracy, the theorist employs a definitional device to respond to a substantive objection. It is unclear whether the fault for this should be laid at the door of the critics of judicial review or their defenders. Both attempt to gain support for their views through the rhetorical advantages of claiming that their views are in accordance with democracy. That can in turn lead to the dispute becoming a terminological one: with Dworkinians claiming that judicial review is 'democratic' and their opponents claiming it is not.[11]

Thirdly, when the debate is couched in 'democracy-supporting terms', it tends to assume that all the important values at stake can be captured by the ideal of 'democracy'. It is true that democracy is a vague ideal and at times it is used in this comprehensive manner. However, it is more usual for philosophers to seek to provide a justification *for* democracy which does not assume it is basic. In such instances, democratic decision-making is defended in relation to other more basic ideals such as freedom, equality, and dignity.[12] These ideals may themselves at times provide moral support for non-majoritarian decision-making procedures. Moreover, they may suggest normative considerations that favour judicial review and those that count against it. The attempt to fit one's justification into the rubric of being supportive of 'democracy' fails to recognize the complexity of normative issues that are involved in a consideration of this issue.[13]

Finally, and perhaps most seriously, there is a tendency in this debate to adopt an understanding of democracy itself that fails to take account of internal tensions within this ideal. This is a problem that besets both the proponents and critics of judicial review.

Consider, for instance, a recent characterization of democracy by a critic of judicial review: democracy, Lenta claims, involves ensuring that 'citizens are permitted an equal say in the content of political decisions'.[14] However, all representative democracies fail to meet this condition, as elected representatives have much more power than citizens to determine political decisions. The arguments of those opposing judicial review often fail to establish the superiority of *representative* democracy over judicial review, but rather make the case for a form of direct democracy that is simply impossible to achieve in most large nation states that exist today.[15]

---

[11] See the caution, for instance, issued by Lenta, 2004a: 4.

[12] Dworkin's discussion of democracy in *Freedom's Law*, for instance, considers the justification of democracy against the background of ideals of positive liberty, equality, and community (1996).

[13] See Christiano, 2000: 525 for a similar point raised in his critique of Waldron.

[14] Lenta 2004a: 4–5.

[15] See Andrea Sangiovanni 'Majoritarianism and Unelected Institution'. Unpublished paper presented at Political Theory Colloquium, University of Cambridge, 12 February 2003. Sangiovanni argues convincingly that many objections to judicial review made by Waldron apply equally to representative democracy: Waldron often conflates 'the people' and 'their representatives'.

Furthermore, as Raz aptly notes, in relation to the ideal of self-government, '[a]rguing one's case before a learned and impartial tribunal gives one more power over the determination of one's rights than being one among the multitude in a participatory democracy, with equality of political power to all'.[16] That may be particularly true in the case of those in the minority for whom majoritarian institutions may fail to offer an opportunity to participate adequately in decision-making and thus to reach decisions with which they identify.

The most serious difficulty with the claim that judicial review is 'undemocratic', however, is the fact that the procedural features of democracy which are focused upon—in the form of majoritarian decision-making—require that certain conditions be guaranteed to ensure that in actual fact the decisions that are reached represent the will of the majority. Fairness of procedures and protections for many fundamental rights are examples of crucial background conditions required for democratic decision-making. These conditions can themselves be threatened by purely majoritarian systems, and, it is thus unclear why institutions—such as judicial review—that are set up to protect the very background conditions for procedural democracy are themselves branded as being 'undemocratic'.[17]

In the face of considerations such as these, Dworkin suggests that we look beyond majoritarianism to a definition of democracy that recognizes the fundamental value or point of democracy.[18] In his view, this is to achieve a system which best treats all members of the political community as individuals with equal concern and respect.[19] In deciding which institutions we should have, democratic constitutional theory ought to be orientated towards results: '[t]he best institutional structure is the one best calculated to produce the best answers to the essentially moral question of what the democratic conditions actually are, and to secure stable compliance with those conditions'.[20] In some cases, it may be possible to entrust the legislature with placing limits upon its own power. In other cases, however, considerations may favour the judiciary. The fact that, in these instances, the courts are not generally accountable to an electorate does not matter; what is important is that 'courts are reliable at making good decisions about democracy'.[21] Where the courts make correct decisions which protect the conditions of democracy, '[n]o moral cost has been paid'.[22]

In my view, Dworkin goes too far in this passage, by claiming that there is no moral cost where courts strike down the acts of majoritarian institutions. By

---

[16] Raz, 1998: 45.

[17] Kavanagh, 2003: 451, 473 distinguishes between formal and effective participation in politics. 'People who have little political power or influence, and are not persistently outvoted by powerful groups, will effectively be disenfranchised in normal politics, despite their possession of the formal right to participate. Given the disparities of power and wealth in society, having an equal right to participate does not mean that one's actual ability to participate effectively is equal.' Institutions—such as the judiciary—which protect participation rights may thus be of importance in establishing the very participatory democracy that critics of judicial review write so eloquently about.

[18] Dworkin, 1996: 15.   [19] Ibid: 17.   [20] Ibid: 34.   [21] Waldron, 1999: 292.

[22] Dworkin, 1996: 32.

redefining democracy in the way he does, it is tempting to imagine that all conflicts of value have disappeared. However, as Waldron points out, Dworkin's
response does not capture the force lying behind the position of those critical of
judicial review.

To illustrate this, he considers a thought experiment in which the Queen of
England decides to impose a system of proportional representation upon the
people of Britain. Let us assume for the purposes of argument that her decision is
right about what constitutes the best method of democratic decision-making.
Waldron argues that, in such an instance, we would have the correct decision
being made but one that was made by an illegitimate method of decision-making.
And Waldron's contention is that the method of decision-making matters. 'If a
question comes up for political decision in a community, a member of the community might reasonably ask to participate in it on equal terms with his fellow
citizens.'[23] Critics of judicial review are concerned about the fact that judicial
review removes some political power from individual citizens to determine certain
key features about their society and places it in the hands of the judges.[24] To deny
there is *any* moral loss in a system that allows for judicial review is not plausible: it
fails properly to engage with the claims of those who are critical of judicial review.
However, to recognize there is *some* loss does not entail that judicial review is
'undemocratic' nor that it is morally unjustified. Critics of judicial review fail to
pay sufficient attention to the losses involved in an unrestricted majoritarianism.

Thus, I have sought to argue in this section for a 'rights-based' justification of
judicial review which should accept that there are competing values at stake in
determining which institutions should have the final say on questions concerning
fundamental rights in our society. That recognition in no way, however, implies
that judicial review is 'undemocratic' or unjustified. I now turn to consider two
arguments offered by Waldron that challenge rights-based justifications of judicial
review and attempt to establish that the final locus of decision-making concerning
fundamental rights should rest with majoritarian institutions.

3 Disagreement, Rights, and Judicial Review

3.1 Judicial review undermines rights

Waldron's first important argument is that the very values underlying rights would
not support the institution of judicial review. To protect rights through judicial
review would thus in some sense be self-defeating. In support of this argument, he
contends that the idea of rights is based on 'a view of the human individual as
essentially a thinking agent, endowed with an ability to deliberate morally, to see
things from others' points of view, and to transcend a preoccupation with his own

---

[23] Waldron, 1999: 293.   [24] See also Lenta, 2004a: 13.

particular or sectional interests'.[25] The attribution of a right is an act of faith in the agency and capacity for moral thinking of individuals. Rights protect choices and the attribution of a right assumes that the person in question has the wherewithal to make choices. Since the point of arguments about rights has to do with the respect owed to a person as an active thinking being, we cannot say that 'our conversation takes *his* rights seriously if at the same time we ignore or slight anything that *he* has to say about the matter'.[26] Waldron says that these considerations suggest that rights-bearers should decide what rights they have, and that there is something disrespectful about a view which holds that questions about rights are 'too hard or too important to be left to the right-bearers themselves to determine, on a basis of equality'.[27] Whilst judicial review is supposed to be protecting such rights, in fact it undermines the very basis of the rights it supposedly protects.[28]

A number of mistaken assertions lead Waldron to this conclusion. First, Waldron argues that rights are justified by a view of people as thinking agents who are able to transcend their own viewpoints and consider the interests of others. In this statement, Waldron fails to distinguish between moral agents—those who are required to act in accordance with the obligations imposed by rights—and moral patients—those who are bearers of rights. Whilst moral agents must be thinking beings with a certain ability to act rationally, we need not make assumptions about the rational agency or altruism of individuals in order to attribute rights to them. As long as a being has certain fundamental interests, it makes sense to see them as bearers of rights. Most moral and legal systems, for instance, would attribute rights to children and those adults with severe cognitive deficiencies despite their inability to be the active, thinking agents Waldron envisages.[29]

Whilst Waldron is wrong to hold that only moral agents can have rights, it is clear that those who are only able to be moral patients would not benefit from having the particular rights involved in participating in the political system.[30] The capacity of moral agents to deliberate and act rationally indicates that they do indeed have an important interest in being able to participate in the decision-making of their communities. Recognition and protection of this interest is important and will mean that, in general, agents will have rights to participate in the decision-making of their communities. However, this reasoning provides no warrant for the claim that this interest in participation is more important than any

---

[25] Waldron, 1999: 250.   [26] Ibid: 251.   [27] Ibid: 252.

[28] Raz, 1998: 45 construes Waldron's argument as saying that since people have the capacity to 'figure out what rights they have, including the capacity to see things from others' point of view, it is appropriate for each person to be able to decide what his or her rights are'. He points out that this argument could be run in reverse: 'since people have the capacity to figure out what rights other people have, including the capacity to see things from others' point of view, it is appropriate for each person to be able to decide what rights other people should have. I will decide the scope of your rights and you will decide mine.' Both arguments, he contends, are equally unconvincing.

[29] This is a point upon which Waldron may disagree but he cannot claim that his view is accepted as an uncontroversial foundation for rights. I discuss this point further below.

[30] It may be necessary to appoint representatives who act to protect their interests. However, a young child or dog fails to experience a loss through not participating in the political system.

of the other fundamental interests of moral agents.[31] Moreover, participatory rights come with a serious risk of abuse: they may allow some participants to jeopardize the very participatory rights of other moral agents. To ensure fair and equal participation as well as the respect for other important rights, it may be necessary to create institutions that are not majoritarian in character. The mere capacity to be a moral agent fails to justify an absolute participatory right or an unrestricted majoritarianism.

Secondly, Waldron argues that his theory is one that allows and takes seriously fundamental disagreements about rights. Yet, in providing his case for participation rights, and against judicial review, he assumes a particular controversial theory of rights. He claims that rights protect choices and the attribution of rights requires an assumption that a person can make rational choices. That makes Waldron a proponent of a particularly controversial theory analysing the formal features of rights, namely, the Will Theory of rights.[32] Moreover, he argues that a theory of rights assumes that human beings are able to transcend their personal or sectional interests. Yet, a number of theories of rights, such as that of Hobbes or Gauthier, are premised precisely on the fact that human beings are essentially preoccupied with realizing their own interests.[33] Thus, instead of rising above the disagreement, Waldron in fact takes a firm position on one side of the debate. That may be inevitable, but it is unclear as a result why his theory is preferable as a means to resolve disagreement about rights.

Finally, Waldron claims that we do not respect people or take their rights seriously if we ignore what they have to say about rights. It is important to point out that the institution of judicial review does not 'ignore' what individuals have to say about their rights. The legislature and executive are provided with the first opportunity to act in accordance with their own understanding of these rights. If an individual in the society disagrees with this understanding, she is provided with an opportunity to challenge the majoritarian understanding of these rights in court. There is an opportunity for all opinions to be canvassed in court. Some of these opinions may in fact be drowned out in majoritarian institutions. Thus, far from ignoring individual opinions about rights, courts in fact often enable a range of opinions to be heard.

Respecting individual opinions about rights, however, need not require that any one opinion be determinative. In cases of opinions that are harmful to one's self or others, it can be precisely because of our respect for individuals and their

---

[31] Thus, contra Liebenberg, 2006 (drawing on the work of Nancy Fraser) and Davis, 2006, fundamental rights are not justified only in relation to the value of participation but rather represent critical protections for all the most fundamental interests of individuals, enabling them to realize the sources of value in their lives (see Chap 1). This wider focus also has the benefit that it can provide a justification for ascribing fundamental rights to those who cannot, or may not wish to, participate in social life.

[32] The leading competitor to this theory is the Interest Theory of Rights: see Kramer, Simmonds, and Steiner, 1998. In an earlier essay, Waldron (1984) seemed to prefer the Interest Theory.

[33] See Hobbes, 1991 and Gauthier, 1986.

rights that these opinions may not be followed.[34] In the face of disagreement about rights, some individual opinions will inevitably not be followed, but that does not necessarily evince disrespect for those individuals.

The question thus arises as to how we should proceed in the face of disagreement about rights. This section has sought to establish that there is nothing uncontroversial in the foundational moral case for rights which requires support for participatory majoritarianism in all circumstances and which undermines the case for judicial review. Waldron recognizes that there is a competitor to his 'rights-based solution to disagreement about rights'.[35] It is to his criticisms of 'rights-instrumentalism' that I now turn.

3.2 Rights instrumentalism

Waldron characterizes rights-instrumentalism as follows: it is the view that, in the face of disagreement, 'one chooses whatever decision-procedures are most likely to answer the question "what rights do we have?" correctly'.[36] The instrumentalist would charge that the participatory approach is overly optimistic about rights-bearers' abilities, and argues that the responsible way to proceed is to adopt institutional procedures that can best ensure the protection of rights and minimize the possibility of their being violated.

According to Waldron, rights-instrumentalism faces two central difficulties. First, it presupposes that we possess the truth about rights in designing authoritative procedures to settle questions concerning the truth about rights. The reason for this is that, in order to argue that judicial review is more likely to protect rights than majoritarian institutions, Waldron claims, it is necessary to assume knowledge of the content of rights.[37] Yet people disagree about the content of rights and it is precisely in relation to this problem that instrumentalism was proposed as a solution. Waldron concludes that '[t]here seems then something question-begging about using rights instrumentalism as a basis for the design of political procedures among people who disagree on issues such as this'.[38]

In response to this objection, Waldron considers a modified version of the rights-instrumentalist approach. The aim of political procedures, according to this view, is to 'choose or design political procedures that are most likely to get at the truth about rights, whatever that truth turns out to be'.[39] We do not need to agree upon the content of rights, according to this view, but we must agree upon the epistemological conditions that are most likely to lead to the truth in an

---

[34] For examples, consider the case of *Laskey, Jaggard and Brown v The United Kingdom* (1997) 24 EHRR 39, which disallowed consensual sado-masochistic practices; and *Christian Education South Africa v Minister of Education* 2000 (4) SA 757 (CC), which disallowed corporal punishment in schools despite parental approval of it on religious grounds.

[35] Waldron, 1999: 252.   [36] Ibid: 252.

[37] Raz, 1998: 46 puts the point as follows: '[h]ow could one justify the claim about the likelihood of it being respected if one did not know what it is?'   [38] Waldron, 1999: 253.

[39] Ibid: 253.

enquiry about rights. In response, Waldron objects, that there are in fact disagreements not only about the content of rights but about the best way in which to make moral decisions. Some think that scholars would be best placed to make decisions; others think that academic casuistry distorts our thinking about democratic matters. Some think that the problem of majoritarian institutions relates to distorting self-interest; others contend that decisions are best taken only by those who have a sufficient stake in the matter to decide responsibly. There is thus no 'uncontroversial moral epistemology', and no consensus about *paths* to moral truths that would allow for a non-question-begging defence of political procedures for use among those who disagree about which claims are true or not. Both versions of instrumentalism thus fail, according to Waldron, to provide a solution to the problem of how we can design procedures to resolve disputes about rights where people disagree about rights and the best way to reason about rights.

Thus, Waldron concludes that we should reject rights-instrumentalism and maintain instead the 'non-question-begging view' that rights-bearers have the right to resolve disagreements about rights among themselves and on roughly equal terms.[40] Participation is a right, according to Waldron, 'whose exercise seems peculiarly appropriate in situations where reasonable rights-bearers disagree about what rights they have'.[41]

3.3 Disagreement as justification for judicial review

Waldron's central argument against rights instrumentalism and in favour of his view is beset by many difficulties but illuminates a key point: if we disagree on every issue, then there can in fact be no shared moral basis upon which to decide who has the authority to make decisions in our societies. He contends that there is a disagreement on every matter of substance as well as about the best way to arrive at decisions. It is important to point out that, if this is true, then members of a society will also disagree about whether they should use the participative procedures suggested by Waldron. Such a method of decision-making is no more uncontroversial than any other method and, in his fervour to reject judicial review, Waldron has undermined the basis for his own participatory majoritarianism.[42] If there is disagreement about everything, then there are in fact no authoritative methods by which to resolve any dispute, and no procedure can be said to be better than any other procedure.[43] As such, no justification can be given for

---

[40] Waldron, 1999: 254.   [41] Ibid: 232.

[42] The self-defeating nature of Waldron's argument has been pointed out by many commentators. Raz, 1998: 47, for instance, states that '[h]aving declared that rights instrumentalism does not take seriously the problem of disagreement, Waldron seems oblivious to the fact that if valid the same charge can be levelled against his solution as (quite likely) against all others'. See also Kavanagh, 2003: 467; Christiano, 2000: 513, 520; and Sangiovanni, 2003: 8.

[43] Waldron, 1999: 302 seems to admit as much in his discussion of rights constitutive of democracy. He says that 'if people disagree about the conditions of democracy, an appeal to the legitimacy of majority-decision to settle that disagreement may be question-begging'.

adopting any particular system and it is merely coercive power that dictates whether a democratic or tyrannical regime is set up.

In the face of an objection such as this, Waldron continues to recommend that we use participatory majoritarianism in a pragmatic way to solve disagreement. Such use would not involve privileging majoritarianism: '[I]f we choose one of the procedures which are up for decision as the procedure for making that very decision, we do so simply because we need a procedure on this occasion and this is the one we are stuck with for the time being.'[44] It is difficult to make sense of Waldron's claim that proceeding in this way avoids privileging majoritarianism: if one uses a method of decision-making to decide upon the legitimacy of decision-making procedures in general, this seems to load the dice in favour of the original decision-making procedure. Moreover, this pragmatic solution fails to provide us with a reason to respect the outcome of the pragmatic procedure as authoritative.[45] If disagreement goes all the way down, and determines legitimacy, then we are required to give up upon the legitimacy of our institutions.

Waldron appears to think that in the face of widespread disagreement about rights, the only solution lies in participatory majoritarianism. However, it is important to recognize that disagreement can, in certain circumstances, contrary to what Waldron claims, be the very reason for assigning final decisions concerning fundamental rights to judges. The decision in South Africa concerning whether the death penalty should be a lawful punishment for certain serious crimes provides a good illustration of this point.

The drafters of the South African Constitution could in fact have placed a provision concerning the death penalty in the Constitution.[46] Instead of doing so, they placed abstract rights in the bill of rights and then left it to the Constitutional Court to decide this matter. What could plausibly explain their reasoning? One possible explanation, I shall suggest, is that the drafters considered that leaving such a decision to the Constitutional Court would be a better way of dealing with disagreement on this matter. To understand this point, it is important to draw on some recent work by Cass Sunstein.[47]

Sunstein argues that, in the face of disagreement, those designing a Constitution may well have recourse to what he terms 'incompletely theorized agreements'.[48] People often agree about abstractions—such as the right to life—whilst disagreeing about the implications of those abstractions—whether capital punishment should be abolished. On the other hand, at times, they agree about the importance of certain institutions—such as the separation of powers—without agreeing on their reasons for doing so. In the face of these disagreements, constitution drafters reach 'incompletely theorized agreements': they are incompletely theorized in the sense that people who accept the principle need not agree on the higher-level theories

---

[44] Ibid: 301.   [45] See Kavanagh, 2003: 451, 469 for these objections.

[46] The drafters did discuss the death penalty but decided to leave it for the Constitutional Court to decide. See *S v Makwanyane* 1995 (3) SA 391 (CC) [20]–[25].   [47] Sunstein, 2001b.

[48] Chap 2 of his book deals with the role of such agreements in constitutional law.

that support them nor upon the lower-level practical implications thereof. Abstract provisions in Constitutions such as rights to 'freedom of speech' or 'life' or 'not to be discriminated against' often reflect the agreement of citizens, whilst being compatible with a large range of disagreement as to the practical meaning of these provisions.

The virtues of such agreements, Sunstein argues, are three-fold. First, they enable a consensus upon certain issues that form the foundation for a stable social order and reflect a common basis for argument. They are often what makes it possible to engage in a process of constitution-making at all.[49] Secondly, they enable individuals to display a degree of mutual respect towards one another and to avoid, at least temporarily, challenging each others' most fundamental commitments. Thirdly, such agreements reduce the costs of enduring disagreements. Even if a particular decision goes against an individual's view about a particular matter, there remains a common basis upon which to argue. That may mean that the individual may succeed in the future.[50]

It is plausible to suggest that the Constitution drafters in South Africa were aware that they could reach an incompletely theorized agreement about the right to life and the right not to be subjected to cruel, inhuman, and degrading punishment. Yet, they could not reach agreement about the implications of these rights for the concrete issue of capital punishment. It was thus not an issue that was ripe for decision-making at the level of the Constitution. To resolve this problem in a principled way, however, they needed to settle upon a procedure to resolve this deadlock. They were not able to reach agreement on the substance of the dispute but could reach agreement about a procedure by which such a dispute was to be determined. The procedure that was agreed upon was judicial review.

Judicial review may thus be an important feature of a democratic society that helps the society to deal with disagreement. A majoritarian decision-making procedure to resolve the problem of the death penalty would have reflected the deep divisions about this issue in the society. It is precisely because a majoritarian procedure is more participative that it was seen to be less attractive as a decision-procedure on this issue.[51] A decision by parliament could have threatened the stable consensus on the values in the South African Constitution and forced individuals to confront each other's fundamental commitments. By placing the Constitutional Court in charge of the decision, the matter was removed from the ordinary political fray and thus from the suggestion that individuals with distinct views in the polity were in direct conflict with each other. The court procedure allows a fair hearing to both sides, and allowed the South African Constitution to provide the common basis upon which both sides were to argue. In this way, the consensus upon constitutional values in South Africa was strengthened, helping

---

[49] Sunstein, 2001b: 56.   [50] These reasons are drawn from Sunstein's account, ibid: 58–60.
[51] Klug, 2000: 14 writes that '[c]onstitutional courts in this perspective may in some situations function as key institutions in consolidating the democratic transition, maintaining social peace and stability while addressing, or at least "judicialising", often severe problems of political and economic dislocation'.

to heal the wounds of a divided past, and provide a common shared framework in which future decisions were to be made.

3.4 The limits of disagreement

The discussion thus far has sought to demonstrate why, at times, it is desirable to allocate final decisions to Constitutional Courts precisely because of large-scale disagreement in society. Disagreement thus does not automatically support majoritarian decision-making. In making this case, I have had to involve reference to shared standards and values. The discussion thus far represents a denial of Waldron's point that our institutions must be founded upon recognition of legitimate disagreement on all foundational issues: without doing so, one would be unable to provide a non-question-begging justification for why others should assent to any argument.

The fact that Waldron engages in argumentation and a process of justification suggests that he regards there as being at least some shared standards of correctness against which his arguments can be tested. Disagreement that is meaningful presupposes certain shared standards of assessment. There must be certain shared rules of language to be able to make sense of what others are saying. To engage with what they say, shared standards are required which enable us to evaluate their claims.[52] In order for it to make sense to have common procedures of decision-making in a society, there must also be some common purposes and ends for which people have come together. Thus, when Waldron takes disagreement to extremes, he leaves us without any basis for explaining why individuals would want to join a political community or even engage with each other in majoritarian decision-making bodies. He provides us with no basis upon which to understand why in fact it is important to respect disagreement at all.

Once we recognize the need for certain standards of assessment, and certain shared substantive commitments, the question arises as to how to identify the content of these without unnecessarily curtailing disagreement in society. I shall argue in the next section that we need to identify what I term 'thin' standards of assessment and shared substantive commitments. We should try to provide arguments for our positions, and take account of those who oppose these 'thin' commitments. Having done so, I shall seek to make a general case as to exactly why the institution of judicial review is supported by such a 'thin' theory of justification.

4 A Thin Rights-based Theory of Judicial Review

Any theory that is to justify the reasons for assigning decisions in a society to certain institutions must have some tools to work with and Waldron deprives us of any such tools. To avoid this result, it is necessary to outline certain values and

---

[52] Davidson, 1986: 205 argues that such shared standards are in fact necessary to make ourselves intelligible to one another.

standards of assessment upon which to assess the legitimacy of fundamental institutions and features of our society.[53] Since there is a diversity of opinion within society, these values should be of such a type that they can command widespread agreement amongst diverse individuals.[54] Such a theory attempts to avoid as far as possible bringing in assumptions that cannot be justified from the perspectives of different individuals. Rawls terms this the liberal principle of legitimacy: 'our exercise of political power is fully proper only when it is exercised in accordance with a constitution the essentials of which all citizens as free and equal may reasonably be expected to endorse in the light of principles and ideals acceptable to their common human reason'.[55] As has been mentioned before, agreement is not necessarily an indication of truth, but it is desirable if all, or most, members of society are to accept the basic institutions and features of a society. That would also have the added benefit of leading to greater stability and social cohesion.

We thus must make reference to 'thin' assumptions that are restricted to the bare essentials required to justify allocating decisions concerning fundamental rights to a particular institution. Such a theory would require at least two elements.[56] The *first* element is a limited range of shared values that represent the fundamental rights of individuals in the society. Chapters 1 and 2 have sought to outline a thin theory which justifies granting certain basic civil and political rights—such as freedom of speech—and socio-economic rights—such as being guaranteed the necessary conditions to survive—which are necessary conditions for all individuals in the society to live lives that are valuable to them. Since the decisions taken in a society impact upon the ability of individuals to achieve what is valuable to them, individuals will have a stake in contributing to those decisions. Rights to vote and participate in political decisions would thus be important to ensure that individuals can play a part in the decision-making of their societies. Moreover, through allowing individuals to participate equally in decision-making processes, societies demonstrate their respect and commitment towards valuing each individual.[57] Thus, in most cases, the principle of equal importance will require that individuals be enabled to participate equally in decision-making for a society (usually through exercising the vote).

[53] This a central feature of John Rawls' project in *Political Liberalism*, 1993 and I draw heavily on his account in this section.

[54] Theorists such as Waldron typically overstate the disagreements in modern pluralistic societies and there in fact appears to be widespread agreement within constitutional democracies for guarantees of basic human rights and institutional structures such as the separation of powers. This too is an important requirement for Rawls' project.

[55] Rawls, 1993: 137. I only discuss the considerations relevant to my purposes in this chapter; Rawls, 1993 provides a much more extensive discussion of some of the issues raised in this section.

[56] Strictly speaking, there is a need for a third element as well and that is an account of the modes of reasoning appropriate for these institutions to employ in the course of their functioning. This is relevant to how judges, for instance, should interpret the Constitution. Rawls, 1993 develops his theory of public reason to provide such an account.

[57] This point is underlined by the many examples in recent history—for instance, apartheid South Africa—where black people (and women) have been excluded from the vote, this being a sign of their inferior status in these societies.

However, equal participation may, under certain circumstances and conditions, come to threaten important features of individual lives and thus lead to treatment inconsistent with an assumption of equal importance. Where equal participation leads or is likely to lead to a clear undervaluing of some individuals in a society, then the principle of equal importance may support a departure from equal participation.

For instance, the majority in a society may decide that the society will offer no welfare support to indigent individuals, being prepared to allow those with little or no income to starve. Since such a society would show utter disregard for an indigent person's life, such a society could legitimately be prevented from making such a decision. The value of ensuring that each individual has an equal say would here be overridden by the value of ensuring that each individual be guaranteed the very preconditions for her survival. Thus, the demands of the principle of equal importance may at times conflict and, in such circumstances, we are required to evaluate which option would have less of an impact upon the equal treatment of individual lives. In the example I have provided, it is evident, in my view, that allowing an individual life to wither away due to starvation is far worse from the point of the view of the principle of equal importance than depriving individuals of the ability to participate equally in decision-making. Allowing someone to starve would affect the very existence of an individual, lead to severe suffering, and inhibit her ability to achieve any of her goals. Depriving individuals of equal participation in relation to such fundamental rights would still allow those people to exist, and to live lives that achieve many or most of their purposes. Moreover, if judicial review is the institutional mechanism through which final decisions on subsistence rights are made, this would not exclude individuals from decision-making in general, even in relation to matters concerning food; it would merely entail that the majority of individuals cannot have the final say in relation to a small, circumscribed area where those very decision-making powers could lead to grave violations of the principle of equal importance.

The above argument thus attempts to establish that it is in fact possible to establish principled limits to the decision-making powers of majoritarian institutions that are rooted in the normative theory I have developed. The question, however, still remains as to which institutions should be required to make final decisions upon matters relating to fundamental rights. The *second* element of the thin theory of judicial review thus involves developing a shared basis upon which to evaluate the institutions that would be most likely to lead to the best decisions concerning fundamental rights. That requires the development of at least a partial epistemology regarding how best to arrive at decisions and a comparison between the virtues of the differing institutions in the society. In this chapter, the choice that is being evaluated is that between allocating final decisions about fundamental rights to majoritarian institutions—such as the legislature—or to courts.[58]

---

[58] Other possibilities do exist, but cannot be considered here. The countermajoritarian difficulty is regarded as most acute in relation to the overriding of legislative decisions by courts and, hence, I focus on contrasting the legislature with the judiciary.

It could be argued that since there can be disagreement about the interpretation of rights, such decisions should be left up to the majoritarian institutions themselves to decide. However, if rights are at times to constrain majoritarian institutions, then it seems important to recognize that such constraints must be imposed by a body independent of those institutions. What kind of body is best placed to make such decisions?

As has been indicated in Chapter 3, reaching final decisions about unconditional rights involves fairly difficult and complex judgements. These matters concern questions of fundamental importance to each individual, and thus it is likely that individuals would agree that the *best* possible decisions should be made regarding such matters.

To justify placing final decision-making authority beyond the reach of majoritarian institutions would require showing why such an alternative procedure would be best placed to protect the guarantees that are required for a society to continue to exist that is founded upon recognition of the equal importance of individual lives. To do this, it is necessary to introduce a set of 'thin' considerations concerning the practices that are likely to lead to the best decision-making about complex issues. Considerations such as the need for time, thoughtfulness, a lack of bias, and a lack of expediency would be standards that could, it is submitted, command widespread agreement amongst diverse individual people. These epistemological considerations, I shall argue in the final section, provide good reasons to favour judicial review when a society is concerned with deciding questions relating to fundamental rights.

Before undertaking this task, it is important to make two preliminary points. First, proponents of judicial review do not contend that representative institutions should be excluded from decision-making concerning fundamental matters of a society; rather, the argument concerns whether judges should be entitled to scrutinize the decision of majoritarian bodies as to whether they succeed in arriving at a weighting of interests that best reflects the equal importance of individuals. The judiciary does not in general replace the decisions of a majority but would represent a check on such decisions. Judicial review can thus be seen in a less antagonistic light as an institution which collaborates with majoritarian institutions to arrive at the best decision-making concerning fundamental rights.[59]

Secondly, to decide the question as to whether judicial review is desirable, it is necessary to have regard to certain general features of the differing institutions. This raises the question whether we consider the history of an institution and how it actually *does* function in contrast to how an institution *should* function. Making a case for or against judicial review is an enterprise that engages values. We are concerned to contrast different institutions for a particular purpose to ascertain whether they are best suited to perform a particular function. Even a discussion of

---

[59] The idea of a collaboration between majoritarian institutions and the judiciary is discussed in the context of socio-economic rights in Wesson, 2004: 295 and Lenta, 2004b: 575.

the descriptive properties of these institutions in this context will involve an implicit understanding of how they should function. Moreover, the actual practices of these institutions are infused with an understanding of how they ought to function. Analysing how they do function already provides us with some indication of how we consider that they should function. The descriptive and evaluative are intimately connected in this analytical enterprise.[60]

That does not imply, however, that we are forced to accept the actual practices of these institutions. The animating vision underlying these institutions may be mistaken; alternatively, the vision may be sound yet the institutions may fail to live up to these ideals. Courts and legislatures have different institutional features and these are largely determined by the functions we think such institutions ought to perform. The actual functioning of these institutions may only imperfectly mirror our reasons for setting them up in the way we have.

However, provided that we have not set them an impossible task, the failure of the institutions to live up to their ideal instantiation does not so much provide a reason for dismissing them as for reforming them. The fact that a police force is corrupt does not make the case for doing away with the police force. Similarly, the failure by courts, on occasion, to deliver decisions that are not biased against particular groups provides us with an argument to try and remedy this defect.[61] It is important to develop institutions in a way that tries to ensure that they function optimally in relation to their distinctive role. Thus, in providing an account of the general differences between the legislature and judiciary, I will be providing an account that engages both with how these institutions do function and how they ought to function. Having made these preliminary remarks, I now wish to provide an argument for why final decision-making powers about questions concerning fundamental rights should be assigned to the judiciary rather than majoritarian institutions such as the legislature.

5 Reaching Optimal Decisions Concerning Fundamental Rights: The Judiciary or the Legislature?

One reason for not assigning final decision-making powers to legislatures has already been provided. That is the point that constraints upon majoritarian bodies would be fairly ineffective if policed by such bodies themselves. The key claim to be established here is that there are certain broad epistemological considerations that render the judiciary more likely than majoritarian institutions to reach better decisions about individual entitlements and the basic structure of a society. An exhaustive discussion cannot be engaged in here nor is this the focus of this book;

---

[60] See, for instance, the discussion of the separation of powers and the appropriate function of the judiciary in *South African Association of Personal Injury Lawyers v Heath* 2001 (1) SA 883 (CC) at [22]–[46], which fuses the descriptive and the normative.

[61] One way to do so, for instance, would be to ensure that a diverse judiciary is appointed.

however, I shall elaborate briefly on a range of factors that support judicial review to show the manner in which this case can be made.

5.1 Time

Good decision-making on complex issues requires reflective deliberation about those issues over a period of time. Quick, intuitive judgments without deep reflection may lead to arbitrary and flawed decisions.

Majoritarian institutions usually have a sharp limit of time upon which to discuss complex matters. Representatives are usually busy with a wide range of matters. Debating time is severely limited. Discussion in the public realm about issues is usually conducted today through radio, television, or newspapers. Such discussion does not allow for arguments of great complexity to be developed at any length. Sound-bites are required which inevitably leads to a simplistic portrayal of complex issues. That may in the end affect the decision-making of representatives.

Whilst the hearings of a court are often limited in time, judges do not have any fixed deadlines as to when to reach their decisions (except in urgent cases). As such, they are able to engage in deliberation for some time. At the level of the highest courts in a society, there are usually a number of judges who jointly decide cases concerning fundamental rights. This allows for discussions to take place between judges and for them to revise their views if necessary out of the public spotlight. The courts are also not governed by the rules of the media and politics, which impose hefty time constraints upon debate and encourage emotional and rhetorical flourishes to win debates. In courts, detailed and lengthy submissions can be made in relation to complex matters and a careful, reasoned judgment must be written when deciding such matters, forcing judges to articulate clear reasons for their conclusions.

5.2 Politics and principle

Good decisions are made by considering the balance of factors involved in a decision and reaching the conclusion most favoured by this balance. Of course, different people would achieve this balance in different ways.[62] However, clear distortions of this balance that are not concerned with the best reasons for a decision would negatively impact upon optimal decision-making.

In Pitkin's famous study of representation, she states that '[t]he modern representative acts within an elaborate network of pressures, demands and obligations'.[63] The political representative has a constituency in which he represents the interests

---

[62] The difficulties of balancing evidence and normative considerations is one of the 'burdens of judgement' that Rawls identifies as leading to a situation in liberal societies in which we are unlikely to reach agreement on complex moral matters. See Rawls 1993: 54–8.   [63] Pitkin, 1967: 219–20.

of thousands. Such interests may conflict and it is often difficult to assess what these interests are. It is one of the virtues of majoritarian institutions—such as the legislature and the executive in modern democracies—that they operate in the political realm, and representative politicians seek to influence the public to vote for them. Their policies are as a result driven often by popularity rather than by principle. Moreover, the opinion of a representative on a measure 'may be shaped by party leaders or other colleagues, by friends or effective lobbyists or even by the mail . . . Issues do not come before him in isolation; issues are interrelated and he may wish to compromise on some in order to gain on others.'[64] Leaving decisions about rights to such a body would lead to such decisions reflecting these various pressures upon the politicians rather than being mandated by the best understanding of the principle of equal importance. As a result, such a procedure could easily lead to the undermining of that principle and basic rights in such a community.

Judges, once appointed, are generally not up for election by the people and do not have to tailor their opinions to popular doctrines. One of the central features of the judiciary is its independence. In the Canadian case of *R v Valente*,[65] three conditions for the independence of the judiciary were outlined: first, there must be security of tenure; secondly, there must be financial security; and finally, there must be administrative control by judges over decisions that bear directly and immediately upon the exercise of the judicial function. In *R v Generaux*,[66] it was held that independence involves not only freedom from interference by the legislature and executive but also by any other external forces, such as business or corporate interests or other pressure groups.[67] Judges are thus required to have a guaranteed structural and financial independence and cannot be fired due to an unpopular decision.[68] They do not, as a result, have any strong incentive to reproduce opinions that may simply be popular or meet the needs of a particular lobby group. They also would not need to compromise rights in one decision in order to make gains in others.

It is true that, in some countries, judges are elected. Moreover, in some cases this epistemological advantage could be challenged as a result of highly political appointment procedures in such countries as the United States. In such circumstances, judges may have to adopt certain political stances in order to be appointed. Once appointed, however, they are free to vary their opinions, and there are instances in the United States where judges have disappointed the politicians that appointed them.[69] Nevertheless, highly politicized appointment procedures may be criticized for failing to place judges sufficiently beyond the realm of the politics

---

[64] Ibid: 220.   [65] (1985) 24 DLR (4th) 161.   [66] (1992) 88 DLR (4th) 110.

[67] Ibid. 128 c–d. See the discussion of these cases in *De Lange v Smuts* 1998 (3) SA 785 (CC).

[68] See, for instance, s 165(2), (3), and (4) of the South African Constitution and the discussion of the centrality of independence of the judiciary in *Heath*, n 60 above, at [25].

[69] One of the most famous instances of this is the refusal of certain justices appointed by the Republicans to overrule the *Roe v Wade* abortion decision. See Dworkin, 1996: 5.

of expediency. In order to ensure that the benefits of an independent judiciary are achieved and that judges are not susceptible to the ordinary demands of political life, it is preferable for alternate appointment procedures to be devised.[70]

5.3 Expertise

The best decisions in an area are often made by those most qualified to do so. Qualifications can include expertise in a particular area as well as a training in the skills of reasoned justification.

It is one of the virtues of legislatures that elected representatives may have different areas of expertise. Some may be lawyers, but others will be doctors, economists, and farmers. Many of these individuals may be unaccustomed to decision-making about fundamental rights. Moreover, they may not be used to separating out their own partisan interests and views from those that are justifiable to a range of different individuals.[71] One of the demands of political life is being able to make a partisan case for a particular course of action. On highly emotive questions concerning issues such as those surrounding abortion, homosexuality, or pornography, for instance, representatives may simply vote for what they personally believe, in a way that is unsupported by any acceptable 'public reasons'. Decision-making in this way is unlikely to be justifiable to a range of different individuals, nor is it likely to be good decision-making, as individuals are not forced to challenge their own views.

Judges are, however, usually lawyers who have been trained since their student days to reason about matters of fundamental rights. Such training does, and should, usually involve separating out illegitimate 'personal reasons' from those that can be offered legitimately as a basis of public justification. It should also involve ensuring that lawyers are particularly adept at protecting the fundamental interests of individuals. Judges should be chosen who have a record that displays a commitment to the protection of fundamental rights. Moreover, there are certain qualities and skills that are required to exercise judicial power. In the *Heath* case, Chaskalson P identifies these as including 'independence, the weighing of information, the forming of an opinion based on information, and the giving of a decision on the basis of a consideration of relevant information'.[72] Partisanship is inconsistent with exercising judicial power.[73]

There is of course no guarantee that judges will not make decisions according to their own personal views or that they will not dress up such views in the cloak of

---

[70] The Judicial Services Commission in South Africa, representing a broad section of the community, is better suited for this purpose, in my view. See s 178 of the South African Constitution.

[71] Michael Moore, 2002: 218, in fact argues in similar vein that '[p]assionate commitment to a point of view is quite consistent with the legislator's job'.   [72] *Heath*, n 60 above, at [34].

[73] Ibid at [40].

respectable public reasons.[74] However, given the fact that a judge should be trained in deciding questions concerning fundamental rights and practised at distancing her personal reasons from the case before her, judges are better placed than elected representatives to make decisions that exclude 'illegitimate reasons' from their deliberations. Rawls thus sees a supreme court as likely to be the exemplar of public reason. 'Citizens and legislators . . . need not justify by public reason why they vote as they do or make their grounds consistent and fit them into a coherent constitutional view over the whole range of their decisions. The role of justices is to do precisely that and in doing it they have no other reason and no other values than the political.'[75]

5.4 Bias

To reach optimal decisions, it is necessary to have relevant information before one, and to make the decision which is most justified on the basis of this information. To the extent that decisions are not made according to the best reasons for a decision and rather on the basis of favouritism or an unjustified predilection, they are likely to be worse decisions.

In relation to this epistemological ground, there are several concerns that arise with majoritarian decision-making.

5.4.1 Informational bias

Politicians often present distorted information to their constituents in order to support their case.[76] Where there are huge disparities of wealth between the opposing sides, one case often receives vastly more coverage than another case, and people are led to believe that the distortions presented are true. Moreover, politicians often focus entirely on arguments in favour of the proposition they defend and often fail to give a fair characterization to opposing arguments. This can have dangerous effects for democracy and the protection of fundamental rights.[77]

The courts (at least in an adversarial system) require that two sides of a case be presented in the best manner possible. In fact, in some cases, where there is no contestation of the case, a court can and will appoint a representative to argue the opposing case.[78] All relevant information is to be placed before a court and in the

---

[74] Lenta, 2004a: 21–2 raises this point in his argument. Nevertheless, he does not confront directly the argument that the institutional features of the judiciary I describe render them more likely to make better decisions concerning the basic structure of a society than representatives in the legislature would. Instead, he seems content with making the very contentious point—which many would dispute—that the history of judicial decision-making fails to show that such epistemic advantages have made a difference in decision-making.   [75] Rawls, 1993: 235.

[76] Pitkin, 1967: 220.

[77] Sunstein, 2001b: 16–22, has a fascinating discussion about what he terms cascade effects in which law, policy, opinion, and behaviour shift rapidly in a particular direction. One direct cause of this is what he terms 'informational cascades', where individuals lacking much private information rely on the information provided by the statements and actions of others. The fact that representatives generally have greater access to information on public questions may lead their opinions to be more influential and thus increase the likelihood of such cascade effects.

[78] See, for instance, *Khosa v The Minister of Social Development* 2004 (6) SA 505 (CC).

event of the court not having access to the information it requires, procedures often allow the court to request and receive such information.[79]

The latter point, it can be responded, in fact favours legislatures and executives in decision-making in that they often have greater financial and investigatory powers than a judiciary does. This may in fact be true and thus, in most circumstances, we allow majoritarian institutions to make the initial decisions concerning particular matters. However, the problem in relation to basic rights is the possibility that the majoritarian institutions will distort the information for their own ends and use their powers to gather information that only supports their case. The judiciary is required to ensure that it has adequate information presented to it from both sides, and thus is better placed to correct for distorting bias. It reviews decisions of majoritarian institutions and can thus reap the benefits of obtaining the information that forms the basis of the judgments made by such institutions as well. It is also, though, able to acquire additional information if it suspects that the majoritarian institutions have presented a one-sided point of view concerning a matter that affects fundamental rights.

5.4.2 The position of minorities

Representative institutions take decisions on the basis of a majority vote. As a result, they are well set up to reflect the opinions of the majority of citizens. However, there is a clear institutional inclination towards deciding matters on the basis of the interests of a majority. In relation to matters of fundamental rights, there is often a delicate balance to be struck between the interests of different individuals. The interests of perpetual minorities may simply be ignored by majoritarian institutions, and, even if they are taken into account, they may be misconstrued through the prejudices of those in the majority. Discrimination and ethnic factors may further contribute to distorting the judgement of the majority.[80]

The sidelining of minorities may not necessarily take place through deliberate discrimination by majorities; rather, it may be that the interests of minorities are simply not taken into account adequately by the democratic process. Consider most modern democracies in the developed world. Political parties generally appeal to the middle class to be elected, and thus the concerns of the middle class are dominant. Homeless people may also be voters, but their numbers may be insufficient to have an impact on party policies or to warrant serious concern by political parties. Thus, their interests are sidelined and not placed firmly on the political agenda. Scant attention can be paid to the homeless as there is little

---

[79] See, for instance, *Prince v President of the Law Society of the Cape of Good Hope* Case CCT 36/00 available at <http://www.constitutionalcourt.org.za>.

[80] This is probably the most famous ground upon which judicial review has been justified. I here draw attention to the epistemological problems that this ground raises: the fact that the majoritarian bias of representative institutions is likely to have a distorting effect on decision-making. For others who raise this argument, see for instance, Dworkin, 1996: 34; Kavanagh, 2003: 473–4, 481; and Moore, 2002: 219.

political cost to doing so. In due course, in such a political community, it is quite possible that the fundamental interests of the homeless will not be adequately protected.[81]

Of course, judges may be biased too. Yet, the training and nature of the institution is such that it encourages decision-making that is not based upon any particular prejudice but on firm public reasons. In South Africa, as in most countries, the very definition of a proper exercise of judicial power is that the law be applied 'impartially and without fear, favour and prejudice'.[82] There is no clear institutional bias in favour of the majority; if anything, due to the institutional bias of majoritarian institutions, it is arguable that judges should be trained to be particularly vigilant in cases where minorities are affected.

To avoid the sidelining of minorities, it is necessary to have some procedure that ensures that the vital interests of the marginalized are protected in a democracy. Judicial review offers this opportunity as the judiciary does not face the same pressures as politicians do to focus primarily on the interests of the majority. To achieve the aim of protecting the interests of all citizens, it is necessary to have a judiciary that is drawn from all sectors of the population. A diverse judiciary will be one that is also likely to be more sensitive to the range of considerations that arise in complex determinations concerning the rights of citizens. Due to the structural problems of majoritarian institutions, the judicial protection of fundamental rights by a suitably constituted judiciary is crucial if democracies are to treat each individual with equal importance.

5.4.3 Eloquence

Given that majoritarian and participatory politics is usually conducted through parliament and the media, it tends to be influenced strongly by those who can eloquently put forward their views. Those who have difficulty expressing themselves in public or those who are naturally shy will as a result rarely be able to convince others. Thus, matters of fundamental rights can end up being decided by the fact that there are good speakers on a particular side of the debate.

---

[81] See Chapter 7 for a real-life example of this phenomenon, which I experienced in the United Kingdom. The case may be different in a country like South Africa, where substantial numbers of individuals are badly off; however, for a variety of other reasons the interests of such people are still often ignored. One central reason for this is the conflict between the interests of the representatives (who are often well off) and their constituents (who are not). A stinging indictment of political leaders failing to promote the interests of the majority in India is offered by the former cabinet secretary, TSR Subramanian: '[v]ery few, if any, of the ministers has any interest in developmental matters or in the economic or social transformation of India. Genuine alleviation of poverty, and the upliftment of the rural masses, was the last thing on their minds. Their only interest was their own future—aside from feathering the nest' (see Randeep Ramesh 'The last thing on their minds' *Guardian* (Thursday 13 May 2004)).

[82] Section 165(2) of the South African Constitution. See also *R v Valente*, n 65 above, at 169–70: '[i]mpartiality refers to a state of mind or attitude of the tribunal in relation to the issues and the parties in a particular case. The word "impartial" ... connotes absence of bias, actual or perceived.'

Although the quality of counsel may vary (together with the standards of their arguments), eloquence is not usually a sufficient ground upon which to win a case where judges are presiding. The content plays a much greater role, and an excellent lawyer with a weak case will often lose. Questions of fundamental rights would thus be less dependent upon the eloquence or otherwise of the group whose rights are affected.

Such a point is of even greater importance in relation to groups who cannot speak or represent themselves at all. In majoritarian politics, young children, the mentally ill, and non-human animals generally require eloquent representatives in order for their interests to be taken into account. Without such representation, the interests of such groups may simply be ignored. However, in courts, the interests of all those affected by a particular issue must be canvassed, and a diligent judge should ensure that the interests of those who cannot speak are taken into account in his decisions.[83] That may involve appointing representatives for the interests of such individuals in court.[84]

5.5 Accountability and justification

Better decisions are made by decision-makers who know that they are required to justify the decisions they make according to high standards. Allowing decision-makers absolute discretion is less likely to produce good decisions, and requiring them to justify their decisions to other branches of government can improve the quality of decision-making.

In a system without judicial review, the decisions of elected representatives are binding, whether they are able to meet certain standards of justification or not. Often, the only standard required will be whether the policy is able to win popular approval or not.[85] However, there are reasons for thinking that a system of parliamentary sovereignty may at times fail to protect even the interests of the majority. In modern democracies, individuals only elect officials every few years. Many people become disaffected with a government before its end of term. The government may on occasion make mistakes and adopt policies that are at odds with the interests of all its citizens, even the majority. Since it is elected for several years, the effects of such wrong-headed policies can indeed be severe for a society if left uncorrected.

The central duty of the judiciary where judicial review exists has been said to involve ensuring 'that the limits to the exercise of public power are not

---

[83] Representatives, often referred to as curators, are appointed to represent the interests of those who cannot speak for themselves.

[84] In fact, this is an area where judges can improve their performance. Both majoritarian and judicial institutions have often failed to take sufficient account of the interests of those who cannot speak. My argument suggests that because of the nature of the institutions in question, the judiciary may be more likely to offer adequate protection to such individuals. This is an area where the theory suggests there is definite room for improvement, particularly in the case of non-human animals.

[85] See Michael Moore, 2002: 218.

transgressed'.[86] The judicial review of legislation and executive policies thus requires that a government must justify its policies in accordance with a particular standard and ensure that such policies do not infringe upon the vital interests of individuals. It represents a safeguard to all citizens that the majority party will not violate their wishes in a way which places their very lives in peril. The structural independence, impartiality, and expertise of the judiciary render it particularly suitable for performing such a role. *Pharmaceutical Manufacturers Association of South Africa*[87] and *Minister of Health v Treatment Action Campaign*[88] are cases where the judiciary arguably helped to protect the interests of the whole society against wholly unreasonable government action.[89]

5.6 General versus particular decision-making

General decision-making across a range of cases can obscure the problems that may arise in particular instances to which that general decision may apply. General decision-makers may simply overlook or fail to give sufficient weight to the problems that may be faced in particular cases.

Legislative decisions, in particular, have the virtue of being general and applying to a range of cases. They may, however, overlook the dire effect that such policies may have in particular situations.[90] Judicial decision-making concerning fundamental rights, on the other hand, usually arises as a result of a particular instance

---

[86] *Heath*, n 60 above, at [25].

[87] *Pharmaceutical Manufacturers Association of South Africa and another In Re: Ex Parte Application of the President of the Republic of South Africa* 2000 (2) SA 674 (CC). This case involved a situation where the President made an error by bringing an Act into force—that regulated the registration and control of medicines for human and animal uses—before the Schedules to the Act had been prepared. These Schedules were an essential part of the regulatory structure of the Act, in the absence of which all potentially dangerous substances would be left completely unregulated.

[88] 2002 (5) SA 721 (CC) ('TAC'). This case will be discussed in detail in Chapter 5.

[89] It could be argued that, in a system of judicial review, a Constitutional Court is placed in a position where it is in fact unaccountable. However, Constitutional Courts are required to justify their decisions in written judgments and to provide clear reasons for their decisions. Were these decisions to be patently unreasonable, individuals in society would lose respect for the court and thus the institution would be weakened. The Constitutional Court cannot decide matters without them being brought before it, and individuals would not bring matters to court were they to expect a capricious judgment. There is of course finally the possibility of a constitutional amendment where the decision of a court is unconscionable: courts would undermine their own powers if they forced legislatures continually to pass such amendments. These considerations thus suggest that there are in fact constraints on judicial decision-making that render judges accountable for providing reasoned decisions that can be accepted by others in the polity.

[90] In addition, a diligent voter is often presented with a difficult problem: she may wish to vote for a party that largely represents her interests, yet be wholly opposed to certain particular policies it has. She may recognize that such policies are objectionable and agree they should be struck down by a court; yet on balance she prefers this party's policies to that of others. Thus, a party with the majority vote overall may lack majoritarian support for some of its policies. Since judges review particular cases that come before them, they are not concerned with whole political programmes but the conformity of a particular action of the government with basic rights. The institution of judicial review is thus well-placed to ensure that the party political system never allows certain policies to hold sway that

in which it is argued by an individual that the general law has dire consequences for the individual or group concerned. A society concerned to protect individual rights must be concerned about the effect upon individuals of general laws and policies. Though judgments are often general in nature, they usually begin from a consideration of the effects of a general law or policy upon a particular individual or group. Thus, the nature of judicial decision-making renders it more likely to have particular regard to such effects and their impact upon individuals than the legislature.

I have thus far considered a number of epistemological factors which provide support for the view that judges are more likely than majoritarian institutions to reach better decisions concerning fundamental rights and the basic structure of a society.[91] Of course, judges may fail to act in the manner I have described and bad judges may be appointed. The appointment procedure is crucial in that it will determine whether in fact judges are merely pawns acting as surrogates for political parties, or whether in fact the epistemological benefits I have canvassed can be achieved through the judiciary. I have attempted to sketch broad grounds which can provide reasons for assenting to the fundamental claim that a supporter of judicial review on rights-respecting grounds must make: that the judiciary is better placed than majoritarian institutions to reach final decisions about disputes relating to the foundational principles of a society.

6 Socio-Economic Rights and Judicial Review

Whilst a number of writers accept the legitimacy of judicial review for final decisions concerning civil and political rights, they object to it where decisions concerning social and economic rights are concerned.[92] One of the most important objections that has been made concerning the involvement of judges in decisions relating to socio-economic rights has been that it is inappropriate for judges to decide how the budget of a society is to be allocated.[93] The legislature and executive have access to a wide range of expertise on economic matters. Judges are not traditionally experts on economic policy or on the complex issues involved in determining a budget. It is claimed that they are not therefore best placed to make determinations concerning the overall allocation of resources.[94]

---

violate fundamental rights. In some instances, judges may in fact be acting in accordance with majority wishes, yet the party system obscures this fact.

[91] The list of reasons is not meant to be exhaustive but to illustrate the way in which a thin theory of judicial review can be justified.

[92] According to Tushnet, 2004, this is the conventional wisdom amongst scholars of constitutional law in the United States. It is not possible to provide detailed responses to the many authors who have objected to judicial involvement in socio-economic rights determinations, but I rather outline in broad terms my principled responses to such objections. For an excellent and more detailed treatment of this subject, see Pieterse, 2004.   [93] See, for instance, Tushnet, 2004: 1896.

[94] See, for instance, Mureinik, 1992: 465, who raises this objection in order to rebut it. See also *TAC*, n 88 above, at [37] where it was held that 'courts are not institutionally equipped to make the

In response, judicial review in a number of countries has for many years involved judges making determinations on civil and political rights. The realization of many of these rights also requires massive expenditure, which has an impact on the overall distribution of resources. For instance, recognizing a right to a fair trial will mean imposing on the government the costs of running an effective criminal justice system; similarly the right to vote requires the holding of regular elections.[95] Yet, judges have generally acquitted themselves well in interpreting and enforcing these rights, and their role in this regard has not generally met with accusations that they are unqualified for the job, despite the resource implications of their decisions.

The first response thus emphasizes that judicial duties in relation to socio-economic rights will not differ greatly from those they perform in relation to civil and political rights. Courts are not criticized for ordering the provision of legal representation to the unrepresented, or for ordering that all are provided with the vote in a society: why then should they be criticized for ordering a state to ensure that people are provided with enough food to avoid malnutrition? The rationale for this distinction seems to lie in the fact that the critics regard socio-economic rights as in some way inferior to civil and political rights and as not warranting equal protection. I have shown in Chapters 1 to 3 that there is no justifiable normative basis for this contention and that the same normative foundations support both types of rights.

Some have argued, however, that the question is one of degree, noting that it is the 'size of the budget consequences' that matters.[96] It has been claimed that 'court orders enforcing socio-economic rights will have significant budgetary implications on nearly every occasion that the court finds against the state whereas in the case of other rights budgetary impact will be a more occasional or less severe consequence of the order'.[97] It is not in fact true that significant budgetary implications will invariably follow from orders involving socio-economic rights: the enforcement of negative duties associated with socio-economic rights—for instance, preventing the state from demolishing houses or evicting persons—will not necessarily attract major budgetary consequences. In relation to positive duties, the exact nature of the budgetary consequences will depend on the order that is made and the context: the extension of an existing feeding scheme, for instance, may cost less than the creation of a new feeding programme. Moreover, it is not clear that there is necessarily a significant difference in all societies between the amount spent on the positive obligations imposed by civil and political rights as opposed to those imposed by socio-economic rights.[98]

---

wide-ranging factual and political enquiries necessary … for deciding how public revenues should most effectively be spent'.

[95] Mureinik, 1992: 466; and recently, see Lenta, 2004b: 569.   [96] Tushnet, 2004: 1896.

[97] Lenta, 2004b: 567.

[98] Consider, for instance, the expense involved in maintaining an electoral system that realizes the right to vote or that involved in the running of the court system. Will such expenses always be significantly higher than, for instance, expenditure on a feeding scheme?

However, let us accept for purposes of the argument that the budgetary consequences of enforcing some positive obligations in terms of socio-economic rights are greater than those that generally result from the positive obligations flowing from civil and political rights. Does size in fact matter as to whether the judiciary should enforce socio-economic rights claims?

The size of budgetary consequences does not, in any general way, affect the argument presented in this chapter as to when the judicial review of majoritarian decisions is justified; as a result it does not provide a strong principled argument for the judiciary to adopt a hands-off approach to adjudicating claims based on socio-economic rights. Perhaps, it will even be more important where there are significant budgetary consequences for the judiciary to be vigilant in ensuring that the fundamental interests of individuals are protected, as it is here that governments are most likely to baulk at protecting these interests.

The size of the budgetary consequences will, however, be a consideration that needs to be taken into account by the judiciary in translating conditional rights into unconditional rights. The greater the size of the budgetary consequences, the more likely the factors discussed in Chapter 3, such as scarcity and sacrifice, will be engaged, and thus conditional rights may not be fully able to be implemented in certain circumstances. Where factors such as scarcity and sacrifice play a significant role in decision-making, judges may well consider it appropriate to give strong weight to the decisions reached by other branches of government given their particular competences and the difficulties of the balancing process. What the size of budgetary consequences does not do is impact upon the urgency of human need, nor provide a reason for other branches of government to fail to prioritize the interests protected by socio-economic rights. Thus, the judiciary will, irrespective of the size of the budgetary consequences, retain an important role in ensuring that policies of the government accord with their obligations in terms of socio-economic rights provisions (as occurs with civil and political rights).[99]

However, this response does not defuse a more general objection to judicial review that maintains that judges should not be the ones determining the overall allocation of resources irrespective of the type of right involved.

This objection is mistaken in two central ways. First, if the objection does not wish to destroy the institution of judicial review of fundamental rights, then it must involve the contention that one can separate out questions of resource allocation from fundamental rights review. However, in general, there will be resource implications to the enforcement of fundamental rights. Even orders in relation to negative duties will require enforcement by agencies and, as such, have an impact on the distribution of resources. Thus, if a society is justified in recognizing fundamental rights, and has good reasons for granting judges review powers, then the society is justified in allowing its judges to ensure that resources are allocated in accordance with the demands of fundamental rights.

[99] See Chaps 6 and 7 for a more detailed discussion of what the judiciary would be required to do to enforce socio-economic rights.

It may be responded, however, that the objection is in fact a general one against the judicial review of fundamental rights where that could involve resource implications. However, the justification for judicial review outlined in this chapter does not disappear where fundamental rights have resource implications: it often becomes stronger. The manner in which resources are allocated—particularly relating to socio-economic rights—often has a severe impact upon the most fundamental interests of individuals. It involves providing shelter, food, and water to individuals without these basic commodities and is thus where the best decision-making is required. It is where the equal importance of individuals is most at stake. If the claim advanced in this chapter is correct—namely, that judicial review can lead to better decision-making concerning fundamental rights—then it is of particular importance that such review occurs where it matters most: where resource allocation is involved.

Moreover, this objection mistakes the very nature of judicial review. Granting judges the power of judicial review does not entail that the judges will suddenly decide to draw up the budget themselves without regard to the expertise of the legislature and executive. The point is that the original decisions are made by those democratically elected and hopefully with the greatest expertise. Judges are given the power to *review* such decisions as to their conformity with the set of priorities mentioned in the Constitution.[100] In the *TAC* case, the Constitutional Court of South Africa recognized correctly that determinations concerning socio-economic rights 'may have budgetary implications, but are not themselves directed at rearranging budgets'.[101]

Where it is found that the budget does not sufficiently make provision for the priorities the government is required to realize in the Constitution, the court then has several options regarding the remedy it can give. Where it feels unable to make decisions regarding allocation as a result of a lack of expertise, it can send the policy back to the executive for a reallocation of resources that meets the priorities in question.[102] It may on occasion be able to ascertain that there are already sufficient resources in the coffers such that competing needs would not be prejudiced by an order requiring the provision of some service.[103] In other cases, it will have the power to pronounce upon a clear mis-allocation of resources and order that

---

[100] Mureinik,1992 claims that the review should be based on the question: 'given the constitutional commitment to eradicate starvation [for instance], is this statute or this administrative programme or even the annual Budget justified?'(at 471). Mureinik believes in a limited form of judicial review—for sincerity and rationality—that requires the government to justify its actions in relation to constitutional standards. He does not, however, specify the content of these rights, and sets the standards very low (sincerity and rationality). The approach I have defended is congruent with Mureinik's approach and can be seen as a development thereof. It attends more closely to the content of rights, and recognizes differing thresholds of urgency. Moreover, this recognition would lead to more stringent standards of justification than those proposed by Mureinik, particularly in cases where the government seeks to justify its failure to realize interests of a high degree of urgency.

[101] TAC, n 88 above, at [38].

[102] The order in *Grootboom* (see Chap 5) is essentially an example of this first kind of remedy.

[103] The *TAC* order provides an example of such a case.

this be remedied. Judges are thus required to evaluate the allocation of resources against an area in which they have expertise: the application of human rights standards.[104] Where the allocation is found wanting, judges have a variety of remedies open to them that will allow them to draw upon the expertise of other branches of government where this is necessary.

7 Conclusion

In this chapter, I have offered a defence of the institution of constitutional judicial review. I have argued in favour of a rights-based theory of judicial review and against Waldron's attempt to suggest that such a theory is ultimately incoherent. The self-defeating nature of Waldron's arguments leads us to recognize the importance of developing a thin theory of shared values and of good decision-making. Such a theory in turn requires an understanding of the normative underpinnings of fundamental rights, and certain principles about how decisions should be taken. A decision then must be made concerning which institutions in a society are best placed to reach optimal determinations concerning fundamental rights. I argued that a number of widely accepted epistemological considerations concerning good decision-making support the view that the judiciary should be responsible for reaching final decisions about the fundamental rights of individuals in a society.

Chapters 5 and 6 will situate the philosophical discussion thus far within the real-life context of contemporary South Africa. The real-life context will highlight the importance of involving the judiciary in adjudicating claims based on socio-economic rights by demonstrating in practice the blind spots of majoritarian institutions and how judicial intervention has led to important improvements in policy for those who are most needy and vulnerable. However, for rights to realize their full potential such interventions must be made upon sound legal doctrine and in a way that reflects the normative importance of these rights. The real-life context will thus require us to draw out the implications of the philosophical theory defended thus far for legal doctrine in an applied context. That context will also allow for a greater understanding of the important distinction between conditional and unconditional rights and the practical obligations that arise from the theory I have proposed. The concluding chapter of this book will seek briefly to draw out further policy implications of this theory both for developed countries, such as the United States and the United Kingdom, and for developing countries,

---

[104] This is a critical point, missed by many writers. Steinberg, 2006: 282, for instance, writes that socio-economic rights are 'essentially about the allocation of resources'; this leads her to recommend an extremely cautious approach to judicial involvement in their interpretation (a similar point is made by Wesson, 2004: 293). However, socio-economic rights are rather fundamentally about the realization of a range of fundamental interests of individuals. The role of the judiciary is not to sit in the abstract and determine the allocation of resources in a society: just like with civil rights, it is rather to ensure that any such allocation is able to meet the most urgent fundamental interests of individuals that are protected in the constitution of a society.

such as India and South Africa. In this way, it is hoped, that the universal implications of this philosophical theory will become evident.

The focus of the discussion in the applied chapters will be on a sub-set of fundamental rights which I shall term 'subsistence rights'.[105] These rights include rights to adequate housing, food, water, and health care. These rights have traditionally been neglected and scant attention paid to their content. The philosophical theory that has been developed also indicates the great normative importance of these rights: once this is recognized, these rights have the potential to assist in developing a legal framework to address one of the most pressing problems of our world at present, namely, the widespread socio-economic deprivation. Using a philosophical theory to develop the content of rights that have historically been badly understood can show the usefulness and validity of such a theory. Moreover, I shall be concerned particularly with the positive obligations that such rights place upon a society. Such obligations engage several of the factors I have identified in translating conditional socio-economic rights into unconditional obligations. As such, it is instructive to consider the consequences of the philosophical theory I have developed for a society in which such rights are legally recognized.

I shall concentrate the applied discussion on the case of South Africa, where socio-economic rights have been expressly included in its Bill of Rights. There are at least three important reasons for doing so. First, South Africa is a country which has a large problem of removing people from dire poverty. Historically, there has been no social security net and currently 34.4 per cent of the population live below the international poverty line of USD 2 per day.[106] South Africa is also a country that has considerable wealth: mining, agriculture, and tourism are amongst a range of thriving areas of economic activity. In 2006, the Minister of Finance indicated that South Africa had a budget overrun of ZAR41 billion, a small budget deficit, and that a large amount of money would be used for social spending.[107] It is consequently a country where needs are large, where there are also significant resources available to meet such needs, yet such resources remain limited. This combination leads it to be a useful example through which to understand the practical implications of recognizing socio-economic rights in a Constitution in situations of what may be termed moderate scarcity.[108] It is a context in which socio-economic rights are of great importance but in which the constraints upon the realization of such rights also have to be taken into account. Such a context is relevant and applicable to many, if not most, countries in the world.

---

[105] In this book I shall use the term 'socio-economic rights' to denote mainly 'subsistence rights'. In general legal parlance, however, the term refers to a wider set of rights, including, for instance, labour rights and the right to education, which are not the focus of this book.

[106] See data in Chap 7; it has been estimated that as many as 57 per cent of people live below the national poverty line (see <http://www.sarpn.org.za/documents/d0000990/index.php>).

[107] See <http://business.iafrica.com/budget_2006_2007/budget_news/904189.htm> for an overview of the budget.   [108] See Rawls, 1999a: 110.

Secondly, in South Africa, socio-economic rights are not just abstract ideas; they can have real-life practical consequences. Depending upon how such rights are interpreted, it is possible that the recognition of subsistence rights could assist in the task of helping to remove large segments of the population from living in absolute poverty. It is thus instructive to consider thus far the impact these rights have had and to develop an understanding of the impact they ought to have on the society.

Finally, South Africa is a country in which legal doctrines are currently being shaped and have not yet become deeply entrenched. Law in the past served to enshrine injustice; there is a desire now to use law as a tool to assist in the transform-ation of the society[109] and to adjudicate competing interests fairly.[110] South Africa, unlike most other countries in the world, also has a number of key deci-sions that have indicated a jurisprudential approach towards enforcing socio-economic rights through the courts. In Chapter 5, I shall thus focus upon these decisions of the South African Constitutional Court and criticize its current approach towards the interpretation of subsistence rights. In Chapter 6, I shall attempt to show that the analytical framework and philosophical foundations that have been developed in the first four chapters of this book can provide a useful and attractive alternative approach to the interpretation of subsistence rights in South Africa and beyond.

---

[109] See, for instance, Klare, 1998 and Liebenberg, 2006.　　　[110] Klug, 2000: 13–14.

5

Judicial Review in Practice: The Reasonableness Approach and its Shortcomings

1 Introduction

The last chapter considered the justification for allowing judges to make final decisions concerning fundamental rights and thus often to render the acts of the majoritarian branches of government invalid. The courts in South Africa are expressly given these powers of judicial review in its Constitution.[1] In fact, it is one of a few countries in which judges may review legislation or executive policies for failure to conform with the socio-economic rights provisions in the Constitution,[2] and in which such provisions are placed on equal terms with their civil and political counterparts.

The manner in which socio-economic guarantees would be included in the Constitution was heavily debated in public and in academic writing at the time of the Constitution's drafting. Some critics challenged whether these rights could, in fact, be given a meaningful role in a constitutional democracy.[3] Others argued that when these rights became operational, judges would inevitably overstep the boundaries of their legitimate function.[4] As a result, several voices proposed adopting the Indian Constitution's model of including socio-economic provisions as directive principles designed to guide state policy but which are not directly justiciable.[5] Others contended that socio-economic rights deserve full recognition in the Constitution and offered arguments to show how they could be rendered directly justiciable.[6]

---

[1] Sections 167(4) and (5), 169(a), and 172 of the Constitution of the Republic of South Africa Act 108 of 1996 (henceforth 'the Constitution').

[2] The inclusion of enforceable socio-economic rights in constitutions has only been a trend in recent years, particularly in the constitutions adopted from the 1980s onwards in Eastern Europe (Hungary, for instance) and South America (Argentina, for instance) after transitions from authoritarian governments to democratic ones.

[3] See, for instance, the objections considered by Haysom,1992.   [4] See Davis, 1992.

[5] In recent years, however, the Supreme Court of India has sought to employ these directive principles to interpret, and thus enlarge, the content and scope of the fundamental rights that are contained in the Constitution. See, for instance, *Olga Tellis v Bombay Municipal Corporation*, AIR 1986 SC 180.   [6] See, for instance, Mureinik, 1992.

The Constitutional Assembly ultimately decided that socio-economic rights were of sufficient importance that they should be included directly within the Bill of Rights. Judges were given the power to review acts and policies for their conformity with these rights. Unlike in Europe—where judges must infer such rights from the nature of the state[7]—and in India—where judges protect such rights through an expansive interpretation of the right to life[8]—in South Africa, judges are faced with the task of interpreting express provisions establishing rights to adequate housing, food, water, and health care. The impact and meaning of these rights for South African society will thus in large measure depend upon the approach that judges adopt to their interpretation. The important task of this chapter will thus be to understand and critique the Constitutional Court's approach towards interpreting subsistence rights. The focus of the discussion will be on the positive obligations that flow from these rights. It will be shown that the approach adopted by the court attempts to circumvent the task of providing content to socio-economic rights; the failure to provide content to such rights places the fledgling jurisprudence on socio-economic rights in South Africa on shaky theoretical foundations but, more importantly, may entail that such rights fail to have any significant practical effect on the lives of those who are most vulnerable. The shortcomings of the South African Constitutional Court's approach suggest the need for an alternative approach towards providing content to these rights, which is the subject of Chapter 6.

2 Constitutional Interpretation in South Africa

The Constitutional Court of South Africa ('the Court') outlined its theoretical approach to constitutional interpretation in two of the early cases it decided. In *S v Zuma*,[9] Kentridge AJ explained that the judges would be adopting a purposive and generous approach to interpreting the Bill of Rights. He cautioned, however, that:

[w]hilst we must always be conscious of the values underlying the Constitution, it is nonetheless our task to interpret a written instrument. I am well aware of the fallacy of supposing that general language must have a single 'objective' meaning. Nor is it easy to avoid the influence of one's personal intellectual and moral preconceptions. Yet, it cannot be too strongly stressed that the Constitution does not mean whatever we might wish it to mean.[10]

In *S v Makwanyane*,[11] Chaskalson P continued to explicate the Court's approach to constitutional interpretation which 'whilst paying due regard to the language

---

[7] See, for instance, the decision of the German Federal Constitutional Court, which recognizes that the right to a minimum subsistence level is derived from the social state principle in the German Constitution 40 BverfGE 121 (133) quoted in De Wet, 1996.

[8] See, for example, *Shantistar Builders v Narayan Khimalal Totame & others* (1990) 1 SCC 520.

[9] 1995 (2) SA 642 (CC).   [10] Ibid at [17].   [11] 1995 (3) SA 391 (CC).

that has been used, is "generous", and "purposive" and gives expression to the underlying values of the Constitution'.[12] He went on to say that provisions of the Constitution must be construed in their context which, in *Makwanyane*, included 'the history and background to the adoption of the Constitution, other provisions of the Constitution itself and, in particular, the provisions of Chapter Three of which it is part'.[13] The judgment goes on to recognize that the social context of a case—such as, in that case, the high level of criminal activity in South African society—also has to be taken into account. Judge Chaskalson emphasized the fact that the Constitution must be interpreted 'in the light of our own history and conditions with due regard to the aspirations articulated in it'.[14]

How then should one determine the context in which a provision of the Constitution is to be viewed and its purpose? It is often argued today that context-ual interpretation is desirable without much thought being given as to how one ascertains the context in which to view a provision. There has, for instance, been some criticism of how the Constitutional Court has interpreted the historical con-text in which to interpret the Constitution.[15] In determining context, what is required is an ability to distinguish relevant from irrelevant considerations. Relevance must to some extent be determined in relation to the values at stake in a particular case. Similarly, regarding the purposes of a constitutional provision, these must be derived from a consideration of the deeper values underlying a Constitution. A Constitution itself usually explains which values are of central importance. As such, it is with reference to these values that the particular pur-poses of provisions are to be determined. The Constitution identifies human dignity, equality, and freedom as the central values underlying the Bill of Rights.[16]

2.1 Challenges for the value-based approach to constitutional interpretation

In an extra-judicial lecture,[17] the Chief Justice of South Africa, Arthur Chaskalson, considered the relationship between these three values, with a particu-lar focus upon the notion of human dignity. He traced the history of the notion of dignity and the importance that is often placed upon it in justifying rights. Chaskalson argues that the values of dignity, equality, and freedom are often regarded as being in conflict. He contends, however, that it is possible to interpret these notions such that they reinforce rather than conflict with one another.

---

12 Ibid at [9].

13 At [10]. Chapter Three was the Bill of Rights in the Interim Constitution of South Africa Act 200 of 1993.

14 This particular statement of the approach to constitutional interpretation appears in Chaskalson, 1998: 7.   15 De Vos, 2001.

16 Section 7(1) reads as follows: 'This Bill of Rights is a cornerstone of democracy in South Africa. It enshrines the rights of all people in our country and affirms the democratic values of human dig-nity, equality and freedom.' See also ss 1, 9, 10, and 36(1) of the Constitution.

17 Chaskalson, 2000.

Equality, for instance, must be interpreted to mean equality of worth (or dignity), and he cites Dworkin's principle that everyone must be treated with equal concern and respect as an elaboration of this idea.

Two of the difficulties faced by the value-based approach to constitutional interpretation are apparent in Justice Chaskalson's lecture. First, he claims in a footnote '[f]or purposes of this lecture it is not necessary to define exactly what is meant by human dignity'.[18] Although it is true that a one-line definition of dignity may well be impossible, some attempt to define the value was of crucial significance to his lecture. If the value has no content, and can be anything one makes of it, then it is trivial that it can be reconciled with freedom and equality. A reconciliation between these values is only meaningful if each has some core meaning that can be shown to complement rather than conflict with the other values. Furthermore, if the notion of dignity lacks a core content that is independent of the other values, then it cannot serve to guide constitutional interpretation, with the values of equality and freedom doing all the work.

Thus, if a value-based approach to interpretation is to work, then continual work needs to be expended in trying to understand these values. It is unrealistic to expect the court to lay out a comprehensive theory in one judgment.[19] One would also expect that such a theory would be subject to revisions as a result of discussions amongst the judges, within civil society and in academia. Nevertheless, the process of constitutional interpretation requires that a well-reasoned approach towards determining the content of constitutional values be adopted.

Secondly, it is important that judges develop an approach not only to the theoretical understanding of core constitutional values, but also to bridging the gap between theory and practice. This point can be illustrated by considering Dworkin's principle of 'equal concern and respect', which Chaskalson invokes to expand upon the notion of dignity. Whilst Dworkin sees his principle as foundational to a society, he recognizes that there are different interpretations of this principle.[20] Much of his work concerns arguing for what he regards as the best interpretation thereof. For instance, he argues that in relation to distributive justice, 'equality of welfare' is a possible but mistaken interpretation of the principle. He defends 'equality of resources' as the best interpretation of the principle. The practical consequences of these interpretations are very different, and so it is of great importance to choose between them in order to decide how the abstract principle of 'equal concern' is to impact practically upon the society.

This discussion of Chaskalson's lecture has thus sought to highlight some of the challenges that are faced in the application of a value-based approach to constitutional interpretation. The central difficulty relates to determining the content of

18 Chaskalson, 2000: 198.
19 Nor would this necessarily be desirable: see the discussion between Currie, 1999 and Roederer, 1999.
20 Dworkin, 2000: 2. Rawls, 1999a: 5, for instance, also distinguishes between a shared common concept of justice and different understandings (what he terms conceptions) of this shared concept.

these abstract values. A number of different conceptions of such values can be offered, and they can be combined in different ways. Different understanding of these values can lead to divergent concrete applications, and it is thus not always easy to ascertain the practical consequences of enshrining certain rights in the Constitution. In order for a value-based approach to constitutional interpretation to work, it is thus necessary to have a political theory concerning the values and reasons that lie behind the recognition of fundamental rights. Such a theory allows for content to be attributed to rights and for the development of principles that can be of clear application in particular cases.

By and large, the Constitutional Court has sought to reason about the values and interests protected by the Constitution and on this basis to afford relief. It has employed the values of dignity, equality, and freedom so as to interpret the Bill of Rights. The problem comes in seeing whether it has given sufficient content to these values and the rights themselves in order to reach its conclusions. In this regard, the Court has been charged with failing to develop a political philosophy of rights and employing fuzzy reasoning concerning the foundational values of dignity, equality, and freedom that has been termed 'rainbow jurisprudence'.[21]

In the rest of this chapter, I shall focus on the Court's jurisprudence on socio-economic rights, and, in particular, upon three seminal cases: *Grootboom*, *TAC*, and *Khosa*. I shall argue that it has not displayed a principled understanding of the reasons for the inclusion of socio-economic rights in the Constitution. It has failed to provide sufficient content to these rights to enable it to reach the conclusions it has arrived at, and its decisions are thus theoretically weak. It can also be argued that the inadequacy of the theoretical reasoning has affected the practical outcomes of the cases and led the Court, in general, to offer weak remedies to those whose socio-economic rights have been violated. The discussion will seek to highlight the need for greater content to be given to socio-economic rights. The next chapter will offer an alternative approach to determining the content of these rights based upon the political philosophy developed in this book.

3 *Grootboom*: Reasonableness and the Minimum Core

3.1 The decision

Government of the Republic of South Africa v Grootboom ('*Grootboom*')[22] concerned a group of extremely poor people (the respondents) who felt compelled by the desperation of their living conditions in the informal settlement of Wallacedene[23]

---

[21] Cockrell, 1996: 11.   [22] 2001 (1) SA 46 (CC).

[23] Yacoob J describes the conditions faced by the residents of Wallacedene as 'lamentable'. He outlines their circumstances at [7] as follows: 'A quarter of the households of Wallacedene had no income at all, and more than two thirds earned less than ZAR500 per month. About half the population were children; all lived in shacks. They had no water, sewage or refuse removal services and only 5% of the

to move onto vacant land that was privately owned and that had been earmarked for formal low-cost housing. Eviction proceedings were successfully instituted against these people, and the resulting court order was implemented in a manner 'reminiscent of apartheid-style evictions',[24] destroying their possessions and materials in the process.

The respondents landed up on the Wallacedene sports field, with nothing other than plastic sheeting to protect them against the elements. They instituted legal action against the government, demanding that the municipality fulfil its constitutional obligations towards them, which they claimed would involve the provision of at least basic shelter. The High Court granted relief to some of the respondents. The government then appealed against this decision to the Constitutional Court. In arriving at his decision, Yacoob J (in whose judgment all the justices concurred) engaged in an analysis of two constitutional rights: section 26 and section 28(1)(c). I shall focus on his approach to section 26. That section reads as follows:

26. (1) Everyone has the right to have access to adequate housing.
    (2) The state must take reasonable legislative and other measures, within its available resources, to achieve the progressive realisation of this right.
    (3) No one may be evicted from their home, or have their home demolished, without an order of court made after considering all the relevant circumstances. No legislation may permit arbitrary evictions.

In considering how this right should be interpreted, it was argued before the Court that guidance should be taken from the interpretations given to socio-economic rights under the International Covenant on Economic, Social and Cultural Rights ('the Covenant').[25] The Committee responsible for the interpretation and application of the Covenant ('the UN Committee') has released a number of General Comments that attempt to give content to the rights recognized in the Covenant.[26] The UN Committee has held that socio-economic rights contain a minimum core obligation that must be fulfilled by state parties. Such an obligation requires every state party to fulfil certain minimum essential levels of the rights in question, and a failure to do so constitutes a *prima facie* failure to discharge its obligations under the Covenant.[27] In his judgment, Yacoob J refers to the approach adopted by the UN Committee. He does not reject the minimum core approach outright (and thus leaves room for its adoption in future); however, he levels several criticisms against this approach and concludes

---

shacks had electricity. The area is partly waterlogged and lies dangerously close to a main thoroughfare. Mrs Grootboom lived with her family and her sister's family in a shack about twenty metres square.'

[24] *Grootboom*, n 22 above, at [10].   [25] Ibid at [26].
[26] The General Comments that are of particular importance in this context are General Comments 3 and 4. They are reprinted in Eide, Krause, and Rosas, 1995: 442ff.
[27] See General Comment 3 at [10].

that it is not 'necessary to decide whether it is appropriate for a court to determine in the first instance the minimum core of a right'.[28]

Instead, he holds that 'the real question in terms of our Constitution is whether the measures taken by the state to realise the right afforded by section 26 are reasonable'.[29] Reasonable measures involve the establishment and implementation by the state of a coherent, well-coordinated, and comprehensive programme directed towards the progressive realization of the right of access to adequate housing. Moreover, '[a] court considering reasonableness will not enquire whether other more desirable or favourable measures could have been adopted, or whether public money could have been better spent ... It is necessary to recognise that a wide range of possible measures could be adopted by the state to meet its obligations.'[30] In order to comply with its obligations, the state will be required not merely to legislate but also to act in a way that is designed to achieve the intended result. Furthermore, a reasonable programme must be balanced and flexible and 'make appropriate provision for attention to housing crises and to short, medium and long term needs. A programme that excludes a significant segment of society cannot be said to be reasonable.'[31]

Yacoob J went on to consider whether the housing programme that had been adopted by the state was reasonable. He found that the state had instituted an integrated housing development policy whose 'medium and long term objectives cannot be criticised'.[32] However, the housing programme lacked any component providing for those in desperate need. Yacoob J found that the absence of such a component was unreasonable and thus concluded that '[t]he nationwide housing programme falls short of obligations imposed upon national government to the extent that it fails to recognise that the state must provide for relief for those in desperate need'.[33]

3.2 Theoretical difficulties with the reasonableness approach in *Grootboom*

The central line of reasoning in *Grootboom* involves the finding that, in order to pass constitutional muster, governmental action in relation to housing (and other socio-economic entitlements) must be reasonable. The fact that in its housing programme the government failed to provide for those in desperate need in the short term was held to be unreasonable. As a result, the government's housing programme was declared to be unconstitutional. In this section, I wish to evaluate the cogency of the Court's reasoning, and demonstrate that in order to render the court's approach coherent there is a need to think more precisely about the

---

[28] *Grootboom*, n 22 above, at [33]. I shall consider the objections of the court to this approach in more detail in Chap 6.   [29] Ibid.

[30] Ibid at [41].   [31] Ibid at [43].   [32] Ibid at [64].

[33] Ibid at [66]. I shall consider the reasons Yacoob J provides for his finding of unreasonableness in more detail below.

content of this right. In so doing, I shall attempt to show that the Court must recognize a minimum core obligation—something it attempts to avoid—in order to reach the conclusion it arrives at in *Grootboom*.

3.2.1 Reasonableness

In order to ascertain whether the Court's reasoning is persuasive, it is essential to gain a clearer understanding of what is meant by the notion of 'reasonableness'. Reasonableness is not a very well-defined notion, though it appears in a number of aspects of the law. The use Yacoob J makes of it in this context is reminiscent of its use in administrative law, where there has been much recent work on the notion of reasonableness.[34] Administrative review also involves review by the judiciary of the decisions made by another branch of government. It is thus relevant to consider the meaning of reasonableness in administrative law.[35]

Hoexter writes that the notion of reasonableness is designed to refer to that which lies within the 'limits of reason' and allows for a legitimate diversity of views. What is reasonable is not only that which is correct, but also those decisions that lie in between correctness and capriciousness. A reasonable decision is one that is supported by reasons and evidence, which is rationally connected to a purpose, and is objectively capable of furthering that purpose. A reasonable decision generally also reveals proportionality between ends and means, benefits and detriments.[36] The notion of reasonableness is thus designed to allow scope for the substantive judicial review of decisions by another branch of government whilst retaining a sense that there is a margin of appreciation, which the original deciding body has in making a decision. A court will only substitute its decision for that of the body with the initial task of deciding a matter if that decision falls outside the margin of appreciation given to that body.

This doctrine is important as it allows for the retention of a separation of powers, and the idea that the body which has been delegated a decision or has the greatest institutional competence will have the choice between measures that fall within the range of the reasonable. In the context of socio-economic rights, reasonableness allows the legislature and executive a margin of appreciation in deciding on the measures that need to be taken in realizing socio-economic rights. As has already been mentioned, doubts have been raised about the institutional competence of courts in making judgments on socio-economic rights[37] as well as the

---

[34] One recent commentator has in fact referred to the approach of the court as the 'administrative law model of socio-economic rights'. See Sunstein, 2001a. This reading has been supported by some writers (see Davis, 2006) and challenged by others (see Wesson, 2004 and Steinberg, 2006).

[35] There is indeed much discussion about the exact nature of the reasonableness test in administrative law. I cannot attempt to resolve the debate here, and refer to the sense of reasonableness that seems to me most appropriate to the current context and that allows for a significant form of substantive review.

[36] I rely here on the excellent account by Hoexter, 2002 at 509–13; see also Wade and Forsyth, 2000, and Elliott, 2001.   [37] See, for instance, Mureinik, 1992.

legitimacy of judicial decision-making in this area.[38] It is not therefore surprising that the Constitutional Court sought to centre its decision on the doctrine of reasonableness, which allows it to demonstrate appropriate deference to the legislature and executive.

Nevertheless, in understanding the role of reasonableness, it is crucial to recognize that the word 'reasonable' qualifies the word *measures* in section 26 and not the right itself. In other words, the right is not just a right to have the government act reasonably when it comes to socio-economic provision in society. Deference is not owed to the government in defining the content of the right to have access to adequate housing, but only in allowing it a 'margin of appreciation' to decide which *measures* it will adopt in fulfilling its obligations. In giving effect to the right, the *measures* the government adopts must be reasonable in relation to the objective it seeks to achieve, which is to realize the right of access to adequate housing. This enquiry requires the specification of some content to the right, independently of the notion of reasonableness.

The reasonableness or otherwise of governmental action must therefore be judged in relation to the ends, purposes, or obligations that the Constitution imposes. Now, the government construed its obligations under the Constitution in a particular way in *Grootboom*. In the Housing Act of 1997, the purpose of its housing programme was described as aiming to ensure that:

all citizens and permanent residents of the Republic will, on a progressive basis, have access to—

(a) permanent residential structures with secure tenure, ensuring internal and external privacy and providing adequate protection against the elements; and
(b) potable water, adequate sanitary facilities and domestic energy supply.[39]

The government enacted legislation and instituted detailed and systematic programmes to achieve this end. The government's programmes were targeted towards fulfilling what it saw as its obligation to provide access to housing as defined in the Housing Act for an increasing number of people over time. If we attempt to assess the programme in light of the government's objective, it is not clear that there is any basis upon which to judge its actions as being unreasonable, except possibly that the rate of building was too slow.[40] At most, the Court could have ordered that the rate of delivery be increased on this approach.

However, instead of accepting the government's interpretation of its obligations and then judging reasonableness in light thereof, Yacoob J commences his enquiry into the reasonableness of the government programme as follows: 'this Court must decide whether the nationwide housing programme is sufficiently

---

[38] See, for instance, Davis, 1992.
[39] See the definition of 'housing development' in the Housing Act 107 of 1997.
[40] See *Grootboom*, n 22 above, at [58], where Yacoob J points to statistics which demonstrate that the backlog of housing is being reduced by only 2,000 units a year.

flexible to respond to those in desperate need in our society and to cater appropriately for immediate and short-term requirements.'[41] This statement invokes the assumption that there is already an obligation upon the government to respond to desperate needs within South African society and to cater to people's short-term requirements. If the right in section 26(1) did not imply such an obligation, there would be no point in asking this question. The question would rather be whether the nationwide housing programme is reasonably designed to ensure that an increasing number of people have access to adequate housing over time. The answer to that question would not, however, have led to the Court's conclusion that the failure to deal with short-term needs in the housing programme is unreasonable. This point becomes clearer upon a more detailed analysis of Yacoob J's reasoning.

3.2.2 Reasonableness and the necessity for a minimum core

What reasons then did Yacoob J give for his finding that the housing plans of the government were unreasonable? He provided two main lines of argument. First, he claimed that the failure to meet short-term needs would exert pressure on existing settlements and lead to land invasions which would in turn frustrate the medium- and long-term objectives of the national housing programme. Secondly, he stated that the absence of a component dealing with those in desperate need may have been reasonable if the housing programme would have resulted in affordable housing for most people within a reasonably short time. Yet, owing to the scale of the problem, this level of housing could not be provided speedily. Thus, people in desperate need would be consigned to their fates indefinitely unless temporary measures were taken to alleviate their situation. 'Housing authorities are understandably unable to say when housing will become available to these desperate people. The result is that people in desperate need are left without any form of assistance with no end in sight.'[42] Such a situation was clearly regarded by Yacoob J as unacceptable and hence his finding of unreasonableness.

Does reasonableness perform the work that Yacoob J claims it does? The first argument he provides attempts to establish that the failure to meet short-term needs would be self-defeating. However, there is a strong burden to be borne by Yacoob J's version of this argument: it is not obvious that the failure to meet basic needs will in all probability result in land invasions. There are many other contingent factors upon which the likelihood of such a result would depend: the government could, for instance, adopt strict policing measures and deal heavy-handedly with any attempts to invade land.[43] Those actions could deter land invasions. It is

---

[41] *Grootboom*, n 22 above, at [56].

[42] Ibid at [65].

[43] Arguably, its actions in response to the land invasions in Kempton Park, Johannesburg during 2001 were designed to demonstrate that it would not tolerate such activities. See <http://www.sabcnews.com/features/ year_in_review/bredell.html> for a report on these events.

not therefore clear that a policy directed towards long-term housing provision for greater numbers of people that lacks a component dealing with short-term needs would necessarily be self-defeating in the way suggested by Yacoob J.

However, there is an argument which could serve to establish that the failure to meet short-term needs is in fact unreasonable in the sense of being self-defeating. Such an argument would require that the constitutional obligation be stated in a way which is more onerous than the idea that the government merely has to increase the number of people that have access to housing over time. It would require that the obligation upon the government is to ensure that, in the long-term, *each* person can have access to adequate housing. Indeed, the wording of section 26(1) suggests that 'everyone' has this right. If this is so, then it makes no sense to ignore basic needs now for a benefit that will accrue in the longer term, because it can be predicted with virtual certainty that the effects of short-term deprivation would preclude some from ever being able to enjoy the longer-term benefit (due to death or chronic ill-health, for instance). Thus, if the aim was to achieve long-term housing for *all*, then it would be self-defeating to ignore any-one's short-term needs. The upshot of this argument would involve recognizing an obligation to meet short-term needs, and thus involve the imposition of a min-imum core obligation upon the government. The reasonableness test would lead to recognition of a minimum core obligation.

Yacoob J sought to avoid recognizing a minimum core obligation; hence, let us consider his second argument based on reasonableness. This argument turns on the claim that it is unacceptable for people in desperate need to be left without any form of assistance with no end in sight. Why should this claim lead to a finding that the government programme was unreasonable? If the main constitutional obligation imposed by section 26 involves the provision of long-term housing to an increasing number of people over time, then there is no basis upon which to judge that government policy is unreasonable for its failure to provide for those in desperate need. The latter goal is simply one not recognized by the Constitution on this construction of section 26. Yacoob J's reasoning in this argument seems to be based on some notion of proportionality. However, the problem with propor-tionality in this context is that it involves balancing means and ends. If the end is the gradual increase in access to long-term housing, then this provides the only basis upon which the means can be assessed. Other interests such as having one's basic needs met do not even enter the picture on such an analysis. They cannot therefore provide the basis for a finding of unreasonableness.

The only basis upon which a proportionality argument could succeed is if one of the purposes of the Constitution is to meet people's basic needs. The measures adopted by the government could then be weighed against this end to determine whether or not they were reasonable. A government programme that failed to make provision for such needs would be unreasonable in the sense that it made no effort to realize a constitutional obligation. However, acceptance of this point would involve recognizing a minimum core obligation to meet basic needs.

What distinguishes Yacoob J's eventual conclusion from that which would be reached on an approach recognizing a minimum core obligation, is his claim that it may have been acceptable not to cater for basic needs 'if the nationwide housing programme would result in affordable houses for most people within a reasonably short time'.[44] In this passage, he gestures towards engaging in a balancing process, weighing some people's short-term needs against the benefits that would accrue to a greater number over a reasonable period of time. I have argued in this section that in order to engage in this balancing process at all, it must be recognized that one of the obligations upon the state is to meet people's basic needs. Moreover, the balancing process involved will be one of weighing up the relative merits of different constitutional obligations and attempting to work out which course of action is most consistent with the constitutional values of dignity, freedom, and equality. It is doubtful that there would be many cases in which it would be acceptable to ignore completely the short-term needs of some. The effect of not protecting people from the elements can have a dire impact on their lives, and affect their basic ability to live and be free from impairments of their physical functioning and freedom.[45] These interests are so weighty that it seems difficult to imagine many situations in which it would be justifiable to ignore these short-term needs in favour of the provision of decent housing even to most people.[46] Recognition of a minimum core obligation would ensure that the Court would be stringent in evaluating the defences offered by a government for not meeting these basic needs.[47]

3.2.3 Dignity and the minimum core

It could be argued that Yacoob J recognizes the insufficiency of reasonableness, and uses dignity as the end against which government action must be measured. He states at one point that '[i]t is fundamental to an evaluation of the reasonableness of state action that account be taken of the inherent dignity of human beings ... Section 26, read in the context of the Bill of Rights as a whole, must mean that the respondents have a right to reasonable action by the state in all circumstances and with particular regard to human dignity. In short, I emphasise that human beings are required to be treated as human beings.'[48]

Such writing is indeed powerful rhetorically, yet it is important to analyse what it actually means. The last sentence offers us very little guidance: what does it

---

[44] *Grootboom*, n 22 above, at [65].

[45] On the effect of homelessness on freedom, see Waldron, 1993b.

[46] The urgency and seriousness of these interests suggest that the main defence that could persuasively be offered by the state for failing to fulfil its minimum core obligations would be that there are not sufficient resources to do so. Section 26(2) and section 36(1) (the limitations clause) would allow for such a defence. What is interesting about the *Grootboom* case is that the state did not make this argument. There would thus have been no real bar to the court ordering the government to give effect to such an obligation.   [47] See Chap 6 for a development of this idea.

[48] *Grootboom*, n 22 above, at [83].

mean to have to treat a human being as a human being? Similarly, the notion of dignity is invoked, yet little content is given to it.

There has recently been a profusion of academic writing in South Africa relating to the use of dignity in South Africa's constitutional jurisprudence in general, and in the interpretation of socio-economic rights in particular. Some have argued the notion has little content and stands 'to be used in whatever form and shape is required by the demands of the judicial designer'.[49] Others argue that the concept has sufficient meaning to be useful in developing the court's constitutional jurisprudence.[50] Even some of the latter writers, however, concede that the 'concept alone does not go very far towards explaining the vision of the transformed society in any detail, nor the means by which such society ought to be achieved'.[51]

The notion of dignity may, depending on its theoretical underpinnings, have different implications. Libertarian theorists, for instance, would generally argue that the obligations of a state must be directed towards protecting only those interests of human beings that are concerned with personal security and the freedom to pursue their own projects. Respect for the dignity of a human being, on this view, requires emphasizing the free choice of individuals and thus their responsibility for improving their own positions. The recognition of socio-economic entitlements on such a view could be said to restrict the freedom of other individuals in society through the imposition of a large tax burden. Moreover, these rights could be said to show disrespect towards the very individuals they are supposed to assist by treating them paternalistically and suggesting that they cannot help themselves. Such a position would generally be opposed to socio-economic rights or, at least, would support a very restrictive interpretation of those rights. I shall term this notion: 'dignity as freedom'.[52]

Many liberal theorists would disagree with this approach and argue that the obligations of the state must be directed towards protecting all of an individual's most fundamental interests, including liberty and security interests, but also interests in having access to certain material resources.[53] This vision of dignity recognizes that the capacity for free choice is only one important aspect of a person. It embraces a concern for the person as an integrated whole, a union of voluntary and involuntary aspects of the self. It recognizes too that the capacities of choice themselves require certain material conditions in order to be exercised in a manner that is valuable to an individual.[54] As such, this conception of dignity does not place overriding emphasis upon personal responsibility. It focuses instead upon ensuring that individual lives are treated with equal *importance*: that entails, on

---

[49] Davis, 1999b: 413.   [50] See Cowen, 2001: 54; Liebenberg, 2005b; Woolman, 2005b.
[51] Cowen, 2001: 55; see also, Liebenberg, 2005b: 9.
[52] Nozick, 1974 would be the most famous proponent of such a view.
[53] Nussbaum, 2000a: 71–4.
[54] Rawls, 1999b: 179, for instance, distinguishes between liberty and the worth of liberty: 'liberty is represented by the complete system of the liberties of equal citizenship, while the worth of liberty to persons and groups depends upon their capacity to advance their ends within the framework the system defines.' In South Africa, see Liebenberg, 2005b: 9–10 and Woolman, 2005b: 14–17.

this view, concern that individuals are each guaranteed the general conditions necessary for leading valuable lives. That would mean that both liberty interests and socio-economic entitlements require protection in order for individuals to be capable of attaining what they regard as valuable. As a result, respect for the dignity of a person on this view would involve protecting the whole range of basic interests that a person has. I shall term this view: 'dignity as integrity'.

The problem with the Constitutional Court's use of dignity in passages such as the one I have quoted above is the idea that dignity can be used without further development to support its conclusion. It invokes the notion of dignity without recognizing that different interpretations of this value may lead to opposite conclusions. It does seem clear from *Grootboom* that the Court does not share the libertarian vision of dignity. Yacoob J states at one point that '[a] society must seek to ensure that the basic necessities of life are provided to all if it is to be a society based on human dignity, freedom and equality'.[55] This suggests that the values in the Constitution support the notion of 'dignity as integrity' rather than 'dignity as freedom'. If this is so, however, then 'dignity as integrity' would support recognition of a minimum core obligation upon the government to ensure that, at least, the basic needs of all are provided. Yet, Yacoob J attempts to arrive at his conclusion on the basis of reasonableness alone without recognizing such an obligation. Thus, we can conclude that the notion of dignity can be used in one of two ways: either it lacks sufficient content to provide an anchor for the notion of reasonableness, or it can have adequate content to guide decision-making but would involve recognizing a minimum core obligation to meet basic needs. Only the latter option will allow the Court to reach the conclusion it does in *Grootboom*.[56]

Thus, the preceding discussion has sought to illustrate that Yacoob J cannot reach his desired conclusion through the notion of reasonableness alone and must in some way recognize a minimum core obligation to meet basic needs.[57] An

---

[55] *Grootboom*, n 22 above, at [44]. See also *Soobramoney v Minister of Health, Kwazulu-Natal* 1998 (1) SA 765 (CC) at [8].

[56] This work could be seen to develop the notion of equal dignity through understanding the content and implications of the notion of equal importance that lies at its centre. However, the way in which the notion of dignity is used in South Africa (and beyond) generally leaves the value and its implications under-specified. The notion of worth has underpinned reactionary ideologies (Nazism saw all and only Aryans as having equal worth) as well as progressive ones, and may have morally objectionable consequences, particularly if its scope is too restrictive (see Fredman, 2005: 190 for a critique of the use of dignity in Canada's equality jurisprudence). I cannot hope to deal with this exhaustively here but much writing on dignity exhibits serious shortcomings by failing to deal with a number of central questions: first, what is the ground of worth? Is it, for instance, rational agency, or sentience? Secondly, who is entitled to be treated with dignity: does the notion include the mentally ill and infants? What about non-human animals? Thirdly, in the context of socio-economic rights, what is the level of provision required in a society that treats individuals as having equal dignity? Finally, how does dignity assist us in balancing the sometimes competing demands of freedom and equality?

[57] In fact, several international academics see *Grootboom* as exemplifying a minimum core approach to socio-economic rights (see Chapman and Russell, 2002: 19). It is strange that the court is so concerned with distancing itself from this approach.

enquiry into reasonableness does not in and of itself dictate whether short-term needs should be met. Reasonableness review rather involves an enquiry into the mode of reasoning of the government and the relationship between the measures adopted and constitutionally mandated purposes. Yacoob J is thus forced to stipulate the meaning of reasonableness in order that he can reach his desired conclusion. In attempting to avoid recognizing a minimum core obligation, Yacoob J ends up smuggling an obligation to meet short-term needs into the very notion of reasonableness itself. It would certainly be more transparent and theoretically coherent to recognize what he is actually doing outright.[58]

3.3 Critique of the remedy in *Grootboom*

3.3.1 *The order*

The 'reasonableness approach' of the Court unfortunately is not only theoretically deficient but could also arguably have had a negative effect on the eventual order[59] that was made, which is of the most crucial significance to those unable to meet their basic needs.

At the end of its judgment, the Court decided to refrain from making a mandatory order and Yacoob J stated that 'it is necessary and appropriate to make a declaratory order'.[60] This order established that the state is constitutionally obliged to create a comprehensive and coordinated programme designed so as progressively to realize the right of access to adequate housing. Such a programme must include relief for those who have no access to land, no roof over their heads, and who are living in intolerable conditions or crisis situations. Further, the Court declared that the programme in place at the time in the Cape Metropolitan area did not meet the government's constitutional obligations as it unreasonably failed to make provision for those who fell within the above categories of those in desperate need.[61]

---

[58] Steinberg, 2006; 269–71 charges that the minimum core approach inherently involves judicial activism and violates the constraints of judicial minimalism, which involves (in the words of Cass Sunstein) 'saying no more than is necessary to justify an outcome, leaving as much as possible undecided'. In section 3.2, I have sought to show that the Court could not reach its decision purely on the basis of reasonableness: accepting the existence of a minimum core obligation was necessary in order to justify the outcome of the decision. Consequently, the adoption of the minimum core approach would not exhibit an unwarranted activism but merely lead to adequately justified decisions: the approach does not exhibit 'intense judicial activism'. I agree with Davis, 2006: 323–4 that the judicial role in socio-economic rights cases 'cannot helpfully be analyzed in terms of the binary opposites of activism versus restraint developed from a history of controversy about judicial rewriting of the text'.

[59] The Court made two orders in this case. The one order sought to deal specifically with the plight of the community in Wallacedene, and essentially rendered a settlement agreement between the parties an order of court. See *Grootboom v Government of the Republic of South Africa* CCT 38/00. The second order was made at the end of the judgment in *Grootboom* and represents the main order of court arrived at as a result of considering the government's constitutional obligations in terms of the right to have access to adequate housing. I shall focus my discussion on the latter order.

[60] See *Grootboom*, n 22 above, at [96].   [61] Ibid at [99].

The order thus requires that the state adopt reasonable measures to provide relief for people in desperate need. The first important point to recognize about this order is its lack of specificity. The state must 'provide relief'. This gives the state little guidance as to what it is required to do in particular to meet basic needs. Since the reasonableness standard is slippery, it can provide the grounds for state delay, obfuscation, and much else.

Imposing a minimum core obligation would have had the benefit that the state would have been provided with a more definite standard against which to judge its behaviour. Thus, instead of merely being implored to be 'reasonable', the state would have been required to ensure that people have 'effective protection from the elements and access to basic services, such as toilets and running water'.[62] These two things may in the end turn out to be identical, but the latter formulation grants vulnerable people greater protection and greater certainty as to what they are entitled to. It also renders the state more certain about its own obligations.

There are two additional aspects of the order that deserve criticism. The first is that the Court imposes no time limit on the state's actions in regard to the development of a programme to meet short-term needs. Had they recognized a minimum core obligation, and the urgency of the interest protected by such an obligation, it seems more likely that they would have been inclined to impose a time limit upon the government. However, the Court could have done so even within the framework it adopted, and so must be criticized for allowing too much leeway for delay and inefficiency in the provision of people's most basic needs.

Finally, there is a real question about the introduction of supervisory mechanisms for the enforcement of socio-economic rights. The Court refers to the fact that the Human Rights Commission will monitor and report on the compliance of the state with its obligations in terms of section 26.[63] However, it is arguable that the Court itself should have retained a residual supervisory role in this regard. It could have done so through crafting its order so as to allow the Human Rights Commission, or an alternative body with *locus standi*, to approach it speedily in respect of the required governmental action under section 26. The failure to craft such an 'easy access' order means that any body wishing to have judges review government action or inaction in relation to housing would have to institute a new case and go through the High Court once again with all the time delays and expense that this entails. If an understanding of the urgency of the fundamental interests protected by socio-economic rights were at the centre of the Court's reasoning, it is at least arguable that the Court would not have been willing to withdraw completely from the process of ensuring that these interests were protected. It is thus possible that placing these interests at the centre of its reasoning may have made it more willing to adopt a residual supervisory role.

---

[62] See Chap 6 for the suggested formulation of the minimum core standard in *Grootboom*.

[63] *Grootboom*, n 22 above, at [97].

3.3.2 *The implementation of the order*

The necessity for the Court to provide clear content to its orders and to retain some form of supervisory jurisdiction in cases dealing with socio-economic rights can be demonstrated by considering how the government has in fact proceeded in implementing the Court's order in *Grootboom*. Kameshni Pillay found that the order in *Grootboom* had not been fully implemented by the government in a study conducted two years after the judgment was handed down.[64] Pillay wrote at the time that 'there has been little tangible or visible change in housing policy so as to cater for people who find themselves in desperate need or crisis situations'.[65] The Western Cape provincial administration spent almost a year deciding on where the locus of responsibility lay with regard to the implementation of the *Grootboom* judgment, and even then, it failed to make systematic policy changes so as to cater for all people in crisis situations. The implementation of the judgment in the Cape initially focused specifically on the *Grootboom* community and did not go beyond this in establishing a comprehensive programme that caters for all those in crisis situations. Moreover, the government interpreted the judgment narrowly as referring only to those affected by such events as floods or fire, and did not see the judgment at that time as mandating the adoption of a policy designed to meet the basic accommodation needs of everyone without a roof over their head.

The decision in *City of Cape Town v Rudolph*[66] confirms the failure by the City of Cape Town municipality to understand (or take seriously) its obligations in terms of the *Grootboom* decision. The *Rudolph* case concerned the attempted eviction of around 50 individuals who had moved to live in a public park as a result of having nowhere else to go.[67] These individuals claimed in a counter-application that the City of Cape Town was failing to comply with its constitutional obligations towards them in terms of their right to adequate housing.

Selikowitz J found that these people were 'living in intolerable conditions or crisis situations' and, consequently, the government had to take reasonable measures to cater to their needs.[68] The Judge found that the City of Cape Town had failed to implement any emergency programme to cater for those in desperate need. The City denied that 'people who live in cars; in the streets; under the stairs at school; in the bushes; or at places outside wherever they can find shelter at night, and who have literally nowhere they may lawfully live, are living in intolerable conditions or that they are in crisis situations'.[69] This led to a finding by the judge that the City had 'displayed, and continues to display an unacceptable disregard for the order of the Constitutional Court',[70] and that its housing programme failed to comply with its statutory and constitutional obligations. This

---

[64] See Pillay, 2002. For a longer version of this paper, see Pillay, 2003.
[65] Pillay, 2002, at 14.   [66] 2004 (5) SA 39 (C) ('first *Rudolph* decision').
[67] The judge details their individual stories at 79–81.   [68] *Grootboom*, n 22 above, at [99].
[69] First *Rudolph* decision, n 66 above, at 84.   [70] Ibid.

time, however, he directed the City to comply with its obligations. The judge ordered the City within four months of the date of the court's order to deliver a report showing the steps it had taken to comply with its obligations. Thus, the failure by the Constitutional Court to exercise supervisory jurisdiction in *Grootboom* effectively led to at least a three-year delay in the implementation of the *Grootboom* judgment.[71] It led to further lengthy litigation and another order of court, which in this case involved the supervision by the court over the implementation of its judgment. In the interim, thousands of people continued to suffer from exposure to the elements.

In a subsequent judgment evaluating the reports of the City,[72] the court found that 18 months after the initial order the City had finally acknowledged its obligations to provide for those in desperate need. The structural interdict had led to this acknowledgement as well as some action on the part of the City. Nevertheless, the City still had not adequately complied with the initial order, though it had attempted to justify its failure to comply. The court in this subsequent judgment declined to supervise further the implementation by the City of its order and issued a declaratory order finding that the City had not fulfilled its constitutional duties. It remains to be seen whether the failure to supervise the full implementation of the court order was a wise decision on the part of the Court.

I have thus attempted to demonstrate two key points in this discussion of *Grootboom*. First, I have attempted to show the inability of the reasonableness approach alone to generate the conclusions that the Court wishes to reach. Greater attention needs to be paid to the obligations imposed upon the government by the right. Secondly, I have suggested that the weakness of the order and the poor record of the Government in implementing it may in part be explained by the failure of the Court to provide sufficient content to the right in question. This critique of the Court's reasonableness approach can be broadened and extended in relation to the *TAC* decision, to which I now turn.

4 *Treatment Action Campaign*: Reducing Rights to Reasonableness

4.1 The decision

The issues in *Minister of Health v Treatment Action Campaign* ('*TAC*')[73] arose as a result of the South African government's policy toward the provision of nevirapine, an antiretroviral drug that considerably reduces the likelihood of HIV transmission from mother to child at birth. The United Nations estimates that

---

[71] See Chap 7 for a brief discussion of the eventual policy response of national government to *Grootboom* in 2004.

[72] *City of Cape Town v Rudolph* (unreported decision of the Cape High Court, 5 December 2005, henceforth the 'second *Rudolph* decision').   [73] 2002 (5) SA 721 (CC).

5.5 million people are infected with HIV/AIDS in South Africa, with the number growing steadily; 29.5 per cent of pregnant South African women are infected with the virus.[74] Newborn children often become infected with the virus at birth when it is transmitted from the mother to her child (referred to as vertical transmission). It was estimated that in 2005 alone vertical transmission was responsible worldwide for about 700,000 children becoming infected with the virus.[75] Nevirapine is administered by giving a single tablet to the mother at the onset of labour and a few drops to the baby within 72 hours after birth. In July 2000, the manufacturers of nevirapine offered to make it available to the South African government free of charge for a period of five years in order to reduce the risk of the vertical transmission of HIV.

Despite this offer, until May 2001 people could not gain access to nevirapine in the public sector. Thereafter, a shift in government policy made nevirapine available at a small number of research and training sites throughout the country. The purpose of this restricted access was to evaluate the possible effectiveness of a future nationwide programme to combat mother-to-child transmission of HIV by studying the results of a comprehensive programme instituted at these sites. At the sites, the government offered a package of testing and counselling, dispensing nevirapine, and follow-up services to pregnant women. Two research sites were to be established in each of South Africa's nine provinces over a period of two years.[76]

The *Treatment Action Campaign*, a non-governmental organization lobbying for universal access to antiretroviral drugs, pressed the government to accelerate its programme to provide nevirapine beyond these research and training sites. The government, however, maintained its position that nevirapine would be made available only at the research sites. This entailed that 'for a protracted period nevirapine would not be supplied at any public health institution other than one designated as part of a research site'.[77]

The first issue in this case concerned whether the restriction of nevirapine to research sites constituted a violation of certain rights in the Constitution. The relevant rights are section 27(1)(a) read with section 27(2), and section 28(1)(c).[78] Section 27 reads as follows:

27 (1) Everyone has the right to have access to—
  (a) health care services, including reproductive health care;
  (b) sufficient food and water; and
  (c) social security, including if they are unable to support themselves and their dependants, appropriate social assistance.

---

[74] This statistic is based on the most recent estimate from UNAIDS: see <http://data.unaids.org/pub/GlobalReport/ 2006/200605-FS_SubSaharanAfrica_en.pdf>.

[75] See <http://www.avert.org/motherchild.htm>.   [76] *TAC*, n 73 above, at [16].

[77] Ibid at [17].

[78] I shall be concerned primarily with s 27(1) in this chapter and thus do not consider the court's approach to interpreting the rights of children in s 28.

(2) The state must take reasonable legislative and other measures, within its available resources to achieve the progressive realisation of each of these rights.

(3) No-one may be refused emergency medical treatment.

The second issue concerned whether these rights obliged the government to 'plan and implement an effective, comprehensive and progressive programme for the prevention of mother-to-child transmission of HIV throughout the country'.[79] Proceedings were initiated in the High Court where it was found that government policy concerning the provision of nevirapine across the country was unreasonable and thus constituted a violation of the Bill of Rights.[80] The government appealed against this decision to the Constitutional Court.

In a unanimous decision, the Court confirmed its approach in *Grootboom* that the question in terms of the Constitution was whether the measures taken by the state to realize socio-economic rights were reasonable. In this particular case, it had to be determined whether the policy to confine nevirapine to the research and training sites was reasonable in the circumstances.[81] After systematically rejecting four objections by the government to the provision of nevirapine, the Court considered the government's policy in light of the factors outlined in *Grootboom* that are of relevance in determining reasonableness. On the basis of medical evidence, the Court found that the provision of nevirapine would reduce the risk of vertical transmission of HIV without presenting any health risks to the mother or infant. Since the drug had been offered to the health department free of charge for five years, cost was not a factor. The government argued that it could only provide a comprehensive package of services which included substitutes for breast-milk at dedicated research sites. Without such a comprehensive package, nevirapine would not be maximally effective because the virus could be transmitted by breastfeeding.

The Court, however, found on the basis of medical evidence that nevirapine could still be effective even if administered without the full package of breast-milk substitutes and support services. Since in such conditions nevirapine could save the lives of a significant number of children, it would not be reasonable to withhold the drugs on the basis that the full comprehensive package was not available. Moreover, the Court held that the best must not be the enemy of the good, and thus waiting for the best programme to be developed for a protracted period of time before deciding to extend the use of nevirapine beyond the research sites was not reasonable.[82]

The Court thus concluded on the basis of this analysis that the policy of confining the provision of nevirapine to research sites was unreasonable and in contravention of the state's obligations under the Constitution. The second issue was whether the programme instituted by the government to prevent mother-to-child

[79] *TAC*, n 73 above, at [5].

[80] The court a quo's judgment is reported as *Minister of Health v Treatment Action Campaign* 2002 (4) BCLR 356 (T).   [81] *TAC*, n 73 above, at [47].

[82] Ibid at [81].

transmission of HIV represented a reasonable attempt to realize its obligations in terms of the Constitution. The Court found that, since it was not reasonable to restrict nevirapine to the research sites, the policy as a whole had to be reviewed. Specifically, counsellors would have to be trained regarding the use of nevirapine, and the government would have to take reasonable measures to extend the testing and counselling facilities beyond the areas where they already existed.[83]

As a result of these findings, the Court engaged in a discussion as to the appropriate remedies it could provide in cases concerning socio-economic rights. The Court held that where state policy is inconsistent with the Constitution, the function of the courts is to ensure that the other branches of government fulfil their constitutional obligations. 'Where a breach of any right has taken place, including a socio-economic right, a court is under a duty to ensure that effective relief is granted.'[84] To accomplish this, it found that the courts have a wide jurisdiction to make any order that is just and equitable.[85] Significantly, the Court held that this jurisdiction could include the power to grant mandatory relief and the power to exercise some form of supervisory jurisdiction to ensure that the order is implemented. The Court decided, however, that in this case there was no need to exercise supervisory jurisdiction, but considered it appropriate to make a mandatory order. The Court ordered the government without delay to extend the provision of nevirapine beyond the research and training sites where this is medically indicated, and ordered it to extend testing and counselling services to hospitals and clinics which are not research sites.

4.2 Theoretical difficulties with the reasonableness approach in *TAC*

4.2.1 *Reasonableness and the content of rights*

The first and second *amici curiae*[86] in the *TAC* case submitted arguments to the Court in which they contended that there were two separate causes of action in cases dealing with socio-economic rights. In the previous cases dealing with socio-economic rights—*Soobramoney*[87] and *Grootboom*—they claimed that the Court had proceeded on the assumption that sections 26(2) and 27(2) were 'exhaustive of its [the government's] positive duties under those sections'.[88] However, the *amici* claimed that a proper interpretation of the Constitution would allow for a separate cause of action to arise where section 27(1)(a) is read alone with section 7(2) of the Constitution.[89] The structure adopted in section 27 creates 'free-standing individual rights on the one hand and imposes positive

---

[83] Ibid at [95].   [84] Ibid at [106].   [85] In terms of s 172(1)(b) of the Constitution.

[86] For sake of brevity, I shall refer to them as 'the amici' in what follows. The first *amicus curiae* was the Institute for Democracy in South Africa (IDASA) and the second *amicus curiae* the Community Law Centre (CLC).

[87] *Soobramoney v Minister of Health, Kwazulu-Natal* 1998 (1) SA 765 (CC).

[88] Amicus Brief at [8].

[89] Section 7(2) reads: 'The state must respect, protect, promote and fulfil the rights in the Bill of Rights.'

duties on the state towards fulfilment of those rights on the other'.[90] These rights have a minimum core to which every individual is entitled immediately. The *amici* employed several arguments in support of this case, ranging from linguistic and structural features of the rights in the South African Constitution to policy-based arguments.

The Court, however, rejected the approach of the *amici*. It stated that implicit in the contention of the *amici* was the claim that the content of the right in sub-section (1) differs from the content of the obligation in subsection (2). This argument 'fails to have regard to the way subsections (1) and (2) of both sections 26 and 27 are linked in the text of the Constitution itself, and to the way they have been interpreted by this Court in *Soobramoney* and *Grootboom*'.[91]

The latter charge against the approach of the *amici* does not appear to have much argumentative force and seems to be simply an assertion of the Court's authority. Seeing that the Constitutional Court has the power to overrule its precedents, the *amici* could be taken to be challenging the Court's approach in the previous cases on socio-economic rights and recommending that it modify that approach. It is no answer to such a challenge to claim that the submission of the *amici* fails to have regard to the very approach they are impugning.

However, the linguistic and structural argument is more convincing. The Court argues that sections 26(2) and 27(2) require the state to take 'reasonable legislative and other measures within its available resources to achieve the progressive realisation of this right'. The reference to 'this right', they claim, is clearly aimed at the section 26(1) and 27(1) rights. This wording, together with the inclusion of these sub-sections within the same overall section of the Bill of Rights, provides evidence that the two sub-sections are linked and meant to be read together. The Court argued that this defeated the approach of the *amici*, who contended that the Constitution conferred on each person two distinct causes of action: one under sections 26(2) and 27(2) and another under sections 26(1) and 27(1) read with section 7(2).

From a purely formal point of view, the Court's approach here seems to be a more natural construal of the relationship between sections 27(1) and (2) than the approach adopted by the *amici*. Yet, it is interesting to note that the Court's argument also raises difficulties with its own approach. The Court is clearly eager to emphasize that the rights referred to in sections 26(2) and 27(2) are the rights in sections 26(1) and 27(1), respectively.[92] This argument implies that the reasonable measures that the state adopts must be assessed in relation to whether or not they are aimed at the progressive realization of the rights expressed in sections 26(1) and 27(1). If this is so, then an enquiry into the reasonableness of the measures adopted by the state must also involve an enquiry into the content of the rights contained in sections 26(1) and 27(1). The problem with the Court's approach in the *TAC* case is that it fails to provide an analysis of what the right to health-care

---

[90] Amicus Brief at [14].   [91] *TAC*, n 73 above, at [29].   [92] Ibid at [30].

services involves. What are the services to which one is entitled to claim access? Do these services involve preventative medicine, such as immunizations, or treatment for existing diseases, or both? Does the right entitle one to primary, secondary, or tertiary health-care services, or all of these?[93] The enquiry concerning the reasonableness of the measures adopted by the government cannot be conducted in a vacuum and requires that some content be given to the right to which these measures are designed to give effect.

4.2.2 Did TAC *involve a violation of a negative obligation?*

At least in the *Grootboom* case, there was some analysis of what the right in section 26(1) is designed to achieve.[94] In the *TAC* case, however, there is barely any analysis of the right in section 27(1). The only statement the Court makes on this matter places reliance on the analysis in *Grootboom*, where it was held that there is at least a negative obligation on the state to desist from impairing the right of access to adequate housing. In this case, the Court held that the 'negative obligation' recognized in *Grootboom* applies equally to section 27(1). The Court went on to find that '[t]his is relevant to the challenges to the measures adopted by government for the provision of medical services to combat mother-to-child transmission of HIV'.[95] The Court thus appears to identify the violation of section 27 that took place as involving the government's failure to comply with its negative obligation to desist from impairing a person's right to have access to health-care services. How does this analysis fit with the facts of the case?

The distinction between negative and positive obligations may be outlined as follows: a negative obligation consists in having a duty not to interfere with the ability of individuals to do something they are entitled to do; a positive obligation, on the other hand, involves having a duty to act in a particular way to provide something for individuals. In this context, a negative obligation would require the state not to interfere with a person's freedom to acquire the drugs that they wish to use; a positive obligation would require the state to provide such drugs for use by individuals.

Ultimately, the Court finds that the policy of the government was unconstitutional owing to the fact that doctors at public hospitals and clinics other than research sites were '*not enabled*' to prescribe nevirapine to reduce the risk of mother-to-child transmission of HIV and that the policy 'failed to *make provision* for counsellors at hospitals and clinics other than research and training sites'(my emphasis).[96] The Court's own language suggests that in the *TAC* case it was concerned primarily with a failure to fulfil the positive obligations upon the state to

---

[93] I do not suggest that the court was required to answer all these questions in this case but it did require some analysis of the right in order to reach the conclusion it did: that access to nevirapine fell within the entitlements conferred upon people by s 27(1)(a).

[94] *Grootboom*, n 22 above, at [34]–[38].   [95] *TAC*, n 73 above, at [46].

[96] Ibid at para 2(c)(i) and (ii) of the order.

provide life-saving medication to patients. A closer analysis of the situation confirms this result.

The government did not ban the use of nevirapine in public hospitals beyond the research sites. If doctors could get hold of the drug through their own means, they could, and indeed in some cases did, prescribe the drug.[97] It thus does not seem that the violation consisted in the government impermissibly interfering with the liberty of doctors to prescribe drugs to their patients. Rather, it was that the government was required to make the drug available for doctors to prescribe—a positive action on its part—and it failed to do so. The same point holds true in relation to the training of counsellors. Of course, the liberty of the doctors to prescribe the drug was pretty formal in the absence of the positive obligation being fulfilled. By failing to provide the drugs, the government was effectively denying people the treatment, and so impairing their access to such treatment. Nevertheless, any breach of a negative obligation arose as a result of a failure to perform a positive obligation: the primary violation was a failure to act where this was required by the Constitution. Moreover, the Court's decision to issue a mandatory order requiring the government to make nevirapine available to hospitals beyond research sites and to train counsellors in the administration of nevirapine provides support for the contention that the failure in question concerned a breach of the state's positive obligations.

If this is so, then the Court's discussion of the content of the right in section 27(1) is inadequate. The failure of the government is not best characterized in terms of a failure to fulfil a negative obligation to its patients. We need to understand what the government is required to do in terms of that section.

The normative content of the right to health-care services has been analysed by the United Nations Committee on Economic, Social and Cultural Rights in its General Comment 14,[98] and by a number of writers.[99] No doubt the task of specifying the content of this right is a difficult matter, and the Court should not attempt to provide in one case a final and exhaustive definition of what is included therein. What could have been expected, however, was some further specification of the obligations imposed by the right in relation to this particular case.

For instance, the South African Constitution requires that when interpreting rights, a court must consider international law.[100] Thus, the right could have been interpreted in light of the International Covenant on Economic, Social and Cultural Rights, which provides specifically in article 12(2)(a) that there be provision for the 'reduction of the still-birth rate and of infant mortality and for the healthy development of the child'. The UN Committee has interpreted this article

---

[97] See paras 124–5 of the Applicant's Founding Affidavit where Ms S Mthathi of the Treatment Action Campaign explains that there were situations in which public hospitals were able to provide nevirapine to their patients despite the official government policy against doing so.

[98] See the General Comment Collection at <http://www.unhchr.ch/tbs/doc.nsf>.

[99] See, for instance, Hunt, 1996; Toebes, 1999; and Chapman, 2002.

[100] Section 39(1)(b) of the Constitution.

as requiring states to adopt measures designed to improve child and maternal health, and to extend sexual and reproductive health-care services. Recognizing such an obligation to provide the services necessary for healthy child development could well have provided the basis for the decision to require the government to make nevirapine available beyond the research sites.[101]

Similarly, an argument could have been made to determine the content of section 27(1)(a) in accordance with article 12(2)(c) of the International Covenant, which provides for the 'prevention, treatment and control of epidemic, endemic, occupational and other diseases'. The UN Committee has interpreted this article to involve at least the provision of urgent medical care in cases of epidemics.[102] The Court could have reached its decision to provide nevirapine through recognizing that section 27(1)(a) imposed at least this obligation upon the state.

The Court has thus approached socio-economic rights cases by claiming that the test in terms of the Constitution is whether the measures adopted by the government were reasonable. This approach is guilty of failing to integrate sections 27(2) and 27(1): it focuses the whole enquiry on section 27(2) without providing a role for section 27(1). Yet, section 27(1) is in fact the right, and the Constitution directs us to evaluate the reasonableness of government policy in relation to an understanding of what the rights in question demand of the government.

4.2.3 Reasonableness and its content

This structural point is also mirrored by a further substantial complaint against the reasonableness approach. By focusing on the notion of 'reasonableness', the Court has demonstrated that it will scrutinize the government's policy and conduct for its ability to meet this standard of justification. This development ties in with a prominent argument for constitutionalism: that it resists a culture in which authority is to be respected for its own sake, and promotes an environment in which all decisions of those in positions of authority, even those of the legislature, must be justified.[103] An emphasis on justification, in turn, has certain salutary effects on laws and policies: it requires a high degree of accountability and thus provides incentives for public servants to consider carefully their reasons for making decisions, thus helping to expose any weaknesses thereof.[104]

---

[101] Steinberg, 2006: 272 argues that this definition is too wide and that 'any definition of the content of socio-economic rights runs the risk of over- or under-inclusivity'. The latter claim is trivial: the laying down of any principles or definitions runs this risk. As with all adjudication of law and constitutional rights, the judicial process allows courts to refine the content of rights over time and on a case-by-case basis (this is one of its advantages). It also does not seem to me that the content offered above would require the government to provide 'infant musical education' as Steinberg contends: this is not usually included within the ambit of health-care services, which is the context of the discussion. However, the content of the right to health-care services derived from the International Covenant represents only one of the possible ways in which the Court could have proceeded in TAC in order to justify its decision adequately. The alternative is to provide no content at all to socio-economic rights: this chapter represents a sustained argument against adopting such an approach.

[102] General Comment 14 at [16].　　[103] See Mureinik, 1994.

[104] See Mureinik, 1992.

The distinctive role of rights, however, is not simply to draw attention to a failure in the justification of government policy. It is a particular *type* of failure that we are concerned with: a failure to address adequately certain vital interests that people have. One of the main theoretical defects of the approach to adjudicating socio-economic rights that has been adopted by the Constitutional Court is its failure to place the fundamental interests of individuals at the centre of its enquiry in such cases. Instead, it has attempted to focus the enquiry on a more abstract and procedural notion which can tend to obscure the vulnerabilities of individuals in particular cases. As I have argued, the Constitutional Court's approach focuses upon whether the measures adopted by the government meet the standard of 'reasonableness' in relation to constitutionally mandated ends. Those ends cannot themselves be determined by the reasonableness enquiry and, thus, the approach on its own fails to generate any useful conclusions.

Moreover, an enquiry into reasonableness does not place the vital interests of individuals at its core. Yet, it is difficult to find adequate reasons for including socio-economic rights in the Constitution without recognizing that they are designed to protect the fundamental interests of individuals in having access to such essential goods as housing, food, and health care. Thus, the roots of the reasonableness approach do not clearly correlate with the purposes for specifically including socio-economic rights in the Constitution. As a result, it does not cohere well with the purposive approach to constitutional interpretation expressly adopted by the Court.

It may be objected, however, that the reasonableness approach has the benefit of developing doctrine slowly and on a case-by-case basis. From an analysis of these particular cases, it will be possible eventually to discern general guidelines for decision-making on reasonableness. The alternative requires the court to assign specific content to rights which may well be controversial and rigidify the law too quickly. By limiting its decisions to the narrow confines of particular cases, a court can also avoid making general pronouncements that may in future lead to incorrect decisions in different circumstances.[105]

In response, however, it has not been argued that it is desirable for courts to determine the entire content of a right in any one particular case. Nevertheless, it is important to recognize that even if a court wishes to confine its pronouncements to particular cases, it will be necessary for it to provide a certain amount of general content to a right that will enable it to reach the decision it does in that case. For it may be questioned how decisions are to be made in particular contexts without some general principles to guide decision-making.[106]

---

[105] 'As limited creatures we should be careful about taking too many steps at one time and perhaps wisdom counsels modesty and the development of the law in an incremental fashion' (Roederer, 1999: 503). In this paragraph, I touch on the debate between those in favour of what has been termed judicial minimalism and their opponents. See, for instance, Sunstein, 1996 and 1997; Dworkin, 1997; Currie, 1999; Roederer, 1999, and Steinberg, 2006.

[106] See the comments in Chap 3 on the value and importance of principles.

Consider the notion of reasonableness: what is considered reasonable will vary in large measure with the circumstances which we are evaluating.[107] That is one of the strengths of the approach that no doubt encouraged the Court to adopt it. However, the very context-bound nature of this approach requires that it involves at least some general standards that can be used to appraise government action in a variety of contexts. Otherwise, the enquiry into reasonableness is empty. For instance, in *Grootboom*, it was stated that a government programme that was reasonable must be balanced and flexible. That general standard can then be applied to a variety of cases to see whether they are in fact balanced and flexible.[108]

A contextual determination of reasonableness thus presupposes certain a-contextual standards that guide our appraisal in different contexts. If we analyse what is involved in the reasonableness enquiry more closely, I have argued that it involves evaluating the justifiability of the links between policies that are adopted and ends that are constitutionally endorsed. It becomes evident in this context that the very contextual sensitivity of reasonableness rests upon the fact that different circumstances allow for different conclusions concerning these linkages. However, in any such enquiry, it must be possible to specify the ends that are being aimed at in a way that is general and not specifically related to the particular context. The very benefits of the reasonableness approach rest upon our ability to identify general ends against which government policy must be evaluated. In this context, those ends are provided by the obligations imposed by sections 26(1) and 27(1). An approach that rejects the need to determine the content of these rights thus leaves the reasonableness approach empty.[109]

As a result of the emptiness of the Court's current approach, reasonableness stands in for whatever the Court regards as desirable features of state policy. The problem with such an approach is that it lacks a principled basis upon which to found decisions in socio-economic rights cases. Apart from the need to avoid *ad hoc* decision-making, there are two additional reasons why such a foundation is of particular importance in the context of socio-economic rights.

First, there have been fears expressed that the Court will overstep its legitimate role in this area by prescribing policy decisions to the government. As a result, the Court requires a method of delineating its role in cases concerning socio-economic rights. Although sensitive to this issue, the Court's current approach of

[107] The court seems to recognize this point in *TAC* at [24].

[108] It is unclear that the court has correctly identified flexibility as being 'reasonable' in all circumstances. In *Soobramoney*, for instance, the government adopted a policy towards rationing the provision of health-care resources that was fairly inflexible, yet it seemed reasonable in light of the desire to use the available resources in the best possible manner. This demonstrates the difficulty of providing content to such a vague notion as reasonableness.

[109] This point is borne out most strongly perhaps by the fact that defenders of the reasonableness approach are forced to refer to other values in giving it content: Steinberg, 2006: 281, for instance, is constrained to admit that only a 'standard of reasonableness that *incorporates concepts of proportionality, fairness, equality and dignity*, is likely to offer considerable protection to the interests of the poor' (my emphasis).

stipulating a meaning for the broad and vague concept of reasonableness places no clear restrictions on its role in such cases. A clearer enunciation of the principles upon which such litigation is to take place will offer just such a specification of the standards the Court is to use in assessing the state's policies. This in turn will help demarcate the scope of its own decision-making powers through articulating clearly the fundamental interests that trigger judicial involvement in the socio-economic affairs of the legislature and executive.

Secondly, there is a need for the Court to clarify the state's obligations imposed by socio-economic rights. The state would not then be left with a completely amorphous standard by which to judge its own conduct, but would be able to assess its conduct against clearer benchmarks. The current system of invoking the vague notion of reasonableness does not provide a perspicuous and principled basis for the evaluation of the state's conduct by judges or other branches of government in future cases. As a result, it is likely that the purposes for including such rights in the Constitution will not be realized and instead confusion will prevail.

4.3 Critique of the remedy in *TAC*

4.3.1 *The practical inadequacy of the order*

It is difficult to avoid the conclusion that in placing reasonableness at the centre of its decisions, the Court has to develop and stipulate a specific meaning for this broad, amorphous concept. It has been argued that there are a number of good theoretical reasons why the Court should not concentrate all its interpretive energy upon developing the notion of reasonableness but supplement its approach by focusing upon the interests at stake in socio-economic rights cases. Such a focus would also have made it clear how urgent it was in this case that individuals be offered effective and robust remedies. It is plausible to suggest that a justification that placed the very lives of new-born infants at its centre may have led the Court to adopt a stricter approach than it did.

One example of the Court's overly cautious approach was its decision not to order the government to provide breast-milk substitutes to mothers. Although confronted with evidence about the problems of such a programme,[110] the Court also had clear evidence that HIV can be transmitted from mother to child via breastfeeding.[111] Under such conditions, it is strange and indeed disappointing that there was not at least an order to include formula feeding within the comprehensive programme to be developed by government where this is medically indicated, and can be appropriately fulfilled. The lack of such an order means that the

---

[110] The Court expressly deals with this matter in *TAC*, n 73 above, at [128] where it considers the problems relating to such a programme where the mother does not 'have easy access to clean water or the ability to adopt a bottle-feeding regimen because of her personal circumstances'. However, it is unclear why the government should be absolved from providing breast-milk substitute in cases where the problems mentioned by the Court do not exist or can be remedied without substantial cost.

[111] Ibid at [51] and [57].

government can avoid having to provide breast-milk substitutes as part of the comprehensive programme it is required to develop by the Court, and this could have a dire impact on the health of thousands of babies. The failure to place the critical interests involved at the heart of the enquiry could provide a possible explanation for the Court's failure to make a slightly more ambitious order.

The Court's theoretical discussion in *TAC* of the relief it could impose is mostly commendable and suggests that it wishes to have a wide range of remedies open to it. The order was mandatory and more specific than that offered in *Grootboom*. Nevertheless, the failure to exercise supervisory jurisdiction in this matter does not appear to have been well justified. The Court decided not to exercise such jurisdiction on the basis of an expression of good faith in the government. It stated that 'the government has always respected and executed orders of this Court. There is no reason to believe that it will not do so in the present case.'[112]

However, this was a strikingly bad moment to express good faith in the government's ability to deliver medication expeditiously. The policy of the government in relation to HIV is notable for its very slow progress in coming to terms with the health crisis facing the country. There has been a tremendous amount of bungling and a high degree of reluctance expressed to provide nevirapine. At one point prior to the release of the judgment, the Minister of Health threatened to disobey the court order on national television.[113] The case also concerned the very serious matter that this drug has the potential to prevent children from being infected by a life-threatening disease. It was, as a result, of the utmost urgency that nevirapine be dispensed immediately. Under these conditions, the Court should have been prepared to ensure that its order was implemented as soon as possible. Whilst it may have been politically important to show confidence in the government, the importance of the interests concerned provided support for a more stringent approach. It is arguable that the failure of the reasonableness approach to place the interests involved in sharp focus may have played a part in shaping the measured and overly cautious approach of the Court.

In reality, there were already signs several months after the judgment was released that the government in several provinces had made little attempt to comply with the Court's order. Two provinces in particular, Mpumalanga and Limpopo, had failed to make any progress in making nevirapine more widely available, despite reports by doctors and nurses that there was the capacity to do so. This situation is tragic and could have been avoided had the Court adopted a more robust approach and sought to supervise the implementation of its order.[114]

---

[112] *TAC*, n 73 above, at [129].

[113] I personally heard her make this threat on a South African Broadcasting Corporation news bulletin in April 2002.

[114] See the articles 'Provinces Stonewall Action' and 'TAC: We Want to Help' in the *Mail & Guardian* (20–26 September 2002). For further criticism of the court's failure to make a supervisory order and the consequences thereof, see Heywood, 2003; Pieterse, 2004: 415; and Swart, 2005: 224.

4.3.2 The role of supervisory jurisdiction

Some writers have recently contended that the main problem with the court's approach to socio-economic rights thus far has been its failure to exercise supervisory jurisdiction. The problem it is claimed is not with the judgments themselves but with 'the state's subsequent implementation of them'.[115] If the Court 'were to exercise supervisory jurisdiction in cases of this nature . . . it would be able to ensure that judgments such as Grootboom and TAC are given their full effect. In this way, the initially vague prescriptions of such cases would become increasingly concrete.'[116]

The problems with this view are three-fold. First, the executive can only understand how to implement a judgment, if the judgment provides guidance as to what is required. Vague exhortations to be reasonable provide the state with little concrete idea as to what is required of it and thus more concrete specifications can provide the state with a standard against which to evaluate its programmes. Without such guidance, it is likely that the state will come back to the court with an inadequate programme which in turn will lead to more time-wasting and individuals who remain destitute.

That leads to the second objection, which is that supervisory jurisdiction really provides no substitute for a conception of the content of socio-economic rights. [117] One has to know what has to be implemented, in order to supervise the implementation thereof; or, at least, one has to have some determinate standards against which to evaluate what the government is doing in order to exercise effective supervision. Thus, supervisory jurisdiction provides no alternative to providing content to socio-economic rights and in fact is incoherent without a theory of content.

Finally, the process envisaged by writers such as Wesson is a two-stage process. The court releases a vague judgment. The executive produces a programme which is then evaluated and the court's order becomes more specific over the period of this interaction. The major benefit here is that there is a relationship of collaboration between the state and the judiciary in the realization of socio-economic rights.[118] It seems that there could be value in such a process; however, it is important to understand that such a process is only applicable in a limited set of circumstances. Such circumstances, in my view, arise where the court has already outlined a general standard which a state's programme must comply with and the court wishes to evaluate whether the state has correctly applied this standard in practice. The process also presupposes that there is time, which may not be the case. The urgency of meeting the needs before the court will have to be evaluated on a case-by-case basis to determine whether the initial judgment must be

---

[115] Wesson, 2004: 306.   [116] Ibid: 307.

[117] Ibid: 305–7 seems to think that supervisory jurisdiction alone can remedy the defects with the Constitutional Court's reasonableness approach. It cannot do so for the reasons indicated in the text.

[118] Ibid: 307.

implemented immediately (and warrants a more concrete and detailed order) or whether a time period may be set within which the state is given an opportunity to outline concrete steps by which it proposes to comply with the court order.

Thus, supervisory jurisdiction is not in and of itself the solution to the defects in the Court's reasonableness approach. Supervisory jurisdiction is rather an important remedy that needs to be considered when the government's fulfilment of its positive obligations concerning the fulfilment of rights is in question.[119] Supervisory jurisdiction can be regarded in various ways: it can be seen as a form of managerial device, where the judiciary attempts to ensure that other branches of the government comply with its orders. This could be seen to be a 'competitive' conception of supervisory jurisdiction. It can also serve to establish a relationship of collaboration between the judiciary and other branches of government, allowing each to bring their skills to bear on a particular problem relating to socio-economic rights.[120] This can be seen to be a more 'cooperative' conception of supervisory jurisdiction.

Given the Court's authority to ensure compliance with its orders, other branches of government may resent supervisory jurisdiction and see it as the Court's assuming final control over their performance of their duties. The Court is to a large extent reliant upon the other branches of government to comply with its orders: there are few effective measures the Court can take where the other branches of government simply refuse to comply with its orders.[121] Supervisory jurisdiction thus needs to be applied carefully and should attempt to co-opt the other branches of government into the process, the Court promoting a cooperative conception over a competitive one. However, where there is a clear unwillingness on the part of other branches of government to comply with court orders, a more combative approach on the part of the Court would be in order.

No doubt, supervision also increases certain costs to the State and requires the preparation of reports. Nevertheless, as has been demonstrated in India,[122] where a right involves the imposition of positive constitutional obligations, there may be a need to supervise implementation of these obligations over a fairly lengthy period of time to ensure that the government is adopting policies consistent with its obligations. Novel remedies such as interim orders and the appointment of

---

[119] It need not apply only to socio-economic rights; supervisory jurisdiction could be exercised for instance in ensuring compliance with a right to legal representation. See Budlender and Roach, 2005 for a discussion as to where such remedies are appropriate.   [120] Wesson, 2004: 307.

[121] Non-compliance with no explanation creates a constitutional crisis, and displays contempt for the courts. Such a course should not be adopted by a democratic government that respects the rule of law unless the order of the court is unconscionable and in fact contrary to the foundations of the constitutional order. All the orders of the Court thus far have been in pursuance of the values underlying the constitution. It is possible for contempt of court proceedings to be employed against state officials to ensure compliance though, for obvious reasons, this would be a remedy of last resort. In South Africa, courts have thus far ruled against such contempt proceedings: see *Jayiya v MEC for Welfare, Eastern Cape* 2004 (2) SA 611 (SCA).

[122] See, for instance, the fascinating action on the right to food, *PUCL v Union of India* (Writ Petition no 196 of 2001) discussed in Chap 7.

dedicated commissioners to oversee the implementation of these rights need to be considered.[123] This can allow for a helpful engagement between the different branches of government in the process of ensuring the realization of constitutional rights and enhancing a culture of accountability.[124] Conceived in this way, supervisory jurisdiction may not only be indicated in cases where the government is reluctant to perform its obligations but in cases where the courts may be of assistance to other branches of government in understanding and fulfilling their obligations.

Thus, socio-economic guarantees may amount to very little if other branches of government do not understand their obligations and are not committed to implementing these obligations. A decision by a court to supervise the implementation of its order need not involve excessive interference with the workings of other branches of government but should be designed to assist them to comply with what they are constitutionally mandated to do. Since such supervision may be necessary to ensure the effectiveness of socio-economic rights, any worries about the legitimacy of the Court's role in this area are misplaced.[125] Rather, a failure to retain such a supervisory element in the order can display an undue deference by the Court to the other branches of government and evince an unwillingness on its part to retain responsibility for the effectiveness of its orders.[126]

5 An Alternative Reading of the Jurisprudence?

5.1 The equality approach

In recent academic literature, a number of commentators have challenged the reading of the socio-economic rights jurisprudence of the Constitutional Court as importing an administrative law notion of reasonableness into the jurisprudence on socio-economic rights.[127] These commentators suggest that the key reasoning underpinning the decision in *Grootboom* is that programmes run by the state should not exclude a significant sector of society from the national housing programme, *a fortiori* where such a group is poor or otherwise vulnerable.[128] Wesson contends that even a searching administrative law review would not have led the court to find that the government's housing programme was unreasonable. Something else must have been at work. I have identified this as being an implicit

---

123 See Chap 7.

124 In this way, supervisory jurisdiction could be a method of achieving a 'dialogical model' of the relationship between the judiciary and other branches of government as is envisaged by Davis, 2006.

125 As the court itself recognizes in the *TAC* judgment, n 73 above, at [106]. The Court is charged with the task of protecting fundamental rights and, in doing so, is empowered to make any order that is just and equitable in terms of s 172(1)(b) of the Constitution.

126 See Wesson, 2004: 307 and Swart, 2005: 240.

127 See Sunstein, 2001a; Roux, 2003; and Wesson, 2004.

128 Roux, 2003 at 97; Wesson 2004 at 293.

minimum core obligation. Wesson identifies this extra element as the notion that programmes must not exclude a significant sector of society.

What then is meant by a significant sector of society? Wesson takes this to mean 'groups of people who cannot be expected to meet their socio-economic needs independently on the basis of their own resources'. The mere fact that a group is vulnerable, however, does not mean that it automatically has a claim to public resources.

What is required therefore is a contextual examination of whether the group in question . . . has a legitimate claim to inclusion in a socio-economic programme from which others already benefit. This, it is submitted, is the paradigm form in which socio-economic claims will be brought before the courts. In practice, it means that the state must account for, or explain why, it has allocated resources in a particular manner.[129]

Roux sees this as akin to the enquiry the court conducts in cases relating to unfair discrimination.[130] Such an analysis is focused wholly on whether a social programme unreasonably excludes a particular group in society.

The Court's assessment is thus not directed at such issues as whether the state might have adopted less restrictive measures in pursuing the programme in question but at whether the claimant group has an equal or better claim to inclusion relative to other groups that have been catered to.[131]

I agree with these authors that administrative law analysis alone cannot provide a full explanation of the socio-economic rights jurisprudence of the Court thus far. However, I do not believe their approach (I shall refer to it as the 'equality approach') towards these decisions provides the best understanding of the court's reasoning; nor do I believe it provides the basis for developing a coherent and substantive analytical framework for the interpretation of the socio-economic rights in the Constitution. In particular, this approach tends to conflate questions concerning who is entitled to benefit from socio-economic rights (the question of scope) from the question of what individuals are entitled to (the question of content). In the last section of this chapter, I shall endeavour to show how the reasonableness approach of the Court has led to a similar confusion in the *Khosa* case.

5.2 The deficiencies of the equality approach

According to the equality approach, the ratio for the decision in *Grootboom* is that government programmes should not exclude a significant sector of society.

---

[129] Ibid: 293. The last sentence represents a misconception concerning the enquiry in socio-economic rights cases. See Chap 6 and the statement by the Court in *TAC*, n 73 above, at [38] that its judgments may 'in fact have budgetary implications but are not in themselves directed at rearranging budgets'.   [130] A similar approach seems to be taken by Fredman, 2005.
[131] Roux, 2003 at 97.

Yet, the point about the government's housing programme in *Grootboom* is not that it *excluded* those in the Grootboom community: in fact, they would have eventually been eligible under such a programme for housing provision. In this respect, the Grootboom community was no different to many others in South Africa who were waiting for government housing. The problem in *Grootboom* was rather that the existing programme did not adequately address their urgent need in the short term to be provided with shelter (though it would address more extensive needs of theirs in the longer term).[132] The government programme at the time was effectively silent about their situation.

The problem in the *Grootboom* case was thus not an unreasonable exclusion: it was inadequate provision. The same is true of the *TAC* case. The problem in that case was not fundamentally one of discrimination; it was a lack of recognition that the government had an obligation to devise a programme for all South Africans to prevent mother-to-child transmission of HIV. Since the government recognized no obligation to provide nevirapine, in its view, it could offer the drug in whatever way it deemed fit (if it decided to do so at all). The core of the *TAC* case was not therefore a problem of unfair discrimination: it was a problem of failing to recognize the content of the duty imposed by the Constitution upon the government.

The 'equality approach' thus seeks to focus the whole enquiry upon the group that is excluded. It takes its inspiration from the non-discrimination provisions of the constitution. These provisions generally, however, focus upon discreet groups of people that have been disadvantaged as a result of characteristics such as race, sex, and sexual orientation.[133] The groups are, in general, readily identifiable and the cases, in general, would be concerned with unjustifiable exclusions of person on grounds of a particular characteristic that marks them out. The non-discrimination provisions also function in an essentially comparative manner: we compare the benefits and burdens of groups in society with one another.

Cases that fall to be determined in accordance with the socio-economic rights provisions of the Constitution are different. They are not essentially comparative: rather, they relate to defining the nature of the entitlements contained in these provisions and the corresponding obligations of the state. They are concerned primarily with *what* the state is required to do to realize the entitlements in question rather than with *who* is the beneficiary of the entitlements.

Once the entitlements have been defined, it is possible to define a group of individuals whose entitlements are not being met; however, the definition of the vulnerable group is parasitic upon the definition of vulnerability. The group is only constituted once a definition of the entitlement is forthcoming. The content

---

[132] Perhaps sensitive to this problem, Wesson attempts to qualify his view by claiming that exclusion means 'not being specifically or adequately catered for' (2004 at 293).

[133] Section 9 outlines all the prohibited grounds of discrimination. The test whether differentiation amounts to unfair discrimination is based upon whether the differential treatment is based upon an attribute or characteristic of persons in such a manner that impairs the fundamental dignity of those persons: see s 9 of the Constitution and the equality test outlined in *Harksen v Lane* 1998 (1) SA 300 (CC) at [42]–[54].

of the right thus determines those who are entitled to claim under its provisions. Thus, if there is an entitlement to be free from starvation, then it is those who are starving that can claim the entitlement.[134]

Wesson's approach requires that we be able to define the vulnerable groups independently of a consideration of the content of the rights. This leads ultimately to incoherence since the constitution of the group is dependent upon a conception of the content of the rights.

Moreover, in a case such as *Grootboom*, understanding that the class of beneficiaries includes all those unable to meet their needs through their own resources is not helpful: the problem in *Grootboom* was rather that there are varying levels of need amongst those within this class. The government's programme in *Grootboom* was in fact designed to meet the needs of the class identified by Wesson (otherwise, the individuals could have provided housing for themselves); it failed, however, to cater to a sub-group of this class whose needs were particularly urgent. Again, we see the failure of the equality approach to adequately explain *Grootboom*, as it is a conception of interests and the relative urgency of interests that is important.

The deeper reason for the problems faced by the equality approach can be seen most clearly in cases where there are no existing entitlements in the country: no one, prior to *Grootboom*, had a right even to temporary shelter in South Africa. Similarly, there is currently no universal right in South Africa being implemented by the state to a subsistence level of food. The problem in such cases is that the equality approach simply provides no guidance: since no one has such entitlements, arguably the state is not discriminating against any group and the demands of equal treatment are met. Equality as a comparative notion has difficulty where there is no standard against which to compare. Part of the task of socio-economic rights is to provide the standard which defines the entitlements of individuals to certain goods within a society. Only a far richer notion of equality together with a conception of value (as has been outlined in Chapters 1 to 3) can generate normative conclusions concerning the content of socio-economic rights.[135] That normative content, I have argued, in turn involves giving priority to those whose needs are most urgent.[136]

---

[134] Since Wesson's proposal is based upon a notion of 'vulnerable groups', such groups are going to be defined in terms of vulnerability. Vulnerability will in turn be based on a conception of interests and urgency. It seems likely as a result that the approach will be consonant with the conclusions of the minimum core approach discussed in Chap 6.

[135] Any approach based on achieving substantive equality needs to provide a conception concerning what needs to be equalized. There is a robust debate in political philosophy on this issue and proponents of the various views (welfare, resources, and capabilities) could arguably provide a standard as to what should be equalized. The standard of provision would arguably on most views exceed that required by socio-economic rights. See Chap 2 for reasons why I have chosen to focus on the minimal implications of the principle of equal importance, rather than developing a full theory of substantive equality.

[136] Ultimately, Wesson's objection (2004: 305) to the minimum core approach seems to be that he is uncomfortable with judges making decisions concerning constitutional priorities such as the

To be meaningful, the equality approach, like the reasonableness approach, would require more development. However, one of the central difficulties with using the equality approach is its attempt to reduce questions concerning the *nature* of entitlements to questions concerning the beneficiaries of those entitlements. Equality jurisprudence is fundamentally about *who* has access to a certain level or standard of entitlement. That standard is defined and then we consider the justification for inclusions and exclusions. Socio-economic rights in the Constitution already define who is entitled to them: it is 'everyone'. The general question in relation to the socio-economic rights provisions relates to *what* 'everyone' in society is entitled to. These are distinct questions which should not be conflated.

The reasonableness approach of the Court was initially proposed as a response to the what-question: determining the content of these rights. However, recently, the Constitutional Court has attempted to use the reasonableness approach to propose an answer to the question of the beneficiaries of these rights as well as the question of their content. The next section involves a consideration of the *Khosa* case, which further explains and tries to disentangle the confusing range of issues that the Constitutional Court now attempts to deal with under the notion of 'reasonableness'.

6 *Khosa*: Reasonableness and the Confusion of Scope and Content

6.1 The decision

Khosa v Minister of Social Development[137] concerned a number of Mozambican citizens ('the applicants') who had acquired the status of permanent residents in South Africa after living in the country since 1980. All of these people were destitute and thus would have been entitled to pension grants as well as other social assistance grants—such as child-support grants—but for the fact that they were not South African citizens.[138] The applicants challenged the constitutionality of prevailing legislation (the Social Assistance Act 59 of 1992) that limited social assistance grants to South African citizens. They argued that section 27 of the Constitution guaranteed the right to social security for 'everyone'. This, they argued, included permanent residents and thus the legislation excluding this group was unconstitutional.

'balance between shorts and long-term aims (in the context of housing)'. Apart from contradicting the *Grootboom* decision, his view, in the absence of a viable alternative, fails to provide any real role for the judiciary in socio-economic rights cases (which, I argue in Chap 6, is precisely to scrutinize government decision-making for its conformity with constitutional priorities) and would effectively render such rights non-justiciable.

[137] 2004 (6) SA 505 (CC) ('*Khosa*').   [138] Ibid at [3]–[4].

After confirming the approach towards the content of rights in *Grootboom* and *TAC*, Mokgoro J, writing for the majority, went on to consider the beneficiaries of the right to have access to social security. The Court reasoned that certain rights such as political rights (section 19 of the Constitution) and the right to have access to land have been expressly limited to citizens (section 25(5) of the Constitution). However, section 27 does not contain such a limitation—it applies to 'everyone'. Since there was no indication that section 27 was limited only to citizens, Mokgoro J held that the word 'everyone' could not be construed as referring only to citizens.[139]

The Court then raised the question whether the exclusion of permanent residents from having access to social assistance grants was reasonable. In reaching a conclusion on this matter the Court considered a number of factors: 'these include, the purpose served by social security, the impact of the exclusion on permanent residents and the relevance of the citizenship requirement to that purpose'.[140]

Mokgoro J held that the reason for the inclusion of a right to social security was that 'as a society we value human beings and want to ensure that people are afforded their basic needs'.[141] Such a purpose included within its ambit the needs of non-citizens.

The majority of the Court then found that there were no good grounds for differentiating between citizens and permanent residents in relation to social assistance benefits. Permanent residents have made South Africa their home and, like citizens, have lived in the country legally for a considerable length of time. In most respects, permanent residents also have similar obligations to citizens; it thus seems unclear why they should not be entitled to similar benefits.[142] The cost to the state, on the evidence, also did not seem to place an inordinate burden on it.[143] The impact, however, of the exclusion of permanent residents forces them into relationships of dependency with their families, friends, and communities. For them, 'the denial of the right is total and the consequences of the denial are grave. They are relegated to the margins of society and are deprived of what may be essential to enable them to enjoy other rights vested in them under the Constitution.'[144] In light of these considerations, the Court concluded that 'the exclusion of permanent residents is inconsistent with section 27 of the Constitution'.[145] In light of this, the Court ordered that the words 'or permanent residents' be read into the legislation (after the citizenship requirement) so as to allow for benefits to be allocated to permanent residents.

Ngcobo J wrote a minority judgment in which he found the exclusion of permanent residents to be justifiable. He explicitly recognized that this was a case concerning scope rather than content and that the question was therefore how this case should be decided. He considered several possibilities but ultimately

---

[139] Ibid at [47].   [140] Ibid at [49].   [141] Ibid at [52].   [142] Ibid at [59].
[143] Ibid at [60]–[62].   [144] Ibid at [77].   [145] Ibid at [85].

commenced his analysis with the right in section 27 that he agreed is available to everyone. In order to restrict the class of person to whom the right is available, he conducted an analysis in terms of the general limitations clause (section 36).[146] For a range of reasons Ngcobo J found that the requirements of section 36 were met: the crucial question ultimately for Ngcobo J was whether everyone within the state's borders is entitled to the socio-economic rights in the Constitution. He found that the state has advanced 'compelling reasons for limiting the benefits to citizens. The need to reduce the rising costs of operating social security systems, the need to prevent the availability of social security benefits from constituting an incentive for immigration and the need to encourage immigrants to be self-sufficient.'[147]

6.2 Reasonableness: confusing distinct issues?

The reasoning of the majority in *Khosa* is curious: the reasonableness approach that had previously been applied to the question of the normative content of the socio-economic rights is here applied to the question of who is entitled to such rights. The sheer vagueness of reasonableness suggests that it can provide the solution to a range of enquiries. However, the overarching nature of the enquiry can lead to confusion between distinct issues. Being concerned with the beneficiaries of rights, *Khosa* would be more of a candidate for the equality approach discussed above. The nature of the case explains why the court had difficulty in deciding whether the case should turn on section 9 considerations or section 27 considerations.[148] The case was effectively a section 9 case: a discreet group could be identified who were excluded from a statutory scheme.

A closer analysis of the reasoning in this case compared to that of *Grootboom* and *TAC* exhibits their differences. In the latter cases, the holding appeared to be that the subjects of the rights are entitled to reasonable government action to realize their socio-economic rights. The structure of reasoning would be that X (the subject of the right) is entitled to Y (reasonable government action) from Z (the government). In *Khosa*, the question concerned the ambit of X: who is entitled to the reasonable government action? The court answers this by saying that the enquiry concerning Y (what one is entitled to) will determine X (who is the subject of the right). The majority in *Khosa* thus appears to conflate two separate questions: the question of scope and the question of content.[149] Being entitled to the government implementing programmes to combat HIV, for instance, does not tell us who is entitled to benefit from those programmes. Are only citizens entitled to benefit?

---

[146] 2004 (6) SA 505 (CC) ('*Khosa*'), at [113].   [147] Ibid at [126].

[148] The court effectively finds that unfair discrimination exists in this case: see para [77].

[149] Iles, 2004: 464 argues that the difference impacts upon whether the Court should have decided the case under the internal limitations clause or the general limitations clause.

It is no doubt true that there is a connection between the questions of scope and content. As has been argued in Chapters 1 to 3, the content of a right relates to the fundamental interests that a being has. The subjects of a right would logically seem to extend to all those who have these fundamental interests. From the perspective of recipience, this account is correct: beings with a subjective consciousness will have fundamental interests, and those fundamental interests will ultimately impact upon the content of their rights.

However, from the perspective of the agents who are responsible for realizing these rights, matters are not so clear. Our world and our communities have been divided into spheres of responsibility: South Africa is responsible for its citizens, Botswana for its citizens, and Namibia for its citizens. There may be no deep ethical basis to this division of labour between countries and communities; though, it may represent a method through which rights can best be realized.[150] The rights of non-citizens may thus exist but not be claimable against the state in which they are non-citizens. In a world of bounded communities, to determine when a non-citizen has a claim against the state in which he is resident raises a set of practical and normative considerations relating to how we determine the boundaries of entitlements within our communities. These may in turn be wholly separate considerations from the question of what these beings are entitled to.

It is consequently important to distinguish between considerations that relate to the beneficiaries of a right and those relating to content. Contribution to a community does not seem to have an impact upon content yet it may have an impact on scope. By conflating the reasonableness enquiries, we may be led to think that contribution to a community grants a greater content to one person's rights over another. Rendering reasonableness the basis for decisions on quite distinct issues thus can lead to a conflation of these issues.

6.3 Reasonableness and the purpose of section 27

The focus on reasonableness also distracts from the true ethical base of the court's decision-making. The Court in *Khosa* located its reasoning within the context of the purpose of section 27, which was said to involve the protection of the basic needs of people within South Africa. The fact that the Court indicates that there is a universalist justification for these rights could, however, form the basis of an extension of such rights further to include all people within the borders of South Africa, including illegal immigrants and temporary residents.[151] The court in *Khosa* did not discuss this issue in detail but indicated that, given the tenuous

---

[150] This is debatable but I raise it as a possible argument here. See, for instance, Goodin 1988a and some of the comments in Chap 2.

[151] The decision is also criticized by Williams, 2005: 468–1 for failing to provide an adequate basis for distinguishing between the entitlements of permanent residents, temporary residents, and illegal residents.

nature of the links these people have to the country, there may be a justification for denying them social assistance benefits. In relation to illegal immigrants, this seems clearly justifiable, as it would make no sense for the law to regard their presence as illegal in one respect and then to provide them with social assistance benefits, thus treating them as legal in another respect.

In relation to temporary residents, matters are not so simple. Temporary residents often become permanent residents and legally reside in the country. As such, if they become destitute whilst in the country, it is unclear why the temporary nature of their stay should in any way entail that they are less needy than others. If the criterion upon which benefits is distributed is one of need and dignity, then the automatic exclusion of temporary residents does not appear to be clearly justifiable.

This reasoning applies *a fortiori* in the case of particularly urgent needs such as those suffering from acute health conditions. Whilst social assistance benefits may be said to be linked to permanence and one's contribution to a community, health care is a requirement of all who fall within the borders of a country. Anyone anywhere can become ill at any time. To allow someone to die or suffer merely because they are temporarily or even illegally resident in a country runs counter to basic universalist principles of political morality relating to need and vulnerability.[152] Many societies, such as those in Europe, provide medical assistance for anyone who falls upon hard times within their countries. This is not dependent on their status in the country (for example, as a tourist). Common humanity and solidarity dictate that a sick person should be treated irrespective of who they are or why they are in a country.[153] At international law, this principle extends to the obligation on an army to treat the wounded enemy soldiers it captures.[154] Thus, it is submitted, in the case of particularly urgent needs such as access to treatment for acute health conditions (even if not in the case of social assistance grants), the judgment in *Khosa* should be extended to all persons within South Africa irrespective of their status.[155]

---

[152] Chapters 1 to 3 provide a justification for such a view or, alternatively, for the idea that the basis of this duty lies in human vulnerability, see Goodin, 1998.

[153] Where a person suffers from a chronic condition or one that requires medical treatment over a long period, it may be argued that this kind of care is similar to a social benefit and that the same legal regime should apply: treatment of such conditions should only be available to those with more permanent connections to the political community concerned. Tourists and illegal immigrants may well not qualify for such treatment.

[154] Article 3(2) of the Geneva Convention Relative to the Treatment of Prisoners of War. The same is true of prisoners, for whom society often has little sympathy. See the discussion in the case *Van Biljon v Minister of Correctional Services* 1997(4) SA 441 (C).

[155] The question of scope also includes the question of our duties to non-human animals. Animals under human control may well have a right to medical treatment from those within whose care and control they fall. It could also be argued that the term 'everyone' in s 27(1) should include non-human animals to the extent that they are capable of having these rights attributed to them. Currently, the scope of the rights in the Constitution are not recognized as extending beyond human beings, a position which the argument in this book suggests should be challenged.

6.4 Reasonableness and the limitation of rights

Finally, placing too much store on the question of reasonableness leads to some difficult structural questions in the Constitution relating to limitations. This arises from the fact that the term 'reasonable' is used both in the internal limitation clauses of sections 26(2) and 27(2) and in the general limitations clause of section 36. The *Khosa* decision considered the question whether it is possible to distinguish between the enquiries in these different contexts. After raising this question, both the majority and the minority declined to decide it.[156]

It is unlikely that the indeterminate notion of reasonableness can be shown to bear an inherently different meaning in these two contexts.[157] It would also be extremely confusing for these notions to bear entirely different meanings. However, in my view, some guidance can be given as to the distinction between these two enquiries by considering the differing functions of the internal limitation and the general limitations clause. The internal limitation is focused on a particular right: for example, the right to have access to adequate health-care services. It is suggested that the enquiry requires us to consider whether, in the context of this particular right, and the competing priorities in relation to this particular right, the measures taken by the State are reasonable.

Section 36, on the other hand, involves a more global enquiry. It requires us to situate the right to have access to health-care services and the measures adopted by the state against other rights that people have in the Bill of Rights and the obligations that they impose on the state. It allows for the consideration of legitimate government purposes other than those relating to the particular right that is in focus, and requires a broader consideration of the impact of a measure on the society beyond the particular sphere of a particular right.

This is an important and significant distinction. The Bill of Rights requires us first to focus on a particular context—of health care for instance—and to consider the interests at stake in this context, and the measures that the State is required to adopt to alleviate suffering in this area. Policies and decisions can be adopted in this context that may address the problems relating to health care or fail to do so. *TAC* is an example of a case where there was no need for a wider enquiry: the state failed to adopt a reasonable (or even rational) policy relating to the health care of individuals, and there were virtually no ramifications for other policy areas because of the negligible costs of rolling out a drug that had been offered to the

---

[156] *Khosa*, n 137 above at [83]–[84] and [105]–[106]. The question raised in the text arises in connection with the positive obligations flowing from socio-economic rights. In *Jaftha v Schoeman* 2005 (2) SA 140 (CC) at [34], the Court found a role for the general limitations clause in socio-economic rights cases by finding that 'any measure which permits a person to be deprived of existing access to adequate housing' would need to be justified in terms of the general limitations clause.

[157] For alternative constructions of the relationship between s 36 and the internal limitations of socio-economic rights, see Liebenberg, 2005a: 33–54 to 33–56; De Vos, 1997: 79–80; Pieterse, 2004: 41–8; and Iles, 2004: 455–7.

state free of charge. The failure to adopt a comprehensive programme for rolling out the drug was therefore patently unreasonable.

However, the existence of the section 36 enquiry suggests that a consideration of the health-care context alone may not be enough. Given the intersections between rights, and the links between rights and other governmental purposes, it may, for instance, be that health-care rights will have to be limited for the purpose of ensuring adequate housing for all. This is where section 36 may assist the Court in determining the reasonableness of governmental action considered holistically.[158]

7 Conclusion

The problems with the reasonableness approach of the Constitutional Court can be summarized as follows. First, reasonableness alone lacks the content necessary to make determinations on matters concerning socio-economic rights. It thus leads to decisions that are not adequately justified. Secondly, it deflects the focus of the constitutional enquiry from the urgent interests at stake in these cases and allows these to be overshadowed by a general balancing of multiple considerations. Thirdly, the contextual nature of a determination of reasonableness requires certain a-contextual standards or principles to determine how it is to be applied in particular cases. The deeper foundations of the content the Court has ascribed to reasonableness are not transparent and often appear to be stipulations. Fourthly, the vagueness of the notion does not help provide any certainty as to the nature of the government's obligations in terms of the Constitution. That leaves other branches of government without clear guidance as to the nature of their obligations to realize socio-economic rights and, similarly, impacts upon how judges in lower courts adjudicate particular cases. Fifthly, reasonableness does not provide a principled criterion to determine the circumstances in which it is legitimate for judges to interfere with the decisions of other branches of government. Finally, as a result of its vagueness, reasonableness is used to perform distinct normative tasks which are often conflated, thus leading to errors in decision-making and a complex, confusing array of enquiries being included within its ambit.

This discussion of *Grootboom*, *TAC*, and *Khosa* has sought to highlight the fact that in order to remedy these problems, it will be necessary to pay greater attention to the content of subsistence rights. Providing content to these rights will require reference to the reasons for including socio-economic rights within the Constitution. The development of such an approach requires a political philosophy of socio-economic rights.

---

[158] See also the discussion in Chap 6 relating to the objection concerning the particular as opposed to the holistic focus of socio-economic rights claims.

In the next chapter, I shall seek to show how the political philosophy that I have defended in the first half of this book can be used to work out a viable and robust approach to the adjudication of socio-economic rights. Such an approach will place the interests at stake clearly in view and question the extent to which government policy succeeds in realizing these interests. The 'interests-based' approach will also lead to the important recognition that socio-economic rights protect interests of differing degrees of urgency for individuals, and that the more urgent interests are to be prioritized by the government in their policies.

6

Political Philosophy in Action: Developing the Minimum Core Approach to Socio-Economic Rights

1 Introduction

In the last chapter, I took issue with the current approach of the South African Constitutional Court to the interpretation of socio-economic rights. The Court, it was shown, has generally adopted a purposive approach to interpreting the Bill of Rights; yet, when it came to developing an approach to interpreting socio-economic rights, the Court has shown little willingness to engage with the reasons for their inclusion in the Bill of Rights. It has largely, as a result, failed to provide very much content to these rights. In this chapter, I hope to put forward an alternative approach to interpreting socio-economic rights that is explicitly derived from considering the justification for recognizing these rights that is defended in this book.

The purposive approach to interpretation requires some background theory that explicates the normative underpinnings of fundamental rights. In the first three chapters of this book, I developed a political justification for socio-economic rights. That justification is a general philosophical one that is applicable to a wide range of societies. The first task of this chapter is thus to demonstrate its suitability as a background theory upon which to build a jurisprudential approach towards interpreting fundamental rights and socio-economic rights in particular.

I shall then attempt to draw out the implications of the political philosophy I have developed for legal doctrine by demonstrating that the philosophical theory supports 'the minimum core approach' to interpreting socio-economic rights that has been advocated by some at the international level. The foundations of the approach have not been attended to in much detail and I shall seek to offer a more adequate justification for the approach. The approach has also been seriously underdeveloped and this has led to several objections being lodged against it, many of these being contained in judgments of the South African Constitutional Court. In offering responses to these objections, I hope to develop and modify this approach. The focus will remain on South Africa in this chapter, though the approach that is advocated towards the interpretation of socio-economic rights is applicable to other domestic jurisdictions, and can also assist in the interpretation of socio-economic rights at the international level. The whole discussion will be designed to show that the modified minimum core approach that I advocate offers a well-motivated, robust, and useful analytical framework for interpreting socio-economic rights. Most importantly, it can also serve to realize the important ethical purposes that lie behind the recognition of such rights: ensuring that each person is able to have access to the necessary prerequisites for living a life of value.[1]

2 Linking Political Philosophy and Legal Doctrine

Thus far, the theory that I have proposed in Chapters 1 to 3 offers a political philosophical approach towards fundamental rights. It is not immediately obvious how such a theory relates to the interpretation of constitutional rights. In this section, I shall argue that several features of the political philosophy of rights developed in these earlier chapters render it particularly apt for the purpose of interpreting fundamental rights in a constitution.

First, any diverse society will include within it many different understandings of what it is to live a good life. An attempt to impose a detailed and comprehensive theory of value on the society would be likely to meet with significant opposition, and to cause social strife. In South Africa, for instance, the apartheid government attempted to impose its own specific conception of the good life on the whole society by, for instance, educating people in what it regarded as a superior language (Afrikaans) and attempting to promote its own brand of Christianity in the education system. Some of these measures led to the Soweto uprising of 1976 and ultimately played a part in the demise of apartheid.

The theory of value that I have developed attempts to capture two broad general sources of value—experiences and purposes—that are applicable to a wide range of diverse beings. Further shared interests can be identified through considering the general necessary conditions that such beings require in order to have positive experiences and to fulfil their purposes. A 'thin theory' of the good is proposed that only partially informs us about the good for each individual. This in turn allows for diversity in the content of the experiences and purposes individuals value. The theory aims to be generally applicable in that the fundamental interests

---

[1] The political philosophy I employ suggests that non-human animals must also be guaranteed these necessary prerequisites for living lives of value to them. Whilst our obligations towards non-human animals may in general require us not to interfere with them, there may be certain positive obligations upon a state as well. For instance, animal shelters may have to be funded by the state, and national parks be established to allow animals their own space in which to lead their own lives. The subject of my book involves developing an approach towards interpreting and enforcing socio-economic rights. In most countries in the world, such rights are in general limited to human beings and the focus of this chapter will henceforth be upon human beings. Whilst my theory shows that this is an unjustified limitation, a detailed working out of the theory's implications for non-human animals must await another occasion.

it identifies are those that are shared by a wide range of diverse individuals. The theory also aims to be such that it can command widespread agreement despite the diversity of individuals it applies to. As such, it appears wholly appropriate for application to a diverse society like South Africa whose Bill of Rights demonstrates a recognition that the document was written for a society in which there are diverse forms of the good.[2]

Secondly, the theory I have proposed provides principled criteria as to which values should determine how beings are to be treated. Value resides in general characteristics of beings rather than whether they belong to a particular race or sex. The theory I have developed attempts to explain and justify its decision to attribute rights to sentient beings and thus does not rely on an arbitrary categorization to determine the scope of its application. Most countries have in recent years attempted to move away from arbitrary categorizations and to prohibit unfair discrimination.

The essence of apartheid in South Africa, for instance, involved classifying individuals into different racial groups and determining their entitlements on this basis. It often invoked pseudo-religious justifications for doing so. Fundamental to the rejection of apartheid was the recognition that the treatment of persons by a state should not vary in relation to irrelevant personal characteristics such as the colour of one's skin. Underlying this ethical position lies the recognition that it is not justifiable for a society to treat beings differently on the basis of any characteristic that cannot be shown to be relevant to the course of action embarked upon. The theory I propose provides a deep normative base upon which to reject unfair discrimination. This also allows the theory to provide a principled basis upon which to critique a constitutional order that allows for differential treatment on arbitrary grounds: perhaps an important blindspot today, for instance, remains the failure to extend anti-discrimination provisions to other species.[3]

Thirdly, an adequate theory dealing with the entitlements conferred on people by socio-economic rights must be able to deal with the different levels of individual need. The theory I have proposed distinguishes between interests with differing levels of urgency and provides a principled understanding of how to determine two different thresholds of need. As such, the process of determining the content of these rights can be sensitive to the differing positions of individuals in a society, and the obligations of the state can vary accordingly.

South Africa, as with many other countries in the world, has a very significant divide between rich and poor.[4] Those who are 'very poor' comprise about 50 per cent of the South African population (23 million people), earning less than ZAR353 per month (about £30). A further 16.6 per cent of the population earns

---

[2] See, for instance, ss 15, 16, and 18 that protect rights to freedom of religion, speech, and association, rights which protect the ability of persons to live diverse lives.

[3] See Singer, 1995, who shows convincingly that discrimination on the grounds of species is very much akin to discrimination on grounds of race or sex.

[4] Given South Africa's history, that divide resulted in large measure from the apartheid policies of deliberately privileging whites over blacks. Whites were provided with better education, and offered

roughly three times more than the average person who is 'very poor'. These two groups together collectively earn 10.6 per cent of the income in South Africa. The next economic bracket (16.6 per cent of the population) earns 17.2 per cent of the income. Finally, the highest earning 16.6 per cent of the population earns 72 per cent of the income.[5] These statistics make it clear that there is a high concentration of wealth in the hands of a small percentage of the population, but they also serve to show that there are different economic positions occupied by different groups in the country. If we were to break down those classed as 'very poor', the situation of individuals and households would also differ in terms of their capacity to meet the two thresholds that I have outlined in Chapter 1.

Fourthly, the theory I have proposed places at its centre the notion that a society is required to treat each being with equal importance. That idea is also conjoined with the theory of value I have developed to give some determinate content to what that 'importance' can be said to consist in. Constitutional interpretation generally involves invoking reference to core constitutional values such as dignity, equality, and freedom.[6] The theory I have developed could thus provide the basis for giving more determinate content to values such as 'dignity' and help to trace the steps from such values to more concrete conclusions.

Fifthly, one of the important formal features of my theory is the distinction between the notion of conditional and unconditional rights, and the desirability of distinguishing the two phases of an enquiry into the content of rights. In general, constitutional law has had to grapple with how to capture in legal doctrine the idea that fundamental rights are not absolute. In many constitutions, particularly those adopted recently, this idea is captured through the inclusion of clauses limiting fundamental rights.

In the South African bill of rights, for example, the constitutional analysis of fundamental rights proceeds in two stages. First, there is the question as to whether a right included in the Bill of Rights has been violated. This enquiry effectively involves consideration of the scope and content of the conditional right in question. Secondly, if there has been a violation of the conditional right, it must then be determined whether the violation constitutes a justifiable limitation of that right.[7] That question involves an overarching enquiry as to whether a limitation is 'reasonable and justifiable in an open and democratic society based on human dignity, equality and freedom'.[8] This enquiry is a general one as to the unconditional obligations of the state, and involves reference to a variety of relevant factors.[9]

---

many more opportunities for advancement than black people were, which translated into general economic privilege.

[5] Terreblanche, 2002: 36.   [6] See s 1(a) of the South African Constitution.

[7] It seems that this two-stage analysis occurs in the German Constitution (as well as in Canada). The approach I have taken is similar to that adopted by Alexy in relation to German constitutional rights. See Alexy, 2002 at 345–6: '[I]t is a hallmark of all balancing models that more is *prima facie* required than definitively.'   [8] Section 36 of the Constitution.

[9] These factors include: 'the nature of the right; the importance of the purpose of the limitation; the nature and extent of the limitation; the relation between the limitation and its purpose; and the less restrictive means to achieve the purpose.'

The reasons for distinguishing between conditional and unconditional rights provide a powerful normative underpinning for this two-stage structure for thinking of rights. Moreover, the factors and proposed framework discussed in Chapter 3 for making decisions about unconditional obligations provide further guidance to the enquiry concerning when the limitation of fundamental rights is justifiable. The dual structure of my theory is thus congruent with the manner in which a rights enquiry should be structured in constitutional law, and can help develop an understanding of the substantive issues at stake there.

In relation to socio-economic rights in particular, this structure has a specific relevance. Consider, for instance, the main provision relating to the right to housing in the South African Bill of Rights. It reads as follows:

26. (1) Everyone has the right to have access to adequate housing.
    (2) The state must take reasonable legislative and other measures within its available resources to achieve the progressive realisation of this right.

The first sub-section can be regarded as being akin to a conditional right in my classification. It represents a statement that individuals have important interests in having access to housing and that the state has an obligation to protect this interest. The second sub-section, however, recognizes that the right in sub-section (1) cannot confer an immediate entitlement that each person should have a house. That section provides an understanding that there are constraints upon what can be achieved in realizing the conditional right in sub-section (1) and provides an indication of at least one major reason that can justify a failure to provide for the interests protected there: namely, resource scarcity. The general limitations clause in section 36(1) allows for additional factors to be brought in when determining the unconditional obligations of the state. Again, the theory that I have proposed fits well with the particular structure of subsistence rights in the South African constitution[10] and provides an understanding of several important factors that must be taken into account in any assessment of the state's unconditional obligations.

Finally, the theory I have proposed in both its structure and its substance does not distinguish sharply between civil-political rights and socio-economic rights. That distinction was in large measure a political one, embodied in the fact that the International Bill of Rights is split between a Covenant on Civil and Political Rights and a Covenant on Economic, Social and Cultural Rights. My theory places the focus upon the interests which lie behind each right, and it is evident that the interests protected by both sets of rights have a similar level of importance for human beings.

In recent years, courts and international bodies have emphasized the important links between fundamental rights. Reflecting these developments in thinking, the South African Constitution, for instance, was drafted in such a way that there is

---

[10] The internal limitation in s 26(2) is similar to that included in the International Covenant.

no neat division between civil-political rights and socio-economic rights in the Bill of Rights. Though the socio-economic rights are generally qualified, so too are some of the civil and political rights.[11] The Constitutional Court has also emphasized the indivisibility of these rights in a number of its judgments: '[t]he proposition that rights are interrelated and are all equally important is not merely a theoretical postulate. The concept has immense human and practical significance in a society founded on human dignity, equality and freedom.'[12] Thus, the political philosophy that lies behind fundamental rights must be able to explain the source of this interconnectedness and allow for an understanding of the deeper values involved. That is yet one more reason why the normative theory I have proposed is well suited to assist in developing a compelling and viable interpretation of constitutional rights. I now turn to the task of considering in more detail the implications of this philosophical theory for the development of a legal framework for the interpretation of socio-economic rights.

3 The Case for a Minimum Core Approach

3.1 The United Nations and the Minimum Core Approach

The United Nations Committee on Economic, Social and Cultural Rights (the 'United Nations Committee') has over the past 20 years been developing an understanding of the content of socio-economic rights, and the obligations that they impose upon states. The development of this content has largely taken place through the Committee's General Comments. General Comment No 3 of 1990 contains the general principles that govern the obligations of state parties to the International Covenant on Economic, Social and Cultural Rights.[13] This approach has been developed, modified, and concretized in subsequent general comments in relation to particular rights in the Covenant. This section shall consider some of the main features of the Committee's approach with a particular focus on the notion of a minimum core obligation.

The UN Committee has provided various categorizations of the obligations imposed by socio-economic rights on state parties. In General Comment 3, it recognized the distinction between obligations of conduct and obligations of result. Obligations of conduct require the taking of action 'reasonably calculated to realise the enjoyment of a particular right'. Obligations of result require '[s]tates to achieve specific targets to satisfy a detailed substantive standard'.[14] Obligations of

---

[11] See, for instance, the right to free speech in s 16.

[12] *Grootboom* 2001 (1) SA 46 (CC) at [83]. See also [23].

[13] Henceforth referred to as 'the Covenant'. See the General Comment Collection at <http://www.unhchr.ch/tbs/doc.nsf>.

[14] See Maastricht Guidelines on Violations of Economic, Social and Cultural Rights in Chapman and Russell, 2002: 345.

result effectively focus on the state of affairs that is sought to be achieved; obligations of conduct upon the actions necessary to reach the state of affairs. In relation to the theory developed in this book, the conditional right may often be seen as imposing an obligation of result: a certain state of affairs must be realized. When we come to translate this into an unconditional obligation, we need to consider the conduct necessary to reach that state of affairs. Consequently, it seems that in practice socio-economic rights typically impose both obligations of conduct and obligations of result.

General Comment 3 also recognized an obligation upon states to take steps through deliberate, concrete, and targeted action towards the fulfilment of the rights which must be accomplished as 'expeditiously and effectively as possible'.[15] There is also an obligation to avoid deliberately retrogressive measures. Any retrogressive measures would involve the 'most careful consideration and would need to be fully justified by reference to the totality of the rights provided for in the Covenant and in the context of the full use of the maximum available resources'.[16]

In more recent general comments, the committee has adopted and modified Henry Shue's framework concerning the range of obligations that flow from fundamental rights. This analysis was discussed briefly in Chapter 3, but involves the recognition that three key obligations can be said to flow from abstract socio-economic rights: obligations to respect, protect, and fulfil the rights. In some of the general comments, the committee has split the obligation to fulfil into two parts: an obligation to facilitate and an obligation to provide.[17]

It is important to recognize that obligations to respect, protect, and fulfil only make sense against the background of a conception of the content of these rights. Thus, I have argued that a society is required to guarantee individuals the general necessary conditions to be able to realize a diversity of purposes. An obvious implication of such a guarantee is that where people already reach this threshold, the state must not deprive individuals of these conditions. Similarly, it must ensure that third parties do not jeopardize people's access to these conditions; and finally, it will be necessary to provide these conditions where they do not exist. These obligations thus flow from a conception of content, something not always entirely clear in the Committee's analysis.[18] They also represent a more concrete specification of the abstract rights, the obligations necessary to give practical effect to them.[19]

Perhaps, one of the most important features of the approach adopted in the 3rd General Comment has been the adoption of what may be termed the 'minimum core approach' to socio-economic rights. This approach, it will be argued, provides the key to providing clear content to these rights, and ensuring that they

---

[15] General Comment No 3 at [2] and [9].   [16] Ibid at [9].

[17] See for instance, General Comment 12 on the right to adequate food at [15].

[18] The Committee does provide normative content to the rights in its General Comments; however, the relationship between this content and the obligations identified in the General Comments is not always entirely clear.   [19] See the discussion in Chap 3.

have enforceable practical implications for government policy that benefit the worst off in society. The Committee found that a 'minimum core obligation to ensure the satisfaction of, at the very least, minimum essential levels of each of the rights is incumbent upon every State party'.[20] A State party in which any significant number of individuals is deprived of essential foodstuffs, primary health care, shelter, and housing is *prima facie* failing to discharge its obligations. The Committee went on to qualify its statement by recognizing that such an obligation must be considered in light of the resource constraints faced by a country. It concluded: '[i]n order for a State party to be able to attribute its failure to meet at least its minimum core obligations to a lack of available resources, it must demonstrate that every effort has been made to use all resources that are at its disposition in an effort to satisfy, as a matter of priority, those minimum obligations.'[21]

The first question that arises concerns the reasons that the Committee decided to introduce the idea of a minimum core obligation into the interpretation of socio-economic rights. The Committee provides two fairly elusive reasons: first, it mentions that it became necessary to recognize such an obligation as a result of its experience in examining the reports of states concerning their compliance with the Covenant; secondly, it makes the following claim: '[i]f the Covenant were to be read in such a way as not to establish such a minimum core obligation, it would be largely deprived of its raison d'etre.'[22]

The first reason is, however, inadequate as it fails to explain the problems that the Committee had experienced and why recognition of a minimum core obligation would serve to rectify such difficulties. The second reason provided by the Committee is essentially incomplete: it requires an understanding of the purposes behind the Covenant and an explanation as to why recognition of a minimum core obligation is necessary to realize these purposes. As a result, the motivation for introducing a minimum core obligation into the discussions concerning socio-economic rights is not clear from the statements in the General Comment. That has caused uncertainty as to the purpose of recognizing a minimum core obligation.[23] A reconstruction of the reasons for such an approach is thus necessary in order to understand why it is of importance to the enforcement of socio-economic rights.

3.2 Early specifications of the minimum threshold

The UN Committee describes the minimum core obligation as a duty upon states to realize 'minimum essential levels' of a right. This provides us with the first intimation of the normative basis of this approach: there are different levels to the

---

[20] General Comment no 3 at [10].
[21] Ibid. What follows in this chapter can be seen as an attempt to justify and develop some of these terse statements. [22] Ibid.
[23] Arguably, that uncertainty has led to several of the objections the South African Constitutional Court has raised as a justification for not following the approach.

realization of a right, some of which are more 'essential' than other levels. Can more be said about the justification for such an approach, and greater content be given to the notion of what constitutes the 'minimum essential' levels of a right? [24]

The authors who initially advocated a minimum core approach proposed the following understanding of the minimum essential level of a right.[25] Their inspiration for this account lay in Henry Shue's idea that it is possible to identify a list of 'basic rights' that are prerequisites for the exercise of all other rights.[26] Applying this idea to the Covenant itself, they developed the notion that there was a *'platform of effective self-provision*, which could put the poor on the *"threshold" of further* progressive steps of development... toward assurance of the higher standards and the longer lists of rights found in the economic/social Covenant' (author's emphasis).[27] They give the example, for instance, of people living in rural Botswana where malnutrition hinders the strenuous efforts that are necessary to bring in a good crop for year-long food security.[28] Without a basic level of nutrition, it thus becomes impossible to achieve more adequate levels of nutrition or health. Thus, essential levels of a right are those that are necessary in order for individuals to be able to provide higher levels of socio-economic well-being for themselves in future.

Whilst these authors have touched upon issues of importance in identifying 'essential' levels of a right, they have not in my view succeeded in identifying correctly the general content of this threshold. There are three problems with their account. First, the justification for their threshold is derivative. The argument is essentially instrumental: the essential levels of a right represent those levels of well-being that must be realized in order for individuals to obtain for themselves higher levels of that right or certain other rights. However, that is only a good argument if there is a good justification for realizing these other thresholds or rights. The authors do not provide such an account or any understanding of what these higher levels consist in. The theory I propose seeks to understand the general justification of subsistence rights, and to derive the conception of a minimum threshold from this general justification. As such, it offers the hope of attaining a more thorough and comprehensive justification for recognizing such a threshold.

Secondly, the threshold that is identified by these authors is purely instrumental to the attainment of higher levels of rights. The theory I propose, however, is able to recognize that there is also some intrinsic value to the satisfaction of these minimal needs. Being free from threats to one's survival entails that one is not subject to severe negative experiences and can achieve some positive experiences as

---

[24] This is important as one of the factors that has led the South African Constitutional Court recently to decline to follow the minimum core approach was the uncertainty as to how to determine what the content of such an obligation is: see *Grootboom*, n 12 above, at [32] and [33].

[25] As far as I am aware, the first explicit attempt to develop a minimum threshold approach was the article by Andreassen, Skålnes, Smith, and Stokke in 1987. They build on this article in Andreassen, Smith, and Stokke, 1992. The approach was also alluded to in the Limburg Principles published in the Human Rights Quarterly, 1987.   [26] Shue, 1980: 19.

[27] Andreassen, *et al.*, 1992: 260.   [28] Ibid: 261.

well as some of one's purposes. Since my account posits value in having positive experiences, avoiding negative experiences and the realization of purposes, the theory is thus able to provide a better account than these authors do of the reasons for the desirability of attaining this threshold.

Finally, these authors focus their threshold upon the notion of being able to be in a position of effective self-provisioning. However, there are many individuals—the mentally or physically disabled, for instance—who are unable to provide for themselves. Yet it is still of great importance to develop an account of the essential levels of provision that they require. I thus turn to providing an alternative account of the normative foundations of the minimum core approach based on the political philosophy I have developed.

3.3 Distinguishing two thresholds of interests

In the second chapter, I sought to ground the justification of fundamental rights in the principle of equal importance which requires protection for certain significant interests that creatures have.[29] Even amongst these central interests of individuals, it was recognized that there are two different thresholds of urgency that can be identified. The idea of urgency is to be understood in relation to the sources of value identified in Chapter 1. The greater urgency of the first threshold is justified as a result of the greater impact that the failure to realize such a threshold has on the ability of individuals to have positive experiences and realize their purposes.[30] In order to understand these points more clearly, and their implications, I shall focus on the right to have access to adequate housing: section 26(1) of the South African Constitution. In relation to this right, there are two central interests, of differing degrees of urgency, that individuals can be said to share in having access to adequate housing.

The first is the most urgent interest in being free from general threats to one's survival. This interest is of greatest urgency, as the inability to survive wipes out all possibility for realizing the sources of value in the life of a being. I shall refer to this in what follows as the first threshold of provision or the minimum core. In this context, the threshold would amount to having at least minimal shelter from the elements such that one's health and thus one's ability to survive are not compromised. Continual exposure to the cold could, for instance, lead to severe health

---

[29] This substantive claim is to be distinguished from the claim in analytical jurisprudence that the essential feature of all rights is that they protect interests. Several features of my theory do in fact require reference to the Interest theory of rights and favour it. One instance would be the attribution of rights to children and non-human animals. On the debate between interest and will theories of rights, see Kramer, Simmonds, and Steiner, 1998. I cannot hope in this book to discuss this matter.

[30] Scanlon, 1975 points to the importance of the notion of urgency in our moral thinking and suggests a naturalist and conventionalist approach towards developing the content of this notion. The account in Chapter 1 provides the basis for developing the naturalist approach by ranking features of our lives in relation to their relative importance for the fulfillment of the two sources of value identified.

problems that may be fatal; the same would be true of continual exposure to wet conditions, such as was experienced by the Grootboom community in their initial dwellings on water-logged land. Thus, it makes sense to identify one 'minimal' interest at this point which involves ensuring individuals are not exposed to the general conditions that threaten their survival.[31] In the context of housing, that formula can be made more concrete so as to require that individuals can at all times have access to accommodation that offers protection from the elements, sanitary conditions, and access to basic services such as sanitation and running water. This more concrete specification is derived from attempting to understand in relation to housing what would be necessary in order to ensure that the minimal interest of individuals is met.[32]

The minimal interest that I have identified thus far is not, however, all that is protected by section 26(1). The preamble to the Constitution states that one of its aims is to '[i]mprove the quality of life of all citizens and free the potential of each person'. Human beings have an interest in living in an environment that does not impair their development but enables them to be in a position to flourish and achieve their goals. It is not only survival that matters: we need protection for our interest in the general conditions that are necessary for the fulfilment of a wide range of purposes.[33] In specifying the human interest in housing, the Indian Supreme Court in *Shantistar Builders v Narayan Khimalal Totame*[34] stated that the human being requires 'suitable accommodation which would allow him to grow in every aspect—physical, moral and intellectual'. This in turn would naturally involve providing a much more extensive form of housing than that required to meet the minimal interest.[35] Such a higher standard of housing would, for instance, meet all the requirements of adequacy identified by the United Nations Committee in General Comment No 4.[36] I shall refer to this threshold as the second threshold of provision.

---

[31] This formulation accords with and gives content to the approach of Sen and Nussbaum, 1993: 41, who talk of satisfying 'certain crucially important functionings up to certain minimally adequate levels'.

[32] Steinberg, 2006: 271 clearly misunderstands the normative basis of my approach to socio-economic rights when she states that the content of the right as described above is derived from a 'utilitarian calculus of social good'.

[33] In *City of Johannesburg v Rand Properties* (Case 04/10330, High Court of South Africa, as yet unreported), Jabhjay J expressed his understanding of this second threshold as follows at [49]: ' "Adequate housing" encompasses more than just the four walls of a room and roof over one's head. Housing is essential for normal, healthy living. It fulfils deep-seated psychological needs for privacy and personal space: physical needs for security and protection from inclement weather; and social needs for basic gathering points where important relationships are forged and nurtured. In many societies, a house also serves an important function as an economic centre where essential commercial activities are performed.'   [34] AIR 1990 SC 630 at [9].

[35] By failing to draw the distinction between minimal and maximal interests, the Indian Supreme Court confused the matter by regarding its statement concerning the more extensive interest in housing as an expression of the basic needs of a human being.

[36] At [8]. These include legal security of tenure, availability of facilities and infrastructure, affordability, habitability, accessibility, location, and cultural adequacy.

It is obvious that the more extensive interest includes the minimal one. There are three reasons, however, why it remains important to distinguish the two interests and the consequent obligations that flow from recognizing that each is deserving of protection. First, it allows us to understand that there is not only one threshold against which improvements in people's lives can be measured. Recognizing the maximal interest alone would suggest that, unless it is fulfilled, people's lives are not significantly improved. The fact that there is a minimal interest allows us to understand that people's lives can be improved through the provision of housing that falls short of realizing the maximal interest in housing.[37] The central defect in the government's housing policy in *Grootboom* can be understood to have been the failure to recognize the minimal interest in housing, and that it had obligations under section 26 to protect this interest.

Secondly, the distinction allows us to recognize that there are differences between the two interests, and that the minimal interest has an urgency and must be prioritized in a way that the maximal interest does not. The minimal interest reflects the respect in which people are most vulnerable, and most needy. It is the respect in which their very lives are threatened which would negate completely any source of value in their lives. Whilst the realization of the maximal second interest is a medium- to long-term goal, the urgency of the first interest strongly justifies recognizing an unconditional obligation to realize it as a matter of priority.[38]

Finally, the second interest generally fails to be protected if the first interest is not protected. In other words, one cannot claim that one wishes that everyone should have a house fully conducive to their flourishing, without protecting their short-term interests. Some people will die in the interim and thus their right to adequate housing will be essentially meaningless. Others will be unable to flourish in the housing that they eventually receive, because of the impairments (such as ill-health) they experience as a result of the failure to meet their minimal needs previously. Thus, it cannot make sense to recognize an obligation to meet the second interest, without imposing an obligation to meet the first interest.[39] Distinguishing the two interests allows us to take cognizance of this fact.

The minimum core approach can thus be understood to derive from this normative foundation for fundamental rights. Minimum core obligations are those obligations to meet the 'minimum essential levels of a right'. The UN Committee fails clearly to specify what these are, what this threshold entails. Through an account of minimal interests that are of particular urgency in human life, it is

---

[37] It could be argued that the court in *Grootboom* (n 12 above, at [52]) recognized this minimal interest where it held that people's 'immediate need can be met by relief short of housing which fulfils the standards of durability, habitability and stability encompassed by the definition of housing development in the Act'.   [38] I shall discuss the notion of priority later in this chapter.

[39] That is the important insight lying behind the original approach to defining the minimum core outlined above and defended by Andreassen, *et al.*, 1987, 1992.

possible to understand the importance of imposing a minimum core obligation to realize such interests.

This account implies that the idea of a core aspect to a right is not necessarily a novel idea of application only in the field of adjudicating socio-economic rights. There is good reason for such a notion to be recognized when there are any interests protected by a right that differ in their degree of importance for human beings. Wherever this is true, the notion of a minimum core obligation will be of use. Thus, for instance, it is arguable that the South African Constitutional Court has recognized that there is a core aspect to the right to privacy.

In *Bernstein v Bester*,[40] Ackermann J considered the rationale behind the protection of the right to privacy in an attempt to determine the scope of the right. He claimed that '[p]rivacy is acknowledged in the truly personal realm, but as a person moves into communal relations and activities such as business and social interaction, the scope of personal space shrinks accordingly'.[41] His discussion of German law on this topic led him to conclude that in Germany a 'very high level of protection is given to the individual's intimate personal sphere of life and the maintenance of its basic preconditions and there is a final untouchable sphere of human freedom that is beyond interference from any public authority. So much so that, in regard to this intimate core of privacy, no justifiable limitation thereof can take place.'[42] Ackermann J approved of a similar approach for South Africa, which regards the right to privacy as related fundamentally to the most personal aspects of a person's existence.

In *Investigating Directorate: Serious Economic Offences v Hyundai Motor Corporation*,[43] Langa DP held that 'Ackermann J characterises the right to privacy as lying along a continuum, where the more a person inter-relates with the world, the more the right to privacy becomes attenuated'.[44] The judge was at pains to point out, however, that the right to privacy applied 'beyond this established "intimate core" ... in the social capacities in which we act'.[45] Here it is evident that, in the context of a civil right, the Court adopts an approach that recognizes that there is a core interest protected by the right to privacy. The right applies beyond this 'intimate core', but there is a central and most important area to which the right to privacy can always be applied and which can rarely be limited.

Thus, the idea of a core aspect to a right is not necessarily a novel idea of application only in the field of adjudicating socio-economic rights—the Constitutional Court has made use of a similar notion in another context—nor is the idea of a minimum core of particular application at the international level.[46] There is good

---

[40] 1996 (2) SA 751 (CC).   [41] Ibid at [67].   [42] Ibid at [77].
[43] 2001 (1) SA 545 (CC).   [44] Ibid at [15].   [45] Ibid at [16].
[46] Mclean, 2006 argues that differences between the functions of the Committee at the UN level and a Constitutional Court at the domestic level may render the minimum core of greater relevance to the international level. I do not find this argument convincing for the reason stated in the text and because I see it as an obligation that is capable of being realized as a matter of priority within states rather than as a purely 'aspirational goal'. Construing socio-economic rights as aspirational goals

reason for such a notion to be recognized whenever there are interests protected by a right that differ in their degree of importance for human beings. The concept has primarily been developed in relation to socio-economic rights as a result of the fact that in this context it appears most evident that there are interests that can be classified as having greater urgency and that must be realized as a matter of priority so that individuals can be free from threats to their survival.

3.4 An alternative interpretation of section 26(1)

I wish now to demonstrate how the minimum core approach can provide the basis for a coherent and plausible interpretation of section 26 in the South African Constitution and, in particular, address the difficult issue concerning the relationship of sections 26(1) and (2). The first important phrase in section 26(1) is the requirement that each person have 'access' to 'adequate' housing. The word 'access' is important in indicating protection for the minimal interest in housing as it suggests that people must at all times have a place to which they can gain entry. 'Access' to adequate housing thus does not necessarily imply the ownership of a house, but that those in desperate need are able to gain access to shelter that protects them from the elements and realizes their other minimal interests.

What then does the term 'adequate' housing mean? Yacoob J says very little about what constitutes 'adequate' housing in *Grootboom*. He claims that section 26 requires the following conditions to be met: 'there must be land, there must be services, and there must be a dwelling.'[47] However, he fails to specify what level of provision of these particular goods would meet the requirements of the right. How big must a piece of land be? How big must a dwelling be? Must it be waterproof? Must it be a two-bedroomed house of brick and mortar? Many more questions are left open about what 'adequacy' entails.

It has been claimed that the notion of adequacy adds a qualitative dimension to the right of access to housing.[48] The question that arises is how this dimension is to be understood. An important point to recognize is that adequacy is partly a relational notion: one needs an understanding of the interests that are at stake in order to determine whether a particular level of provision is adequate or not. In relation to an interest in being free from general threats to survival, a tent or iron shack may be 'adequate'. In relation to an interest in being provided with the general conditions necessary to realize one's purposes, these are inadequate.[49]

---

is usually what leads them to be taken less seriously and to be considered idealistic notions with little relevance to policy.

[47] *Grootboom*, n 12 above, at [35].   [48] Liebenberg, 1996: 41–39.

[49] The conception of flourishing people have, and their corresponding choices, will play an important role in determining what they consider to be fully 'adequate'. Nevertheless, to the extent that this requires provision beyond the threshold of the 'maximal interest' I have identified, individuals and not the state will be responsible for ensuring that their own standards of adequacy are met for the reasons discussed in Chap 2.

Thus, adequacy is a concept that admits of varying degrees. It can be understood as involving a range from the provision for minimal needs to the provision of an environment in which human beings have the general conditions necessary for them to realize their goals and flourish.

There is a second scale upon which adequacy can be measured. There are certain requirements in all societies that people have if they are to survive and not be subject to serious ill health, and thus adequate accommodation must at least meet these universal requirements. However, there are also requirements people have that are relative to the particular culture or society in which they live. The UN Committee has recognized in General Comment 4 that one of the requirements for adequate housing is that it be 'culturally adequate'.[50] The level of development of a society will also determine what constitutes adequate housing. Thus, fully adequate housing will be such that it is 'adequate according to the level of economic development that obtains in society'.[51]

Adam Smith famously pointed out that there are many resources that are not strictly speaking necessary in order to live at all; yet they are required to live a life of dignity within one's community. His famous examples are of a linen shirt and leather shoes which 'the poorest creditable person of either sex would be ashamed to appear in public without'.[52] Similarly, Amartya Sen[53] points out that, 'to lead a life without shame, to be able to visit and entertain one's friends... requires a more expensive bundle of goods and services in a society that is generally richer and in which most people have, say, means of transport, affluent clothing, radios or television sets'. The range here is between the meeting of absolute, invariant needs and the meeting of needs that are socially determined and central to living a life of dignity within a particular society.

'Adequacy' can thus be judged in relation to three standards: whether an individual is able to meet their survival interests; whether they have access to the general conditions necessary in all societies to realize a wide range of purposes; whether they have access to the general conditions in their particular society to realize a wide range of purposes. There is a close relationship between the second and third standards I have identified. If the culturally variable range of needs is not met, they are likely to impair the ability of people to realize their purposes within a particular society. Since people live within societies, it is likely that they will be unable to live well, achieve their goals and have positive experiences if they are forced to live below standards that are regarded as acceptable by those communities. Thus, for purposes of simplification, it is possible to define one 'maximal interest' of individuals in having access to the general conditions that are necessary for the fulfilment of a range of purposes within a particular society.

---

[50] At [8].   [51] Fabre, 2000: 124.
[52] Quoted in Sen, 1981: 18. Obviously, his examples relate to the particular society and time in which he lived.   [53] 1987:18.

3.5 Section 26(2) and the notion of progressive realization

The understanding I have provided of the two standards upon which to judge adequacy is of great significance when interpreting the notion of 'progressive realization' in section 26(2). That section requires the state to take reasonable measures in order to achieve the 'progressive realization' of the right to have access to adequate housing. It is important to recognize that there is a fundamental ambiguity in the notion of 'progressive realization'. One way of understanding this notion could be that it imposes an obligation upon the government to make housing accessible to a greater number of people over time. Progressive realization thus involves simply more people gaining access to housing over time.

There are several problems with this interpretation. First, the right in section 26(1) which is to be realized progressively vests immediately in everyone. The failure to offer temporary alleviation for the plight of the homeless would result in some never being able to enjoy the 'full realization' of their right (as some people would succumb to the elements). For these people, their right of access to adequate housing would be effectively negated.

Secondly, this interpretation is unable to capture the important point that some are at a greater disadvantage than others in South African society. Consider a situation in which the government focused its housing programme on those who could afford to repay loans that it granted for the purpose of building houses.[54] It seems that such a programme would constitute 'progressive realization', on the first interpretation thereof, even though it completely ignored those who are most significantly deprived—who cannot afford the loan repayments. Such a case would demonstrate the failure to recognize the priority that some interests have over others.

An alternative interpretation, however, exists, and fits very well with section 26(1). It involves understanding the notion of 'progressive realization' to comprise two components: the first component is a 'minimum core obligation' to realize the levels of housing required to meet the minimal interest I have identified; the second component is a duty on the state to take steps to improve the adequacy of the housing in accordance with the standards I have developed. In other words, progressive realization means the movement from the realization of the minimal interest in housing to the realization of the maximal interest. Progressive realization involves an improvement in the adequacy of housing for the meeting of human interests. It does not mean that some receive housing now, and others receive it later; rather, it means that each is entitled as a matter of priority to basic housing provision, which the government is required to improve gradually over time. Such an interpretation makes sense of the idea that the socio-economic

[54] In relation to land reform, the government has shifted resources away from the poorest of rural workers to those who are relatively well off. Roux, 2002 argues that the *Grootboom* decision is deficient in that it would not provide a remedy for the worst off in such cases.

rights enshrined in the Constitution have an aspirational dimension but, like other rights, provide strong protections for certain urgent interests.[55]

In light of this interpretation, I turn now to an analysis of what Yacoob J had to say in *Grootboom* about progressive realization. First, Yacoob J stated that the drafters of the Constitution 'contemplated that the right could not be realized immediately'.[56] However, what was contemplated, in my view, was that the 'full realization' of the right could not be realized immediately and not that it could not be *partially* realized within a short space of time.

Secondly, Yacoob J states that 'the goal of the Constitution is that the basic needs of all in our society be effectively met and the requirement of progressive realisation means that the state must take steps to achieve this goal'.[57] A natural reading of this claim suggests that Yacoob J mistakes the ultimate purpose of including socio-economic rights in the Constitution. It is not the ultimate goal of the Constitution that only the minimal needs of people be met.[58] The goal of the Constitution is loftier than that, recognizing a wider human interest in housing that provides people with the general enabling conditions to fulfil a wide range of purposes. Indeed, section 26 is phrased so as to require the provision of 'adequate housing' and not merely 'basic housing'. It is in respect of this maximal interest that the state has the duty to take steps to ensure that each will in time be provided with housing that meets the maximal standard of 'adequacy'.

Finally, Yacoob J referred approvingly in his judgment to the way in which 'progressive realization' is understood by the UN Committee. The Committee claims that the notion of 'progressive realization' imposes 'an obligation to move as expeditiously and effectively as possible' towards the full realization of the right, and to refrain from taking deliberately retrogressive measures.[59] Yacoob J claimed that the meaning of the phrase in the Constitution is consistent with this interpretation.

However, the Committee's interpretation of this phrase, in my view, cannot be divorced from its interpretation of the Covenant to include a minimum core obligation to meet minimal essential levels of these rights. Thus, in its view, the state has a duty to take steps towards the *full* realization of the right, but is at the same time under an obligation to ensure that each is guaranteed the essential levels of provision required by the minimum core. These two are fundamentally inter-twined in the interpretation given by the Committee. Yacoob J attempts to divorce the one element from the other. I have argued against the coherence and desirability of this interpretation of 'progressive realization' and have attempted to show how such an interpretation significantly weakens the protection that socio-economic rights provide for individuals.

---

[55] The subsequent discussion will clarify the nature of the protection offered by such rights.

[56] *Grootboom*, n 12 above, at [45].   [57] Ibid.

[58] Since Yacoob J is not clear about what he means by basic needs, it is possible that he has a more extensive conception which covers all of the thresholds I have identified. Such a view would not be subject to the above-mentioned objection.   [59] See General Comment 3 at [9].

3.6 The relationship between the minimum core and obligations to respect, protect, and fulfil

What is the relationship between the minimum core concept and the concrete framework of obligations to respect, protect, and fulfil that the Committee has recognized flow from socio-economic rights? The conditional right at the first threshold would involve guaranteeing individuals the general conditions to be free from threats to survival. This understanding of the content of the minimum core would then give rise to the following obligations: a society will be required not to interfere with the enjoyment of those conditions by individuals (respect); to prevent third parties from jeopardizing the enjoyment of those conditions by individuals (protect); and to assist individuals to gain access to those conditions where they do not currently have such access (fulfil). The focus of the discussion in this book will be on the last of these obligations as it is in respect of these positive obligations that there is the greatest lack of clarity concerning what is required of a government.

However, it has been suggested by some authors that the negative obligations imposed by socio-economic rights, even in relation to the second threshold of provision, should always be recognized as being part of the minimum core obligations of a government. For instance, Chapman and Russell argue as follows: '[s]ince the obligation to respect is fundamental and apparently cost-free, it is a short step to assign the respect-bound obligations to the category of minimum State obligations.'[60] This statement, in my view, represents a conflation of different considerations and, again, suggests why it is of importance to have a clear conception of the normative underpinnings of socio-economic rights.

First, there is no reason relating to the fundamental interests of individuals to prioritize negative duties over positive duties. Both arise from a more general abstract duty to guarantee individuals the thresholds I have identified. The one duty is no more 'fundamental' than the next. Once this is understood, negative duties that are not related to the first threshold should not be assigned to the 'minimum core', whose justification lies in its being of greater urgency than the second threshold.

Secondly, giving normative priority to negative obligations may have unwarranted practical implications. Thus, for instance, a government may decide to implement a programme that realizes the first threshold of provision for all, but involves the interference with some people's enjoyment of a higher level of socio-economic provision. To assign negative duties to the minimum core would mean that such a programme would be *prima facie* impermissible; however, at times, giving priority to the interests of the worst off may involve interference with the higher levels of socio-economic goods enjoyed by the better off. Such interference

---

[60] Chapman and Russell (eds), 2002: 11.

should not be prevented by an unwarranted assertion that negative duties have a greater priority over positive duties.[61]

Perhaps, a real-life example akin to such a situation occurred in the case of *Minister of Public Works v Kyalami Ridge Environmental Association*.[62] In this case, the government had attempted to provide temporary housing on state land to individuals rendered homeless by severe flooding. Existing property owners in the area of the housing scheme complained that the government had failed to consult them in setting up this scheme. They also claimed that the government's scheme would violate some of their environmental rights and interfere with their property rights in that the value of their properties would be reduced and the character of their neighbourhood changed. The Constitutional Court ruled that the government had acted in pursuance of its constitutional obligations to provide temporary relief for those in desperate need and had thus acted lawfully. Effectively, the court held that the positive action taken by the government to provide individuals with temporary housing trumped the interests of the owners to avoid having their property and other interests interfered with.[63]

Finally, the difference between negative and positive duties lies largely in the fact that negative duties may be translated more readily into unconditional obligations without engaging many of the difficult countervailing normative considerations that arise in translating positive duties into unconditional obligations. Thus, to the extent that negative duties are 'cost-free', they do not raise the questions of scarcity and sacrifice that are raised in connection with positive duties. This does not mean that the one has more normative significance than the other and, consequently, the negative duties should not be assigned automatically to the minimum core.

This section has thus sought to demonstrate two important points. First, the political philosophy I have developed supports a variant of the 'minimum core approach' to constitutional rights in legal doctrine. Secondly, the minimum core approach is able to provide a viable and attractive interpretation of socio-economic rights such as those contained in the South African Constitution. However, there are a number of objections that have been raised against adopting the 'minimum core' approach. Through responding to these objections, I hope to develop the approach and clarify its implications.

---

[61] It is important to qualify this claim by recognizing that interference with the second threshold will generally be undesirable and have a negative impact on social stability. It would also often be self-defeating for a state to increase its problems by reducing more people to the first threshold. Nevertheless, there may be occasions where such interference may be warranted.

[62] 2001 (3) SA 1151 (CC).

[63] The realization of socio-economic rights may, at times, conflict with existing property rights that generally impose obligations of non-interference. I argue later on in this chapter that property rights have the same normative base as socio-economic rights, and thus do not automatically take priority over such rights as libertarians, for instance, would claim.

4 Objections to the Minimum Core Approach

4.1 General standards and the minimum core

The Constitutional Court has, in both the *Grootboom* and *TAC* judgments, lodged several objections against the minimum core approach and been at pains to distance itself from this approach.[64] In *Grootboom*, Yacoob J's central claim was that in order to determine what the minimum core of a right is, one must first identify the needs and opportunities for the enjoyment of the right.[65] As a result, he identified three problems that arise in determining the content of a minimum core obligation: first, a court requires sufficient information about these needs and opportunities to determine what the minimum core should be. The UN Committee responsible for monitoring the International Covenant had extensive information after examining the reports provided by states over many years. Yacoob J claimed, however, that the Constitutional Court lacked comparable information and so could not determine the minimum core. Secondly, the needs in the context of the right of access to adequate housing are diverse. This makes it difficult to fix upon a precise definition for a minimum core. Finally, difficulties arise as to whether the minimum core should be defined generally or with regard to specific groups of people, and this undermines the very notion that there is one particular minimum core.[66]

The presentation of these arguments is not particularly clear in the judgment and I have tried to outline them in as fair a way as possible. In my view, these arguments exhibit confusion as to the nature of a minimum core obligation, which arises from failing to draw a crucial distinction. This is the distinction between the invariant, universal standard that must be met in order for an obligation to be fulfilled, and the numerous particular methods that can be adopted in order to meet this standard and thus comply with a constitutional obligation. In general, courts attempt to identify general principles and rules that specify the obligations of a government or individuals that apply beyond the facts of particular cases. This is a crucial role of the Constitutional Court in particular[67] which, as the chief interpreter of the Constitution,[68] is responsible for expanding upon the nature of the obligations imposed by constitutional rights.

---

[64] The attitude of the Court towards this approach is at odds with that expressed by most academic authors who have written on the socio-economic rights contained in the South African Constitution who have supported the recognition of minimum core obligations. Few, however, have considered the requirements of the approach in any detail. See Scott and Maklem,1992: 77; De Vos, 1997; Van Bueren, 1999; Scott and Alston, 2000; Roux, 2002; Liebenberg, 2003 and 2005a; and Pieterse, 2004; opponents of the approach include De Wet, 1996, Wesson, 2004, and Steinberg, 2006.   [65] *Grootboom*, n 12 above, at [32].

[66] These arguments are laid out in [32] and [33] of the judgment.

[67] See, for instance, Alexy, 2002: 86.   [68] See s 167(3) of the Constitution.

Consider, for example, the right to vote.[69] In *August v Electoral Commission*,[70] Sachs J held that 'the *right to vote* by its very nature imposes positive obligations upon the legislature and the executive. A date for elections has to be promulgated, the secrecy of the ballot secured and the machinery established for managing the process.'[71] In this statement, Sachs J explains the general standard that state conduct must meet in order to comply with its obligations in terms of the right to vote. There are a number of ways of meeting these obligations: the state could, for instance, decide to conduct the ballot via a secure computing system, or, alternatively, use the traditional ballot boxes. Whichever method is adopted, however, must meet the standard, of ensuring the secrecy of the ballot.[72]

The function of a court in relation to socio-economic rights can be understood in a similar manner. The right is stated at an abstract level. In giving content to the right, a court engages in the process of specifying general principles that define the obligations placed upon the state by the right. Recognizing the role of a constitutional court in defining general principles allows us to see how such a court can determine the content of a minimum core obligation. The role of the court in this respect would be to set the general standard that constitutes the minimum core obligation of the state.

An example of such a standard would be for the Court to hold that every person in South Africa must have access to accommodation that involves, at least, protection from the elements in sanitary conditions with access to basic services, such as toilets and running water. As is evident, the standard incorporates the duty to protect the minimal interest that individuals have in housing. The setting of this general standard, however, still raises significant questions as to the measures that will be adopted to realize it in particular cases: protection from the elements could involve the provision of tents or the provision of corrugated, galvanized iron such that people could build their own shacks. The Constitution allows the legislature and executive some leeway in deciding exactly what measures are to be taken to realize the right. The reasonableness of the particular measures must be assessed against the general principles the Court interprets as defining the content of the right.

A minimum core obligation should be understood in light of the distinction I have argued for. It does not represent any particular means by which a socio-economic right can be realized; rather, it represents, the standard of socio-economic provision necessary to meet people's minimal interests.

---

[69] Section 19(3) of the Constitution.   [70] 1999 (3) SA 1 (CC).   [71] Ibid at [16].

[72] The court has, in many cases, given content to rights at the level of general principles. Government action in the particular circumstances of each case is then tested against this general standard. See, for instance, *Dawood v Minister of Home Affairs* 2000(8) BCLR 837 (CC), in which the right to dignity was held to protect people's ability to form marriage relationships and to honour the obligations that they assume towards one another in terms of such relationships. In giving content to the right to equality, the court has also laid out a fairly detailed test which incorporates a number of principles, against which particular actions are to be measured: see *Harksen v Lane NO* 1998 (1) SA 300 (CC).

Replies to Yacoob J's arguments now become evident. First, in order to specify the standard that the government must meet in order to comply with its obligations, it is not necessary for the Court to have wide sources of information such as that open to the UN Committee. Such information may be necessary in order to decide on the particular actions that the state is required to take in particular circumstances. However, it is not necessary in order for us to understand what the minimal interests of people are. The community in *Grootboom* was quite clear about this: what they wanted was protection from the elements, and an environment that would not be injurious to their health. Few people would have difficulty specifying the nature of their minimal interests and Yacoob J overstates the matter when he depicts this question as involving enormous complexity.[73] Thus, no vast sources of information would be necessary to determine the minimum core, if it is understood in the way I have suggested.

Secondly, it is clear that the minimum core of a right, on the conception that I defend, is not to be defined with reference to specific groups, but is a wholly general notion applicable across the human species. Yacoob J is therefore mistaken in making statements such as his claim that 'a [m]inimum core obligation is determined generally by having regard to the needs of the most vulnerable group that is entitled to the protection of the right in question'.[74] In fact, the minimum core is to be specified in relation to the minimal interests we all share. It is the vulnerable who are less able to meet these interests by their own means and therefore require greater assistance from the state.

This last point also offers the basis for a response to Yacoob J's claim that the needs in the context of section 26 are diverse and that this fact presents difficulties in defining the minimum core. The fact that some need access to land, some need land and houses, and others need financial assistance is not relevant to the determination of the minimum core. Each is entitled to the same level of provision; the differential needs people have will determine in what way the government is required by the Constitution, if at all, to assist them. Let us specify the minimum core obligation imposed by section 26 to require that the government ensure that each person in South Africa is able to gain access to shelter that is sufficient to protect her from the elements.[75] It then becomes clear that those who have such shelter have no basis upon which to claim it from the government. Those who have land, but no shelter, could claim building materials, for instance. Those with neither land nor shelter could claim both (or at least access to sheltered accommodation). Nevertheless, the general obligation of the state does not vary: it is the same in respect of each person. What differs in an unequal society is how far off

---

[73] There may indeed be some theoretical difficulties in analysing the concept of need, but there are some fairly clear-cut general standards we share in judging what constitutes a minimal need that could serve to define a minimum core obligation. Political philosophy can help to clarify these standards, something I have attempted to do in this book.

[74] *Grootboom*, n 12 above, at [31].

[75] For purposes of illustration, I leave out the full definition I offered above.

from the minimum core each person lies, and therefore what must be provided for each to alleviate her need.

Thus, Yacoob J's contextual approach to socio-economic rights has the merit of recognizing that the particular actions required of the state in order to meet its constitutional obligations will differ according to the particular circumstances: the weather, for instance, will determine what form of shelter is required to protect people from the elements. The problem with this approach is, however, that it fails to recognize that people share basic interests that can be specified independently of context: in relation to housing, one of these interests includes, at least, the ability to be protected from the elements. What meets this formula will differ according to context but the human interest it protects does not.

4.2 The minimum core cannot be a general standard

Danie Brand argues that understanding the minimum core as a general standard is suitable for the international enforcement of socio-economic rights, but is not that useful for the domestic context where we must be 'far more specific, particular, concrete, context-sensitive and flexible in our thinking about basic standards, core entitlements and minimum obligations'.[76] He considers the case of a particular individual, Kas Maine,[77] whose early life involved a large degree of relative economic independence as a result of being party to a sharecropping agreement. Later in his life, he became dependent for his survival upon his family and the state. Brand argues that the minimum core content of the right to food—which he identifies as freedom from hunger—for Maine and his family changed throughout his life, and was dependent upon Maine's situation and the different relationships he found himself in. At different stages of his life, he would have held different minimum entitlements.

In the early stages of his life, in which he could provide food for his family as a result of the sharecropping agreement, his minimum entitlements would have been to a legal remedy to protect his position in case the agreement failed. The minimum duty of the state would have been to ensure that there was a legal framework to protect sharecropping agreements. When the state decided to prohibit sharecropping agreements, the minimum entitlement transformed into a negative right against the state to be left alone to produce food for his family through the sharecropping agreement. Later in life, however, when he was too old to farm and the apartheid laws had left him destitute, he would have had a positive right to the provision of food by the state.

---

[76] Brand, 2002: 101.

[77] Maine was a black sharecropper. Sharecropping agreements usually involved a landed white farmer and a landless black farmer. In return for the labour, implements, and expertise of the black farmer, the harvest on the white farmer's farm was to be shared in proportion to the economic inputs made by each to the farm: see Brand, 2002: 103. The example is taken from a book by Van Onselen,1996.

Brand concludes that what matters in the domestic context are 'the specific entitlements and specific duties of conduct implied by the minimum standard of freedom from hunger, in real-time, specific situations'.[78] These entitlements, however, cannot be fixed as they depend upon the specific relationships within which people find themselves and the circumstances of a particular case, including issues of dependency, distribution, and capabilities. 'Every time Kas's personal situation changed, whether because of external circumstances of a political or economic nature, or because of his own waning abilities, the minimum assistance to gain access to food that he could as of right expect from the state changed . . . In South Africa, where the right to food is now justiciable and liable to judicial enforcement in specific, individualized cases, the core content is of necessity a shifting concept.'[79]

Brand raises several important issues which an adequate theory of rights must be able to deal with. Yet his conclusion that the minimum core is 'a shifting concept' is not warranted on the basis of the concrete example he gives. The primary problem with Brand's analysis is his desire to specify the core content at too concrete a level. In so doing, he obscures the common human interest in each of the different situations Maine finds himself in, and is thus led to conclude that the minimum core must shift according to circumstance. At certain points, however, he is more circumspect and appears to recognize that his analysis involves drawing out the implications of a general standard for specific situations.[80] Maine's situation exhibits the need for certain general a-contextual standards—a requirement that everyone be free from hunger, for instance—to determine the concrete obligations that exist in each particular circumstance. The alternative is to have a mass of ad hoc obligations whose justification remains obscure. Such a model would also be entirely unsuitable for constitutional rights analysis where the implications of abstract rights are traced in concrete situations.

This confusion of standards and their application may have arisen owing to the fact that Brand does not distinguish between conditional and unconditional rights. Thus, he attempts to determine the content of entitlements and obligations in one overarching enquiry that considers all relevant features of a situation at once. As has been argued, the problem with such an analytical strategy is that it can fail to highlight the common human interests that exist in a variety of specific situations. Arguably, Brand falls into this trap.

In Chapter 3, I laid out several different factors that must be taken into consideration in moving from conditional to unconditional obligations. That analysis implies that the obligations of the state may vary in relation to their concrete implications for individuals in specific cases. The case of Kas Maine shows the importance of some of these factors. First, there is the question of effectiveness. As I have pointed out, a conditional right does not inform us how a state must fulfil

---

[78] Brand, 2002: 105.   [79] Ibid: 106.
[80] See the first quote in the paragraph immediately above.

its obligations but identifies the interests that must be realized. The state is required to ensure that the conditional obligations can be effectively realized. Considerations of effectiveness will determine who bears responsibility for performing the unconditional obligations that flow from the right.

During Maine's early life, he was able to realize the needs of his family for food, and thus the most effective assignment of responsibility for meeting their needs was to leave their food provision to him. That would have required the state to desist from impairing his efforts, and to enact a legal framework that would protect his ability to provide his family with food. Government intervention in prohibiting sharecropping agreements rendered him less able to provide for their needs, and deprived him of the general liberties necessary to achieve his own goals in life without providing any alternative opportunities for him. As such, these actions would have been prohibited by a minimum core entitlement to food.

Later in his life, where Maine was unable to meet his own needs, it is clear that positive intervention would have been required of the state. Allocating responsibility to him for meeting his own needs, in such a situation, would simply have been ineffective. Thus, in Maine's later life, the meeting of his family's need for food had to be assigned to others or assumed by the state.

Effectiveness itself implies a second requirement and that is a more concrete specification of duties. Such a specification can involve all of those duties identified by Shue[81]—duties to respect, protect, and fulfil—and such duties can be both negative and positive in nature. Brand draws our attention to the importance of giving a more concrete specification of duties in individual situations; however, he fails to recognize the importance of also identifying more abstract duties that can serve as the foundation of the concrete ones. Thus, the source of many of the state's concrete duties throughout Maine's life was its minimum core obligation to ensure that he (and his family) had sufficient food to be free from hunger. The nature of those concrete duties, however, changed in accordance with changes in his circumstances.

Thus, Brand's analysis, like that of the *Grootboom* Court, correctly highlights the fact that in determining unconditional obligations and the particular actions the state is required to take, it will be necessary to consider the concrete circumstances of each case.[82] Yet Brand fails to recognize that these concrete obligations arise precisely because there is a common human interest in having certain basic needs satisfied. Identifying these interests allows us to identify the relevant features of each situation and to tailor state actions to such a situation. Moreover, identifying general factors such as effectiveness and the assignment of duties also can assist us in reaching determinate conclusions about what is required in each individual case. The two-tier structure I have proposed thus has the benefit of offering a clear, structured way in which to approach the application of socio-economic rights to particular situations.

---

[81] 1980: 52.   [82] This will include the particularities of each country or culture where relevant.

4.3 Can the minimum core be enforced as an individual right?

A further objection to the minimum core approach attacks Brand's very understanding of how the minimum core is to operate. Brand envisages socio-economic rights as individual rights where individuals can claim particular goods from the state. If the court finds in favour of the individual, then it will, on this view, grant an order requiring the government to provide the minimum core to particular individuals. Yet, such an individualized model of litigation poses two significant problems.

First, individualized relief would effectively prioritize those individuals who are able and willing to bring their claims to court. If successful in their litigation, such individuals would be entitled to a court order requiring the government to provide them with shelter as a matter of urgency. That would render them effectively better off than others, and so, rather than ensuring the equal importance of persons, such a system of adjudication would lead to greater inequalities.

Secondly, it is highly inefficient to have courts make orders requiring the provision of goods to particular individuals. Imagine a situation in which a number of individuals each sue the government for basic shelter. The courts make separate orders requiring the government to provide these individuals with such shelter. If this is repeated in many cases across the country, there will be a number of ad hoc orders made against the government requiring it to provide shelter for a number of specific individuals. In trying to meet its obligations in terms of these court orders, the government will be prevented from developing any coherent policy initiative in relation to the provision of shelter for all in the society. Moreover, such inefficiency would in turn lead to a violation of the principle of equal importance. For, in fulfilling this array of individual orders, it is likely that the government will not be able to realize effectively the rights of others (who also live in similar desperate conditions). Thus, the provision of relief to some individuals on an ad hoc basis may in fact make other individuals worse off.

In *Grootboom*, the Court was very concerned about these problems arising: it recognized that 'hundreds of thousands (possibly millions) of South Africans live in appalling conditions throughout our country'.[83] Yacoob J held that the initial movement of the community from Wallacedene onto the land earmarked for low-cost housing could not be said to be a 'deliberate strategy to gain preference in the allocation of housing resources'.[84] Yet he recognized that 'the effect of any order that constitutes a special dispensation for the respondents on account of their extraordinary circumstances is to accord that preference'.[85] In light of a government undertaking to provide temporary accommodation for the respondents, the Court did not have to make a special order in relation to these particular individuals.[86] Nevertheless, in Yacoob J's judgment, he held

---

[83] *Grootboom*, n 12 above, at [80].   [84] Ibid at [81].   [85] Ibid at [81].
[86] As a result of the government's failure to live up to its promise, the court ultimately made an order enforcing this undertaking, and specifying what had to be provided. See *Grootboom v Government of the Republic of South Africa* CCT 38/00.

that '[n]either section 26 nor section 28 entitles the respondents to claim shelter or housing upon demand . . . However, section 26 does oblige the state to devise and implement a coherent, co-ordinated programme designed to meet its section 26 obligations.'[87]

Although the Court's response has not been fully developed, it correctly recognizes that there are powerful arguments against providing individual relief in socio-economic rights cases. However, there are also several good arguments in favour of individual relief.[88] First, in this work, I have tried to demonstrate the importance of considering the impact upon individuals of a failure to fulfil a person's minimal interests. Rights, on this view, are thus fundamentally concerned with individuals and their plight, and litigation based upon such rights should in large measure be concerned to remedy injustices faced by individuals. If courts are unable to offer individual relief, then rights litigation in some sense becomes divorced from its purpose and may no longer be an effective tool for protecting individuals.

Secondly, part of the function of courts has traditionally been to be concerned with the plight of individuals, and their relationship to the law. If a court cannot provide individual relief in specific circumstances, then there is the discomforting possibility that courts may be led to turn their back on severe suffering. Finally, the lack of individual relief may well discourage individuals from bringing cases based upon socio-economic rights to court. Individual claimants 'will understandably wish to see something geared more to their situation and are unlikely to wish to bring constitutional cases purely to serve as constitutional triggers for general policy processes'.[89]

These competing considerations suggest that it is not desirable to adopt an overly rigid policy in relation to individual relief. The matter should to some extent be decided in accordance with the Constitutional Court's wide remedial powers, to make any order that is just and equitable.[90] The fact that these rights must be realized effectively and be applicable to all equally will entail that, in interpreting what is 'just and equitable', courts will not generally favour orders which require the government to realize these rights in an ad hoc fashion.

Individuals may indeed approach the courts where there is a failure to fulfil their rights. Where there is already a programme to fulfil such rights, and the government has unjustly excluded particular individuals from this programme, then they may succeed in having individual relief provided. Such relief, however, will generally require that the government, in the application of its programme, should treat them equally. Where there is no programme, individuals will generally be provided with relief in an indirect manner. The courts will order the government to develop a programme to provide shelter to all individuals who are

---

[87] *Grootboom*, n 12 above, at [95].
[88] I am indebted to Prof. Sandra Liebenberg for an enlightening discussion of these issues.
[89] Scott and Alston, 2000: 254–5.   [90] Section 172 of the Constitution.

similarly situated (as it did in *Grootboom*), and then individuals can claim their shelter under such a programme. There is thus an ambiguity in the Court's claim that section 26 does not entitle individuals to claim housing 'on demand'. In a sense this is true, in that individuals cannot generally come before courts and claim an entitlement to shelter tomorrow. Yet, in another sense it is false, in that individuals can demand that the government institute a programme that will lead them to be sheltered along with others within a reasonable period of time.

Thus, individual claims may highlight areas in which government policy has failed to treat individuals equally or with sufficient respect for their importance. Any remedy will benefit individuals, and thus there will be benefits to litigants on the basis of these rights. Yet, these benefits must occur in an orderly, systematic way taking into account all those with similar needs. As such, the relief granted should not generally involve any special orders to the individuals who brought the case; rather, it should seek indirectly to benefit the litigants through the general order that is made.

However, there will be circumstances in which it will be appropriate to grant individual relief despite the difficulties I have raised. That will be a matter for the discretion of the Court and will depend on several factors: the urgency of the need, the ease with which it can be addressed, and the effect that providing individual relief will have on developing an effective programme to meet the needs of other individuals who are similarly situated. A flexible approach that allows for exceptional circumstances in which individual relief may be provided can thus help to balance the various normative considerations that arise in this area.

In a similar vein, a further objection is often put forward arguing that the approach I have defended renders it very difficult for individuals to achieve success in cases based on socio-economic rights. Litigants are not merely required to prove a violation of rights in their own case, but also in relation to all those who are similarly situated.[91] This makes the difficulties of prosecuting such a case very pronounced.

It is important to recognize that this objection will not arise in many cases based upon socio-economic rights which involve the failure to extend a government programme to particular individuals or communities. Where there is a general policy failure, it may well be necessary for litigants to make a case for their position. The *Grootboom* and *TAC* cases provide evidence that it is possible to do so. The Court also has wide investigatory powers[92] and thus can use them to bring the necessary evidence to court if the individual litigants cannot do so. Furthermore, procedural rules can be designed such that the burden of proof upon individuals is lessened in such cases, and the primary responsibility to prove that their policies conform with the Constitution is shouldered by the

---

[91] See Liebenberg, 2003: 177.

[92] Section 173 of the Constitution—which recognizes the inherent powers of Courts to regulate their own process—could be used to develop these powers.

government.[93] This makes sense as the government is the better-resourced party, and also the one that has or should have intimate knowledge of the policy area that is at issue in a particular case.

Imposing such a responsibility on the government may well require modification of the existing structure of the constitutional enquiry. Currently, those complaining of a rights violation bear primary responsibility for showing that such a violation exists, whereas the government is only required to justify limiting a right in terms of the limitations enquiry. The new position I propose suggests that those claiming that a right has been violated should still bear responsibility for showing at least that there has been a *prima facie* violation of their conditional socio-economic rights in their individual circumstances. The government can then be required to provide evidence of people similarly situated in order for decisions to be made about whether there is a general violation of rights. It can also be expected to justify the inability to realize conditional rights by raising some of the factors discussed in Chapter 3 that are relevant for translating conditional rights into unconditional obligations.[94] Such a procedural change would help ensure that individuals are not deterred from bringing socio-economic rights claims as a result of an overly onerous burden of proof being placed upon them. It would also require evidence from the party that is best placed to produce it.

4.4 The minimum core and self-standing rights

The Constitutional Court raised further objections to the minimum core approach in the *TAC* case. As I have already mentioned in Chapter 4, the *amici* in the *TAC* case argued that there are two separate causes of action which arise in cases concerning socio-economic rights. They tied the notion of a minimum core obligation to the cause of action that arises under section 27(1) rather than that arising under section 27(2). Yet the argument for a minimum core approach does not in any way depend upon there being a separate right conferred on everyone in terms of section 27(1). The *amici* brief need not have joined two issues: the self-standing nature of the right in section 27(1) and the establishment of a minimum core obligation.

The conflation of these two claims led the Court, in its rejection of the idea that there are two separate rights created by sections 27(1) and (2), to reject the claim that the state has minimum core obligations in fulfilling socio-economic

---

[93] Naturally, these comments apply where the government is the defendant, and separate rules would have to be devised if socio-economic rights claims apply between private parties. I cannot deal with this issue more fully here.

[94] In the context of the South African Constitution, that would mean that the individual would have to show that his or her right in ss 26(1) or 27(1) has been violated. The government would be required to satisfy the courts that its failure to realize the conditional rights in those sections could be justified in terms of either the internal limitations of the rights (ss 26(2) or 27(2)) or the general limitations clause. See Liebenberg, 2005a: 33–54 for a similar, albeit not identical, position concerning the burden of proof.

rights. The Court, for instance, treated the minimum core 'as possibly being relevant to reasonableness under section 26(2) and not as a self-standing right conferred on everyone under section 26(1)'.[95] Indeed, it seems that the most important point the Court wished to make in its discussion of these issues was its conclusion that section 27(1) 'does not give rise to a self-standing and independent positive right enforceable irrespective of the considerations mentioned in section 27(2)'.[96]

However, recognition of this fact does not require a rejection of the minimum core approach, which does not require that there be two rights. It merely requires an understanding that one right can involve different levels of provision; the state can be obligated to prioritize the effectuation of a minimum threshold of a right whilst having to increase its level of effectuation progressively over time. The interpretation that I have provided thus provides a structural integration of sections 27(1) and 27(2) by explaining what progressive realization means in section 27(2) in relation to the urgency of the interests protected by section 27(1).

4.5 The minimum core is rigid and absolutist

The Constitutional Court provided one argument against the *amici* in *TAC* which involves more complex considerations. The Court claimed that in fact a purposive reading of sections 26 and 27 supported its approach to these sections. It reasoned that the minimum core approach requires everyone to gain access to the minimum core immediately. However, the context in which socio-economic rights are to be interpreted, it held, is one where '[m]illions live in deplorable conditions and great poverty. There is a high level of unemployment, inadequate social security and many do not have access to clean water or to adequate health services'.[97] Under such conditions, it found that it is 'impossible to give everyone access even to a "core" service immediately. All that is possible, and all that can be expected of the state, is that it act reasonably to provide access to the socio-economic rights identified in sections 26 and 27 on a progressive basis.'[98]

In this argument, the Court essentially charges that the minimum core approach is rigid and absolutist. Moreover, it cannot deal with the exigencies of the real world, and the limitations imposed by scarcity. The Court's own approach is designed to avoid these shortcomings by being flexible and sensitive to the difficulties of realizing these rights. However, the Court has not offered a fair characterization of the minimum core approach. In the next section, I shall offer a response to this objection through examining what exactly is entailed by the notion that the minimum core of a right must be addressed as a matter of 'priority'.

---

[95] *TAC* 2002 (5) SA 721 (CC) at [34]. The reference in this quote is to ss 26(1) and (2) as the court was referring to its discussion of the minimum core in *Grootboom*.   [96] Ibid at [39].
[97] Ibid at [35], quoting *Soobramoney* at [8].   [98] Ibid.

5 The Notion of Priority and the Minimum Core

The minimum core approach does require us to take a rigid stance in one respect: it requires us to recognize that it is simply unacceptable for human beings to have to live without sufficient resources to be free from threats to their survival. A state must exert great effort to rectify such a situation, and we must be intolerant of such living conditions. Such rigidity may indeed be a feature of the minimum core approach; but such rigidity occurs in exactly the right place. A society that recognizes the equal importance of each individual should have a principled and strong commitment to eradicating such terrible living conditions as a matter of urgency. One of the main ideas behind constitutional rights is to protect the most fundamental interests of the individual; there is none so vulnerable as those who lack basic shelter, food, water, and health care. The fact that, on the interpretation of socio-economic rights that I support, the Constitution takes a strong approach to eradicating such conditions does not, however, imply that it is out of touch with reality.

The first important point to recognize is that the minimum core approach is a means of specifying priorities. It involves the injunction that any government programme must, as a matter of priority, address those in a condition where their minimal interests cannot be satisfied.[99] The state cannot merely treat individuals in such situations as representing one problem to be dealt with amongst many others. The conditions the Court describes eloquently in *Soobramoney* are indeed the background conditions that this approach addresses. It embodies the understanding that there are millions living in deplorable poverty; but it also involves the recognition that there are some who are more vulnerable than others, some whose very survival is threatened by the conditions in which they live and by their lack of access to such goods as food and water. Such individuals are to be given priority in terms of the minimum core approach such that the threat to their survival is removed.

5.1 Lexical priority

However, it is necessary to develop a clearer understanding about what it means to treat the minimal interests of individuals as having 'priority'. Otherwise, it is unclear what the implications of the minimum core approach are. I shall distinguish two different notions of priority, only one of which I shall defend in the current context. First, let us consider the notion of 'lexical priority'. John Rawls

---

[99] For a similar understanding of what the minimum core approach demands, see Scott and Macklem, 1992: 77, who state that 'in effect, a priority of attention is mandated for people who would not be able to meet the most basic of health, nutrition and housing needs without direct government assistance'.

explicates this notion as follows: '[t]his is an order which requires us to satisfy the first principle in the ordering before we can move on to the second, the second before we consider the third, and so on. A principle does not come into play until those previous to it are either fully met or do not apply. A serial ordering avoids, then, having to balance principles at all: those earlier in the ordering have an absolute weight, so to speak, with respect to later ones, and hold without exception.'[100]

In the current context, saying that the minimum core should be given lexical priority would entail that the government would have to devote all its attention initially to ensuring that the minimum core of each individual is realized, and only then could it turn to matters beyond the minimum core. Roux outlines a similar notion of priority that specifies 'the temporal order in which government chooses to meet competing social needs'.[101] He criticizes the *Grootboom* decision for failing to hold that 'the state's short-term relief strategy should take precedence *in time* over the long-term housing strategy. Rather, the ruling was that the two strategies should be pursued in tandem . . .'.[102]

An approach to socio-economic rights that accorded the minimum core lexical priority or temporal priority is subject to a number of pressing objections. First, unfortunately, there are a number of people whose health situation makes it very difficult and expensive to raise them even to the standard required by the minimum core. Examples include persons with severe mental and physical disabilities, as well as those requiring expensive medical care.[103] An approach based on lexical priority would hold that it is justifiable to prevent the state from raising the standard of living of the majority of individuals in a society beyond the minimum threshold as long as a small number of people remain below that threshold. Such an approach has no reference to the costs of raising everyone above such a threshold or the sacrifices necessary to achieve the minimum threshold for all. Though the needs and interests of that small number of people need to be considered, and special weight given to them, to hold back everyone else on the basis of the vast expenditure and research necessary to improve the lots of such people would place a disproportionate burden upon other members of society. Such a situation would involve a violation of the principle of equal importance by failing to place equal burdens upon individuals in a society.[104] Moreover, such an approach has little regard for the reasons people fall below this threshold. In many cases, even with a vast expenditure of resources, the people in question would not be brought up to this minimum threshold. Everyone in the society would be brought down, often for a very minimal benefit to others.

Secondly, as was argued in Chapter 3, a theory that ensures only minimal interests are satisfied is one that is essentially self-defeating. Such minimal interests—as

---

[100] Rawls, 1999a: 38.   [101] Roux, 2002: 46.   [102] Ibid: 47.
[103] Nozick, 1974: 210 lodges a variant of this objection against Rawls's Difference Principle.
[104] See Chap 3 for a discussion about sacrifice and the principle of equal importance.

I have identified them—are generally necessary *means* to living a good life.[105] Where the realization of such interests entails that most of a society's resources are devoted to this purpose, the realization of such needs can lose its point for everyone. It is necessary for there to be resources available to retain a space beyond the basic in order for individuals to have the opportunity to realize their ends. A theory that led only to such an equality of the minimal would elevate the means to a valuable life to the status of ends in themselves and thus have a poverty of ambition, mistaking what is of ultimate value in people's lives.[106]

Thirdly, by providing for the more expansive interests I have identified, individuals are given the resources by which to maintain themselves for the long term well beyond the minimum threshold. To force the state to spend all its resources immediately upon realizing the minimum core would be to prevent it from adopting strategies to ensure that people in future would not fall below the minimum core. Such a policy would be short-sighted and fail to invest in any long-term solutions for the situations that people find themselves in.[107] In the words of the President of Brazil upon introducing a project to eradicate hunger: '[i]f we restrict ourselves only [*sic*] to these [short-term] policies, whilst the structural policy continues to generate unemployment, to concentrate income and to enlarge poverty—we will waste resources, deceive society and perpetuate the problem'.[108]

Finally, Rawls himself recognizes the drawbacks of the concept of a lexical order which he says 'appears to offend our sense of moderation and good judgment'.[109] Further, he recognizes that such principles must be fairly particular, apply to a limited sphere of operation, and establish definite requirements that can be fulfilled. Otherwise, 'later principles will never come into play'.[110] Rawls' principle of equal liberty, he contends, is a candidate for such lexical priority as it may satisfy these requirements.[111] Even if we accept this, however, it is not clear that such a notion of priority would be helpful in relation to socio-economic entitlements. In light of scarce resources and the different needs people have, such a notion of priority would lead to a situation where interests beyond the minimum core would seldom, if ever, have resources devoted to their fulfilment.

5.2 Weighted priority

In light of these serious problems with the notion of 'lexical priority', it is preferable, in my view, to define an alternative notion of priority. Such a notion has two

---

[105] In Chap 1, I developed the 'thin' theory of the good in terms of which the good life in a pluralistic society is to be understood.

[106] For a similar point, see the discussion in Chap 3 of Michelman, 1975.

[107] See also Wesson, 2004: 304.

[108] See Hunger Zero website found at <http://www.fomezero.gov.br/download/programa_FZ_Ingles.doc>.   [109] Rawls, 1999a: 38.

[110] Ibid.

[111] Rawls admits, however (ibid: 476), that even liberty interests 'may not always appear to be controlling. The realization of these interests may necessitate certain social conditions and degree of fulfilment of needs and material wants, and this explains why the basic liberties can sometimes be restricted.'

components. The first component involves the fact that those interests which have priority are those which we have particularly strong reasons to value and which require strong countervailing considerations to outweigh them. This view seems closer to the notion of priority that a strong 'right' has for Dworkin: '[i]n most cases, when we say that someone has the "right" to do something, we imply that it would be wrong to interfere with his doing it, or at least that some special grounds are needed for justifying any interference'.[112] Scanlon[113] also recognizes the problems of rendering rights as absolute moral bars, and prefers a 'balancing view, according to which such a right merely represents one important value among others, and decisions must be reached by striking a proper balance between them'. Thus, I propose to understand this notion of 'priority' as referring to a reason which has great importance to us and which can only be overridden by considerations that are of equivalent weight. [114]

The second component of this notion involves a point made by Parfit.[115] He outlines what he terms the 'priority view', which holds that benefiting people matters more the worse off these people are. He contrasts this with the utilitarian view that the moral importance of each benefit depends only on how great this benefit is.[116] His own view holds that the moral importance of each benefit depends also on 'how well off the person is to whom this benefit comes. We should not give equal weight to equal benefits, whoever receives them. Benefits to the worse off should be given more weight.'[117] Parfit is nevertheless at pains to point out that this priority to the worse off is not absolute. 'On this view, benefits to the worse off could be morally outweighed by sufficiently great benefits to the better off.'[118] Thus, this view of priority does not accord absolute priority to the interests of the worst off, yet it provides special consideration for such interests.

---

[112] Dworkin, 1977: 188.   [113] Scanlon, 1984: 146.

[114] Raz, 1986: 186ff rejects the idea of rights as involving reasons that are of great importance to us that can be balanced against other competing considerations. Instead, he argues that rights represent the grounds for imposing duties. Duties, in turn, have pre-emptive force: they 'replace rather than compete with the other reasons which apply in the circumstances' and are thus absolute within a particular domain (at 186). The domain itself may, however, be limited and of little importance. There are three important reasons why Raz's account is inappropriate in the current context. First, his aim is to provide an account of all rights, some of which are trivial and others of great importance. My project is limited to fundamental rights that always protect interests of great importance. Secondly, Raz does not distinguish between conditional and unconditional rights and claims that the protection of certain interests is sufficient to generate rights. In my account, unconditional obligations do in fact have peremptory force within a certain domain. I have provided arguments, however, to demonstrate that the protection of fundamental interests alone does not justify an unconditional obligation, which is arrived at only through the interplay of different normative considerations. Finally, it is unclear how Raz can avoid bringing in the idea of reasons with different strengths when determining which rights we have. My account explicitly recognizes the special importance of protecting fundamental interests without rendering that duty absolute. It is thus preferable in the current context to provide an alternative notion of priority to the lexical ordering approach.   [115] Parfit, 1997.

[116] A utilitarian view could lead to conclusions similar to those of Parfit—giving priority to the worst off—through factoring the notion of diminishing marginal utility into the overall utilitarian calculus.   [117] Ibid at 213.

[118] Ibid. He continues (at 213): 'If we ask what would be sufficient, there may not always be a precise answer. But there would be many cases in which the answer would be clear.'

These two ideas are compatible in that the according of special weight to the interests of the worst off requires a justification which I have argued is rooted in the particular importance of the first threshold for individuals. That in turn explains why rights which protect such interests have a particular strength and can only be outweighed by other weighty considerations. Two important implications flow from this reasoning: first, rights protecting the first threshold are not absolute; and secondly, there will have to be a justification provided for not realizing these minimal interests, and that justification must meet stringent standards.

It is necessary at this point, however, to explore in a little more detail what such weighty considerations could involve which would allow for the non-fulfilment of minimal interests. There will be few occasions where such justifications succeed in overriding the special weight that minimal interests hold. As with civil and political rights, however, there are always factors which can provide weighty countervailing reasons which justify limiting a right. No doubt all the countervailing reasons cannot be laid out in advance or without reference to specific contexts. The relative strength of the reasons will also vary in relation to specific contexts. However, it is worthwhile mentioning four instances where there may be justification for failing to realize such minimal interests. The first of these involves the scarcity of resources which renders it not possible to realize the minimum core. It is a basic principle that 'ought implies can'. Both the International Covenant and the South African Constitution make it clear that the unconditional obligations of a government will be subject to resource availability.

Secondly, I have mentioned that there are cases where the minimal interests of some individuals can only be met by dedicating a disproportionately vast amount of resources to them. In turn, such a course of action can threaten to deprive most others of the ability to live an existence beyond the minimal. In such an instance, it may be necessary to draw a limit to the resources that are devoted to a particular individual in bringing her up to the minimum core.

Thirdly, the realization of minimal interests must allow at least for some space beyond the minimal, and even beyond the maximal interests I have identified. In order not to be self-defeating, there must be an area of life preserved which can allow individuals to realize their goals and achieve positive experiences. Finally, the realization of the minimum core of a particular right must not prevent the realization of the minimum cores of other rights and liberties.

Thus, I have defended an account of priority that involves giving special attention to minimal interests but does not require that they have absolute weight in relation to competing interests. The notion of priority has not generally been analysed by those who advocate a minimum core approach.[119]

---

[119] Roux, 2002 is an exception and contrasts his notion of temporal priority with another less defined notion of 'priority-setting' which he takes to mean the specification of 'the relative importance that the state accords to competing social needs' (at 46). In the last section, I have attempted to develop a clearer alternative to the idea of lexical or temporal priority with more content than the alternative notion that Roux identifies.

Writers[120] generally assume that the UN Committee in its third General Comment wished states to realize minimum core obligations as a matter of *temporal* priority. That claim is based upon the following statement of the Committee:[121] '[i]n order for a State party to be able to attribute its failure to meet at least its minimum core obligations to a lack of available resources it must demonstrate that every effort has been made to use all resources that are at its disposition in an effort to satisfy, *as a matter of priority*, those minimum obligations'(my emphasis).[122]

However, the General Comment need not be interpreted in this inflexible manner, and could be taken to suggest a more nuanced approach. The UN Committee does not in fact specify what notion of priority is to be applied in interpreting the General Comment. As a result, it is possible to read it in a way that is consistent with the vision of the minimum core I have advocated. The state would thus have to justify its use of resources as displaying a special concern for the minimal interests of individuals. Whilst there could be reasons for not realizing the minimum core, such reasons would have to be of sufficient weight to override the special weight to be attached to the realization of an individual's minimal interests.

5.3 Response to objections

Working with this revised understanding of the minimum core approach, it now becomes possible to offer compelling responses to those objections of the Constitutional Court which have not as yet been resolved. For instance, it now becomes evident that the minimum core approach has much flexibility and is not correctly described as rigid and absolutist. The approach does not require that absolute weight be given to the realization of minimal interests and, where there is a strong justification, it allows for circumstances in which it may be legitimate to fail in this endeavour.[123] This accords with the theory of rights I have developed in which the more urgent the interests, the greater the burden that must be borne to show that there is a weighty justification for not realizing them.

---

[120] Roux (ibid at 47) for instance, appears to make this assumption.

[121] Certain recent statements of the Committee can also be taken to suggest that the minimum core obligation has in fact hardened into a duty that cannot be overridden. In General Comment 14 at [47], the Committee stressed that 'a State party cannot, under any circumstances whatsoever, justify its non-compliance with the core obligations...which are non-derogable'. Similarly, Toebes, 1999: 244 claims that the minimum core represents those elements of a right which are to be realized 'irrespective of a State's financial resources'. Such an approach is vulnerable to the objections raised by the Constitutional Court and those I have outlined in the course of this discussion. See also Wesson, 2004: 303–4 for further objections against an absolute approach to the minimum core.

[122] General Comment 3 at [10].

[123] Although not engaging in this analysis of the approach, several academic authors have also emphasized the need for justification where the minimum core is not met. See, for instance, Van Bueren, 1999: 59, and Scott and Alston, 2000: 250: 'it is for states to demonstrate their societal poverty and patterns of wealth distribution so as to prove that some people simply cannot—yet— have minimum needs met.'

The account I have provided also recognizes the importance of interests beyond the minimal, as well as the importance of setting up long-term projects that can guarantee a level of provision that exceeds the minimum core. The notion of 'priority' I have developed seeks to create a space for the idea that a government programme must devote attention to specific minimum needs without having to focus the entire budget upon their realization. As such, this accords well with a realistic model of governance and embodies the theoretical recognition that minimal interests are of great importance, yet we must not lose site of more expansive human interests as well.

The failure to adopt this analysis has led the Constitutional Court to reject the minimum core approach without recognizing its many virtues. One unfortunate consequence has been the willingness of the Court to make vague and general statements about the capacity of the government to meet minimum core obligations. The Court provides no evidence to show that the government could not provide basic shelter, food, water, and much life-saving health care to everyone within a very short space of time. In the absence of evidence to show that the fulfilment of a minimum core obligation would indeed be impossible, the Court's statement that it is impossible[124] merely strikes one as a pessimistic expression of despair at the severity of the problems facing South Africa.[125] Indeed, it is arguable that the contrary position is true—that with sufficient will and organization, the government in South Africa could ensure within a very short space of time that everyone has access to minimum core goods.[126] That would not involve very extensive provision for people, but require at least, for instance, that everyone has access to basic shelter, food, water, and much life-saving health care.

It is also possible to provide an answer to the Court's objection that the minimum core approach would require the government to do the impossible. A proponent of the minimum core approach is, in the Court's view, committed to recognizing the existence of an absolute right to have one's survival needs fulfilled in all circumstances. However, as I have argued, this claim mischaracterizes the approach. It is clear that the UN Committee envisages circumstances in which it may be proven by states that they cannot fulfil their minimum core obligation.[127] The South African Constitution, too, clearly offers a method of attenuating the obligations of the government where the core content cannot be realized. Since the argument for the core obligation involved integrating sections 27(1) and (2), the proviso 'within available resources' applies also to the minimum core of the right. The general limitations clause (section 36(1)) could also be used for this purpose. Indeed, reference to the limitations clause will be necessary when dealing

---

[124] *TAC*, n 95 above, at [35].

[125] I contend that the court cannot be satisfied with such vague, broad generalizations. It must require the government to provide evidence that meets a certain standard of justification if it wishes to draw such strong conclusions about the government's inability to fulfil minimum core obligations.

[126] It is by no means clear that the problems in South Africa arise from an absolute scarcity of resources; in this context, the problems seem to be rather about the highly unequal distribution of resources.   [127] See General Comment 3 at [10].

with factors such as the extent of the sacrifice required of individuals, which are not adequately covered in sections 26(2) and 27(2). The philosophical approach to interpreting socio-economic rights that I have advocated can thus help to clarify the role of the general limitations clause in such cases.

The Court has thus set up a straw man. Proponents of the minimum core should not claim that it must be fulfilled even where this is impossible. Essentially, the claim that such a core obligation exists commits one to the proposition that the government must prioritize the realization of this core level of provision. If the government claims it is not possible to realize the minimum core of every person, then the court must require proof as to why this is so. In light of the importance of the interests involved, courts would also be justified in requiring that the government provide an indication of how it aims to rectify this situation.[128]

6 Resources, Impossibility, and Rights

The above analysis of how to treat a minimum core obligation under conditions where it is difficult or impossible to fulfil raises an important conceptual question of wider application to analyses of rights. I shall focus on the question of scarce resources but the analysis below is applicable to any case where there are reasons that justify not realizing a right immediately. The question that arises is whether the availability of resources must be considered in the process of defining the very content of a right, or whether that very content is determined independently of the availability of resources. Under the latter scenario, the scarcity of a resource would represent a limitation on the ability to fulfil a right, whose content is determined independently.

6.1 The Court's approach

The Court's approach to this question is not altogether clear. The dominant approach appears to be expressed in *Soobramoney* by Chaskalson P in the following statement:

What is apparent from these provisions is that the obligations imposed on the State by ss 26 and 27 in regard to access to housing, health care, food, water and social security are

---

[128] An example of a government programme that would meet the requirements of the approach advocated here is the Hunger Zero Programme adopted recently by the government of Brazil. That programme seeks to provide immediate access to food for those who lack food at present, whilst at the same time adopting structural policies that can guarantee the self-sufficiency of individuals in the long term. The policy recognizes that short-term policies alone cannot guarantee long-term food security. Equally important, however, is the recognition that the long-term projects cannot alone be pushed at the expense of short-term needs: in the words of the President of Brazil, '[t]he structural policies require years, sometimes decades, to generate consistent results. Hunger kills people every day, produces social and family dissolution, diseases and despair as well as increases in violence.' See

dependent upon the resources available for such purposes, and that the corresponding rights themselves are limited by reason of the lack of resources.[129]

The Court's statement here suggests that the availability of resources must be considered in defining the very content of the right itself. In a separate judgment, Sachs J specifically endorses adapting traditional rights analyses to take account of the problem of scarcity and competing interests.[130] He holds that '[w]hen rights by their very nature are shared and inter-dependent, striking appropriate balances between equally valid entitlements or expectations of a multitude of claimants should not be seen as imposing limits on those rights (which would then have to be justified in terms of s 36), but as defining the circumstances in which the rights may most fairly and effectively be enjoyed'.[131]

In *Grootboom*, too, the Court held that '[s]ection 26 does not expect more of the state than is achievable within its available resources'[132] and, in so doing, suggested that the content of the right itself is to be determined by taking account of available resources. As has been discussed, the approach of the Court in the *TAC* case comes close to viewing socio-economic rights as providing a right to reasonable government action. Since the reasonableness of government action must be determined by having regard to the available resources, the content of the right is partially determined by the resources that are available.

On the other hand, Madala J in *Soobramoney* held that 'the guarantees of the Constitution are not absolute but may be limited in one way or another . . . One of the limiting factors to the attainment of the Constitution's guarantees is that of limited or scarce resources.'[133] His position thus seems to construe constitutional rights as having a content determined prior to a consideration of the availability of resources. The scarcity of resources represents a limitation on the ability to fulfil a constitutional guarantee. The majority judgment in *Soobramoney* can also be interpreted as suggesting that socio-economic rights confer entitlements that go beyond what the government can at present be required to provide: '[g]iven this lack of resources and the significant demands on them that have already been referred to, an *unqualified* obligation to meet these needs would not *presently* be capable of being fulfilled' (my emphasis).[134] In *Grootboom*, the Court claimed that available resources only qualify the content of the obligation in relation to 'the rate at which it is achieved as well as the reasonableness of the measures employed to achieve the result'.[135] This, too, could provide support for the notion that the content of the entitlements conferred by the Constitution is to be determined separately from a consideration of the availability of resources.

Hunger Zero Project Document, n 108 above. For further discussion on the policy implications of the minimum core approach, see Chap 7.

[129] *Soobramoney v Minister of Health, Kwazulu-Natal* 1998 (1) SA 765 (CC) at [11].
[130] Ibid at [54].   [131] Ibid at [54].   [132] *Grootboom*, n 12 above, at [46].
[133] *Soobramoney*, n 129 above, at [43].   [134] Ibid at [11].
[135] *Grootboom*, n 12 above, at [46].

6.2 The importance of conditional rights

I have tried to show that the Court's pronouncements do not clearly endorse one approach over the other. Is there any value then in recognizing that a right exists when it cannot currently be fulfilled? Is it not better only to recognize those rights that are currently capable of being fulfilled?[136] In answering this question, it becomes evident that it is of crucial importance to distinguish between conditional and unconditional rights. The Court's failure to draw this distinction may explain its lack of clarity about this issue.

Conditional rights protect fundamental interests that people have and arise in societies that seek to treat individuals with equal importance. These guarantees are designed to enable people to be free from threats to their survival and to be capable of achieving the purposes they value in the world. If we accept this theory of conditional rights, then it becomes clear that such rights should be recognized even where they are not currently capable of being fulfilled. People have conditional rights by virtue of being creatures of a certain type with certain interests and not in virtue of having control over a certain quantity of resources. The scarcity of resources does not affect whether a person has a conditional right, but rather the capacity to realize that right.[137]

The recognition that people have conditional rights even where there is no ability to realize them is important in that it recognizes that in a world of scarcity, there are often cases where people are not able to acquire what they are entitled to. It suggests that as the scarcity is lessened, there are entitlements that are already in existence which must now be realized. The idea that people have conditional rights even when these are not currently capable of being fulfilled thus helps to express the idea that there is a moral loss, something deeply disturbing that occurs when not all can be provided with life-saving health care, food, water, and shelter. It enjoins us to change this situation as soon as we can so that people can be given what they are conditionally entitled to. If we do not recognize such rights, then the failure to meet basic needs under conditions of scarcity does not violate any claim that people have. The situation does not demand reform as it does in a position where people have conditional rights that are not fulfilled. Thus, the recognition that a person's conditional rights are going unfulfilled—albeit ineluctably—provides a strong sense that there is some injustice or moral tragedy involved in the inability to realize those rights. The fact that we perceive such circumstances to be deeply troubling suggests that we do in fact recognize that there is something morally defective about such a situation. This feature of our moral psychology can in turn be captured by recognizing that people have conditional rights in such situations which are not currently being fulfilled.

---

[136] This question is addressed in Kramer, 2001a: 65–78.
[137] Donnelly, 1982: 394–5 argues that this analysis of conditional rights accords with how cases of impossibility of performance are dealt with in relation to private law rights as well.

Nevertheless, as I have argued in Chapter 3, there are several problems with holding that such conditional rights are in fact unconditional. First, it does not make sense to impose an unconditional obligation where such an obligation cannot be realized. This would violate the basic principle that 'ought implies can'. Secondly, there is no attendance to the overall costs that the realization of such rights may impose on the society. Finally, an unconditional obligation would imply that even a very diligent society, which had made a large effort to realize the basic needs of its people, would be in breach of its obligations if a few people remained below the minimum threshold. Thus, in translating rights from a conditional to an unconditional form, it is necessary to refer to a range of factors relevant to the question whether the state should be unconditionally obliged to ensure that people's fundamental interests are realized in a particular case.[138] Scarcity of resources will be one of the factors that has to be considered, and thus will play a part in determining the content of unconditional obligations. Consequently, the availability of resources should not be considered in determining the content of conditional rights but should be considered in providing content to unconditional obligations.

There are also some textual arguments in the South African Constitution that can be made for adopting this approach. Consider the structure of the principal socio-economic rights in the Constitution. First, there is the recognition of conditional rights in sections 26(1) and 27(1). These rights are expressed in unqualified terms and are recognized as existing no matter what the circumstances. Yet, sections 26(2) and 27(2) stress that what can be required of the state is only that it takes reasonable measures towards realizing these rights, and its obligations are qualified by the availability of resources. Thus, it becomes evident that the practical implications of the rights in sections 26(1) and 27(1) are to be qualified by the factors mentioned in sections 26(2) and 27(2). Nevertheless, the two sub-sections are separate. This can be understood to give expression to the importance of recognizing the distinction between conditional and unconditional entitlements. The rights in sections 26(1) and 27(1) must have their content determined independently of the question as to what the current obligations of the state are in realizing those rights. The reason for this lies in the very justification for recognizing such rights. However, the current and unconditional obligations of the state must take account of scarcity (and other factors). Where such scarcity is lessened, the obligations of the state change accordingly. Scarcity thus determines the extent to which the conditional right can be realized but does not qualify the actual content of that conditional right itself.

It may be objected, however, that there is no practical virtue in recognizing a conditional right that is essentially inchoate. What is the difference between recognizing that such a right exists and cannot be fulfilled, and not recognizing that

---

[138] Recognizing both conditional and unconditional rights thus is not simply a formal distinction but allows us to take account of these substantive moral points as well.

any such right exists? Apart from the theoretical virtues that have been mentioned,[139] there could be certain practical effects to adopting an approach of recognizing conditional rights that are not currently capable of being fulfilled. First, the recognition of an existing entitlement entails that the government is required to modify the current position so as to fulfil people's conditional rights as soon as it can.[140] As such, the government can be expected to make every effort to increase its control over resources so as to enable it to fulfil these conditional rights. Its actions can thus be scrutinized in relation to their successes in removing barriers to the realization of these rights. This accords with a distinction made by Sen.[141] He distinguishes between a right to x (to be free from hunger, for instance), and a meta-right to x (to be free from hunger). The meta-right is a right to have policies that genuinely pursue the objective of making the right to x (to be free from hunger) realizable. Recognizing that several factors preclude the full realization of a conditional right immediately does not imply that these factors defeat any obligation that arises from such a right. The reasons for the right may still require the government to remove the obstacles to the full realization of such a right.

Secondly, the continued existence of these entitlements can also help influence the behaviour of those who have resources available but are not legally obligated to provide for those suffering from deprivation (other countries, for instance). The idea that people are being deprived of something they are entitled to in virtue of their fundamental interests that they share with others may well have significant persuasive power. Finally, the fact that a conditional right exists even when not fulfilled entails that, as soon as the overriding reasons disappear—resources become available, for instance—the government is required to act in order to realize these rights.

An analogy with a temporary suspension order—a remedy developed by the Constitutional Court—is useful in understanding the situation that arises when there is a failure to fulfil the minimum core of a right due to its being impossible to do so. In *Fraser v Children's Court, Pretoria North*,[142] the Court found that the Child Care Act 74 of 1983 was unconstitutional to the extent that it did not require the father of an illegitimate child to consent to its adoption. None of the remedies open to the Court, however, could correct the defect in the interim without causing other severe policy difficulties. New legislation was required to deal with the complex policy matters involved in remedying the existing law. As a result, the Court decided to declare the Act unconstitutional but suspended its declaration of invalidity for two years until Parliament had been able to correct the defect. This order recognized that the current law violated a father's conditional rights. Since it was not possible to improve the situation immediately without causing other undesirable consequences, it maintained the current status quo

---

[139] I have argued for the theoretical virtues of this analysis in this chapter and in Chap 3.
[140] Put more correctly, this phrase means as soon as the defeating reason can be removed.
[141] 1984a: 70.   [142] 1997 (2) SA 261 (CC).

temporarily until the legislature corrected the whole framework. Ultimately, the rights would have to be realized, but at present it was seen to be impossible to do so.

Where the government cannot realize the minimum core of a right, the situation is similar to that which arises in the case of a temporary suspension order. It is important to recognize that there is a grave violation of a person's conditional rights taking place in such a circumstance, which has very serious consequences for individuals. Yet, the government does not have the ability to solve this problem immediately. The obligation to fulfil conditional rights is 'suspended' until the government is in a position to do so. Thereafter, it must immediately fulfil its obligation. The virtue of this analysis is that it preserves the idea that even under conditions of impossibility people retain certain conditional rights to have the minimum core fulfilled, even if such rights cannot be realized due to current conditions. Once these conditions change, the conditional rights transform into unconditional rights and must be fulfilled.

6.3 Distinguishing the minimum core and the pragmatic minimum threshold

There are, however, certain instances, particularly in relation to the right to health care, where the obligation to realize even the minimum core appears to be permanently suspended. This raises a number of important questions relating to the purpose of recognizing a minimum core obligation. If it is impossible to realize the minimum core, is there any purpose in using the concept in such a context?

In answering this question, it is important to return to the reasons for the introduction of the concept by the United Nations Committee. As has already been argued, these purposes were not entirely clear: however, two rationales leading to two different notions are suggested by the comments of the Committee, which need to be distinguished. The first is a concept that arises from the idea that there are urgent interests that must take priority over others; the second is the importance of having minimum benchmarks against which to evaluate state action. In the UN Committee's statements concerning the minimum core, there appears to be a conflation between these two notions. In relation to most subsistence rights, this does not matter; however, in the case of the right to health care, these two concepts come apart and must be distinguished conceptually. The distinction will also have implications for how the right will be realized and enforced.

6.3.1 The principled minimum core

The first notion is what may be termed the 'principled minimum core'. Essentially, this is the primary notion and the one that has thus far been analysed in this chapter. This notion relates to the statement by the UN Committee that the minimum core describes 'minimum essential levels of the right'. The minimum core here refers to the minimum basic resources that are necessary to allow individuals to be free from threats to their survival and to achieve a minimal level of well-being. The minimum core does not encompass the resources necessary to live a decent life or a dignified life in a community, but rather the basic resources that allow people to move beyond starvation, thirst, and homelessness.

One of the key evils sought to be remedied by the UN Committee when adopting the minimum core approach was also the lack of practical benchmarks against which to evaluate the performance of states in meeting the needs of people. This is the second key aspect of the minimum core: the development of a threshold against which state performance can be measured. In relation to food, water, and housing, it seems that the principled minimum core notion can provide such benchmarks. We can determine the amount of food necessary to prevent malnutrition or water necessary to avoid dehydration. Reaching this standard will not, generally, require a very high standard of provision, and the provision of such food will, in most cases, be within the resources of a state party. The state's actions can then be measured against whether it provides this level of food, water, and housing. However, matters are different in the context of health care.

Consider the definition of the minimum core obligation as the duty to ensure that individuals are able to be free from threats to their survival. In relation to health care, the imposition of this minimum core obligation would involve not only primary health care, but also the provision of expensive drugs and treatments such as dialysis and heart transplants that are necessary to preserve life. The imposition of such an obligation could preclude spending on any other area of human endeavour and lead the entire budget of a country to be absorbed by health-care expenditure.[143] The problem with providing such care universally is explained eloquently by Moellendorf:

[t]he cost of providing needed medical resources to all citizens, unlike the costs of providing universal housing and access to food and water, may be limitless since the costs of new technology are high and resource needs will continue to grow as new treatments become available. If the costs of providing needed medical resources to all citizens is limitless, then clearly available resources are insufficient to meet all claims and a system of rationing available resources is needed.[144]

The second problem with focusing all expenditure on the provision of health care services is that it will inevitably affect the realization of other less expensive needs, such as the provision of housing and food. The failure to realize these interests in turn has an impact upon the health of individuals. Thus, focusing expenditure purely on health-care services that meet survival needs can be self-defeating even from a point of view that is concerned to promote the health of individuals.[145]

---

[143] The problems mentioned here will vary in their severity according to the level of development of a country.   [144] Moellendorf, 1998: 332.

[145] The UN Committee has recognized these points by including access to basic food, water, and shelter as part of the minimum core of the right to health. A UNESCO publication has recognized a similar point in relation to other health-care services. The provision of equal access to high-technology care even in industrialized nations, it states, 'would inevitably raise the level of spending to a point

Finally, the vast spending necessary to maintain everyone at the level of the minimum core in relation to health care would ensure that people could only attain a very low standard of living. Few resources would be available for people to use to fulfil their projects and goals beyond those focused on guaranteeing survival needs.

Thus, in the context of health care, it is possible to say that there is indeed a minimum core providing strong reasons for prioritizing the health care necessary for survival and to alleviate suffering. Yet there are strong countervailing reasons in this area generally not to impose a practical obligation upon governments to realize the minimum core fully. In light of this conclusion, it may be objected that the idea of a 'minimum core' loses its usefulness in the context of the right to health-care services. Arguably, we should dispense with this idea and rather focus our energies on defining practical minimum standards against which government action can be measured.

It is important to make two points in response to this objection. First, we should again take account of the distinction between conditional and unconditional rights. The thresholds are specified in relation to conditional rights, and explain what, under ideal conditions, political institutions based upon an assumption of the equal importance of persons should seek to guarantee to each individual. This threshold thus recognizes the crucial importance to individuals of having the health care necessary to survive. The provision of such health care remains a priority (as with other socio-economic rights) and only strong reasons can help to justify the failure to provide such services. Identifying the principled minimum core ensures that these urgent individual interests are recognized and have a central place on the list of concerns that the government is obliged to address. That importance persists even if there are strong reasons why a government cannot afford to realize the entire minimum core. To focus only on pragmatic standards as discussed below loses sight of the urgency that certain interests have for individuals irrespective of resource constraints.[146] Tragic consequences may follow for individuals even if it is simply not possible to assist them in realizing these important interests. The minimum core thus has the virtue of placing these interests in clear view, and, practically, still requiring justification for the failure to realize them.[147]

Secondly, the formulation of any pragmatic minimum standards does not take place in a vacuum. The point is that without some form of principled foundation, the pragmatic standards are likely to be arbitrary. It is thus necessary to have a background theory which determines why the minimum practical standards are

which would preclude investment in preventive care for the young, and maintenance care for working adults': See Brody, 1993 quoted in *Soobramoney*, n 129 above, at [53].

[146] This may be the foundation of the view that the obligation exists irrespective of the resources available to a country. See, for instances, Toebes, 1999: 244.

[147] On the importance of the minimum core approach in placing a burden on the state to justify its failure to fulfil minimum core obligations, see Liebenberg, 2003: 176–7.

determined in the way that they are. Central to any formulation of practical standards in relation to fundamental rights must be recognition of the interests involved, and the differing levels of urgency that must be attached to the realization of such interests. Thus, even though the minimum core may not itself provide the minimum standard against which government action will be evaluated, it remains of importance in helping to define—along with a range of other factors—the practical standards which will be used. There consequently remain good reasons to retain the idea of a principled minimum core even in the case of health care, where it is not fully realizable.

6.3.2 The pragmatic minimum threshold

However, a focus on the principled minimum core alone in the context of health care will mean that we lack practical minimum standards that governments must meet in the provision of health care. Arguably, this is one of the important functions that was envisaged when the notion of a minimum core obligation was initially developed. The terse statement of the UN Committee concerning the problems it faced with state reporting suggests that countries had often attempted to evade their responsibilities in relation to socio-economic rights by pointing to the vagueness of the rights contained in the Covenant and by trying to avoid any specific definition thereof. One of the functions of recognizing a minimum core obligation was thus to identify certain clear obligations imposed by the Covenant, and thus to give a more definite content to these rights. By identifying a minimum level below which government action should not fall, the minimum core obligation ensures that the rights in the Covenant can be enforced and realized. However, if in the case of health care, the principled minimum core can never provide practical standards against which government action can be measured, then it fails to perform this important purpose.

This reasoning suggests that although we should not replace the notion of the principled minimum core, it remains important in addition to define certain practical minimum standards which government action must meet in the sphere of health care as a matter of urgency. I shall term these standards the 'pragmatic minimum threshold'. Defining such a threshold would involve a number of factors—apart from the urgency of the interests that I have already mentioned—only some of which are canvassed here. First, the cost of the treatment required would clearly be of relevance. Secondly, the availability of resources needs to be taken into account. Thirdly, it will be important to balance a preventative strategy focused on preventing health-care problems from arising against a curative strategy that focuses on treating health-care problems as they arise. Fourthly, an attempt must be made to ensure that each individual is offered equal opportunities for treatment. Finally, the impact of a pragmatic minimum on achieving other needs and wants in the society must be considered.

The UN Committee has in fact defined a pragmatic minimum threshold in its General Comment 14 on the right to health care. In this General Comment, the

UN Committee purports to define a core obligation to 'ensure the satisfaction of, at the very least, minimum essential levels' of the right to the highest attainable standard of health in the International Covenant.[148] However, the obligations it identifies in no way go so far as to meet even people's survival needs.[149] Much life-saving health care is left out of the scope of the minimum core.[150] Thus, it is evident that the definition of the minimum core has not only been governed by the 'essential' nature of the interests involved but by pragmatic considerations as well.

The pragmatic minimum threshold is thus arrived at through considering the minimum core as well as other theoretical considerations, together with the resources and capacity available in a particular society. These considerations are then used in the process of formulating a threshold which specifies a pragmatic minimum standard to which governments must devote urgent attention. This standard is a conglomeration of several principled and pragmatic considerations that lacks the simplicity of the justification for the principled minimum core.[151]

Distinguishing the principled and pragmatic strands within the idea of setting minimum thresholds allows us to understand the various important theoretical and practical purposes that such a concept must fulfil. In the case of most other subsistence rights, these purposes (and, consequently, the two concepts) overlap. They do not in the case of health care. Modifications will thus need to be made to our conceptual and policy frameworks in order to give effect to the right to health care.[152]

What then in brief are the implications of a minimum core approach for the right to health-care services in a country such as South Africa? Whilst it is not possible to guarantee all individuals in South Africa the treatment necessary to eliminate all the conditions that generally threaten survival, it is possible for the government to institute programmes that guard against some of the most prevalent threats to survival. These include, for instance, eliminating malnutrition, and

---

[148] At [43]. This definition of the minimum core comes from General Comment 3 at [10].

[149] See General Comment 14 at [43] where the Committee defines core obligations and at [44], where it recognizes obligations of 'comparable priority'. The difficulty of attaining a fully principled basis for the pragmatic minimum core in relation to health care may have given rise to the latter additional category of obligations. For similar accounts of the minimum core in relation to health care, see Hunt, 1996; Toebes, 1999; and Chapman, 2002.

[150] Examples include surgery and treatment of life-threatening illnesses that do not constitute epidemic diseases.

[151] Many authors have failed to distinguish between these different understandings of the minimum core and thus the normative underpinnings thereof have lacked clarity. The following authors seem to have understood the minimum core as a pragmatic minimum threshold. Thus, Eide,1989: 47, for instance, regards the minimum threshold approach as representing 'a pragmatic compromise between the ideal and the realistic'. Brand and Russell, 2002: 14 also state that the notion of minimum state obligations bridges the gap 'between fundamental entitlements and scarce resources'. See also the approach of Andreassen *et al.*, 1987 and 1992.

[152] The term 'minimum core' should be taken to refer to the principled minimum core in this book unless there are indications to the contrary in the text.

ensuring equal and urgent access to and the availability of treatment programmes for HIV/AIDS. In this way, the principled minimum core can play a role in the development of pragmatic minimum standards against which to evaluate government health programmes.

Also, health-care services in many parts of South Africa are in an abysmal state, which has a dire impact on people's health. The Department of Health should thus be obligated to develop pragmatic minimum standards which must be met as a matter of priority within the public health-care system. Such standards will also provide the basic standards which can then be built on over time so as to ensure the progressive realization of the right to health-care services in South Africa.

The right to health care thus requires at least that a number of goals be set for government policy (this need not be done by the courts), a minimum level of service be specified, and that the government establish detailed plans and programmes for an increase in the quality of health care over time with measurable indicators, targets, and deadlines. The reasons for its particular plan and its setting of the pragmatic minimum threshold could be evaluated by courts. Moreover, should the government fail to meet its targets, it would be in breach of its constitutional duty to realize the right to health care progressively over time. Courts need to be prepared to impose obligations upon the government to develop such a plan, evaluate the plan, and to compel the government to implement the plan. In this way, a pragmatic route can be forged for realizing a most important matter of principle: decent health-care services for all.

7 The Availability of Resources

The discussion thus far has demonstrated that the availability of resources is one of the central factors that must be considered when determining the unconditional obligations of a government in the context of socio-economic rights. More thus needs to be said about the interpretation of the phrase 'within available resources' which appears in sections 26(2) and 27(2) of the Constitution. The *Soobramoney* decision of the Constitutional Court[153] is the only decision thus far to be decided largely on the basis of the scarcity of resources and thus warrants further discussion.

7.1 *Soobramoney*

The case concerned a 41-year-old unemployed man from Kwazulu-Natal who was a diabetic. He also suffered from heart and vascular diseases which led him to have a stroke in 1996. That same year his kidneys failed and he came before the Court in the final stages of chronic renal failure. His life could have been

---

[153] See n 129 above.

prolonged by regular renal dialysis and, as a result, he argued on the basis of several constitutional provisions that he was entitled to such treatment.

Each dialysis treatment takes four hours and a further two hours have to be allowed for the cleaning of the machine. There were limited facilities for renal dialysis in Durban and there were not sufficient resources to provide dialysis to all those suffering from renal failure. As a result, the hospital had a policy of only treating acute renal failure, which could be treated and remedied by renal dialysis, or those who were eligible for a kidney transplant. Mr Soobramoney requested that the Court compel the state to make funds available to the renal clinic to provide dialysis for him.

I shall only consider those parts of the judgment concerned with section 27(1). In the majority judgment, Chaskalson P began by explaining the context in which the decision was to take place:[154]

We live in a society in which there are great disparities in wealth. Millions of people are living in deplorable conditions and in great poverty. There is a high level of unemployment, inadequate social security, and many do not have access to clean water or to adequate health services. These conditions already existed when the Constitution was adopted and a commitment to address them, and to transform our society into one in which there will be human dignity, freedom and equality, lies at the heart of our new constitutional order. For as long as these conditions continue to exist that aspiration will have a hollow ring.

He held that the obligations imposed on the state by sections 26 and 27 are dependent upon the resources available for such purposes, and the rights themselves are limited because of a lack of resources. In relation to current budgetary allocations, there were many more patients than could be accommodated by the existing dialysis machines in the public sector. 'This is a nationwide problem and resources are stretched in all renal clinics throughout the land.'[155] The Court held that the guidelines that had been developed were fair and rational: they were aimed at benefiting the most patients and directed towards the curing of patients. On the other hand, if everyone in the condition of Soobramoney were to be provided with dialysis, the current programme would collapse and no one would benefit.

The Court made this last point clear: if Soobramoney were to be provided with dialysis, then others in a similar position would also have to be treated. That would be very costly. The Court took note of the Kwazulu-Natal Department of Health's budget in which there had been significant overspending in the year 1996–1997.[156] It found that if all those with chronic renal failure were to be treated, 'the cost of doing so would make substantial inroads into the health budget. And if this principle were to be applied to all patients claiming access to expensive medical treatment or expensive drugs, the health budget would have to be dramatically increased to the prejudice of other needs which the State has to

---

[154] *Soobramoney*, n 129 above, at [8].   [155] Ibid at [24].

[156] In that year, there had been overspending of ZAR152 million, and in the year of the decision overspending was likely to be at ZAR700 million. See *Soobramoney*, n 129 above, at [24].

meet.'[157] The provincial administration had to make difficult choices in fixing the health budget, and in deciding upon the priorities to be met. Chaskalson P held importantly that '[a] court will be slow to interfere with rational decisions taken in good faith by the political organs and medical authorities whose responsibility it is to deal with such matters'.[158]

Moreover, the State is required to manage its limited resources in order to address all the basic claims upon it. 'There will be times when this requires it to adopt an holistic approach to the larger needs of society rather than to focus on the specific needs of particular individuals within society.'[159] Chaskalson P concluded on this basis that the failure to provide renal dialysis to those suffering from chronic renal failure did not represent a breach of the state's obligations in terms of section 27.

7.2 The pool of available resources

Two important issues arise out of this case which relate to the minimum core approach as well as to the jurisprudence on socio-economic rights in general. The first question relates to the pool of resources that is to be considered as being available for purposes of realizing socio-economic rights claims. The second issue concerns how the division of these resources is to be approached. I shall discuss each issue in turn.

In relation to the first issue, Moellendorf [160] has pointed out that the notion of 'available resources' is ambiguous. 'It may mean those resources that a ministry or department has been allotted and has budgeted for the protection of the right. Alternatively, it may mean any resources that the state can marshal to protect the right.'[161] Moellendorf recognizes that these are two extreme versions of what the term means and it may be held to involve something between these extremes. In *Soobramoney*, he argues, Chaskalson P generally employs the term in its narrowest sense, referring to the resources allocated by the provincial government to kidney dialysis.

This position, he points out, does not accord well with the position the Court adopted in its earlier *Certification* judgment.[162] There, it considered the objection that the inclusion of socio-economic rights in a bill of rights could lead the courts to dictate to the government how its budget should be allocated. Whilst the Court recognized that socio-economic rights might well have direct implications for budgetary matters, it also found that this was true when the enforcement of civil and political rights was at issue. It concluded that '[i]n our view it cannot be said that by including socio-economic rights within a bill of rights, a task is conferred

---

[157] Ibid at [28].   [158] Ibid at [29].   [159] Ibid at [31].   [160] 1998.
[161] Ibid: 330.
[162] *In Re: Certification of the Constitution of the Republic of South Africa, 1996* 1996 (4) SA 744 (CC).

upon the courts so different from that ordinarily conferred upon them by a bill of rights that it results in a breach of the separation of powers'.[163]

The Court in this passage does not limit its role in the adjudication of rights claims to the framework of existing allocations. 'Rather the court may pass judgments on these rights, as with other rights, that require a change in fiscal priorities.'[164] Moellendorf supports such a wider reading of 'available resources', for he claims that the narrow reading would reduce rights to mere 'policy priorities'. Rights, he claims, 'must have some role in guiding policy rather than being merely dependent upon it, if they are to be real rights and not mere priorities'.[165]

Yet, Moellendorf does not attend to the manner in which he uses the term 'priority' and fails to explain what the exact difference is between rights and policy priorities. His reasoning suggests this is a distinction in kind between different types of reasons. Yet, in my view, when the notion of priority is considered properly, the distinction becomes not one of kind but between reasons with differing degrees of strength. Conditional rights are reasons which have a special weight. If we recast Moellendorf's argument in this light, then it becomes evident what the real problem with the narrow interpretation of 'available resources' is.

To construe 'available resources' in the narrowest sense would be to ignore the special weight that should be attached to rights. 'It would be remarkable, for example, for the court to claim that the right to a fair trial need not be protected because those legislating and administering the budget have simply not allowed the resources to provide for fair trials.'[166] That would allow the government to avoid realizing conditional rights merely by virtue of its allocation of the budget. Such allocations may be well-motivated but it is also possible that they can fail to have sufficient regard for the urgent interests of individuals or be based upon the poor management of resources. As I have argued above, in order to defeat conditional rights, it is essential to raise reasons of sufficient weight to do so. Thus, if the allocation of the budget is to provide a sufficient reason for not fulfilling certain conditional rights, then that allocation itself needs to be justified by reasons of sufficient weight to justify the failure to fulfil such rights. This explains why the mere allocation by the government of resources cannot alone be taken to justify the non-fulfilment of rights. There must be good reasons lying behind such an allocation, which take account of the special weight to be attached to conditional rights. The failure to recognize this point will be incompatible with the justification for the inclusion of socio-economic rights in a bill of rights. Thus, since the state may be called upon to justify its allocation of resources, the pool of resources that must be considered as being 'available' must be all those that lie within the control of the state.

That formulation, however, itself admits of various meanings. It is clear that it refers at least to those resources that are owned by the state and can form part of the national budget. Any narrower construal of this phrase is not consonant with a

---

[163] *In Re: Certification of the Constitution of the Republic of South Africa, 1996* 1996 (4) SA 744 (CC) at [77].   [164] Moellendorf, 1998: 331.
[165] Ibid at [77].   [166] Ibid: 331.

purposive approach to interpreting socio-economic rights. What is controversial, however, is whether the notion of 'available resources' can be given an even wider gloss. It is plausible to suggest, for instance, that capital from foreign loans may also be said to be 'available' to a state. The question thus arises as to whether there are any limits to the pool of available resources that should be considered when determining the unconditional obligations of a society.

To some extent, the answer to this question depends upon the particular context with which we are concerned and the branch of government that is making decisions about the realization of socio-economic rights. The judiciary generally lacks expertise in macro-economic policy. It would therefore generally be inappropriate for courts to require the government to take out foreign loans in order to meet their constitutional obligations. There would be legitimate fears of the judiciary straying well beyond its sphere of competence and thus, for judges, the notion of 'available resources' would generally not include higher levels of foreign capital than the government currently has access to. Courts could only recommend that other branches of government consider this as an option for improving the realization of conditional rights, and require that the other branches of government justify their decisions properly in this regard. The executive, however, is well-placed to consider the amount of foreign capital that can be marshalled for the fulfilment of conditional rights, and, as such, a realistic assessment of foreign assistance should be part of its understanding of 'available resources'. The extent to which such capital can be acquired will, however, depend upon a number of economic and political factors determined by such institutions as the International Monetary Fund and World Bank, which lie beyond the control of any one state.

Privately held resources within a state may also lie within its control through its regulatory powers, and its powers to expropriate property. The question thus arises whether the notion of 'available resources' can also be said to include the state's ability to control privately held resources. That question can only be considered here briefly as it requires a lengthy discussion about the nature and role of property rights in a democracy such as South Africa.[167]

The theory I have proposed does provide support for the recognition of limited property rights. Individuals are generally extremely vulnerable and insecure in the absence of private property rights. To some extent that fear arises from the sense that the very resources required for their survival do not lie within their control. The protection of certain basic property rights is thus a necessary condition to ensure that individuals are in the longer term able to be free from threats to their survival. Secondly, private property rights allow individuals to have control over their own lives. It allows them a space of freedom to pursue projects and goals of their choosing. As such, it is an essential general condition for allowing the pursuit

---

[167] I shall sketch a broad resolution to this question, though a more extensive account will have to be left to another occasion.

of a variety of goals. Political institutions based upon the equal importance of individuals would have to recognize these factors and grant some protection to private property rights.

It is important to recognize, however, that private property rights on this account do not have priority over other rights. Their justification derives from the same source, and where they conflict with other rights, a decision will have to be made as to what affects the equal importance of persons more deeply: the suspension of property rights or the abrogation of subsistence rights. Relevant factors will include the urgency of the interests which are not realized, as well as whether abrogating property rights in a particular instance may affect the whole institution of private property.[168]

Determining the 'availability of resources' is thus more complicated than it initially appears as a result of the fact that scarcity is in many instances a result not of natural facts but of human institutions and decisions. As a result, the availability of resources is not a fixed parameter, but its meaning needs to be considered as one question to be determined as part of the overarching enquiry into the content of unconditional obligations. I have argued in this section that the phrase 'available resources' should be interpreted so as to refer to all those resources that lie within the control of the state. In determining what lies within the control of the state, judges should begin with a presumption that involves the protection of existing private property rights, and attempt to consider whether conditional rights can be realized through resources that can be marshalled by the state in its national budget. Where this is not possible, it will be necessary to evaluate whether the fundamental interests of individuals that are not realized in a particular case have sufficient weight to justify state interference with certain private property rights in light of the imperative to treat each person's life as having equal importance.

7.3 The need for a holistic consideration of available resources

The judgment in *Soobramoney* raises another issue of much importance to the adjudication of socio-economic rights claims based upon the minimum core approach. Chaskalson P recognizes that the provision of expensive health-care needs to all could prejudice the realization of other fundamental interests such as having access to housing, food, and social security. Furthermore, he holds that the interests of society will sometimes need to take precedence over those of particular individuals. These comments can form the basis of a further objection to the manner in which cases concerning fundamental rights have generally been adjudicated where such cases have major implications for resource distribution in a society.

---

[168] An interesting example in this area is the clash between the patent rights of pharmaceuticals that have led to very high prices for life-saving medication, and the rights of poorer individuals suffering from illnesses such as HIV to acquire life-saving medication. There are many complexities in the discussion of this case, but the theory I propose would allow for patent rights to be limited in the interests of ensuring that individuals with these illnesses can have access to life-saving medication.

The objection arises from the fact that the rights that are included in a bill of rights usually have a particular focus of some kind. We have, for instance, the right to have access to housing, the right to have access to health-care services, and the right to a fair trial. Particular entitlements are identified by these rights, which individuals can claim in court. Yet, it could be argued, such entitlements are not neatly sealed off from one another. The main reason for this is the fact that each involves the investment of resources. If a court orders the realization of one of these rights, this can affect the realization of other rights. It is thus not possible to adjudicate such claims on a one-by-one basis, but necessary to consider how the overall allocation of resources is affected by each claim, and whether such a claim prejudices the realization of other interests.[169] The problem with litigation based upon individual rights is that it particularizes an enquiry that should be holistic. The focus that rights have is consequently misleading as the enquiry is rather a general one concerning whether the overall allocation of resources in society succeeds in treating every individual with equal importance.[170]

A consideration of the underlying justification of socio-economic rights can, however, help to defuse the force of this objection. The philosophical theory I have proposed recognizes that a society is obliged to realize two fundamental interests that beings have which represent the general necessary conditions for living lives of value. Resource allocation in the society should thus be tied to this aim that, at this general level, need not identify differing rights. However, in order to put this theory into practice, it is necessary to specify what such general conditions consist in. Particular fundamental rights represent the specification of those general necessary conditions. Any holistic consideration of resource allocation must thus involve a consideration of the particular needs and interests that have to be realized. Fundamental rights, and the minimum core in particular, specify those determinate interests which must be given priority in the distribution of resources. The specification of these interests need not, however, imply that their realization is not interconnected.

Recognition of this point provides another important reason for distinguishing between conditional and unconditional rights. Conditional rights specify certain particular interests which must guide the allocation of a society's resources. That provides a further reason why the availability of resources should not be considered when determining the content of these rights.[171] It would be circular to use conditional rights as a guide to the allocation of resources where the very content of such rights is determined by the resources available for their realization.

---

[169] Davis, 1992: 478 puts the point as follows: '[s]hould the judge have to adjudicate upon a dispute such as A's right to a house the decision would not only impact upon A and the state but also upon all citizens whose particular interests, namely whether such money should be used to build a crèche, a hospital or a sporting stadium, would be directly affected by the decision notwithstanding their lack of participation in the litigation.'

[170] I am indebted to O. Ferraz who raises this objection in an unpublished article, 2003.

[171] See the discussion in section 6 of this chapter.

Conditional rights are thus useful for purposes of judicial review, allowing judges to scrutinize whether the government has considered the protection of these fundamental interests in guiding its allocation of the budget.

This approach also has the merit of distinguishing the broad categories of basic needs that individuals have, and considering how government policy fares in relation to each category. Greater specification allows for more particular analysis, more specialized data, and a detailed picture of the situation in each particular sector.[172] Breaking down problems into their component parts can be helpful in developing effective strategies to deal with them. The Constitution can be seen to require that resources be allocated in such a way that the policies and programmes that are developed by the government are targeted towards the fulfilment of the particular rights enumerated in the Bill of Rights.

It is when we turn to the unconditional obligations of a government that the holistic analysis becomes important. A court must thus consider the effect that the realization of a particular conditional right will have on the realization of other rights and interests. In many cases, such a broad enquiry may not be necessary. As *Grootboom* demonstrates, many cases could be decided in relation to the existing budgetary allocations of the government. The question that arises in this context is whether the existing allocations in the housing budget, for instance, are being spent in accordance with constitutional priorities. In the case of *Grootboom*, the answer was that the existing budget should be used to prioritize needs in a different way. Since this enquiry did not involve a reallocation of the national budget, the Court did not have to consider the impact of its judgment on competing needs. As a result, there may be little reason in such instances for it to defer to the government regarding the overall allocation of resources.

In a number of cases, however, it will not be sufficient to look at existing allocations, as was the case in *Soobramoney*. The court will have to consider in such instances whether the overall budget displays sufficient regard for constitutional priorities. In doing so, it must be admitted that such an enquiry is a wide-ranging one that will involve considering competing needs and interests. A holistic judgment will have to be made. The theory of rights I have proposed suggests an overall question that should be asked in making such a judgment as well as a number of relevant factors for such a determination.

In a number of cases, such as in *TAC*, the resource implications of the claim are minimal and would have little effect on other rights and interests. In such cases, judges need not fear that their decisions will have massive consequences for other areas of the budget, and thus judicial intervention is highly desirable. Where the effect on other needs and interests is much greater, and factors such as scarcity and

---

172 Andreassen *et al.*, 1987 and 1992 recognize the need for greater specification of the minimum core approach itself and suggest a particular method of assessing human rights performance.

sacrifice are engaged strongly, judges may be more wary of second-guessing the decisions of the legislature and executive, unless there is a glaring failure to take account of certain constitutional priorities.[173] Where conditional rights are not realized, judges may well declare this to be the case, but seek to work together with the other branches of government in a more collaborative relationship so as to reach a decent accommodation between the various normative and pragmatic considerations that are engaged. Since much government spending does not relate to basic needs, there are also cases where the allocation of resources will not accord with the special weight to be attached to such needs. When making such determinations, courts will need to consider the extent to which the budget meets the priorities that are justifiable within a particular society. Two axes could affect their decisions. First, the greater the government spending on luxuries and the greater the resources a society has, the less excuse it will have for not realizing fundamental rights, and particularly, the minimum core. Secondly, the greater and more urgent the needs are in a society, the less allowance will be made for government spending on luxuries.[174]

In determining whether there are available resources, the proposed approach can thus be summarized in the form of a two-stage enquiry. The first stage is to consider the current allocation of the government to the specific area under consideration and determine whether the policy in such a department accords with the dictates of fundamental rights. If it does not meet these standards and this defect cannot be corrected within existing budgetary allocations, then a court will be required to consider the overall budgetary allocations of the government. Again, the enquiry is whether the budgetary allocations of the government fulfil its duties under the Constitution in giving priority to the urgent interests of individuals. Courts will only be fulfilling their duties to protect the interests of the most vulnerable if they are prepared to make orders that ensure the realization of individuals' most fundamental interests. Courts will often be guided by the extent to which factors such as scarcity and sacrifice are engaged when translating conditional rights into unconditional rights. Where the resource implications are relatively minor, the Court may well be prepared to intervene robustly in the decisions of other branches of government; where such implications are vast, courts may well be less confident in interfering with the decisions of other branches of government. Even in such circumstances, however, it is conceivable that budgetary priorities may fail to accord with socio-economic rights considerations, and courts would be justified in intervening to correct this situation.

---

[173] Where complex interlocking considerations arise, courts will often defer to those with the greatest competence in the area of budgetary allocation. This should not provide an excuse for courts to abdicate their responsibility to ensure that budgetary allocations are determined with reference to constitutional rights.

[174] See Chap 4, where the objection that it is inappropriate for judges to make decisions which have budgetary consequences was considered.

It is here that a collaborative approach between the different branches of government towards the realization of socio-economic rights can be most important.[175] Where holistic determinations have to be made which have large-scale budgetary implications, courts may find themselves with the difficulty of attempting to prescribe the measures through which the state should remedy a violation of socio-economic rights. Courts can, however, declare the existence of such a violation and the need for the state to take steps to remedy it. The court can use innovative orders, including structural interdicts, interim orders, and the appointment of commissioners, to require the other branches of government to explain how they propose to deal with the violation and provide time frames for such programmes to be implemented or amended. The courts will be able to scrutinize the programmes developed by the government or the amendments made to existing programmes for their compliance with the socio-economic rights provisions of the Bill of Rights. Through this dialogue between the different structures of government, cooperative governance will be fostered, and each branch of the government can play an important role in ensuring the development of optimal programmes to realize socio-economic rights. Courts will not, however, be able to abdicate their role of providing content to these rights and an evaluation of state policy against these standards.

The courts should, it seems, afford more discretion to the government in the meeting of the second threshold than the first threshold. However, any defence of resource unavailability that justifies not meeting even the first threshold of provision will require the strictest scrutiny so as to understand why the position of the country is so dire that individuals may be allowed to perish for want of basic socio-economic goods. Such scrutiny should be akin to the scrutiny that would be applied were a government to claim that it could not afford to subsidize an election or court system. It is unlikely that many countries will succeed in being able to justify the failure to meet the first threshold. Some of the policy implications of the minimum core approach for countries with different levels of resources and needs will be discussed in the concluding chapter.

8 Conclusion

In this chapter, I have thus sought to demonstrate some of the implications of the philosophical theory of fundamental rights I have proposed for the legal interpretation and adjudication of claims based on socio-economic rights. I have argued that this theory provides the normative underpinnings for a modified version of the minimum core approach to socio-economic rights. The theory clarifies that

---

[175] Wesson: 2004, for instance, proposes 'a relationship of *collaboration* between the state and the judiciary'. As has already been indicated, I do not agree with features of his approach, but this is a valuable idea.

the minimum core represents a conditional right whose content is determined by the minimal interests of individuals in being free from general threats to their survival. It also provides a viable and persuasive interpretation of the socio-economic rights in the South African Constitution, and is able to respond to a number of pressing objections. The philosophical theory is thus not only well-motivated on a theoretical level but offers the hope of providing an analytical framework within which practical decisions about the content of socio-economic rights can be taken.

7

Conclusion: Implications for Policy in South Africa and Beyond

The philosophical framework defended in this book has sought to show the common normative foundations of socio-economic rights and civil and political rights. The one set of rights is no less fundamental than the other. We thus have no good reason to prioritize a right to free speech over a right to food. Both are of crucial significance to individuals and have important consequences for them. The serious normative import of socio-economic rights is often lost in academic and policy discussions as the focus is placed upon the resource implications of realizing such rights. In turn, these are regarded as providing knock-down arguments against realizing such rights. However, this common method of arguing provides a way of conveniently ignoring the normative import of these rights. For the distribution of resources should be considered in light of the important normative considerations that a society is required to realize: any scarcity of such resources should not obscure the fundamental interests of individuals that are not being realized. Those fundamental interests should in turn guide how these scarce resources are to be used. In many instances, the supposed scarcity is a convenient excuse for favouring the well-off over those who are most in need. Giving effect to the minimum core approach to socio-economic rights has the potential to provide a corrective to such unjust distributions.

Putting the pieces all together, I propose a view of socio-economic rights as rights that protect important interests of individuals, some of which have greater priority than others. In law, the modified version of the minimum core approach that I defend requires the government to give special weight to the realization of those interests that were defined as minimal, and beyond this to take reasonable measures to achieve the full realization of these rights. The state is thus required to justify its use of resources as displaying a special concern for the minimal interests of individuals. The conditional obligations of the government are consequently defined independently of resource limitations, the government's capacity to realize the rights, and a number of other factors. The unconditional obligations of the government, however, are arrived at through an all-things-considered judgment that takes into account the urgency of the interests involved and weighs up many competing factors. The structure of this enquiry thus requires the government to justify its failure to realize the minimum core with reasons of sufficient weight to override the reasons lying behind the protection of that very core. Justification is also required for failing to realize the second threshold of provision beyond the minimum core and a programme needs to be put in place to realize this level of provision over time.

It could be argued that, ultimately, when determining unconditional obligations, my approach in fact calls for an overall assessment akin to the 'reasonableness' enquiry that the Constitutional Court has developed. Although it is true that the final judgment concerning unconditional obligations does involve a broad-based decision involving a number of disparate factors, I have tried to argue for the importance of the two-stage approach, both theoretically, and through a discussion of the recent case law of the Constitutional Court on this topic. The two-stage analysis provides a principled structure to the enquiry concerning these rights that is not present in the cases decided thus far by the Constitutional Court. That structure, moreover, insists that a court (or other decision-making body) place the fundamental interests that are at stake in each case at the centre of its analysis. The fact that there are interests with differing degrees of urgency can then be recognized overtly, and those that need to be prioritized can be focused upon in the overall assessment of a state's unconditional obligations. Moreover, the theory I have proposed helps prevent the reasonableness approach from being vacuous by offering an understanding of conditional rights that specifies the ends against which government policy must be evaluated. It also provides more content than the notion of 'reasonableness' does to the broad enquiry that courts are required to engage in when determining the unconditional entitlements a person has.

This analytical framework is clearly important for the adjudication of socio-economic rights claims through the courts, the understanding of such rights by other branches of government, and the analysis of compliance with socio-economic rights by international bodies. However, the discussion thus far has been conducted at a relatively abstract level and the policy implications of the minimum core approach may be unclear. To understand how this approach can assist in addressing some of the pressing needs in the world currently, the practical implications of such an approach need to be outlined. Moreover, the theory proposed is a general one with universal application.[1] The discussion has thus far focused on the South African case alone and the policy implications of the approach for other countries need to be considered.

This conclusion shall seek therefore to provide a brief analysis of certain policy implications of the minimum core approach to socio-economic rights both within South Africa and beyond. This will help to connect up the theoretical discussion with real practical consequences for our world. I shall focus on two subsistence rights in particular: the right to food, and the right to adequate housing. In relation to each right, I shall consider some of the implications of the minimum core approach proposed here for a developed country with greater resources and

---

[1] The approach itself includes within it sufficient flexibility to take cognizance of contextual factors that may have an impact upon its practical implications in particular contexts.

wealth than South Africa (the United States and the United Kingdom); a developing country with higher levels of need and poverty (and possibly greater resource constraints) than South Africa (India); and finally, South Africa itself, a middle-income country. The application of this theory to each particular context will need to be considered in greater detail than is provided here; this conclusion, however, provides an indication of some of the practical policies that may flow from the adoption of a minimum core approach to socio-economic rights. It also raises a number of interesting issues relating to socio-economic rights that arise in the context of their practical implementation, and provides a clear demonstration of some of the points discussed in the rest of this work.[2] The flexibility and importance of the minimum core approach can thus be demonstrated in a range of contexts that reflect the problems faced by many countries in the international community.

1 The Right to Food in the United States, India, and South Africa

1.1 United States of America

The United States Constitution does not expressly recognize socio-economic rights. In general, it is recognized that the Constitution does not confer such rights on persons.[3] If socio-economic rights are to be recognized, this would have to be through the other rights contained in its Constitution.[4] The Supreme Court has in the past been hostile to finding substantive constitutional rights to social welfare in the Constitution; it has, however, recognized that such rights may be conferred by a statutory scheme.[5] There have, however, been cases in certain states that have effectively recognized certain socio-economic rights.[6] Roosevelt was also instrumental with his four freedoms in recognizing the importance of socio-economic guarantees, and, to this day, social welfare policies and programmes—such as food stamps—continue to exist, though some of these have been cut back in recent years. The United States has signed but not ratified the International Covenant on Economic, Social and Cultural Rights. Consequently, whilst it is recognized that the direct application of socio-economic guarantees in the

---

[2] This book has sought to defend a philosophical theory and corresponding analytical legal framework through which to understand the content of socio-economic rights: this chapter seeks to chart some of the practical applications of this framework, though in no way aims to be exhaustive of the issues that arise in determining policy in accordance with this approach.

[3] See Williams, 2005: 440.   [4] See, for instance, Michelman, 1969.

[5] See, for instance, *King v Smith* 392 US 309 (1968); *Goldberg v Kelly* 397 US 254 (1970); and *Dandridge v Williams* 397 US 471 (1970).

[6] See, for instance, *Callahan v Carey* NY 2d (NY 1989) discussed in Housing Rights Legislation (Report no 1 of the United Nations Housing Rights Programme found at <http://www.unhabitat.org/programmes/housingrights/documents/HS-638.pdf> at 112.

United States may be a long time in coming, it is interesting to consider what the implications of a minimum core view would be for the realization of the right to food in the United States.

Hunger does not manifest itself in the United States in general in the form of severe and acute malnutrition. This is generally due to the fact that there are existing social welfare programmes (such as food stamp programmes) that provide a safety net for the poorest families. When people refer to hunger in America, they refer to 'the recurrent and involuntary lack of access to sufficient food due to poverty or constrained resources, which can lead to malnutrition over time'.[7] Such inadequate food intakes can have harmful effects on learning, development, productivity, physical and psychological health, and family life.[8] To capture the differences between levels of hunger in the United States, certain terminology has been developed by government agencies. Food security is the term used to refer to 'the assured access at all times to enough food for an active, healthy life, with no need for recourse to emergency food sources or other extraordinary coping behaviours to meet basic food needs'.[9] 'Food insecurity' refers to the lack of access to enough food to meet fully an individual's nutritional requirements due to a lack of financial resources. A further category of 'food insecurity with hunger' refers to a more severe form of food insecurity in which the people concerned fairly regularly experience the unpleasant sensation of hunger as a result of not being able to afford sufficient food.

It is estimated that in 2004, 13.5 million households in the United States were food insecure. Of these, 4.4 million suffered from food insecurity to the extent that they were classified as 'hungry' (food insecure with hunger) by the United States Department of Agriculture.[10] In 2004, 38.2 million people lived in food insecurity compared to 33.6 million people in 2001.[11] The problem thus seems to be increasing rather than decreasing.

The United States conference of mayors surveyed 24 cities in 2005 to assess the demand for emergency food assistance that year and the capacity to meet that demand. Requests for emergency food assistance rose by an average of 12 per cent in the survey cities during that year. Eighteen per cent of the requests for emergency food assistance had to go unmet. In almost half of the cities, emergency food assistance facilities may have to turn away people in need due to the lack of resources.[12]

It is interesting to consider the link between the thresholds that have been developed in this book and the categories for measuring hunger in the United

---

[7] See the website of the Food Research and Action Centre (FRAC) at <http://www.frac.org/html/hunger_in_the_us/hunger_index.html>.   [8] Ibid.

[9] Ibid. See also the United States Department of Agriculture definitions at <http://www.ers.usda.gov/Briefing/FoodSecurity/measurement.htm>.   [10] See website of FRAC, n 7 above.

[11] Ibid.

[12] See Hunger and Homelessness Survey (a Report by the United States Conference of Mayors) found at <http://www.usmayors.org/uscm/hungersurvey/2005/HH2005FINAL.pdf>.

States. The categories that have been developed point to the need to indicate the severity of the lack of food and consequently the urgency of need. In general, in the United States, people do not starve to death and thus the food stamp programme could be seen to meet the first threshold of need. However, there are indications, for instance, that only 30 per cent of persons requiring emergency food assistance were recipients of the food stamp programme[13] and, consequently, the coverage of such a programme would need to be increased and improved for the minimum core obligations of the United States to be met fully. Those in the category of 'food insecure with hunger' may also over time suffer from malnutrition, and this can in turn lead to threats to their survival. Even if those in this category fall slightly above the minimum core threshold, nevertheless, there would be reasons to give their interests priority, given the severity of their experiences. Almost one-fifth of requests for emergency food assistance had to go unmet. Consequently, it would appear that the minimum core approach would require the United States to ensure that priority is given to raising all those who are food insecure with hunger above that level. Given the affluence of the country,[14] there does not appear to be any good justification for failure to do so, and it is likely that it would be necessary to discharge such an obligation immediately.

Given the affluence of the United States, however, it would seem that removal of persons from the lowest category of deprivation would not be sufficient. Raising everyone to a level of food security is a readily achievable goal.[15] Whilst priority must be given to those in the worst situation who have not reached the first threshold, the theory of rights defended in this book entitles all to the second threshold of provision (the general conditions necessary to enable individuals to realize a diversity of purposes). A compelling justification would have to be given for not translating the conditional right to the second threshold into an unconditional right. It is not clear what such a justification would be in a country such as the United States and it seems unlikely that any of the factors identified in Chapter 3 would provide a strong justification for such a failure. Consequently, the theory of socio-economic rights defended here would require resource-rich countries such as the United States to guarantee those within their borders access to food that is sufficient for them to live a healthy, active life rather than merely to avoid chronic malnutrition or starvation. Currently, the United States is far from meeting this standard. Developing a rights framework for the recognition of the fundamental interests of people in this regard could assist in creating pressure and urgency for change within the polity. This is what has happened in India through some remarkable litigation in its Supreme Court.

[13] See website of FRAC, n 7 above.
[14] The country has a GDP of US$11, 734 billion (see <http://www.census.gov/statab/www/income.html>).   [15] See FRAC website, n 7 above.

1.2 India

Nearly 50 per cent of the world's hungry live in India. Around 35 per cent of India's population are regarded as food insecure, consuming less than 80 per cent of their minimum energy requirements. Nearly nine out of ten pregnant women aged between 15 and 49 years suffer from malnutrition and anaemia. Anaemia in pregnant women causes 20 per cent of infant mortality. More than half of the children under five are moderately or severely malnourished, or suffer from stunting.[16]

Within this context, it was surprising to find that the issue of hunger was hardly dealt with in public debates and electoral politics prior to 2002.[17] For instance, in a period of six months in 2000, the *Hindu*, one of the best English daily newspapers, did not have a single article on health and nutrition.[18]

Whilst there was a vast need relating to food, India was accumulating food-stocks at an unprecedented rate. In mid-2002, India had 17 million tonnes of food-grain stocks.[19] It was thus clear that there was a sufficient supply of food to meet the needs of people in India: rather, people did not have the purchasing power to gain access to the food they required and the government was not providing them with such food.[20]

In light of this situation, an important and unprecedented case concerning the right to food was launched before the Supreme Court by the People's Union for Civil Liberties (PUCL).[21] Whilst India acceded to the International Covenant in 1976, the Indian Constitution does not contain clearly justiciable socio-economic rights in express language. Rather, it has 'directive principles that lay down some socio-economic goals which the various governments in India have to strive to achieve'.[22] These principles are not enforceable by any court of law.

In recent years, however, the Indian Supreme Court has developed its jurisprudence concerning the right to life to include what it terms the right to a livelihood as well.[23] No person can live without the means of living, the Court reasoned. Consequently, '[i]f the right to livelihood is not treated as a part of the constitutional right to life, the easiest way of depriving a person of his right to life would be

[16] Data is from World Food Programme and can found at <http://www.wfp.org/country_brief/indexcountry.asp?country=356>.

[17] A. Joseph 'Covering the Republic of Hunger' *India Together* (30 January 2006) found at <http://www.indiatogether.org/2006/jan/ajo-hunger.htm>.

[18] J. Dreze, 2003 'Food Security: Beating around the Bush' found at <http://www.righttofoodindia.org/data/jeanhumanscape.pdf at 1>. [19] Ibid at 4.

[20] U. Patnaik, 2004 'The Republic of Hunger' found at <http://www.righttofoodindia.org/data/republicofhunger.doc>; and A. Sen, 2003 'Hunger in India' found at <http://www.righttofoodindia.org/data/amartya.pdf>.

[21] *PUCL v Union of India* (Writ Petition [Civil] No 196 of 2001). The final judgment has not been given in this case though several interim orders have been made. Details of those orders can be found at <http://www.righttofoodindia.org/orders/interimorders.html>.

[22] Jain, 1998: 737.

[23] *Olga Tellis v Bombay Municipal Corporation* AIR 1986 SC 180 at [32].

to deprive him of his means of livelihood to a point of abrogation. Such depriv-ation would not only denude the life of its effective content of meaningfulness but it would make life impossible to live, leave aside what makes life liveable.' [24] Thus, the court recognized that the right to life would 'take within its sweep the right to food, the right to clothing, the right to a decent environment and a reasonable accommodation to live in'.[25] Through the right to life, the court has thus effect-ively recognized a number of justiciable socio-economic rights.

The PUCL petition sought to argue that the right to food of India's citizens entailed that the country's massive food stocks should be used without delay to prevent starvation and hunger. Initially, the petition was focused on the drought in Rajasthan, but over time was extended to involve permanent arrangements to avoid hunger and starvation.

Whilst the Supreme Court has not issued a final judgment in this matter, it has made its jurisprudential stance clear in the following statement on 23 July 2001: 'in our opinion, what is of utmost importance is to see that food is provided to the aged, infirm, disabled, destitute women, destitute men who are in danger of star-vation, pregnant and lactating women and destitute children, especially in cases where they or members of their family do not have sufficient funds to provide food for them'.[26] In light of this finding, between July 2001 and May 2005 the court has issued a number of interim orders that have been of major importance in giving effect to the right to food in India.[27]

First, the court has ordered the government to introduce a midday prepared meal at all government or government-assisted primary schools with a minimum content of 300 calories and 8 to 12 grams of protein per day for a minimum of 200 days in the year. Secondly, it ordered the extension of food security benefits (through a card system) that effectively guarantees food benefits to all those who are below the first threshold, including the aged, infirm, the disabled, destitute men and women, as well as pregnant and lactating destitute women. Thirdly, it ordered the full implementation of another six nationwide food security schemes. Fourthly, it directed the government to increase its budgetary allocations to its schemes that sought to guarantee employment (and thus provide people with the means to acquire food). Finally, it appointed two Commissioners to monitor the implementation of the court's orders and to report back to the courts.

The directions of the Supreme Court in this case show the promise that a mini-mum core approach to socio-economic rights can have even in contexts of massive need. It also, in my view, provides a ringing endorsement of allowing courts to adjudicate socio-economic rights claims. For, as has been documented by a num-ber of authors, the democratic political system was failing to accord sufficient

---

[24]   *Olga Tellis v Bombay Municipal Corporation* AIR 1986 SC 180 at [32].
[25]   *Shantistar Builders v Narayan Khimalal Totame* AIR 1990 SC 630 at 633.
[26] See the summary of the finding of the court at <http://www.righttofoodindia.org/orders/interimorders.html>.   [27] Only some of the Supreme Court's findings will be summarized here.

importance to the right to food of the most vulnerable.[28] The matter was largely ignored in the public sector and there was a lack of coordinated public action surrounding the issue. The *PUCL* case, far from removing the issues concerning the right to food from the public domain, actually placed the realization of the right to food firmly on the political agenda. Public action and activism surrounding the issue has increased.[29]

India, unlike the United States, cannot at present be seeking to realize the second threshold of socio-economic rights for everyone. It is not even meeting the first threshold for vast numbers of people. Consequently, the first step in the realization of socio-economic rights is to guarantee those worst off and most vulnerable in society sufficient food to enable them to be free from threats to survival (starvation and hunger). This was the focus of the *PUCL* litigation, which has led to important orders, where effectively the Supreme Court has forced the government to guarantee all individuals in the society a certain basic quantity of food. The midday meal programme and integrated child development programme has been directed at some of the most vulnerable in society: children, who tend to suffer greatly from malnutrition. Thus far it has reached around 55 per cent of Indian children.[30] These programmes have also been conjoined with programmes to enable people to realize higher levels of nutrition through gaining employment so that they can feed themselves.

The existence of large amounts of grain that was being hoarded by the government rendered arguments concerning the lack of resources impossible to sustain. The court did not, however, shy away from forcing the government to spend significant amounts of money on the right to food: it is estimated that the cost of the employment guarantee programme will amount to roughly 2 per cent of GDP.[31] Some economists have criticized the court for its orders: they have argued that it is

---

[28] See Dreze, 2003, n 18 above, at 1, where he states that 'Looking back at the food situation in India during the last ten years, one lesson stands out: the poor do not count for much in public policy.' See <http://www.righttofoodindia.org/data/jeanhumanscape.pdf>.

[29] Ibid at 5. Steinberg, 2006: 269 is concerned that the minimum core approach will stifle democratic deliberation; Liebenberg, 2006: 30 expresses a similar concern. As the *PUCL* case clearly shows, the needs of the poor are most often marginalized in public debate and modern representative democracies. The involvement of the judiciary in these issues can serve to place them on the agenda and in fact forces a discussion to take place concerning how best to meet the needs of the most vulnerable. The minimum core approach ensures that priority is given to individuals' most urgent interests; however, there remains a large space for discussion and debate concerning economic policy within a nation beyond the minimum core (and indeed about how to provide such a core to all). Moreover, a decent 'constitutional conversation' can only take place about socio-economic rights where there is some idea concerning what the conversation is about: the emptiness of the reasonableness approach means that there is nothing to talk about. It is only by providing content to fundamental rights that such a conversation becomes meaningful, and the judiciary has an important role to play in providing such content and thus stimulating the public discourse concerning the implications of socio-economic rights for a society.

[30] A. Waldman, 'Against All Odds, India Casts a Safety Net' (27 April 2005) *International Herald Tribune* found at <http://www.iht.com/articles/2005/04/26/news/india.php>.

[31] See A. Roy, 'Minds and Intestines' (10 December 2005) *Tehelka* found at <http://www.tehelka.com/story_main15.asp?filename=Cr121005Minds_and.asp>.

economic growth and market forces that should be used to improve the position of the poor. They argue that allowing more foreign investment, privatizing unprofitable state businesses, and cutting red-tape will reduce poverty more than a new government programme.[32] Other economists, whilst not opposed to growth, however, contend that to improve the lot of the poor, growth will have to occur beyond even the most optimistic predictions. Without government intervention, it will take 'forever to get people to an acceptable living standard'.[33] Social welfare entitlements and such measures as the employment guarantee schemes in India are justified in order to guard against hunger and child labour.

It is important to recognize that the normative foundation for the arguments of the economists focused on growth without social welfare is a form of classical utilitarianism that famously lacks sensitivity to the suffering of individuals. It aggregates benefits without 'taking seriously the distinction between persons'.[34] Growth-based economics of this kind promises an improved quality of life for some in a deferred future (the extent of such benefits is debatable) but, from its aggregating focus, ignores the suffering of individuals in the present. Moreover, many of those suffering in the present may not be able to become beneficiaries of the future wealth as their lack of food now will impact upon their ability to survive, function, and contribute economically.

An ethic that considers individuals as being of equal importance cannot callously condone hunger and malnutrition in the present for predicted benefits in the future. It must attempt to alleviate the plight of those suffering in the present whilst casting an eye to the future. This is why an economics whose normative foundations are rights-based cannot promote growth without attending to the suffering of all those in the present. Such an approach requires guaranteeing at least the first threshold of socio-economic rights provision to all, and building upon this over time. This may have a positive by-product for growth, in that many of these people will be able to become productive citizens without having to worry continually about having their basic needs met.[35] Moreover, it will provide a bulwark against economic exploitation as individuals will not be required to work in any unpleasant job that guarantees them merely the barest survival.

The minimum core approach thus has important implications for the economic policies of governments. This should not be surprising: just as tyrannical political systems are not compatible with civil and political rights, so too, unbridled and unregulated laissez-faire economics is not consistent with the protection of socio-economic rights. Socio-economic rights will not dictate the economic policy of the government; but such rights place constraints upon the policies that can be adopted. Such policies cannot abstract from the consequences for the

---

[32] See Waldman, 2005, n 30 above.   [33] Dreze quoted in Waldman, 2005, n 30 above.
[34] Rawls, 1999a: 24.
[35] This is one of the arguments given for the basic income grant in South Africa: see <http://www.big.org.za/index.php?option=faq&task=viewfaq&artid=3>.

fundamental interests of the most vulnerable within a society. The order of the Supreme Court in the *PUCL* case thus provides clear direction to the government: that it may pursue its economic policies, but cannot allow the poor and the destitute to starve in the process.[36]

The order is also fascinating in terms of its implications for remedies in socio-economic rights cases. First, the Court has released a series of interim orders. It has considered various aspects of state policy, and over a period of time evaluated the impact and problems with a number of these policies. Secondly, the Court has not merely left implementation up to the government. It has appointed Commissioners to monitor implementation to ensure that the orders are given effect. In a number of states, the midday meal programme, for instance, was not implemented, and further orders had to be made to ensure the fulfilment of the court's directives.[37] Such monitoring also allows the court to become aware of problems with its orders, to make them more specific, and to identify and remove obstacles to their implementation. The court also recognized the importance of Commissioners working together with NGOs, and other actors in this area.

Finally, as a result of the Court orders in the *PUCL* case, most primary school children in India will have at least one meal a day. The destitute will receive food allowances. This litigation establishes the possibilities for socio-economic rights to make a major impact on the lives of the most vulnerable in society. It is an example of the promise that socio-economic rights hold for establishing a more just distribution of wealth within even the poorest of countries with massive needs.

1.3 South Africa

South Africa is classified internationally as a middle-income country: 11.3 per cent of people live below the international poverty line of USD1 per day, and 34.4 per cent live below the higher poverty line of USD2 per day.[38] Currently, about 35 per cent of the population or 14.3 million people are vulnerable to food insecurity.[39] Data shows the prevalence of underweight children under five years of

---

[36] Steinberg, 2006 demonstrates a failure to understand that rights—whether civil and political, or socio-economic—determine the acceptable boundaries of justice and fairness within which the legislature and executive may exercise their policy-making powers. Consequently, the recognition of fundamental rights in a Constitution—which entails ensuring that the fundamental interests of individuals are protected and realized—will have policy implications. There are, however, a range of policies that are consistent with the recognition of fundamental rights in a Constitution and, consequently, the legislature and executive retain significant policy-making powers. The role of the judiciary in adjudicating rights claims involves evaluating whether the policies adopted by the other branches of government conform to these principled boundaries of justice. Failure to provide any content to fundamental rights renders these principled boundaries meaningless.

[37] See Mahabal, 2004.

[38] Data is taken from the Department of Health website based on 'A Poverty Profile of South Africa' (2005) Statistics South Africa data found at <www.doh.gov.za/docs/reports/2005/mdgd/part2.pdf>.

[39] See the Integrated Food Security Strategy of South Africa at 22–4 found at <http://www.nda.agric.za/docs/Foodsecurity/FinalIFSS.pdf>.

age as being at 11.1 per cent; the number of children suffering from stunting (low height for age) between 12 and 71 months was 23.3 per cent, and the number of children suffering from wasting (low weight for height) was 3.6 per cent.[40] This means that roughly 1.5 million children below the age of six are malnourished. Nationally, South Africa is food secure, with a surplus of maize that is used to supply regional food needs, and, generally, an ample supply of other goods.[41]

South Africa has signed but not yet ratified the International Covenant on Economic, Social and Cultural Rights. However, section 27(1)(b) of the South African Constitution guarantees everyone the right to sufficient food, and section 28(1)(c) guarantees children the right to basic nutrition. A minimum core approach to these rights would insist on a guaranteed safety net whereby those unable to access such rights through their own means are able at least to acquire sufficient food to be free from general threats to their survival. The state would also be required to ensure over time that people have sufficient food to meet the second threshold.

In 2002, the South African government released its Integrated Food Security Strategy (IFSS) that aims to develop a coherent and coordinated approach towards food security that 'stream-lines, harmonises and integrates diverse food security sub-programmes'.[42] The programme is multi-sectoral and places the management of the key priorities identified in the programme within different departments. The programme has many virtues: there is no specific department that focuses on the right to food and this right was therefore being dealt with through a range of unrelated initiatives. Seeking to develop a national strategy towards ensuring food security for all can only help to provide a more coherent, transparent and effective response to the lack of food security in South Africa.[43]

However, as I have indicated, the minimum core approach requires that priority attention be given to those who are most vulnerable and suffer from malnutrition. As was argued in Chapter 5, the Constitutional Court effectively recognizes this aspect of the minimum core approach in its *Grootboom* decision when it requires the government to provide relief to those in desperate need. Measured against this standard, however, the IFSS is seriously deficient.

One of its key priority areas seems to be promising in that the focus is on strengthening safety nets and food emergency management systems. However, it seems that there is little elaboration in the document about how this is to be done. The focus is rather placed on inserting the poor into the economic mainstream— a long-term, aggregating goal—rather than the provision of food—a shorter-term, distributive question. Moreover, when one looks at the policies proposed to improve social safety nets, they mostly relate to acquiring better information

---

[40] These statistics are taken from the National Food Consumption Survey conducted in 1999: it does not appear that more recent data is available. Data can be found at <http://www.sarpn.org.za/documents/d0001538/RSA_MDG_report2005.pdf>.

[41] See the Integrated Food Security Strategy, n 39 above, at 19–20.   [42] IFSS at 11.

[43] See Brand, 2005: 56C-24.

relating to food insecurity. There seems to be no dedicated effort to guarantee food security to those who are most desperate.

Much is left up to social welfare grants, but these are focused, in general, on those with special needs. The Social Relief in Distress grant is available universally but is provided monthly for a maximum of four months at a time. The emergency food parcel programme that existed was due to terminate in 2005, and such parcels were only handed out for three months in the year. The coverage and implementation of these programmes has also been poor.[44] The result is that 'if one is older than 14 years of age and younger than 60 (for women) or 65 (for men), physically and mentally able, not in foster care and not a war veteran, there is no regular state assistance to meet even the most basic of food needs'.[45] These people can literally starve to death in South Africa.

In general, the IFSS is focused upon empowering people to be able to feed themselves through, for instance, increasing income and job opportunities, and increasing the opportunity of poorer people to participate in the productive agricultural sector. As a long-term aim, improving economic access of poorer people to the mainstream economy and enabling them to feed themselves is a worthy objective that cannot be faulted. However, South Africa has an unemployment rate of 26 per cent.[46] Implementing these growth-based policies will take a lengthy period of time and their impact is subject to multiple uncertainties. Even when realized, it is unlikely they will cover all who are in need of food (for instance, those unable to work). In the interim, individuals in the polity will be suffering from hunger and malnutrition. Such individuals cannot be expected to wait for food until the long-term economic policies of the government take effect. They require that their fundamental interests be met as a matter of priority.

This raises the interesting question as to how these needs should best be met: whether in kind through a food stamp programme, or through an income grant.[47] In recent years, a concrete proposal has been favoured by many non-governmental organizations which would guarantee a basic income of ZAR100 (roughly USD18 or GBP10) per month to all South Africans.[48] The grant would be designed to provide the poorest South Africans with more income that could be used to meet their basic needs.

Income support programmes have the benefit of respecting the autonomy of individuals to spend the money as they deem fit. The income grant would also

---

[44] See, for instance, the problems that arose in the case of *Kutumela v Member of the Executive Committee for Social Services, Culture, Arts and Sport in the North West Province* Case 671/2003 (unreported 23 October 2003) (B), where social relief in distress grants were available in theory but could not be accessed by poorer people in practice due to the province not dedicating resources to the implementation thereof.

[45] Brand, 2005: 56C-27. Brand states that more than half of poor South Africans or 11,840,597 people fall within this category.

[46] See <http://www.statssa.gov.za/news_archive/12may2005_1.asp>.

[47] This is an issue that requires a lengthy discussion in its own right. I only seek to draw attention to the issue and some key issues relating to this debate here.

[48] See the Basic Income Grant Coalition website at <http://www.big.org.za>.

allow poorer South Africans to direct the income towards their areas of greatest need. On the other hand, an income grant allows less clear targeting of a particular problem such as hunger than food provision programmes. The income can be spent on other basic needs (or even non-basic wants), making it difficult to gauge the impact of such a grant upon particular ills in the society. Negligent parents, for instance, may squander their child's income grants without providing for their basic needs. The grant will not therefore necessarily have the desired impact of reducing child malnutrition.

Clearly, an in-depth analysis is needed as to the optimal policy method—both normatively and pragmatically—through which a government should provide a safety net for those in desperate need. Perhaps, if it is affordable, the solution is to have both income and in-kind grants such that the values underlying both are realized. What is clear is that currently South Africa lacks any policy that guarantees even the minimum core of the right to food to individuals within its IFSS policy. This represents both a violation of the approach advocated in this book and the reasonableness approach of the Constitutional Court.[49] Urgent action is needed by the government to remedy this defect, the absence of which should result in public interest litigation akin to that which occurred in India.[50]

2 The Right to Adequate Housing in the United Kingdom, India, and South Africa

2.1 The United Kingdom

The United Kingdom until 1998 had no formal bill of rights. All rights that were recognized in the society were statutory or developed through the common law. In 1998, the new Labour government passed the Human Rights Act which allows for a form of judicial review of legislation against human rights norms.[51] The Act effectively incorporates a number of rights from the European Convention on Human Rights into English law. A declaration of incompatibility between the Human Rights Act and a piece of legislation is not determinative, however, and parliament retains the final say in such matters. The Human Rights Act only includes a number of civil and political rights and no express socio-economic rights are included therein.[52] It would of course always be open for courts in the United Kingdom to interpret the right to life to include certain socio-economic

---

[49] This should not come as a surprise given the argument in Chap 5 that the court implicitly smuggles in a minimum core obligation to its analysis in *Grootboom*. It is the minimum core element in *Grootboom* that gives the socio-economic rights provisions some content and teeth.

[50] At the time of writing, the author and a team of colleagues were in discussions concerning launching such litigation.

[51] See the Act at <http://www.opsi.gov.uk/ACTS/acts1998/19980042.htm#aofs>.

[52] It has therefore been criticized as creating an 'unbalanced constitution'. See Ewing, 2001: 103.

rights as the Supreme Court of India has done; whether such a strategy will be adopted remains to be seen. The United Kingdom has signed and ratified the International Convention on Economic, Social and Cultural Rights.[53]

Provision for socio-economic rights in the United Kingdom takes place mainly through legislative and executive schemes dedicated to this purpose. In relation to the right to adequate housing, the United Kingdom passed a Housing Act in 1996 that provides framework legislation relating to housing.[54] That Act contains specific provisions relating to homelessness which were amended in 2002 by the Homelessness Act to extend the eligibility of persons to assistance and extend the range of powers available to local authorities.[55] This legislative scheme places a duty on local housing authorities to provide advice and assistance to homeless people, to assist them in securing accommodation, and, in a range of cases, requires the actual provision of accommodation for those who are homeless.[56] It also identifies categories of persons who have priority needs: these include pregnant women, persons with dependent children, old people, mentally and physically ill persons, and those affected by disasters such as floods and fires.

Homelessness is defined in the Housing Act as the state of being without available accommodation that a person has a right to occupy.[57] Falling within this definition are persons at various levels of need: the most extreme form of homelessness involves what is termed in the United Kingdom 'rough sleeping', where people are literally forced to sleep on the streets.[58] In 1998, there were 1,850 rough sleepers in the United Kingdom. At the end of 2005, the number of rough sleepers had been reduced to 459.[59] There are many people who are homeless yet do not sleep rough: the number of people living in temporary accommodation with no tenure security and assisted by the local authority is around 100,000; 80 per cent of these are in self-contained homes, though they occupy these on an insecure basis, which can be damaging to them and their communities.[60]

In response to this situation, the UK has developed a multi-pronged strategy that seeks to reduce and eliminate homelessness over time. The strategy includes the aim of halving the number of persons in temporary accommodation by 2010, and includes measures to do this by preventing homelessness; providing support for vulnerable people; tackling the wider causes and symptoms of homelessness; helping more people move away from rough sleeping; and providing 75,000 new units for social housing.[61]

---

[53] See <http://www.ohchr.org/english/countries/ratification/3.htm#N13>.
[54] See <http://www.opsi.gov.uk/ACTS/acts1996/1996052.htm>.
[55] See <http://www.opsi.gov.uk/acts/acts2002/20020007.htm>.
[56] Section 193 of the Housing Act delineates the category of people to whom this duty is owed.
[57] Section 175 of the Housing Act.
[58] See the most recent United Kingdom Policy on homelessness termed 'Sustainable Communities, Settled Homes, Changing Lives: a Strategy for Tackling Homelessness' (SCSH), found at <http://www.odpm.gov.uk/index.asp?id=1163057> at 10.
[59] See Department for Communities and Local Government, found at <http://www.odpm.gov.uk/index.asp?id=1150131>.   [60] See SCSH, n 58 above, at 12.
[61] Ibid at 7.

The strategy initially appears to be impressive and aims to achieve the progressive realization of the right to adequate housing. However, the minimum core approach to socio-economic rights requires a priority focus upon the first threshold of provision as well as the progressive realization of the second threshold. In the context of housing, the first threshold requires at least access to accommodation that offers protection from the elements, sanitary conditions, and access to basic services such as sanitation and running water.[62] In the United Kingdom, the government since 1998 has shown significant progress in realizing the first threshold by reducing the number of rough sleepers by 75 per cent. However, 459 people remain, who on a regular basis have no access to shelter which, particularly in the winter, may have a severe impact upon their health.

The minimum core approach would require that urgent attention be given to ensuring access to shelter for these persons. Arguably, the government's strategy is not ambitious enough: it focuses on sustaining reductions in rough sleeping, and the only new measure it proposes is additional funding of GBP90 million for the improvement of living conditions in existing hostels. With the low numbers of people who sleep rough, it could be possible given the reductions in recent years, to set the goal as the virtual elimination of this extreme form of homelessness in the United Kingdom.

Moreover, the strategy says little about the increased investment in new hostels (rather than the refurbishment of existing hostels) which would be necessary to offer rough sleepers temporary alleviation of their plight. The author's own experience of working on homelessness in Cambridge during 2002/3 was that the main existing night-shelter had to turn away at least five people per week (and usually two to three per night).[63] Cambridge, during this period, had between 20 and 40 people who slept rough each night, and the Cambridge University Support for the Homeless group found, after much research, that the best method of ending this problem would be for the council to open an additional night-shelter to sleep up to 40 persons.[64] The main reasons for not doing so appeared to be two-fold: first, there was a lack of priority given to the issue in the Council's budget, and, secondly, the possible locations of the night-shelter were being vigorously opposed by residents in those areas—who were worried about their property prices and a possible decline in safety in their areas—and this opposition could have had severe political consequences for certain councillors.

The author's experience of working on homelessness through democratic institutions in the United Kingdom suggests a strong justification for judicial involvement in the enforcement of socio-economic rights even in resource-rich countries.[65] The number of homeless people in the United Kingdom is very

---

[62] See Chap 6 above.

[63] See 'Strategy "a success" as Homeless Figure Drops' in *Cambridge Evening News* (6 March 2003).

[64] The author functioned as the political officer of this group and, as such, was exposed to a wide range of issues relating to homelessness in the city.

[65] The argument here provides an application of the general case made in Chapter 4 for the judicial protection of socio-economic rights.

small and these people are highly vulnerable. Such persons are politically insignificant for a government in the United Kingdom unless their cause is taken up widely in society. Providing for the needs of the homeless can lead to conflict with the interests of the larger number of middle-class voters, and the latter group is the most significant politically. Since homelessness issues have a relatively low profile in the United Kingdom, they are unlikely to play a major role in electoral politics. Consequently, a democratic government may safely sideline the issue and devote little priority attention to it.[66] The judicial protection of socio-economic rights can provide a corrective to this structural problem of majoritarian government whereby the interests of those who are weak, vulnerable, and not electorally significant can be sidelined in the democratic process. Thus, even in a country like the United Kingdom with a social welfare tradition, the judicial protection of socio-economic rights can be important.[67]

A judiciary that adopted the minimum core approach to socio-economic rights would require strong justification from the responsible government for failure to meet the first threshold of provision. The fact that there are only a small number of people who sleep rough interestingly renders it more feasible to provide them with shelter than in countries with large numbers of homeless people. It appears that in a resource-rich country such as the United Kingdom, it would be difficult to justify a failure to provide the minimum core to individuals, and the government would be directed as a matter of urgency to end rough sleeping.[68] The courts could force the government to devote greater attention and resources to realizing the needs of the most vulnerable in the society. Given the availability of resources in such countries, this would not need to be at the expense of meeting the second threshold of provision and ensuring the end to the wider problem of homelessness for around 100,000 people. The United Kingdom government's strategy here provides an indication of how the progressive realization of the second threshold could be achieved.

---

[66] To its credit, the current United Kingdom national government does not appear to have adopted this course of action. At a local level, however, the experience of the author was that this issue did not receive the priority it deserved.

[67] Such protection may also be important in cases where the government passes laws that, ostensibly, are supposed to deal with a pressing political problem, but have an unconscionable impact upon an unpopular group of people. This has happened in the United Kingdom in relation to asylum seekers, where the government passed a law refusing the claimant any benefits unless their claim was made as soon as reasonably practicable after the claimant's arrival in the United Kingdom. The persons denied these benefits effectively had to exist on the streets with no shelter or food. Given the absence of express socio-economic rights in the United Kingdom, judges have a more difficult time protecting individuals in such cases. For an instance where statutory interpretation and civil and political rights were used to recognize effectively that asylum seekers had a right to support where they were in circumstances of dire need, see *R(Q) v Secretary of State for the Home Department* [2004] QB 36 upholding the lower court decision in [2003] EWHC 195 (Admin) and Elliott, 2003.

[68] There are many problems that relate to rough sleeping such as alcohol and drug addiction, and mental illness. In 2002/3, in Cambridge, unbelievably, there were only two beds available for detoxification: see Cambridge City Council *Single Homelessness and Rough Sleeping Strategy* 2000–2002. Attending to rough sleeping may require that more resources be devoted to substance abuse and better care, for instance, for the mentally ill such that they are not left to fend for themselves on the streets.

2.2 India

In contrast to the United Kingdom, in India there are large numbers of people who sleep rough and large numbers who live in wholly inadequate accommodation. It is difficult to obtain data concerning homelessness in India, as it appears that no effort has been made by the government to collect information concerning the number of homeless people in the last 15 years.

The 1991 census estimates that there were 29,000 homeless people in the capital city of Delhi. That number is regarded as a gross underestimation according to the Housing and Land Rights Network, an NGO focused upon the achievement of the right to adequate housing. They claim that the figure is more likely to be around 100,000 homeless people in the capital.[69] In an unusual bout of cold weather in January 2006, over 300 people died on the streets of northern India. In Delhi, there were only 12 permanent shelters, 16 temporary shelters, 4 portacabins, and 22 temporary tents available to offer shelter to the destitute. These shelters could offer accommodation to a maximum of 6,200 individuals, leaving around 90 per cent of individuals without any access to shelter.[70] The temporary tents represented the government's response to this crisis; however, these too were grossly inadequate, being described as 'constructed of poor quality material, often with gaping holes. They are, by and large, flimsy and crude, and do not provide adequate protection from the cold and rain.'[71] The authorities have been charged by some with indifference and abandoning the homeless to their fate.[72]

It is in fact notable that India seems to lack any adequate strategy for dealing with the homeless and providing shelter. The main National Housing Policy of 1998 estimates the housing shortage in India at 22.9 million units.[73] To meet this need would involve a vast amount of money which the government cannot finance wholly.[74] The focus of the housing strategy is thus on creating strong public–private partnerships for the provision of housing. It thus concentrates on measures whereby finance from the private sector can be drawn to fund housing development and be more accessible to the poor. The strategy does discuss the improvement of slums yet, remarkably, for a national strategy, there is virtually no specific focus on the homeless.

---

[69] See Housing and Land Rights Network Press Release (11 January 2006) at <http://www.hic-sarp.org/news_show_user.php?id=51>.   [70] Ibid.

[71] Ibid. Quote by Ram Kishan, Project Officer for Aashray Adhikar Abhiyan, an organization working on homelessness in Delhi.

[72] See <http://www.wsws.org/articles/2006/jan2006/indi-j25.shtml>.

[73] See National Housing Policy found at <http://pib.nic.in/feature/feyr2003/ffeb2003/f030220031.html>.

[74] The cost is estimated at 1,510,000,000,000 rupees, only 25 per cent of which will flow from banks, financial institutions, central and state governments.

The Indian Supreme Court has recognized on several occasions that the right to life includes within its ambit the right to adequate housing.[75] In giving content to this right, it has stated that it involves the 'right to a decent environment and a reasonable accommodation to live in ... [i]t is not necessary that every citizen must be ensured of living in a well-built comfortable house but a reasonable home particularly for people in India can even be a mud-built thatched house or a mud-built fire-proof accommodation'.[76]

It is clear from the recent spate of deaths as a result of homelessness in Delhi that, for millions, the minimum core of the right to adequate housing has not been realized. India's problem is much more acute than the United Kingdom, and it is likely that realizing the first threshold of provision cannot take place immediately. This situation involves a grave violation of the rights of individuals and, consequently, it is incumbent upon the government to take urgent steps to ensure protection from the elements for those without it. The lack of statistics on homelessness and the lack of priority given to this issue in the National Housing Policy indicate that currently India lacks a strategy to deal with homelessness and to realize the minimum core of individuals as a matter of priority.

The first step in realizing the right to adequate housing in India will thus involve the development of a strategy to provide shelter to those who are destitute. Such a strategy may, of course, be integrated into a general housing policy that looks at longer-term, permanent provision. However, as the National Housing Policy of the government indicates, the provision of adequate housing for all in India requires an outlay of resources that the government currently does not appear to be able to afford. It is doubtful whether a partnership with the private sector will yield sufficient resources to meet the housing shortfall.[77] It thus appears that there is uncertainty even in the longer term as to whether the second threshold of provision (adequate housing) for a large number of Indians will be met.

Despite this situation of vast need and scarce resources, the minimum core approach would not allow the inability to provide the second threshold to serve as a sufficient justification not to attempt to realize even the first threshold.[78] The situation in India is one where prioritization of resources is critical; it is also a society based upon fundamental rights which cannot accept the consignment of large numbers of people to permanent homelessness. Dealing with this situation requires a strategy to provide at least the minimum core within as short a period as

[75] The seminal case in this regard was *Olga Tellis*, n 23 above.

[76] See *Shantistar Builders*, n 25 above, at [9].

[77] It is unclear how the government sees the private sector as making up the 75 per cent of financing necessary to meet the housing shortfall, and it seems a statement of faith on the part of the government that there will really be sufficient incentives for the private sector to finance low-cost housing for the millions who need it in India.

[78] Selikowitz J in *City of Cape Town v Rudolph* 2004(5) SA 39(C) ('first *Rudolph* decision') at 84 made a statement of relevance to this context: 'when funds are short, the need for emergency provisions is exacerbated'.

possible. Tents with holes that do not protect people from the elements fail to meet even the first threshold.[79]

Secondly, there is a duty to take steps to realize the minimum core with urgency. Even if there will be some delay in realizing the first threshold completely, partial realization is better than no realization. Such steps can involve, for instance, 'improving upon and rendering more structurally sound, sanitary and weather-resistant all existing structures, including tents ... and identifying municipal structures that could be used as shelters'.[80]

Finally, the lack of statistical information on the number of people who are homeless and whether they are sleeping rough or not also displays a failure to take the right to adequate housing seriously. In order to develop an effective policy that adequately deals with the problem of homelessness, it is necessary to understand the extent of the problem. The progressive realization of the right to adequate housing also requires measures and indicators against which progress can be measured. Detailed information gathering is thus necessary in order to develop a policy that gives priority to the worst off. Such information gathering should not, however, be used as an excuse to delay interim measures to meet the needs of those with no protection from the elements.[81]

2.3 South Africa

A critique of the *Grootboom* judgment and its aftermath in the courts was discussed in Chapter 5. It was contended there, that to the extent that *Grootboom* contained a viable approach to adjudicating socio-economic rights, it drew on the minimum core approach and its normative foundations. This argument is strengthened by considering two recent developments in the law relating to the right to have access to adequate housing in South Africa.

2.3.1 National Emergency Housing Policy

The first important development is the fact that four years after the *Grootboom* judgment was handed down, the national government finally took notice of it by including within the Housing Code a chapter dealing with the provision of

---

[79] Moreover, it appears that there have been large-scale evictions violating the negative element involved in the right to adequate housing. The obligations to realize the minimum core (as has been argued in Chap 6) certainly involve as a necessary corollary the obligation not to deprive people of shelter they already have without providing an alternative. The deprivation of 130,000 people of their homes in Yamuna Pushta without any attempt at compensation would thus clearly exacerbate the problems of homelessness and be a violation of the right to adequate housing. See <http://www.hic-net .org/articles.asp?PID=191>.

[80] See Housing and Land Rights Network proposals at <http://www.hic-sarp.org/news_show_ user.php?id=51>.

[81] Interestingly, in India, protection from the elements does not only involve protection from the cold in winter but from the heat. See, for instance, 'Indian tsunami victims spurn "model homes"' *Daily Times* (10 March 2005) found at <http://dailytimes.com.pk/default.asp?page= story_10-3-2005_pg4_24>.

housing in emergency situations.[82] The programme describes its objective as being to provide 'temporary assistance in the form of secure access to land and/or basic municipal engineering services and/or shelter in a wide range of emergency situations of exceptional housing need through the allocation of grants to municipalities instead of housing subsidies to individuals'.[83] An emergency housing situation is defined as one where people become homeless in situations which include a 'declared state of disaster'; 'extra-ordinary occurrences' such as floods and fires; where people are 'evicted or threatened with eviction from land or from unsafe buildings'; and where people live in 'conditions that impose immediate threats to life, health and safety and require emergency assistance'.[84]

The policy envisages temporary shelter being provided to people in such conditions which shall be 'basic, simple in form and easy to construct. The structural design should provide the strength, stability, and durability for the anticipated life-span of the shelter, providing basic shelter against the elements. The floor area of a shelter should be at least 24 m^2.'[85] Basic engineering services will also be provided.

In order to render assistance to persons in emergency situations, municipalities are required to apply for a grant which involves an intricate procedure that involves all levels of government. The grant application must be submitted to provincial government, which then collaborates with local government to submit an application to the Emergency Housing Steering Committee (a national government body). That Committee is then responsible for approving the application. The national government then transfers funds to the provincial government, who in turn arrange for the emergency housing to be provided together with local government. There are no time frames constraining this process other than that the Emergency Housing Steering Committee must make a decision within 21 days of the application being submitted to it.[86]

The introduction of this emergency housing programme by national government represents a major advance in its thinking and shows the potential of socioeconomic rights to have an impact upon government policy. Given the increasing housing backlogs in the country, the government recognizes its obligations to provide some form of temporary relief to individuals with emergency housing needs. This accords with the minimum core approach of addressing the urgent needs of individuals. However, although the overall intent of the programme complies with the minimum core approach, it is not clear that the content of the policy does for several reasons.

First, the definition of emergency housing needs in the policy admits of wider and narrower constructions. The first few categories appear to bear out the claim

---

[82] See the policy at 4 (Chapter 12 of the Housing Code) found at <http://www.housing.gov.za/ Content/legislation_policies/Emergency%20%20Housing%20Policy.pdf>.
[83] See Emergency Housing Policy, ibid at 5.   [84] Ibid at 7–8.   [85] Ibid at 17.
[86] See the flowchart of the process described in the policy at 25.

in Chapter 5 that the government had adopted a narrow reading of *Grootboom*, confining its obligations only to those suffering from the effects of natural or man-made disasters. If this is so, the policy fails to cater to all those in desperate need and thus fails to conform with the judgment in *Grootboom*. The category that has the potential to go beyond this reading is that which refers to people living in conditions that pose 'immediate threats to life, health, and safety and require emergency assistance'. However, the ambit of this category is unclear. The Human Rights Commission has questioned whether or not the category extends to those living in informal settlements in intolerable conditions.[87] Moreover, it may be questioned whether the category includes all homeless persons. In accordance with the arguments in this book, all those without protection from the elements (the first threshold) may be said to be in a condition where their life, health, and safety is threatened. The government would consequently have to provide emergency housing assistance to all those who are homeless.[88] It is not clear whether this wider reading represents the intention of the government. If it does, the emergency housing policy has the potential to make a major impact on the lives of the homeless.

Secondly, the programme does not appear to be well-designed to provide adequate short-term relief for those in crisis situations. The procedures it establishes are cumbersome, and it is not clear that they can succeed in making available urgent assistance to people who suddenly land up in a crisis as a result of a natural disaster, for instance.[89] In the second *Rudolph* judgment, the City of Cape Town estimated that it would take between eight and eighteen months to make the application for assistance. The entire process could take two to four years.[90] The Judge recognized that this situation pointed to a serious lacuna in the emergency housing policy: 'it does not make provision for a place where people with exceptional and immediate housing needs can be accommodated temporarily until a more permanent solution can be found for them.'[91]

Consequently, it appears that there still is no programme in place to provide urgent relief to those in desperate need of protection from the elements. The policy does not, as it stands, accord with a minimum core approach to socio-economic rights. Nor, it seems, would it even meet a standard of rationality: the policy that ostensibly is supposed to deal with emergencies creates procedures that render it incapable of doing so. As such the policy appears to be

---

[87] 'The Right of Access to Adequate Housing' 5th Economic and Social Rights Report Series (21 July 2004) found at <http://www.sahrc.org.za/5th_esr_housing.pdf> at 14.

[88] In *City of Johannesburg v Rand Properties* (Case 04/10330, High Court of South Africa, WLD, as yet unreported, henceforth '*Rand Properties*'), Jabjhay J seemed to regard the emergency housing programme as applying to *all* those who are poor and destitute.

[89] See the arguments of Mclean 2006: 21.

[90] *City of Cape Town v Rudolph* (unreported decision of the Cape High Court, 5 December 2005), at 13. The judgment is given in response to four reports delivered by the municipality and responses by the applicants. It is an unreported judgment on file with the author and referred to in what follows as the 'second *Rudolph* judgment'.   [91] Ibid at 22.

self-defeating and it may well as a result fail to pass the Constitutional Court's reasonableness test (that would at least include review for rationality). Moreover, the policy seems to envisage applications for emergency housing on a case-by-case basis: it is unclear why it does not rather provide for proactive budgetary allocations to be made to municipalities in order to deal with emergency housing crises as they arise.

Finally, the Human Rights Commission Report indicates that many municipalities do not have the capacity to engage the application process for emergency grants envisaged by the national government.[92] There are indications that the complex process also renders municipalities unwilling to make such applications.[93] As a result, it appears at the time of writing in 2006 that there have been only 244 beneficiaries of the programme in the Western Cape, and only two emergency housing projects have been approved in the North West.[94] Moreover, it appears that even a major city such as Johannesburg with a higher level of capacity than many other municipalities has not implemented an emergency housing programme.[95] Thus, a more streamlined, user-friendly policy is necessary to enable municipalities to realize the urgent needs of people for housing.

2.3.2 Alternative accommodation

As has been argued in Chapter 6, the minimum core approach involves recognizing a range of more concrete obligations to respect, protect, and fulfil the first threshold. The intersection between positive and negative obligations relating to the minimum core is neatly illustrated through a line of cases in South Africa that have recently sought to establish the principle that, in general, courts will not allow people who are relatively settled to be evicted from their places of residence unless alternative accommodation is made available to them.

In *Port Elizabeth Municipality v Various Occupiers*,[96] a municipality sought an eviction order against 68 people, including 23 children, who had erected shacks on privately owned land and lived there for between two and eight years. The municipality in particular wanted the court to affirm that it did not need to provide alternative accommodation when it sought to evict unlawful occupiers. Sachs J, delivering judgment for a unanimous court, found that 'the integrity of the rights-based vision of the Constitution is punctured when governmental action augments rather than reduces denial of the claims of the desperately poor to the basic elements of a decent existence'.[97]

The Constitution required a balance to be struck between ownership rights and ensuring that individuals have access to adequate accommodation.[98] Judges

---

[92] See report n 87 above at 37.   [93] See second *Rudolph* judgment, n 90 above at 17.

[94] This is based on information on the Department of Housing website, <www.housing.gov.za>.

[95] In *Rand Properties*, n 88 above, at [47] and [53], Jabjhay J found that notwithstanding the adoption of the Emergency Housing Programme, the City had failed in the 'pragmatic implementation of the Programme'.   [96] 2005 (1) SA 217 (CC).

[97] At [18].   [98] At [23].

must balance competing claims by taking account of all relevant factors in a particular context. These circumstances included the availability of alternative accommodation: a 'court should be reluctant to grant an eviction against relatively settled occupiers unless it is satisfied that a reasonable alternative is available, even if only as an interim measure pending ultimate access to housing in the formal housing programme'.[99] Since a municipality has a duty under the constitution to improve access to housing in its area, it cannot merely evict people from their homes without considering a solution to their problems. On this basis, the court refused to allow the occupiers to be evicted until a decent solution had been found.[100]

A similar finding was reached by the Court in *President of the Republic of South Africa v Modderklip Boerdery (Pty) Ltd*.[101] The case concerned a community of around 40,000 persons who settled unlawfully upon the farm of a private company (Modderklip). An eviction order was granted by a lower court but none of the branches of government were prepared to enforce it. Modderklip sought an order of court compelling the state to remove the occupiers. The court found that '[t]he problem of homelessness is particularly acute in our society' and that 'the frustration and helplessness suffered by many who still struggle against heavy odds to meet the challenge merely to survive and to have shelter can never be underestimated'.[102] Private parties had a right to have court orders enforced in terms of the right 'to have any dispute that can be resolved by the application of law decided in a fair public hearing before a court'.[103] The state had an obligation to take reasonable steps to ensure that Modderklip was provided with effective relief. However, to execute this particular court order 'and evict tens of thousands of people with nowhere to go would cause unimaginable social chaos and misery and untold disruption'.[104] In light of this, the Court ordered payment of compensation to Modderklip for the unlawful occupation of its land, but also declared that the current residents were entitled to occupy the land until alternative land was made available to them by the state.

Finally, a remarkable and important decision was reached by a judge in the Witwatersrand Local Division of the High Court in *City of Johannesburg v Rand Properties*.[105] The City Council of Johannesburg wished to evict 300 persons from buildings that it regarded as dangerous and constituting health hazards. The evictions were part of its inner city regeneration programme. The occupiers were generally desperately poor people who earned whatever income they could from opportunities in close proximity to where they lived. The judge found

---

[99] At [28].
[100] Shortly after this case was decided, the court recognized in *Jaftha v Schoeman* 2005 (2) SA 140 (CC) at [33] in unambiguous terms that there is a negative content to socio-economic rights which can only be limited through application of the general limitations clause.
[101] 2005 (5) SA 3 (CC).   [102] Ibid at [36]
[103] Section 34 of the Constitution. Ibid at [39].   [104] Ibid at [47]   [105] See n 88 above.

the conditions in the buildings to be appalling and, at times, disgraceful.[106] Nevertheless, the Court held that 'the mere establishment by a municipality that an occupation is unhealthy or unsafe does not automatically require a Court to grant an eviction order'.[107] Since the Constitution requires everyone to be treated with equal care, 'the actions of the State should be construed as unreasonable, if they fail to respond to the needs of the most desperate and vulnerable individuals in society'.[108]

In light of this, the judge found that the City cannot just wish away its problems in light of its inner city rejuvenation project by evicting people without offering them any alternative. Although the people lived in difficult conditions, at least they had shelter from the elements and access to water. 'The eviction of the occupiers from their current unsafe accommodation will leave them far worse off— they will be without any accommodation at all.'[109] In light of this, the judge found that the City had failed to fulfil its obligations and give adequate priority to those in desperate need; he directed the city to develop a programme that could realize the right to adequate housing of people in the inner city and in desperate need of accommodation; and interdicted the City from evicting the residents of these buildings until such a programme was in place.

The reasoning in all these cases places a particular focus upon desperation and vulnerability. The people were living in conditions that, generally, barely met the first threshold of provision. It is clear from the reasoning of the courts in these cases that they are acutely aware of the plight of these people: should they be evicted, they would be rendered homeless. The reasoning and grounds for the decisions are thus consonant with the minimum core approach.

For instance, Jabhjay J in *Rand Properties* writes eloquently about adequate housing involving more than merely four walls or a roof over one's head.[110] Ultimately, however, the case was about preventing people from becoming homeless, where their living conditions were far from adequate. The Court recognized that having access to shelter from the elements was better than having no shelter at all, even though the shelter people had did not meet the standards of adequate housing. Such reasoning recognizes that there are important interests people have short of having access to 'adequate housing' and that these interests require protection. Rendering people homeless places them in a position of greater desperation even where their existing accommodation leaves much to be desired.

On the whole, however, the courts have been reluctant expressly to recognize a distinction between levels of need. This could result from having placed dignity at the foundation of socio-economic rights and failing to recognize that violations of dignity admit of degree. A person without any home, forced to move from pillar to post with no place of their own, would be suffering from an extremely severe violation of dignity. Where people have access to a home that they can call their

---

[106] Ibid at [18].   [107] Ibid at [29].   [108] Ibid at [54].   [109] Ibid at [57].
[110] At [49].

own, albeit one that is not fully adequate, they suffer from a lesser violation of their dignity. Consequently, there seems no barrier to courts recognizing different thresholds that impact upon dignity to differing degrees. Urgency of need could in fact be explicated in these terms.[111]

Finally, these cases involve an interesting intersection between positive and negative obligations relating to the minimum core. Effectively, they were about evictions and the state having to respect people's existing access to housing. Yet the issues in these cases were closely tied to the state's fulfillment of its positive obligations to provide housing to people in desperate need. Courts would be inclined to allow violations of the obligation to respect socio-economic rights, if the state had provided alternative accommodation, part of its obligations to fulfil such rights. The omission to fulfil its positive obligations meant that the negative obligations of the state not to interfere with people's existing homes effectively became stronger. Both sets of obligations are designed to ensure that people reach at least the minimum core level of being raised from the state of being in desperate need.

3 Conclusion

The Human Development Report of 2005 recognizes that poverty cannot be addressed effectively by strategies focused on aggregate growth alone: the distribution of resources within a society also matters.[112] Justice Sachs eloquently wrote in similar vein in a recent judgment that 'in a society founded on human dignity, equality and freedom it cannot be presupposed that the greatest good for the many can be achieved at the cost of intolerable hardship for the few, particularly if by a reasonable application of judicial and administrative statecraft such human distress could be avoided'.[113]

An understanding of the normative foundations of socio-economic rights provides an important moral basis for these claims. It also provides the basis for developing an approach to the enforcement of such rights which has teeth. A government is required to give priority to ensuring that individuals are free from the general conditions that threaten their survival. Were governments to adopt policies in line with their obligations in terms of the minimum core approach, radical improvements would occur in the economic position of the worst-off in society within a short period of time.[114]

---

[111] The content of dignity would have to be developed for it to perform this role.

[112] See Human Development Report Summary at 26 found at <http://hdr.undp.org/reports/global/2005/pdf/ hdr05_summary.pdf>.

[113] *Port Elizabeth Municipality* case, n 96 above, at [29].

[114] It is recognized that governments also have obligations to assist one another to lift individuals from below the thresholds. This book has focused upon the obligations of states towards those within their midst, but the normative foundations of socio-economic rights also provides reason to recognize an obligation upon the affluent countries to assist the less affluent to realize the fundamental rights of individuals in their midst.

Governments serious about social justice would also aim to ensure that individuals are provided with the general conditions necessary to realize a diversity of purposes. Such a society would establish a baseline of equality for individuals in its midst, and thus truly place itself on the path towards making good its commitment to the equal importance of individuals. The debate could then be had about realizing higher levels of distributive equality.

However, at present, most societies in the world, even affluent ones, are failing to realize even the most basic needs of many individuals in their midst. This work has argued that this sorry state of affairs represents a major violation of the fundamental normative commitments that any just society must make. It has provided an analytical framework through which socio-economic rights can be translated into legal doctrine and policy. Adopting the minimum core approach to the content and enforcement of socio-economic rights holds out the possibility of a proximal future in which no one will be allowed to starve to death for want of food and no one will be allowed to die of exposure to the cold for want of shelter from the elements. This is not a utopian vision but one that is readily achievable. By taking socio-economic rights seriously, attending to the content thereof, and adopting appropriate institutional and enforcement mechanisms, it will be possible to ensure that the vision of a world without absolute poverty can be translated into reality.

Bibliography

Aiken, W. and H. La Follette (eds). 1977a. *World Hunger and Moral Obligation*. New Jersey: Prentice Hall.

Aiken, W. 1977b. 'The Right to be Saved from Starvation'. In W. Aiken and H. La Follette (eds).

Alexy, R. 2002. *A Theory of Constitutional Rights*. Oxford: Oxford University Press.

Alkire, S. and R. Black. 1997. 'A Practical Reasoning Theory of Development Ethics: Furthering the Capabilities Approach'. *Journal of International Development* 9: 263–79.

Alston, P. and K. Tomasevski (eds). 1984. *The Right to Food*. Utrecht: Martin Nijhoff.

Anderson, E.S. 1999. 'What is the Point of Equality?' *Ethics* 109: 287–337.

Andreassen, B., T. Skalnes, A.G. Smith, and H. Stokke. 1987–8. 'Assessing Human Rights Performance in Developing Countries: The Case for a Minimal Threshold Approach to the Economic and Social Rights'. *Human Rights in Developing Countries*: 333–55.

——A.G. Smith, and H. Stokke. 1992. 'Compliance with Economic and Social Human Rights: Realistic Evaluations and Monitoring in the Light of Immediate Obligations'. In A. Eide and B. Hagtvet (eds).

Antony, L. 2000. 'Nature and Norms'. *Ethics* 111: 8–36.

Appiah, K.A. 2001. 'Equality of What?' *New York Review of Books* (26 April 2001).

Aristotle. 1962. *Nicomachean Ethics* (trans. M. Ostwald). New York: Macmillan.

Arneson, R. 1989. 'Equality and Equal Opportunity for Welfare'. *Philosophical Studies* 56: 77–93.

—— 1990a. 'Liberalism, Distributive Subjectivism, and Equal Opportunity for Welfare'. *Philosophy and Public Affairs* 19: 158–94.

—— 1990b. 'Primary Goods Reconsidered'. *Nous* 24: 429–54.

Arthur, J. 1977. 'Rights and the Duty to Bring Aid'. In W. Aiken and H. La Follette (eds).

Attfield, R. 1981. 'The Good of Trees'. *Journal of Value Inquiry* 15: 1.

—— 1983. *The Ethics of Environmental Concern*. New York: Columbia University Press.

Barry, B. 1996. 'Real Freedom and Basic Income'. *The Journal of Political Philosophy* 4: 242–76.

Beitz, C. 1979. *Political Theory and International Relations*. Princeton: Princeton University Press.

Ben-Zeev, A. 1982. 'Who is a Rational Agent?' *Canadian Journal of Philosophy* 4: 647–61.

Bilchitz, D. 1998. *The Mental Lives of Animals*. Unpublished BA (Honours) Dissertation. University of the Witwatersrand.

—— 2001a. 'Which Inequalities are Unjust?' Unpublished MPhil. Dissertation. Cambridge University.

—— 2001b. 'Giving Socio-Economic Rights Teeth: The Minimum Core and Its Importance'. *SALJ* 119: 484–501.

—— 2003a. 'Towards a Reasonable Approach to the Minimum Core: Laying the Foundations for Future Socio-Economic Rights Jurisprudence'. *SAJHR* 19: 1–26.

—— 2003b. 'South Africa: Right to Health and Access to HIV/AIDS Drug Treatment'. *International Journal of Constitutional Law* 1: 524–34.

Brand, D. 2002. 'The Minimum Core Content of the Right to Food in Context: A Response to Rolf Künneman'. In D. Brand and S. Russell (eds).

—— 2005. 'The Right to Food'. In S. Woolman *et al.* (eds).

—— and S. Russell (eds.). 2002. *Exploring the Core Content of Socio-Economic Rights: South African and International Perspectives.* Pretoria: Protea Book House.

Brock, G. (ed.). 1998. *Necessary Goods.* Oxford: Rowman and Littlefield.

Brody, E.B. 1993. *Biomedical Technology and Human Rights.* Paris: UNESCO.

Buchanan, A. 1975. 'Revisability and Rational Choice'. *Canadian Journal of Philosophy* 5: 395–408.

Budlender, G. and K. Roach. 2005. 'Mandatory Relief and Supervisory Jurisdiction: When is it Appropriate, Just and Equitable?' *SALJ* 122: 325–51.

Campbell, T. *et al.* (eds). 2001. *Sceptical Essays on Human Rights.* Oxford: Oxford University Press.

Chapman, A. 1996. 'A "Violations Approach" for Monitoring the International Covenant on Economic, Social and Cultural Rights'. *Human Rights Quarterly* 18: 23–66.

—— 2002. 'Core Obligations Related to the Right to Health and Their Relevance for South Africa'. In D. Brand and S. Russell (eds).

—— and S. Russell (eds). 2002. *Core Obligations: Building a Framework for Economic, Social and Cultural Rights.* Antwerp: Intersentia.

Chaskalson, M. *et al.* (eds). 1996. *Constitutional Law of South Africa (1st ed).* Kenwyn: Juta.

Chaskalson, P. 1998. 'Opening Address'. *Acta Juridica*: 1–7.

—— 2000. 'Third Bram Fischer Lecture'. *SAJHR* 16: 193–206.

Christiano, T. 2000. 'Waldron on Law and Disagreement'. *Law and Philosophy* 19: 513–34.

Christman, J. 1989. *The Inner Citadel.* Oxford: Oxford University Press.

Cockrell, A. 1996. 'Rainbow Jurisprudence'. *SAJHR* 12: 1–38.

Coetzee, J.M. 1999. *The Lives of Animals.* London: Profile Books.

Cohen, G. 1989. 'On the Currency of Egalitarian Justice'. *Ethics* 99: 906–44.

Cowen, S. 2001. 'Can Dignity Guide South Africa's Equality Jurisprudence?' *SAJHR* 17: 34–58.

Cranston, M. 1967. 'Human Rights: Real and Supposed'. In D. D. Raphael (ed).

Craven, M. 1995. *The International Covenant on Economic, Social and Cultural Rights: A Perspective on its Development.* Oxford: Clarendon Press.

Currie, I. 1999. 'Judicious Avoidance'. *SAJHR* 15: 138–65.

Dancy, J. 1993. *Moral Reasons.* Oxford: Blackwell.

—— 2004. *Ethics Without Principles.* Oxford: Oxford University Press.

Daniels, N. (ed.). 1975. *Reading Rawls: Critical Studies on Rawls' A Theory of Justice.* Stanford: Stanford University Press.

Davidson, D. 1984. 'Thought and Talk'. In D. Davidson (ed.).

—— (ed.). 1984. *Inquiries into Truth and Interpretation.* Oxford: Clarendon Press.

—— 1986. 'Judging Interpersonal Interests'. In J. Elster and A. Hylland (eds).

Davis, D. 1992. 'The Case Against the Inclusion of Socio-Economic Demands in a Bill of Rights Except as Directive Principles'. *SAJHR* 8: 475–90.

—— 1996. 'The Twist of Language and the Two Fagans: Please Sir May I Have More Literalism'. *SAJHR* 12: 504–12.

Davis, D. 1997. 'Of Closure, the Death of Ideology and Academic Sand Castles—A Reply to Dr. Fagan'. *SAJHR* 13: 178–80.

—— 1999a. *Democracy and Deliberation*. Kenwyn: Juta.

—— 1999b. 'Equality: The Majesty of Legoland Jurisprudence'. *SALJ* 116: 398–414.

—— 2006. 'Adjudicating the Socio-Economic Rights in the South African Constitution: Towards "Deference Lite"?' *SAJHR* 22: 301–27.

DeGrazia, D. 1996. *Taking Animals Seriously: Mental Life and Moral Status*. Cambridge: Cambridge University Press.

Dennett, D. 1983. 'Intentional Systems in Cognitive Ethology: The "Panglossian Paradigm Defended"'. *Behavioural and Brain Sciences* 6: 343–90.

—— 1984. *Elbow Room: The Varieties of Free Will Worth Wanting*. Oxford: Clarendon Press.

De Vos, P. 1997. 'Pious Wishes or Directly Enforceable Human Rights: Social and Economic Rights in South Africa's 1996 Constitution'. *SAJHR* 13: 67–101.

—— 2001. 'A Bridge Too Far? History as Context in the Interpretation of the South African Constitution'. *SAJHR* 17: 1–33.

De Villiers, B. 2002a. 'Directive Principles of State Policy and Fundamental Rights: The Indian Experience'. *SAJHR* 8: 29–49.

—— 2002b. 'The Socio-Economic Consequences of Directive Principles of State Policy; Limitations on Fundamental Rights'. *SAJHR* 8: 188–99.

De Wet, E. 1996. *The Constitutional Enforceability of Economic and Social Rights: The Meaning of the German Constitutional Model for South Africa*. Cape Town: Butterworths.

Donelly, J. 1982. 'Human Rights as Natural Rights'. *Human Rights Quarterly* 4: 391–405.

Du Plessis, L. and H. Corder. 1994. *Understanding South Africa's Transitional Bill of Rights*. Kenwyn: Juta.

Dworkin, R. 1977. *Taking Rights Seriously*. London: Duckworth.

—— 1983. 'In Defense of Equality'. *Social Philosophy and Policy* 1: 24–40.

—— 1986. *Law's Empire*. London: Fontana Press.

—— 1996. *Freedom's Law: The Moral Reading of the American Constitution*. Oxford: Oxford University Press.

—— 1997. 'Order of the Coif Lecture: in Praise of Theory'. *Arizona State Law Journal* 29: 353.

—— 2000. *Sovereign Virtue*. London: Harvard University Press.

Eide, A. 1989. 'The Realisation of Economic, Social and Cultural Rights and the Minimum Threshold Approach'. *Human Rights Law Journal*: 35–51.

—— and H. Hagtvet (eds). 1992. *Human Rights in Perspective*. Oxford: Blackwell.

Eide, A., C. Krause and A. Rosas (eds). 1995. *Economic, Social and Cultural Rights: A Textbook*. Dordrecht: Martinus Nijhoff.

Elliott, M. 2001. 'The Human Rights Act and the Standard of Substantive Review'. *Cambridge Law Journal* 60: 301–36.

—— 2003. 'Asylum-Seekers Have Human Rights, Too'. *Cambridge Law Journal* 62: 528–31.

Elster, J. and A. Hylland (eds). 1986. *Foundations of Social Choice Theory*. Cambridge: Cambridge University Press.

Ely, J.H. 1980. *Democracy and Distrust: A Theory of Judicial Review*. Cambridge: Harvard University Press.

Ewing, K.D. 2001. 'The Unbalanced Constitution'. In T. Campbell *et al.* (eds).

Fabre, C. 2000. *Social Rights Under the Constitution*. Oxford: Oxford University Press.

Fagan, A. 1996. 'In Defence of the Obvious—Ordinary Meaning and the Identification of Constitutional Rules'. *SAJHR* 12: 545–70.

Fagan, E. 1996. 'The Longest Erratum Note in History'. *SAJHR* 12: 79–89.

—— 1997. 'The Ordinary Meaning of Language—A Response to Professor Davis'. *SAJHR* 13:174–7.

Feinberg, J. 1980. *Rights, Justice and the Bounds of Liberty*. Princeton: Princeton University Press.

Ferraz, O. 2003. 'Social and Economic Rights in the Courts: What Lessons from South Africa?' Unpublished article on file with author.

Finnis, J. 1980. *Natural Law and Natural Rights*. Oxford: Clarendon Press.

—— 1983. *Fundamentals of Ethics*. Oxford: Clarendon Press.

Fish, S. 1989. *Doing What Comes Naturally: Change, Rhetoric and the Practice of Theory in Literary and Legal Studies*. Durham: Duke University Press.

Fishkin, J. 1982. *The Limits of Obligation*. New Haven and London: Yale University Press.

Frankfurt, H. 1987. 'Equality as A Moral Ideal'. *Ethics* 98: 21–43.

Fredman, S. 2005. 'Providing Equality: Substantive Equality and the Positive Duty to Provide'. *SAJHR* 21: 163–90.

Friedman, B. 2002. 'The Birth of an Academic Obsession: The History of the Countermajoritarian Difficulty'. *Yale Law Journal* 112: 153–259.

Gauthier, D. 1986. *Morals By Agreement*. Oxford: Clarendon Press.

Gewirth, A. 1978. *Reason and Morality*. Chicago: University of Chicago Press.

—— 1980. 'Comment on Bond's Article'. *Metaphilosophy* 11: 54–69.

—— 1982a. 'On Rational Agency as the Basis of Moral Equality: Reply to Ben-Zeev'. *Canadian Journal of Philosophy* 4: 667–71.

—— 1982b. 'Why Agents Must Claim Rights: A Reply'. *Journal of Philosophy*: 403–9.

—— 1982c. *Human Rights*. Chicago: University of Chicago Press.

—— 1984. 'Replies to my Critics'. In E. Regis (ed.).

—— 1985. 'From the Prudential to the Moral: Reply to Singer'. *Ethics* 95: 302–4.

Goldsworthy, J. 1997. 'Originalism in Constitutional Interpretation'. *Federal Law Review* 25: 1–50.

—— 2000. 'Interpreting the Constitution in its Second Century'. *Melbourne University Law Review* 24: 677–710.

—— and T. Campbell (eds). 2002. *Legal Interpretation in Democratic States*. Aldershot: Ashgate.

Goodin, R. 1987. 'Egalitarianism, Fetishistic and Otherwise'. *Ethics* 98: 44–9.

—— 1988a. 'What Is So Special About Our Fellow Countrymen?' *Ethics* 98: 663–86.

—— 1988b. *Reasons for Welfare: The Political Theory of the Welfare State*. Princeton: Princeton University Press.

—— and A. Reeve (eds). 1989. *Liberal Neutrality*. London: Routledge.

—— 1998. 'Vulnerabilities and Responsibilities: An Ethical Defence of the Welfare State'. In G. Brock (ed.).

Griffin J. 1986. *Well-being: its Meaning, Measurement and Moral Importance*. Oxford: Clarendon Press.

Hamilton, L.A. 2003. *The Political Philosophy of Needs*. Cambridge: Cambridge University Press.

Hare, R.M. 1984. 'Do Agents Have to be Moralists?' In E. Regis (ed.).

Harrison, R. 1993. *Democracy*. Routledge: London and New York.

Harsanyi, J.C. 1982. 'Morality and the Theory of Rational Behaviour'. In A. Sen and B. Williams (eds).

Hawthorn, G. (ed.). 1985. *The Standard of Living*. Cambridge: Cambridge University Press.

Haysom, N. 1992. 'Constitutionalism, Majoritarian Democracy and Socio-economic Rights'. *SAJHR* 8: 451–63.

Heywood, M. 2003. 'Contempt or Compliance? The TAC case after the Constitutional Court Judgement'. Economic and Social Rights Review 4(1): found at <http://www.communitylawcentre.org.za/ser/esr2003/2003mar_tac.php#tac>.

Hill, J.F. 1984. 'Are Marginal Agents "Our Recipients"?' In E. Regis (ed.).

Hobbes, T. 1991. *Leviathan*. Cambridge: Cambridge University Press.

Hoexter, C. 2000. 'The Future of Judicial Review in South African Administrative law'. *SALJ* 117: 484.

Hunt, P. 1996. *Reclaiming Social Rights*. Aldershot: Dartmouth.

Iles, K. 2004. 'Limiting Socio-Economic Rights: Beyond the Internal Limitations Clauses'. *SAJHR* 20: 448–65.

Ingram, A. 1994. *A Political Theory of Rights*. Oxford: Clarendon Press.

Jain, M.P. 1998. *Indian Constitutional Law*. Agra: Washwa and Company.

Kant, I. 1933. *Critique of Pure Reason* (trans. N.K. Smith). Hong Kong: Macmillan.

—— 1983. *Grounding for the Metaphysics of Morals*. Cambridge: Hackett Publishing Company.

—— 1996. *Practical Philosophy* (ed. M.J. Gregor). Cambridge: Cambridge University Press.

Kavanagh, A. 2003. 'Participation and Judicial Review: A Reply to Jeremy Waldron'. *Law and Philosophy* 22: 451–86.

Kende, M. 2003. 'The South African Constitutional Court's Embrace of Socio-Economic Rights: A Comparative Perspective'. *Chapman Law Review* 6: 137–60.

Kentridge, J. and D. Spitz. 1996. 'Interpretation'. In M. Chaskalson *et al.* (ed).

Klaaren, J. 2003. 'A Remedial Interpretation of the *Treatment Action Campaign* Decision'. *SAJHR* 19: 455–68.

Klare, K. 1998. 'Legal Culture and Transformative Constitutionalism'. 14 *SAJHR*: 146–88.

Klug, H. 2000. *Constituting Democracy: Law, Globalism and South Africa's Political Reconstruction*. Cambridge: Cambridge University Press.

Kramer, M. 1999a. 'Reason Without Reasons: A Critique of Alan Gewirth's Moral Philosophy'. In Kramer, M. (ed.) 1999b.

—— (ed). 1999b. *In the Realm of Legal and Moral Philosophy*. London: Macmillan Press.

—— 2001a. 'Getting Rights Right'. In M. Kramer (ed.) 2001b.

—— (ed). 2001b. *Rights, Wrongs and Responsibilities*. Basingstoke: Palgrave.

Kramer, M., N.E. Simmonds and H. Steiner. 1998. *A Debate Over Rights*. Oxford: Oxford University Press.

Kripke, S. 1980. *Naming and Necessity*. Oxford: Blackwell.

Kuper, A. 2002. 'More Than Charity: Cosmopolitan Alternatives to the "Singer Solution"'. *Ethics and International Affairs* 16(1):107–20.

—— (ed.). 2005. *Global Responsibilities: Who Must Deliver on Human Rights?* London: Routledge.

Laslett, P. and W.G. Runciman (eds). 1969. *Philosophy, Politics and Society* (2nd Series). Oxford: Blackwell.

Lenta, P. 2004a. 'Democracy, Rights Disagreements and Judicial Review'. *SAJHR* 20: 1–31.

—— 2004b. 'Judicial Restraint and Overreach'. *SAJHR* 20: 544–76.

Liebenberg, S. 1996. 'Socio-Economic Rights'. In Chaskalson, *et al.* (eds).

—— 2003. 'South Africa's Evolving Jurisprudence on Socio-Economic Rights: An Effective Tool in Challenging Poverty?' *Law, Democracy and Development* 6: 159–91.

—— 2005a. 'The Interpretation of Socio-Economic Rights'. In Woolman *et al.* (eds).

—— 2005b. 'The Value of Human Dignity in Interpreting Socio-Economic Rights'. *SAJHR* 21: 1–31.

—— 2006. 'Needs, Rights and Transformation: Adjudicating Social Rights'. *Stellenbosch Law Review* 17: 5–36.

Lomasky, L.E. 1981. 'Gewirth's Generation of Rights'. *Philosophical Quarterly* 31: 248–53.

Lyons, D. 1984. 'Utility and Rights'. In J. Waldron (ed.).

Mahabal, K.B. 2004. 'Enforcing the Right to Food in India—The Impact of Social Activism'. *ESR Review* 5(1) found at <http://www.communitylawcentre.org.za/ser/esr2004/2004march_india.php#india>.

Malcolm, N. 1991. 'Thoughtless Brutes'. In D.M. Rosenthal (ed.).

Martin, R. and J.W. Nickel. 1980. 'Recent Work on the Concept of Rights'. *American Philosophical Quarterly* 17:165–80.

Mclean, K. 2006. 'The Right to Have Access to Adequate Housing'. In Woolman *et al.* (eds).

Melden, A.I. 1977. *Rights and Persons*. Oxford: Blackwell.

Michelman, F. 1969. 'Foreword: On Protecting the Poor Through the Fourteenth Amendment'. *Harvard Law Review* 83: 7–59.

—— 1975. 'Constitutional Welfare Rights and "A Theory of Justice"'. In N. Daniels (ed).

Mill, J.S. 1998. *John Stuart Mill On Liberty and Other Essays* (ed. J. Gray). Oxford: Oxford University Press.

Moellendorf, D. 1998. 'Reasoning About Resources: *Soobramoney* and the Future of Socio-Economic Rights Claims'. *SAJHR* 14: 327–33.

Moore, G.E. 1965. *Principia Ethica*. Cambridge: Cambridge University Press.

Moore, M. 2002. 'Natural Rights, Judicial Review and Constitutional Interpretation'. In J. Goldsworthy and T. Campbell (eds).

Mureinik, E. 1992. 'Beyond a Charter of Luxuries'. *SAJHR* 8: 464–74.

—— 1994. 'A Bridge to Where? Introducing the Interim Bill of Rights'. *SAJHR* 10: 31–48.

Murphy, L. 1993. 'The Demands of Beneficence'. *Philosophy and Public Affairs* 22: 267–92.

Nagel, T. 1970. *The Possibility of Altruism*. Princeton: Princeton University Press.

—— 1973. 'Rawls on Justice'. *The Philosophical Review* 82: 220–34.

—— 1975. 'Rawls on Justice'. In N. Daniels (ed.).

—— 1979a. 'What is it like to be a Bat?' In T. Nagel (ed.).

—— (ed.). 1979b. *Mortal Questions*. Cambridge: Cambridge University Press.

—— 1986. *The View from Nowhere*. Oxford: Oxford University Press.

—— 1991. *Equality and Partiality*. Oxford: Oxford University Press.

Neuborne, B. 2003. 'Constitutional Court Profile: India Supreme Court'. *International Journal of Constitutional Law* 1(3): 476–510.

Nickel, J.W. 1982. 'Equal Respect and Human Rights'. *Human Rights Quarterly* 4: 76–93.

Nielsen, K. 1984. 'Against Ethical Rationalism'. In E. Regis (ed.).

Nozick, R. 1974. *Anarchy, State and Utopia*. Oxford: Blackwell.

Nussbaum, M. 1995. 'Human Capabilities, Female Human Beings'. In M. Nussbaum and J. Glover (eds).

—— 2000a. *Women and Human Development*. Cambridge: Cambridge University Press.

—— 2000b. 'Aristotle, Politics, and Human Capabilities: A Response to Antony, Arneson, Charlesworth, and Mulgan'. *Ethics* 111: 102–40.

—— and J. Glover. (eds). 1995. *Women, Culture and Development: A Study of Human Capabilities*. Oxford: Clarendon Press.

O'Manique, J. 1990. 'Universal and Inalienable Rights: A Search for Foundations'. *Human Rights Quarterly* 12: 465–85.

O'Neill, O. 1995. 'Justice, Capabilities, and Vulnerabilities'. In M. Nussbaum and J. Glover (eds).

—— 1996. *Towards Justice and Virtue*. Cambridge: Cambridge University Press.

Parfit, D. 1997. 'Equality and Priority'. *Ratio* 10 (3): 202–21.

Pieterse, M. 1999. 'A Different Shade of Red: Socio-Economic Dimensions of the Right to Life in South Africa'. *SAJHR* 15: 372–85.

—— 2004. 'Coming to Terms with the Judicial Enforcement of Socio-Economic Rights'. *SAJHR* 20: 383–417.

Pillay, K. 2002. 'Implementing Grootboom: Supervision Needed'. *Economic and Social Rights Review* 3 (1): 13–14.

—— 2003. 'Implementation of *Grootboom*: Implications for the Enforcement of Socio-Economic Rights'. *Law, Democracy and Development* 6: 255–77.

Pitkin, H. 1967. *The Concept of Representation*. Berkeley: University of California Press.

Pogge, T. 2002. *World Poverty and Human Rights*. Cambridge: Polity Press.

Putnam, H. 1975. *Mind, Language and Reality*. Cambridge: Cambridge University Press.

Rachels, J. 1977. 'Vegetarianism and "the Other Weight Problem"'. In W. Aiken and H. La Follette (eds).

Raphael, D.D. (ed.). 1967. *Political Theory and the Rights of Man*. London: Macmillan.

Rawls, J. 1982. 'Social Unity and Primary Goods'. In J. Rawls 1999b.

—— 1993. *Political Liberalism*. New York: Columbia University Press.

—— 1999a. *A Theory of Justice* (Rev. Ed.) Oxford: Oxford University Press.

—— 1999b. *Collected Papers*. London: Harvard University Press.

Raz, J. 1986. *The Morality of Freedom*. Oxford: Clarendon Press.

—— 1998. 'Disagreement and Politics'. *American Journal of Jurisprudence* 43: 25–52.

—— 1999. *Engaging Reason: On the Theory of Value and Action*. Oxford: Oxford University Press.

Regan, T. 1988. *The Case for Animal Rights*. London: Routledge.

Regis, E. (ed.). 1984. *Gewirth's Ethical Rationalism*. Chicago and London: University of Chicago Press.

Rodewald, R.A. 1985. 'Does Liberalism Rest on a Mistake?' *Canadian Journal of Philosophy* 15: 231–51.

Roederer, C. 1999. 'Judicious Engagement: Theory, Attitude and Community'. *SAJHR* 15: 486–512.

Roemer, J. 1995. 'Equality of Opportunity'. *Boston Review*. Boston: Michigan State University Press. Online at <http://bostonreview.mit.edu>.

Rosati, C. 1995. 'Persons, Perspectives and Full Informational Accounts of the Good'. *Ethics*: 296–325.

Rosenthal, D.M. (ed.). 1991. *The Nature of Mind*. Oxford: Oxford University Press.

Ross, W.D. 1930. *The Right and the Good*. Oxford: Clarendon Press.

Roux, T. 2002. 'Understanding *Grootboom*—A Response to Cass R. Sunstein'. *Constitutional Forum* 12(2): 41–51.

——2003. 'Legitimating Transformation: Political Resource Allocation in the South African Constitutional Court'. *Democratization* 10(4): 92–111.

Sangiovanni, A. 2003. 'Majoritarianism and Unelected Institutions'. Unpublished paper on file with author presented at Political Theory Colloquium, University of Cambridge, 12 February 2003.

Scanlon, T. 1975. 'Preference and Urgency'. *Journal of Philosophy* 72: 655–69.

——1984. 'Rights, Goals and Fairness'. In J. Waldron (ed.).

——1993. 'Value, Desire and Quality of Life'. In A. Sen and M. Nussbaum (eds).

——1995. 'Comments on Roemer'. *Boston Review*. Boston: Michigan State University Press. Online at <http://bostonreview.mit.edu>.

——1998. *What We Owe to Each Other*. London: Harvard University Press.

Scheffler, S. (ed.). 1988. *Consequentialism and its Critics*. Oxford: Oxford University Press.

Scheuermann, J. 1987. 'Gewirth's Concept of Prudential Rights'. *Philosophical Quarterly* 37: 291–304.

Schwartz, A. 1973. 'Moral Neutrality and Primary Goods'. *Ethics* 83: 294–307.

Scott, C. and Alston, P. 2000. 'Adjudicating Constitutional Priorities in a Transnational Context: A Comment on *Soobramoney's* Legacy and *Grootboom's* Promise'. *SAJHR* 16: 206–68.

—— and Macklem, P. 1992. 'Constitutional Ropes of Sand or Justiciable Guarantees? Social Rights in a New South African Constitution'. *University of Pennsylvania Law Review* 141: 1–148.

Sen, A. 1981. *Poverty and Famines: An Essay in Entitlement and Deprivation*. Oxford: Clarendon Press.

——1982. *Choice, Welfare and Measurement*. London: Harvard University Press.

——1984a. 'The Right Not to be Hungry'. In P. Alston and K. Tomasevski (eds).

——1984b. *Resources Values and Development*. London: Harvard University Press.

——1987. 'The Standard of Living: Concepts and Critiques'. In G. Hawthorn (ed.).

——1988. 'Rights and Agency'. In S. Scheffler (ed.).

——1992. *Inequality Reexamined*. Oxford: Clarendon Press.

—— and M. Nussbaum (eds). 1993. *The Quality of Life*. Oxford: Clarendon Press.

—— and B. Williams (eds). 1982. *Utilitarianism and Beyond*. Cambridge: Cambridge University Press.

Shue, H. 1980. *Basic Rights*. Princeton: Princeton University Press.

——1988. 'Mediating Duties'. *Ethics* 98: 687–704.

Sidgwick, H. 1981. *The Method of Ethics*. Indianapolis: Hackett Publishing Company.

Singer, M.G. 1985. 'On Gewirth's Derivation of the Principle of Generic Consistency'. *Ethics* 95: 297–301.

Singer, P. 1972. 'Famine, Affluence and Morality'. *Philosophy and Public Affairs* 1: 229–43.

——1995. *Animal Liberation* (2nd ed.). London: Pimlico.

Smith, N. 1996. 'The Purpose Behind the Words'. *SAJHR* 12: 90–8.

Spector, H. 2003. 'Judicial Review, Rights and Democracy'. *Law and Philosophy* 23: 295–304.

Sprague, C. and Woolman, S. 2006. 'Moral Luck: Exploiting South Africa's Policy Environment to Produce a Sustainable National ART Programme'. *SAJHR* 22: 337–79.

Steinberg, C. 2006. 'Can Reasonableness Protect the Poor? A Review of South Africa's Socio-Economic Rights Jurisprudence'. *SALJ* 123: 264–84.

Sumner, L.W. 1987. *The Moral Foundation of Rights*. Oxford: Clarendon Press.

——1996. *Welfare, Happiness and Ethics*. Oxford: Clarendon Press.

Sunstein, C. 1996. 'Foreword: Leaving Things Undecided'. *Harvard Law Review* 110: 6–101.

——1997. 'Order of the Coif Lecture: Response: From Theory to Practice'. *Arizona State Law Journal* 29: 389.

——2001a. 'Social and Economic Rights? Lessons from South Africa'. *Constitutional Forum* 11(4): 123.

——2001b. *Designing Democracy*. Oxford: Oxford University Press.

Swart, M. 2005. 'Left Out in the Cold? Crafting Constitutional Remedies for the Poorest of the Poor'. *SAJHR* 21: 215–40.

Taylor, P.W. 1986. *Respect for Nature*. Princeton: Princeton University Press.

Terreblanche, S. 2002. *A History of Inequality in South Africa 1652 to 2002*. Pietermaritzburg: University of Natal Press.

Toebes, B. 1999. *The Right to Health as Human Right in International Law*. Antwerpen: Intersentia and Hart.

Tushnet, M. 2004. 'Social Welfare Rights and the Forms of Judicial Review'. *Texas Law Review* 82: 1895–919.

Van Bueren, G. 1999. 'Alleviating Poverty through the Constitutional Court'. *SAJHR* 15: 52–74.

Van Onselen, C. 1996. *The Seed is Mine. The Life of Kas Maine, a South African Sharecropper 1894–1985*. New York: Hill and Wang.

Van Parijs, P. 1995. *Real Freedom*. Oxford: Clarendon Press.

Van Wyk, D. *et al*. 1994. *Rights and Constitutionalism: The New South African Legal Order*. Kenwyn: Juta.

Vlastos, G. 1984. 'Justice and Equality'. In J. Waldron (ed.).

Wade, H.W.R. and C.F. Forsyth. 2000. *Administrative Law*. Oxford: Oxford University Press.

Waldron, J. (ed.). 1984. *Theories of Rights*. Oxford: Oxford University Press.

——1988. 'When Justice Replaces Affection: The Need for Rights'. *Harvard Journal of Law and Public Policy* 11: 625–47.

——1989. 'Legislation and Moral Neutrality'. In R.E. Goodin and A. Reeve (eds).

——(ed). 1993a. *Liberal Rights*. Cambridge: Cambridge University Press.

——1993b. 'Homelessness and the Issue of Freedom'. In J. Waldron (ed.).

——1999. *Law and Disagreement*. Oxford: Clarendon Press.

Wesson, M. 2004. 'Grootboom and Beyond: Reassessing the Socio-Economic Jurisprudence of the South African Constitutional Court'. *SAJHR* 20: 284–308.

Williams, B. 1972. 'The Idea of Equality'. In P. Laslett and W.G. Runciman (eds).

——1987. 'Interests and Capabilities'. In G. Hawthorn (ed.).

Williams, L. 2005. 'Issues and Challenges in Addressing Poverty and Legal Rights: A Comparative United States/South African Analysis'. *SAJHR* 21: 436–72.

Winston, M.E. 1989. *The Philosophy of Human Rights*. Belmont: Wadsworth Publishing Company.

Wise, S. 2001. *Rattling the Cage: Towards Legal Rights for Animals*. London: Profile Books.

Woods, J.M. 2003. 'Justiciable Social Rights as a Critique of the Liberal Paradigm'. *Texas International Law Journal* 38: 763–93.

Woolman, S. *et al.* (eds). 2005a. *Constitutional Law of South Africa* (2nd ed.). Cape Town: Juta and Co.

Woolman, S. 2005b. 'Dignity'. In S. Woolman *et al.* (eds).

Key:
SALJ—South African Law Journal
SAJHR—South African Journal of Human Rights

Index